Emotional Abuse and Other Psychic Harms

For Chris,

Katherine, Gary, Hermione, Joe, Harriet and Sherko
Felix, Rosie, Ronahi, Cleo, Mirvan and Lilan

Emotional Abuse and Other Psychic Harms

Invisible Wounds and their Histories

Marian Allsopp

palgrave
macmillan

First published 2013 by
PALGRAVE MACMILLAN

Palgrave Macmillan in the UK is an imprint of Macmillan Publishers Limited, registered in England, company number 785998, of Houndmills, Basingstoke, Hampshire RG21 6XS.

Palgrave Macmillan in the US is a division of St Martin's Press LLC, 175 Fifth Avenue, New York, NY 10010.

Palgrave Macmillan is the global academic imprint of the above companies and has companies and representatives throughout the world.

Palgrave® and Macmillan® are registered trademarks in the United States, the United Kingdom, Europe and other countries.

ISBN 978–0–230–30302–7

This book is printed on paper suitable for recycling and made from fully managed and sustained forest sources. Logging, pulping and manufacturing processes are expected to conform to the environmental regulations of the country of origin.

A catalogue record for this book is available from the British Library.

A catalog record for this book is available from the Library of Congress.

10   9   8   7   6   5   4   3   2   1
22 21 20 19 18 17 16 15 14 13

Printed and bound in Great Britain by
CPI Antony Rowe, Chippenham and Eastbourne

Contents

v

Preface

This book is about the concept of 'invisible wounds' or psychological harm, examples of which I locate in a variety of settings in the 'psy' complex – academic, professional and practical – across the Anglophone world. Post-traumatic stress disorder, nervous shock, emotional abuse, attachment disorder and loss are all instances of the wound that have come into being as objects of expert attention and intervention. They are brought together here in what I call 'a genealogy', which traces their emergence and connections within the context of the growth of the 'psy' knowledges, and their institutional organisations, throughout the 20th century.

The orientation of the study is Foucauldian, in the sense that it seeks to make strange that which is taken for granted. In refusing the popular and professional assumptions of an interior life in which invisible wounds can be identified and managed, it attempts to destabilise a whole cluster of ways of thinking about selves and their problems that have become significant (and arguably dominant) conceptions of the soul in western liberalism. It hopes to open out new ways of seeing how our collective understanding of the self and the psyche have been formed – and how particular ways of acting on selves have been made possible, legitimate and a form of government.

This project developed over a number of years; the ideas evolved gradually and the studies of different sites meant a continual reorientation to new literatures and institutional details. This has meant that chapters which presented 'a history of the present' when written, no longer do so. However, the trends described continue very much as they were, and the inexorable progress of the psy has not faltered. The only major recent change in the UK is the demise of the New Labour government, whose policies feature in these chapters. It remains to be seen if the Tory vision of the Big Society makes a substantial difference to our attitudes to selves and their harms.

During my research, I was given advice by two of the most experienced and accomplished sociologists that I could have hoped for: Stanley Cohen and Nikolas Rose. They were unfailingly encouraging and helpful and I trusted their judgement completely. My thanks also go to John Clarke, for his support; to Nicola Lacey, Ruth Nissim, Jim Pye,

Bob Sutcliffe and Frances Kennett for constructive reading; to a series of experts in the field of child welfare who kindly talked to me about emotional abuse, when I was just starting my work: Mark Allsopp, Janet Boucher, Marion Brandon, Peter Clarke, Marian Elgar, Elaine Farmer, Sarah Glennie, David Howe, Christa Laird, Peter Marsh, Teresa Munby, Wendy Rose, Alan Rushton, Dave Seal, Mike Simm and Judith Trowell; and to others, whose work, at a distance, has been a source of inspiration and information for me: Wendy Brown, Peter Fonagy, Nigel Parton, Ian Hacking, Caroline Steedman and Allan Young. Of course, I alone am responsible for what I have written here.

Finally, my special thanks go to my family, Chris, my three girls, their partners and my six grandchildren. As I struggled with accounts of the inner life, they have kept me firmly in touch with the outer one.

1
Introduction

This book is about how the concept of harm, damage or wound is applied as a metaphor to a site often called the self or the soul. This is the social space of the individual subject, which is, paradoxically, placed by our language and culture in a person's interior – a place where we are all said to be vulnerable and endangered by a potentially hostile environment. The book consists of a series of studies which are designed to show how the concept of harm to an inner life emerges from different discursive contexts, and how it does so in distinctly variable versions: psychological, emotional, neurological or social, in more or less stable hybrid forms. Using primary sources which are mostly documentary, the studies range from a look at the psychiatric history of post-traumatic stress disorder (PTSD) and at the story of its rewriting in English tort law; the recent reprised popularity of attachment theory and its marriage to neurology, and a look at the career of the concept of the emotional abuse of children as a social problem category in the legal/administrative processes of child protection. These are introduced by a first chapter which concentrates on the metaphoric content of invisible wounds or psychic trauma and the way it produces particular forms of the self. The studies which follow this are clustered around the literature and practices of the psychiatric, psychological, psychoanalytic, social work and legal professions, in order to show how the work of these professionals makes the concept of a psychic injury visible, discussible, treatable, administrable and justiciable. Through their efforts, it is argued, the concept moves from being a metaphor, hooked on to the palpable reality of a physical wound, to acquire a 'facticity' of its own; it becomes a reality through its achieved status as a social problem category and an ever present risk to self and self regulation at the turn of the 21st century.

1.1 Journey into the interior

It would be an exercise far beyond the scope of this book to try to map all the 'social conditions' under which human beings began, conceptually, to place wounds in an emotional interior, or to describe all the particular political, cultural, technical and organisational contexts in which such ideas and knowledge forms emerged. But while the book concentrates largely on a social problem formation in various discursive and therefore non-concrete locations (mostly professional literature and the academic publications on which it depends), it takes these virtual locations as sites for the making of knowledge, which are as much spaces for productive activity as any factory for frozen food or clinic for pathology – and as full of conflict and ambition, fashion and trend as any other social enterprise. This activity is structured, guided and constrained by the technologies of research, communications and publishing, the availability of funding streams and the organisational form of the academy. And these, in turn, are influenced by government's attitude to particular scientific endeavours as a public good, the size and structure of tertiary education and professional training and the quasi-market conditions which prevail, creating the need for institutions and individuals to produce value for money in the form of publications.

Within the general discursive conditions for the social production of academic and professional ideas, however, there are, also, more idiosyncratic individual influences, and here I must acknowledge the particular concatenation of social circumstances which led to the writing of this book, particularly the development of my own interest in the idea of emotional or psychological harm. This was, indeed, something of a journey. With a background as a professional in child and adolescent mental health, systems therapy and research on social workers' attitudes to risk in child protection,[1] I wanted initially to look in detail at the risk-assessment process in the field of mental health and local authority social work and at how the task of applying the rigid, technical categories of risk management to the indeterminate, turbulent and morally ambiguous world of ordinary people was accomplished. However, from this beginning, I became increasingly interested in what I *thought* was, at the turn of the new century, the smallest category of child abuse, the one least applied to children in the child protection registration process, certainly the one least talked or written about: emotional abuse – a vague puzzling idea and one which would take most work and ingenuity to dress up in the calculus of risk. What was it that was 'at risk' and what would count as evidence in the administrative and legal processing of cases where this cruelty was suspected?

My curiosity about this concept and its application was enhanced by three events. The first occurred when I checked the UK Department of Health statistics for children on the Child Protection Register under the category of emotional abuse. I discovered that in 1999 they formed 19 per cent of the total – a dramatic increase from the middle of the decade and a larger number than those registered for sexual abuse, at 17 per cent, though still considerably less than those said to be physically abused. I was startled and puzzled by this amount; they were a departure from the US figures, where psychological maltreatment remains by far the smallest category. Besides, sexual abuse seemed to receive so much more media attention and professional input in terms of teaching, training and literature in both countries.

Second, I began to investigate the meagre academic and professional literature in this area and discovered a copy of the first US book on the subject by John Garbarino and colleagues (Garbarino *et al.*, 1986) in my university science library – where else? – I found it there, wedged between two other books. On the left was a large medical tome on the physical abuse of children, a photographic compendium of injuries on small, fragile bodies, images which were powerful and quite pornographic in their raw, technicolour detail; on the right was one of the first volumes published on the sexual abuse of children, which consisted in chapters of compelling oral testimony by adult survivors, transcribed into the written word. I was struck by the force and the directness of their visual and oral communication and by the contrasting invisibility and silence of the problem I was interested in. The 'injury' caused by this abuse could not be seen, and nor could the inchoate experience of a small child, who had known no other life, be put into words. How could the intermittently cruel behaviour of parents be observed without continual access to the private world of the family? To be made public and visible, this was a harm which would need a subtle form of policing and the mediation of a certain sort of professional knowledge. It required some convincing theory or stockpile of lay wisdom, which could relate, by inference, observable behavioural signs to an invisible mental state and some causal parental actions or poor familial relationship. It was hardly surprising that the emotional abuse of children had never become the subject of a political and media campaign in the USA and the UK, as had child physical abuse and child sexual abuse, in the 1960s and the 1970s–80s respectively. It lay in a hidden territory, which, as in Foucault's version of the psychoanalytic confessional, could only be known or explored through the arcane knowledge of experts.

And who were these experts? This question triggered the third event: a memory, this time, of a session of an International Society for the

Prevention of Child Abuse and Neglect (ISPCAN) European Congress in Oslo in 1995, where a social work academic from Northern Ireland gave a paper on the urgent necessity of finding a definition that would distinguish between the *emotional* and the *psychological* abuse of children. I was surprised by a paper on this little-discussed form of child abuse, surprised that what was problematised here was the *classification* of this particular form of deviancy, rather than the behaviour it purported to describe. I was even more struck by the vigorous way in which some of the leading players in the child protection field entered into the consequent discussion of taxonomy. I later realised that, at that point, the paper's author had published the only UK monograph on the subject, but that these other experts were about to enter the field. Compared to other social problem categories, the terrain of emotional abuse was as yet hardly occupied and I was witnessing my colleagues laying claim to a strip or two.

It may seem cynical to go from an initial interest in a social problem category straight to the politics of its inception, promotion and public recognition, rather than to the causes, manifestations and consequences of the problem itself – the distress and difficulty located in the child and family. But I had practised a therapy where the way a problem was understood, or framed by the major players, was of primary importance to its maintenance or solution and formed the point of intervention. Also, I was very familiar with the constant reframing or renegotiation of the nature of child and family problems in the eclectic, multi-professional field of child welfare. Here, child psychiatrists, psychologists and psychoanalysts rubbed shoulders with teachers, social workers and lawyers. They met in clinics, courts and case conferences, where difficulties for children and their families were constantly being rewritten in the light of different professional rationalities and organisational imperatives – most especially those entailed by scarce resources.

Of course, these professional rewritings were not infinite. Apart from the limitations imposed by institutional structure, professional rationalities depended on a limited set of knowledges, and the items of this repertoire were often mixed up with each other even in the language and practices of one individual, let alone in those of one profession or institution. On the whole, day-to-day practice and decision making in this area seemed like a thoroughly commonsense affair, in which particular pieces of technical talk were adopted for rhetorical purposes – to prove a point or assert a professional identity. Nevertheless, several broad discourses could be identified in everyday professional practices in the area of emotional abuse and in the academic and professional literature. These partial models, explaining the behaviour of children and families, were sometimes purely behavioural, but more often invoked theories of an interior life – medical (psychiatric, psychological and neurological) theories of the psychic reaction of human beings to sudden loss or shock, often called trauma; socio-medical (psychological and biological) theories of the emotional and behavioural reaction of children to poor, disturbed or dangerous mother–child relationships; socio-legal theories, more feminist, hybrid, rights-based narratives about the depredations of patriarchy and the psychic reactions of victims to abuse of power in all its forms and, lastly, psycho-social and biological theories of child development. And all of these were set in a rich legacy of two centuries of discourse about danger to children from the aberrations of adults, both individually and collectively.

It was clear that if the status of the emotional abuse of children as an administrative category in the world of child protection were to be made problematic, it could be done in two different ways: first by looking at the interprofessional politics of its emergence and growth in considerable institutional detail, which might indicate a sort of social history of this problem category in the form of a classic social constructionist thesis; or, second, by looking more at the genealogy of the concept – at marriage, divorce and death amongst the knowledges that were the ancestors of the idea. These two did not seem to be mutually exclusive in theory, but I chose the second course, because I wanted to think more specifically about the psychological or emotional harm said to be done by this version of abuse and how particular psychiatric, psychological and legal versions of psychic harm contributed to the way it was construed and treated.

At this point, a literature search on emotional abuse in general threw up two self-help books. The first was called *Invisible Wounds,* by Kay Douglas, a writer and therapist from the USA. This was a book for women who felt subjugated and hurt by men, written by one who had shared their pain (Douglas, 1996). This was an attractive metaphor and I began to look for other examples of its use located in the discourses I was already interested in. Apart from the instance of the broken, bleeding heart in literary or religious iconography (not always invisible), the obvious one was psychic trauma. The word 'trauma' is Greek for a wound or a piercing of the body's skin. Its first use, as recorded in the *Oxford English Dictionary,* was in the mid-17th century. In the second half of the 19th century its use was extended to include a form of 'nervous' injury by British neurologists working on the effects of railway accidents. Freud himself first used 'trauma' as a metaphor for psychological harm in his work on hysteria (Breuer and Freud, 1955 [1893–1895]; Freud, 1966 [1892–94]) as did William James, who, in reviewing his work in 1894, described certain reminiscences of shock as 'psychic traumata, thorns in the spirit, so to speak'.

'Trauma' is now part of a flourishing vernacular about shock and psychic hurt, and has emerged in the medical world as the diagnostic category of post-traumatic stress disorder. There is the notion of traumatic attachments in the mother–child relationship and that of spiritual wounds inflicted in racism or hate speech, bullying or harassment, or collective wounds to groups and even nations, an example of which occurs in the discourse of truth and reconciliation commissions looked at in Chapter 2. This language of the wound is also accompanied by its causes and consequences, as in wounding words, psychic pain, mental anguish, damage, sickness, healing and scarring, and its location, as with deep wounds, spiritual lesions, hurting inside and, of course, the notion of vulnerability and so impending danger. I began to think about the power of the physical metaphor of the wound and the work that it does in discourse. How might it help to make the incorrigible, private experience of psychic suffering into a social problem which was discussable, theorisable and even legally actionable? At the same time, how could the dualistic philosophy of the law, in which the mind inhabits its body as a possession, ever accommodate to the idea of harm to an inner life?[2]

Metaphor and interiority

At first, it seemed clear that the metaphor of invisible wounds primarily locates the injury in some kind of mental or emotional space inside an individual. This was underlined by the metaphor of the second self-help book I had found, called *Inward Bound: Exploring the Geography of Your Emotions*, by Sam Keen, a clinical psychologist (Keen, 1992), which was reminiscent of John Sutherland's earlier biography of the distinguished psychoanalyst, Ronald Fairbairn, *Fairbairn's Journey into the Interior* (Sutherland, 1989). If I embarked on a study of invisible wounds, how was I going to deal with the whole topic, even assumption, of human interiority – 'the world passed within', as Charles Taylor put it in *Sources of the Self* (Taylor, 1989)? I was in no danger of making my own journey into the vast and intractable terrain of the interior world of the self or the soul (a space which, though it is continually explored and rewritten, is still as mysterious as the dark continent of Africa was to western explorers in the 19th century). For all I knew it was the

Kingdom of Prester John, a land of myth and legend. I was not going to 'go native'. I was (and remain) agnostic about the nature and location of this interior, seeing the accounts of those who claim to have been there as dependent on the culture and practices of the explorers themselves and their colonising homeland. For example, Foucault saw this tricky, even hostile land, with deep, impenetrable subterranean caves, as created and elaborated in the context of the psychoanalytic confessional, where the esoteric techniques of experts helped the inhabitants to imagine and map their world, making it the subject of systematic 'scientific' knowledge and therefore power and regulation. In the more recent psychological paradigms of cognitive or cognitive-behavioural therapy, the natives are the informants, giving first-hand accounts of the lie of their flatter and less savage land – expert, privileged observers of their own mental behaviour. In both cases, the maps and charts are all produced within the linguistic and therefore social processes by which subjectivities and their worlds are made up. Any precultural psychic interior cannot, by definition, be seen or spoken of. It may be a no-place, though not, according to Freud and Klein, a utopia!

Moreover, not only can it only be broached within a cultural domain, it would, as the last paragraph testifies, be hard to imagine without metaphor. This is a complicated claim which is based on the fact that many of the abstract theoretical constructs which are used to explain human behaviour within a psychological paradigm started life as everyday concepts, and often as metaphors, from which the figurative content has been gradually lost, as they have become abstract, reified, technical categories; they are inferred from certain sets of observable behaviour, which they are then used to explain. Like the language of the emotions (Griffiths, 1997), metaphors of a psychic interior, concepts like depression, stress and, of course, trauma – a psychic wound – and emotional abuse as harm, seem to lack an obvious referent, although they have meaning, embedded in language's figurative history and current social use. Aristotle, the arch-realist, wrote that 'metaphor consists in giving the thing a name that belongs to something else' (Aristotle in Ross ed., 1925: Chapter 21, 1457b1–30). In a realist world, it is the nature or existence of this thing which is problematic.

So any discussion, examination or elaboration of the nature of a psychic interior plunges us further into a figurative world; any consideration of the work that the metaphor of the psychic wound does in discourse to make this interior place public, treatable and administrable, immediately involves *more* metaphors. Most especially, it involves a spatial trope, based on a dichotomy between interior and exterior sites, public and private domains, and on movement between the two; a narrative about 'bringing forth' from incorrigible self-knowledge to vocal expression or visibility in the social domain – the two registers of knowledge of another which, according to Susan Sontag, are the bases of the two modes in which metaphor functions: the 'expressive and the scientific' (Sontag, 1991: 91). But if this book were just about the work of metaphor as something which locates, names and 'brings forth' a 'private place' into the social world, it would simply be part of the process it is writing about.

I have already declared agnosticism about this inner world, however – a suspicion, even assumption, that it is ontologically subjective, a creation of the social domain. In such a case, while metaphor may be said to reveal or make discussable a private place, it also facilitates its creation as a new form of life. The language and practices of the invisible wound can not only be described as revealing a particular form of subjectivity; in the revealing, they also make it. Susan Sontag writes in her introduction to *Aids and its Metaphors* that 'saying a thing is something-it-is-not is a mental operation as old as philosophy and poetry and the spawning ground of most kinds of understanding' (Sontag, 1991: 91). We could add that saying, in metaphor, that a thing is something-it-*is*, creating facticity, seems to be a similarly ancient mental occupation. We are all expert users of this linguistic convention, just as we are all expert users of language in general.

But what is significant in Sontag's formulation is that it catches the *negative* basis of metaphor. For example, in the case of a spiritual or psychological wound, we do not really think that when someone declares or shows extreme distress that their soul or their psyche is pierced or opened up painfully by a forceful object or weapon. But our language and ways of thinking about this process are almost totally taken from the body and its hurts. So, to describe distress, our words for bodily hurts must be qualified by the adjectives like 'mental' or 'psychological'. And to start with, at least, such qualifiers have a certain *dis*qualifying connotation. For example, the qualifier, 'invisible', for a wound, suggests that the wound is *not* a gross bodily lesion after all; that is, *not* a wound. As the critic John Lanchester pointed out in a *Guardian* tribute to Muriel Spark (Lanchester, 2006: viii) 'all metaphors have, to some extent, an anti-realistic effect', and Gilbert Ryle went further when he reminded an Oxford seminar that 'making a mental note' was precisely not to make a note at all (Eagleton, 2001: 163)! The suggestion is that with time and habitual use, these qualifiers lose their disqualifying power; they are taken for granted and become part of a phrase with a unified and technical meaning, not dependent on its supposed metaphorical referent; they can be dropped, and a powerful, often implicit, theoretical context used to provide their intention (Manier, 1980, cited in Steedman, 1995). This process is traced in Chapter 5 on the history of the concept of emotional abuse as a problem category, where these historical stages in the development of a metaphor are identifiable.

So, over time, the figurative content of a metaphor may be lost, especially in scientific programmes of work. In the current use of the word 'trauma' in the psy sciences, for example, there is little qualification. But when Freud first used the wound as metaphor at the beginning of the 1890s in his notes on an edition of lectures by Charcot (Freud, 1966 [1892–94]), he talks of 'traumatic *hysteria*' and '*psychical* trauma' He makes it clear that he is talking about the psychic consequences of a material event, a trauma. (Breuer and Freud, 1955 [1893–1895]: 7) and whether the event is an accident involving physical injury or one which merely causes intense fright, anxiety or shame, is immaterial. The word is then subtly expanded by Freud from this identifiable event, which might perhaps be or cause a physical wound, to include its psychic sequelae (Freud, 1966 [1892–94]: 137). And, gradually, in this concept of psychic trauma, the figurative, physical tropes seem to fade – or do they? Is it just that they are present at a subliminal or habitual level, directing our thoughts and ideas about the inner life, and their practices, in certain ways rather than others?

Certainly, in the case of the metaphor of the wound, this process of theorisation is complicated and the technical expression not entirely detached from its cultural context. This is for two basic reasons. The first is simply the ideological nature of psychology itself, in which so many categories are, like those for the emotions, grounded in the vernacular (Griffiths, 1997: 2–5). (What appears to be objective is sustained by tacit knowledge from introspection or the testimony of subjects within a linguistic and, therefore, social domain which is saturated with figurative understandings.) The second reason is that the processes of figurative loss, abstraction and reification in scientific theorisation also constantly occur in popular usage, for which science itself, far from providing merely abstract ideas, provides a new and fertile source of metaphor. Take the example of trauma again, which as a description purely of damage or hurt to a psychic interior – 'the feelings' – has acquired a legitimacy of its own as a theoretical construct in the psy disciplines. Nevertheless, it has also found its way into self-help literature and back into popular 'psychologised' discourse. Thus in the expressive, figurative language of literature and the everyday, the more recent 'technical'

concept of 'trauma' joins and elaborates the metaphor of 'wounded feelings'; it suggests that a private event might be likened to one which has
some legitimate public status, one which has a name which is lodged
among an array of official diagnostic categories, necessitating medical
attention, if not legal compensation.

Metaphor is clearly not a simple linguistic device; all language functions in complex ways, and the metaphor of the invisible wound is
no exception. First, it covers a large domain of meaning; second, this
domain is constantly enlarging through time and spreading over different social contexts in a sort of 'metaphoric flow' between bodies of
thought (Figlio, 1976: 26), as it migrates between expressive and scientific language and back again; and third, it works to create new meanings
for the concepts it refers to in ways that may have social and political
significance. All of these points are enlarged in Chapter 2.

Techniques of the interior

Although addressing figurative accounts of a wound to some inner site,
it was important to remember that I was not just looking at a linguistic phenomenon, an exercise in syntax and semantics; and whilst it was
tempting to do a sort of cultural 'reading', I decided to confine this to
one chapter only – Chapter 2 – and, even there, I do not attempt to
engage with the millions of accounts of human suffering, present in
world literature since the *Myth of Gilgamesh*, the oldest written story
(Godwin, 2002: 18–22). For I wanted to concentrate on the notion of
psychic *harm* as opposed to *suffering* – suffering-induced (and inducing)
change for the worse; damage to the wholeness and integrity of the soul;
a departure from the normal. For this implies in its study and formulation not just subjective experience, its observation or literary expression;
it entails its very creation by a range of helpful and expert others: it is
shaped by a self-confirming understanding both driven and limited by
skills in intervention and healing – in a word, by technique.

Although the exploration of this inner world is presented in the narratives of those who claim to have been there, these expeditions, as in
the great 'Age of Exploration'of the 15th and 16th centuries, could not
have been envisaged without contemporary technical advances in navi-
gation, boat-building, weapons and the rest – 'ways and means' (Latour,
1988 [84]: 47) – a thoroughly technological, interventive understanding
of being. As in the new forms of microbiology, the method of study is
no more the hermeneutic gaze of subject on object (Heidegger, 1977;
Rheinberger, 2000). These were not just voyages of discovery, but, also,
of colonisation and control. So accounts of psychic hurt had to be seen,

not just in terms of what was related, but of who the explorers were; who were their friends and professional colleagues; who had funded their expeditions and for what purpose; what were they trying to prove; whose account were they trying to disqualify and why; what other expeditions were they trying to pre-empt? Besides this, and most important, what maps did they emerge with to locate and describe what they had seen and by what practices and accomplishments did they try to make this interior territory a part of the known world – not some exotic other, but literally mundane, a place where the same social customs and rules would be as applicable as everywhere else? How did they make this place the subject of regulation?

In fact, I did not have to wait long to discover one such technique. This was a piece of evidence, a picture, with all the truth and immediacy of a travel photograph, taken in the interior and brought back for our inspection. There it was on the page of a Sunday newspaper, a large grey, grainy image of a human brain with its two hemispheres of slightly uneven size. Above it was the headline:

HARSH WORDS CAN DEFORM CHILDREN'S BRAINS FOR LIFE
And below it was the caption: *'An abused child's brain is uneven – the larger hemisphere rules the rest'* (Burke, 2000: 4).

Neuro-imaging: a snapshot of harm to this internal territory; a piece of compelling evidence of the dangers to human development of a discouraging and hurtful social environment.

This was not the picture or the place I had expected. Was the invisible wound located in a psychic or a biological space, or were these indistinguishable? On which side of the rift valley between body and soul had the conflicting accounts of the explorers placed it; where had they located the raging sea of the passions or the still mere of motives (Danziger, 1997)? And if the invisible wound was sited in the body, was it, with all the techniques of modern medicine, invisible; or was it, in fact, a visible wound, sited at a microbiological level – not a metaphor at all?

Obviously, this was just one technique of discovery and one version of the inner world amongst a plurality of techniques and accounts, their form arising contingently in different social situations, with different professional imperatives and different local conditions. With this in mind, it seemed that the best way of resolving my different leanings, and using work already done, was to make a series of studies of different social and organisational contexts in which instances of the invisible wound are created and made visible by the writings and practices of academics and professionals (in the broad sense of the word). The following presented themselves:

1. the development of the concept of trauma in the history of PTSD in psychiatry and tort law – the 'pure' case of the wound, since it does not necessarily involve crime by another or even always arise in an interpersonal context;
2. the career of the concept of the emotional abuse of children as an official problem category in government guidance to local authorities on their statutory duties in child protection, and
3. an account of this wounding relationship in modern developments in attachment theory within the psychoanalytic, neurological and child welfare communities.

These studies would be prefaced by a chapter introducing the metaphor of invisible wounds and its appearance in psychiatric, psychoanalytic and therapeutic literature across a wide spectrum of sites, and attempting to trace the particular form of subjectivity that this metaphor serves to create.

The following case studies could only expose small pieces of the social surface to view, localised snapshots of a potentially vast social problem area, in which discourses appear, merge, part and disappear across time and social space. It was obvious that these were not going to throw up any major generalisations or grand narratives – except perhaps that there can be none – but an emphasis on the contingency and local nature of different assemblages of techniques and practices. Nevertheless, certain key themes seemed clear from the beginning, and from these three main questions presented themselves: first, How has this concept of invisible wounds, in its varying manifestations, grown and changed from a metaphor hooked onto the palpable reality of a physical wound to something which has a reality of its own?; second, To what extent is it made real by its location in the interior of the body rather than in an emotional interior, in a biological rather than a psychological space?; and third, By what route has the threat to this interior space been elevated to a major social risk at the end of the 20th century?

1.2 Invisible wounds: The social problems

That psychic harm is seen as a major social risk is indubitable.[3] Obviously, such a claim involves appeal to social changes and particular discursive shifts over the last quarter-century, which have none of the clarity of the sort of institutional changes that can be pinned down statistically. But the former do manifest themselves in the language and preoccupations of the media, academic and professional literature and, more important, official government documents and guidelines for specialists, which effectively regulate both language and practice in the professions of the wound. In these, psychological harm, as a social problem category, seems to sit at the centre of a Venn diagram, a unique site, where several different major social preoccupations or projects overlap and inform each other. There are, no doubt, many that could be named, but those that seem to stand out can be listed thus:

1. a broad and complex risk discourse (Douglas, 1992; Luhmann, 1993);
2. the increasing use of the language of psychology and individualisation in accounts of social and even political problems (Nolan, 1998);
3. the growth of identity politics with its claims to harm, injury or the uneven distribution of risk (Brown, 1995; Clarke, 2004);
4. our perennial concerns about childhood, child safety, welfare and development (Hendrick, 2003);
5. the socio-political project of producing the flexible, self-motivating, self-appraising, self-governing individual (Rose, 1999) and
6. somewhat paradoxically, the increased disciplinary role of the state (Brown, 1995).

These are the discursive conditions in which the concept of psychic harm has emerged

Risk of psychic harm

The infliction of an invisible wound on another covers an enormous number of cruel and sometimes criminal acts by individuals, sometimes collective, as well as events of unprecedented power and psychological consequences for those involved, which are not due to the destructive intention of an individual or group but to negligence or chance. These can all be construed in the technical language of risk as environmental hazards which threaten us all.[4] Although some of these events are extremely infrequent, they carry highly aversive outcomes, which have, until recently, been largely thought of in their physical form; when we insure against accidents or ill-health, we are usually thinking of the physical kind.[5] But threats to our psyche are gaining more credibility as legitimation of our claims to rights and needs (Douglas, 1992).

It is a commonplace of a particular strand of realist sociological writing that the western world at the end of 20th century was and is a 'risk society' (Bauman, 1994; Beck, 1992; Beck *et al.*, 1994). Reflexive modernity is accompanied by a sense of the essential contingency of self, science and society; the technological project of controlling and exploiting nature is subject to the stochastic character of the world; uncertainty accompanies every human decision, in which, 'for something gained, something is always lost' (Luhmann, 1993). The cosmic bottle is half-empty rather than half-full. And this is said to be accompanied by a breakdown of trust in the willingness and ability of government and big business to respect individual rights; the traditional knowledge of academics and professionals no longer has authority and trust moves to self-help groups and the law – a system which, because it is based on notions of human intentionality, is not ultimately equipped to deal with the problems of risk as an actuarial phenomenon (Luhmann, 1993).

In this context, psychic harm can be said to loom on the horizon as an environmental hazard as real as any spouting volcano – an outcome of natural and technological disasters which are now socially accepted as distressing, debilitating and legally actionable (see Chapter 4). In these particular cases, the medium of the harm is fear for the physical safety of self and those emotionally close. The list of such disasters in the last fifty years is evocative: Hillsborough, the *Torrey Canyon*, the Zeebrugge ferry disaster, Bhopal, the King's Cross fire, the Paddington train crash, and the recent tsunamis; with Lockerbie, 9/11 and 7/7 adding the factor of intentional human agency and a new form of risk called 'terror'. Since a team from the Tavistock Clinic (Garland, 1998) decided to set up shop at the scene of the Zeebrugge ferry disaster, it has become automatic for UK local authorities to set up counselling services for shocked and bereaved victims and distressed rescue workers (Ursano and Norwood, 2003).[6] Powerful and debilitating psychological consequences of fear and horror in participants, witnesses or relatives are what is expected and part of the tally when the economic and social costs of such events are estimated.

By the same token, psychological harm is an expected outcome and cost of the horrors of war, for both the military and civilians involved.[7] Though its presence, in the form of shell shock, was much written about in World War I, such harm was only finally legitimated for the professionals by the compensation paid by the US government to Vietnam veterans in the late 1970s, and by the writing into DSM-III[8] of the new diagnostic category of post-traumatic stress disorder in 1980.[9] In the UK media, it was a feature of the aftermath of the Falklands War and it is notable that part of the discourse of the British press in even contemplating the recent invasion of Iraq was the prospect of psychological as well as physical injuries to our soldiers. The US studies on returning soldiers produce a figure of 1 in 6, rising to 1 in 3 veterans suffering depression or PTSD (CBS News, 2007). It is simply part of modern warfare, though a soul count is not yet used in its memorialisation, in the way that a body count of the dead and injured still serves (Scarry, 1985). In the case of civilians the psychological risks of warfare, ethnic cleansing, genocide and mass rape are incontrovertible and documented in a vast international academic and institutional literature, from UN publications onwards.[10]

Psychic harm is also part of another environmental danger, listed by the technicians of risk as 'crime',[11] a problem involving the effects of human agency. Under this heading are forms of communication in threatening relationships: the crime of psychic assault, a sub-category of grievous bodily harm, which induces fear for physical safety in the victims (Horder, 1998), as do the crimes of harassment and stalking (Best, 2008). There are other forms of verbal communication which are not generally criminalised but which are said to produce different negative emotions in addition to fear, such as shame, humiliation and self loathing (Nussbaum, 2004). Such emotions induced by cruel words over a long period are said to produce a slow death of the spirit or 'soul murder' (Shengold, 1979). Whilst public defamation and libel, one-off events, are judged in civil law for compensation mostly on the basis of consequent loss of goods like reputation and earnings, emotional abuse, hate speech, psychological torture, racism, bullying, harassment at work and other acts are seen as abuses of power, and the cause of 'injury to feelings', which may be justiciable under some interpretations.[12] Current social panics in the UK and USA concentrate on the 'culture of bullying' of young army recruits at Deepcut and Catterick army barracks, the sexual humiliation of Iraqi prisoners at Abu Ghraib, the degradation and mental torture of internees at Guantanamo and the rest. Sexual assault, degrading treatment of the elderly and vulnerable or institutionalised children, and physical and verbal aggression in close family relationships, marital and parental, are also said to have such an effect on mental states (Kennedy, 1993) and, for example, a diagnosis of Battered Wives' Syndrome has been used as mitigation in some cases of women accused of spouse murder.[13]

The threat of psychic, or any, harm to children is thought of as a social problem of particularly high valence, since, for the last two centuries at least, the child has had such a symbolic importance in our culture. After World War II and the shock generated by the poor physical and educational state of the child evacuees who poured out of London, children and families became a prime object of social policy (Rose, 1999). With the start of the Welfare State, childhood, as a social ideal, became elevated to a protected space, watched over by Mother – a nostalgic place of primal innocence and happiness, despite the contemporary theories of Freud and Klein. Images of children at risk are constantly used to enhance political movements and campaigns, from community panics about paedophiles through law-and-order issues and the crisis of the disintegrating family, to matters of global ecology, in which 'children yet unborn' and 'generations to come' are overwhelming objects of concern. Formally, UK Local Authorities have been running a child protection system of increasing cost, sophistication and organisation since 1970; the right to protection was written into the UN Convention on the Rights of the Child (signed by the UK in 1991) and, recently, the government has created a Minister for Children to safeguard their especial interests. Meanwhile, child emotional abuse, that is abuse that does not touch the body, became an official registration category in this system in 1980.[14] In the administrative processing of abuse, it was initially low on the hierarchy of 'dangerousness' implicit in the figures but seems to be rising fast (see Chapters 5 and 6) as a major risk to children and their psychological and emotional development, though it is now coded in another language.

For, here, as elsewhere, 'risk' is being reframed. The official parlance of the Department for Children, Schools and Families (DfES) has for some time avoided the use of the word 'risk'. Children at risk of abuse were administered under a system called 'Child Protection' and now children are no longer just 'protected' but 'safeguarded'. This, it seems, is thought to have more positive and more universal connotations[15] and is twinned, in government-speak, with the reframing of issues of risk in general as those of 'security' – a positive programme for making safe in the face of threats.[16]

It is not only the positive emphasis that is subtly different, however. For example, whilst in the UK 'security' is still very much concerned with 'protection' (protecting borders against unwanted threats such as immigration and protecting the population against terrorism and crime), in the world of international relations the concept of security has migrated away from the realist one of sovereign nation-states, like individuals manning their own boundaries, to become amalgamated with the discourses of human rights and human development.

This amalgam forms the concept of 'human security', which is a universal, individual and communal aspiration across borders, concerned with the 'downside risks' caused by famine and war (often internal) to these same rights and development (Ogata and Sen, 2003).[17] This discourse therefore includes an insistence on positive as well as negative freedoms, the rights of individuals to have their basic needs met and to develop on some optimal path of wellbeing. It is the downside risks to this optimal development which have to be guarded against, not just by protection from threats and curative action in response to calamity but by the empowerment of people (Ogata and Sen, 2003). Psychological health is one such need, and a therapeutic process, by definition, is one which penetrates the boundaries of individuals as well as states. Thus its relationship to empowerment, which invokes the concept of negative as well as positive rights, is somewhat problematic, as discussed in Chapter 2.

The consequences of psychic harm

A general reading of the psy academic, professional and social policy literature and the UK media suggests that these consequences are dire for individuals and society as a whole. For adults, what seems to be threatened by a psychic injury, is varying levels of reactive mental illness, depression, PTSD, dissociative disorder, obsessive compulsive or eating problems, suicidal or other disturbed behaviour (often called maladaptive), signs of unhappiness, restlessness, inability to concentrate, unwillingness to socialise, unprompted aggression, substance abuse, delinquency and the rest, all of which may last for varying periods of time. There is no doubt that psychic harm enlarges the pool of mental health problems, which one in four of the UK population is said to have experienced (Royal College of Psychiatry, 2008), especially in the worrying guise of environmental 'stress', which is apparently the number one complaint of British workers – 'a stress epidemic', Richard Excell of the TUC calls it. (Excell, 2004)

The negative consequences here are seen as twofold and represent a bifurcation in the way that psychological problems are construed and controlled in this country. Stress sufferers either enter the formal medical sector, consuming costly care and treatment, with escalating use of mood- and personality-enhancing drugs, like SSRIs,[18] which are an ever-increasing drain on NHS resources. They may present problems of social control, because of compensatory substance abuse which sometimes accompanies long term psychological problems, in extreme cases supported by delinquency, and problems of depletion of the workforce.

This is less an issue of loss of skills, but more, according to the present UK government – and the last – that of the numbers on Incapacity Benefit.[19] This, in turn, is partly a problem of cost and, also, partly of social order, because a lack of employment is seen to loop back into poor mental health, as well as more traditional satanic activities (Black, 2008).

The alternative is that stress sufferers make their way into the burgeoning alternative medical sector, through self-help books or groups, private counselling or therapy. According to Frank Furedi, the UK has become a 'therapy culture', and this, he thinks, presents us with a meta-problem. The profound discursive shift, manifest in the huge growth in the therapy sector, does not just track our psychic vulnerability to the dangers of our physical and social environment, it creates it. We react to events in ways in which we have learnt are culturally appropriate; we know how victims ought to behave; our lack of emotional resiliency is self fulfilling (Furedi, 2004).

Our psychic vulnerability is also said to pass from generation to generation, one of the results and one of the causes of a crisis in the family and the care and control it is seen to provide. The negative effects of parental mental ill-health and marital conflict on children's health and welfare are a commonplace of our family narrative. In general, we hear, the diagnosis of depression among children is rising rapidly, as, not surprisingly, is their consumption of drugs like SSRIs and Ritalin for hyperactivity (Horwitz and Wakefield, 2007; Wong *et al.*, 2004). Meanwhile, the Health and Lifestyle sections of the Sunday newspapers have taken up the publication of neurological research suggesting that emotional deprivation affects the development of children's brains (Burke, 2000). Neuro-imaging provides powerful visual material for new 'narratives of endangerment', designed, like the government's pro-familial policies, to keep parents on the job.[20]

Consequently, we are told, this sadness and behavioural disturbance in children has significant social outcomes, affecting our collective welfare in complicated ways. Apart from its immediate effects on levels of delinquency and poor educational attainment, it signals poor adult adjustment. If we cannot raise mentally healthy adults, we cannot enjoy the high levels of economic wealth we currently experience. According to the hedonic calculus of some economists (Di Tella *et al.*, 2003; Layard, 2008) we are just not happy enough, too depressed to appreciate what we have got (James, 2007).

In the longer run, mental ill-health may affect our very powers of wealth creation. Unlike World War II paternalism, which rested on a concern for the collective psychological health of the nation, current policy pursues the collective wealth of the nation. The New Labour blueprint for the future was a vision of private individuals and corporations functioning in a global economy, mediated by the state through facilitating partnerships, and by the family and civil society in similar roles (Giddens, 1998). For these individuals (and institutions) to function, people have to be healthy in body and mind. Above all, since paternalism has gone, the contribution of state and family to their welfare is education, teaching and training in order to produce a flexible response to changing work role expectations; participation depends on transferable social and technical skills. These, in turn, rest on the ability of the individual to process information, and to manage the self and the emotions at all times. Training for this begins early. The Personal, Social Health and Economic Education section of the Secretary of State's proposals for the national curriculum (QCA/DFE, 1999) provided a perfect template for the production of such a paragon of reflexivity and control: someone who, for example, has learnt how to mourn the loss of parents in family breakdown by Key Stage Four.

Finally, all this happiness and wealth is still at risk, because even a population of flexible, self-motivating, self-controlled individuals may be adversely affected by the major calamities that the modern world has in store for them, accidental disasters, civil wars, violent bereavement and the rest. Psychic harm may be too much even for these models of psychological health and normality, unless they have the ability to bounce back from trauma, to carry on in the face of overwhelming odds in the form of shock and grief or devastating social circumstances and to survive mentally, where ordinary people would succumb to stress. Probabilistically, of course, such extraordinary people were a statistical phenomenon, the tail of a bell curve, picked up in early epidemiological studies of child developmental psychopathology.[21] But we now learn from further studies that such 'resilient' people exist, a minority of the population, for instance at the level of 40 per cent in a study of New Yorkers exposed to the events of 9/11 (Ahern *et al.*, 2004; Behrens *et al.*, 2007; cited in Young, 2006). Furthermore, such 'trait resiliency' can be measured (Connor and Davidson, 2003) and learned through psychological interventions,[22] or induced through regimes of medication, which promote an optimistic frame of mind (Davidson *et al.*, 2005). But most surely and lastingly it can, literally, be incorporated in the individual by the right developmental experiences[23] (Young, 2006).

In a way, the story is obvious. Stress and risk, those two great reifications of the late 20th century, lurk somewhere in the ether waiting to get us when we are down on our luck, joined now by 'terror' as the hazard for the new century. And their social threat is maximised when the danger is to children, repositories as they are of our uncertain future and icons of human vulnerability to harm and its unjust distribution. Their proper growth and development is crucial to the social production of the self governing individual of the neoliberal state and, further, to a subject who is resilient to shocks both to the individual and to the social system (Young, 2006). This process of development is, paradoxically, so important that it cannot be left to individuals. The child and the family, above all else, have become sites where the disciplinary role of the state can be said to have increased (Brown, 1995), along with the ceaseless occupation of the confessional in the treatment of the psychologically sick in both the alternative and the statutory health markets. For behind all our preoccupation with trauma and treatment is the fantasy of resilience, the inner capacity of an individual to rise above adversity – not impervious to suffering shock and emotional pain but not long-term harmed or altered by it either. On the contrary, 'Resilientman' grows stronger in crisis and difficulty; he bursts the clothing of the normal and the everyday like some psychic superhero who, whatever befalls, by the end of the episode has achieved resolution 'and moved on'.

1.3   Psychic harm: The sociological problem

Metaphysics?

In Section 1.1 of this chapter, I committed myself to a study of the social processes whereby a social problem category is made and, in this case, how it is made visible, how it becomes the object of professional knowledge and techniques, talk, text and social practices. I have also suggested that this study is less a social constructionist theorisation and history of emotional abuse and more a version of a Foucauldian genealogy of the current categories of psychic harm, as elaborated below. This was presented as a choice framed in terms of the subject matter to be covered. But it also has some implications for methodology and the vexed question of metaphysics for researchers in either of these traditions: does their study of the forging of mental categories in the social world imply a theory of knowledge which restricts what they themselves can say or do? The problem seems to be their position in relation to the world they study; whether they can claim the empirical validity of their observations; whether it is they themselves who endow these with meaning – and whether either question matters.

The first question relates to social constructionism, which is an old and sometime honourable activity in sociology (Best, 1989; Sarbin and Kitsuse, 1994; Spector and Kitsuse, 1977) studying the way certain social problem categories are constructed in social process. Over time, the term became conflated with poststructuralist philosophy, and is much used in the United States to denote the nominalist as opposed to the realist side in the 'science wars' or 'culture wars' which have riven the US academy (Hacking, 1999). As such, it has become a position associated with controversy and criticism, from which this book may not be free. If all our categories of knowledge are cultural categories, forged in linguistic and social processes, how can researchers make claims to objective truth?

Not only can they be accused of an absurd omnipotence as they observe and distance themselves from the knowledge of other disciplines – and even, sometimes, their own – an audience to a drama played out in a particular discursive space. Worse, their position is fraught with paradox. Simply put, how can they, with any logical consistency, make other people's truth claims relative and anthropologically strange whilst claiming empirical validity for their own observations? According to Steven Woolgar and Dorothy Pawluch in their well known critique of social constructionism, claiming the empirical validity of descriptions of socially constructed phenomena is simply a contradiction in terms, which has to be managed in social constructionist studies by 'selective relativism' and 'lapses into realism' (Woolgar and Pawluch, 1985: 224). This, the authors suggest, is gerrymandering,[24] doing boundary work, which sustains 'the differential susceptibility of phenomena to ontological uncertainty' (Woolgar and Pawluch, 1985: 216). It is, they assert, the social accomplishment of sociology departments, which all have to manage the contradictions inherent in presenting objective accounts of social phenomena.

There are several solutions to this problem, none of them entirely satisfactory. Ian Hackings's, outlined in the commonsense language of the philosophy department, in his book, *The Social Construction of What*, attempts to rescue a tenable realist position for those who 'do' social constructionism. First he demotes this back to an activity rather than a metaphysical position or a theory of knowledge (Hacking, 1999), identifying a hierarchy of claims for the categories described as 'constructed', from neutral claims for their contingency or lack of inevitability (a historical or ironic approach) through 'reformist', 'rebellious' and 'revolutionary' versions. These run from merely 'unmasking' to claims that such social constructions are undesirable and ought to be abolished (Hacking, 1999: Chapter 1). Second, he reminds us that social problem categories are concepts or 'social kinds', not to be confused with the activity that they purport to describe. And these kinds, he claims, exist only under a description; they are subject to historical contingency; their existence in the social world is not inevitable but an outcome of social circumstances – as, indeed, is the world in which they exist (Goodman, 1979; cited in Hacking, 1999: 44, 45 and 128–131). So these concepts are, for the reasons just given, ontologically subjective. But, since they exist in the world, in the public domain, up for discussion and, in the case of ideas, are observable within the social matrix of their use in public rhetoric, claims making and associated practices, they are also epistemologically objective – they can be known by the researcher, who can make claims to truth.

On one level, this neat argument, based on marking the distinction between ontology and epistemology, which Hacking attributes to the linguistic philosopher John Searle (Hacking, 1997; Searle, 1995), appears to have solved the contradictions managed by ontological gerrymandering, without abandoning the question of metaphysics. But Hacking's shelter from paradox in a realist world seems almost too good to be true. He adds a rider about the contingent changes to a social problem category 'looping back' to influence the behaviour of those so categorised – 'human kinds' emerging and transformed simultaneously with the language that describes them (Rose, 1999: xix). (He calls this process 'making up people', which is hardly a new idea and basically indistinguishable from the old concept of 'labelling' in the sociological study of deviance.) The real difficulty is that he says nothing about the social work done in deciding on how to recognise its concrete instances – that is, in applying the category. There is nothing on the looping-back effects on the internal worlds and practices of the people who make these observations, and thus on researchers themselves. It is as if these categories were the beginning and the end of the social process, not deeply embedded in language as a constantly transformed and transforming cultural institution (Hacking, 1995a).

Nevertheless, Hacking's work does provide a place from which to build some coherent account of what any particular social constructionist account is doing. In Hacking's hierarchy of social constructionist claims, this work on the invisible wound would be low on the radical count (though perhaps it might attain the status of irony!). An argument for the lack of inevitability or of the contingency of its various social forms is certainly being made, although even this seems hardly necessary. For instance, it is a commonplace in the child protection literature that child abuse is a 'socially constructed' concept, mostly described as dependent on contemporary values. However these 'values', seem to transmogrify over time as effortlessly as language does in Hacking's accounts. As stated earlier, this work is more about the effort – about *how* this set of problem categories has been socially produced. If this can be shown, then the question of *whether* they have been will take care of itself.

Another solution to the social constructionist research paradox is to forget about metaphysics and go for a position of irrealism – an indifference to the nominalist versus realist debate and even to metaphysics at all.[25] This might involve a pragmatic assertion that, while selective relativism might be unacceptable, it is a legitimate exercise in academic enquiry to examine only one aspect of a complex problem, holding the other variables constant. After all, agnosticism about the existence and location of the territory known as 'inner life' and its wounds is not denial. It could be claimed that this book simply does not enquire into its ontological status; it is about the 'exploration industry' itself, its claims to discovery and its creation of new versions of the territory called the self through the concept of an invisible wound.

This is an approach which subtly keeps alive the possibility of a realist version of the phenomena under study. However, irrealism might also involve a shift to a more European, poststructuralist stance. Social constructionism was always dogged by its siting within a predominantly realist US academy and the demands of research funders. Metaphysics or a theory of knowledge is only interesting where the observer is taken to be some enlightenment figure who is the hero of his own observations, in which case the validity or consistency of his claims to know the physical and social worlds of his observation are central. If the subject is decentred, as for Foucault, just part of the observing system, produced and reproduced by his own operations, or, in other language, discursively produced, then what is interesting is the story – discourse itself, the conditions for its emergence, its regimes of truth and its fields of power.

This position suggests that I should hastily abandon a first-person narrative in my accounts of invisible wounds and their conditions (which I do at the end of this chapter). It suggests, also, avoiding the term social constructionism, with its metaphysical implications and concentrating on a version of Foucauldian genealogies, or a 'history of the present'. And, if social constructionism involves tracking the forging of a problem category in the crucible of competing professional claims and practices, then it is just a small step to the way that Foucault thought about the emergence of discourses out of the power struggles of people wielding professional rationalities. Genealogy, his name for this history of discourse, is a word which he took from Nietzsche, who saw ideas as arising from everyday and extremely low-level squabbles (Foucault, 1977). Foucault himself was more concerned with knowledge encapsulated in the more formal theories and practices of what he called 'the unsafe sciences' – the human and social sciences (Foucault, 1973), which are also part of the context of this investigation.

Foucault's theorisations, however, bring us to the second question, relating to the place in his philosophy of hermeneutics and the meaning giving observer, rather than the realist researcher. Although his writing assiduously avoided this problem, according to the influential commentary by Dreyfus and Rabinow, it would seem that he never really felt free of metaphysics (Dreyfus and Rabinow, 1982). For Foucault, the archaeologist, discourses were synchronic, discrete, discontinuous and objectively recognizable sets of rules, because their meaning was created by the rules themselves. They were in no way dependent on the meaning given them by an interpreting subject. With the introduction of the genealogical metaphor into his later work, discourses became diachronic, looser, more mobile phenomena, still discontinuous, emerging into a social space and submerging again, criss-crossing the social surface in a series of marriages and divorces, fusions and fissions, which make an ordinary family tree look like a very orderly affair (Dreyfus and Rabinow, 1982). It was in genealogical method that Foucault famously married knowledge and power in their complex interdependent relationship (Foucault, 1979; Foucault, 1980b). And, of course, in his studies of power in the social world, he re-encountered the problem of the interpretive observer, also a subject of power/ knowledge (Dreyfus and Rabinow, 1982).

His answer to this problem of interpretation was to write a very concrete and pragmatic form of history, totally divorced from appeal to subterranean forces and metaphysical explanations. This he called 'genealogy'. The surface of human activity is looked at from high up, from which point a map of all the empirical connections between persons, texts and apparatuses would be apparent. These connections were not interpreted by the observer but rather traced into the past, as one would trace the ancestry of a present, living individual on a family tree. This genealogy was not like the old history of ideas which was, paradoxically, dehistoricised (in which concepts and theories drew their meaning from their own self-contained trajectory, developing according to some internal rationality). Moreover, in contrast to current history, where events and ideas draw their significance from their place within the social context of their time, these events were significant only for what they did or allowed to happen next, rather than for any meaning attributed to them by the genealogist. This method Foucault also called 'a history of the present', in which was mapped a chain of happenings which lead to a current state – inexorably, it would appear, with the hindsight of the present, but, in fact, of course, a random and chancy business – as with evolution.

My approach to my series of studies will be similarly *genealogical*, as described above, mapping the ancestors of present forms of invisible wounds and asking a set of generic 'Foucauldian' questions about what allowed these present forms of life to come into being – necessary but not sufficient conditions for their existence: In this 'history of the present', what are the social conditions under which each form of the invisible wound discussed here was made visible – that is to say, knowable, discussable, treatable, administrable and justiciable?;What were the different regimes of truth which prevailed? What were the discursive conditions under which truths, facts and explanations, theories of the wound, came to be formulated and accepted? What were the different individual and institutional power relations and hierarchies of authority and prestige, technological conditions and practical affordances? What was the political context in which such knowledge emerged?

It should be said that, whilst I have borrowed the concept of genealogy (or historical ontology) from Foucault, I would not claim that what follows is a full Foucauldian analysis of the emergence of these wound categories. True, it is a study conducted at the level of *discourse*, not of everyday speech or social interaction but within the broad context of scientific, professional, policy and legal texts[26] and the practices they enshrine. True, discourse is defined in a Foucauldian way: as a relatively well-ordered, though not necessarily internally consistent, system of knowledge; as consisting of ideas, beliefs, attitudes and practices, linked by certain styles of thought, key concepts and techniques, which construct both their subjects and the truths about the worlds of which they speak and write and, lastly, as an open system, drawing on multiple sources and constantly changing over time. However, whilst I look at the emergence of key concepts and their implied techniques within a literature, I do not fully address these techniques and practices through either history or ethnography – a gap which I regret and hope others may fill.

Besides this, the book does not directly employ a Foucauldian theorisation of power. That is, it assumes it, rather than using it to add to the analysis of the current political conjuncture. What is simply taken for granted here is that discourses are not just sets of *knowledges* but, in their construction of subjects and their worlds, they, also, carry with them relations of *power*. Ways of thinking are linked to ways of acting; human agency, even down to individual action, is shaped and constrained by formally defined capacities and legitimations at the discursive level, though these, in their turn, are changed over time by social action and interaction from which new discourses emerge. It is the emergence which this book addresses as an exercise in what Foucault called 'historical ontology', charting the birth and growth of some of the categories of the wound: PTSD, nervous shock in tort law, emotional abuse and attachment disorders, particular forms of knowledge, which have become fundamental to our ways of knowing ourselves.

As such, these categories are also, as Hacking has observed, involved inexorably in world-making, in our ways of being and in our forms of power. But this 'looping back' of socially constructed categories into the making-up of people and their forms of government is the part of a recursive system which I have largely to assume, rather than examine in any detail, simply because there is a limit to what can be done here. The exception is Chapter 2, where I look at the work done by the metaphor of 'invisible wounds' in the creation of a particular form of subjectivity, but I do not extend this to look at what forms of government or Foucauldian forms of power this version of subjectivity allows. In the main body of his work, Foucault's 'histories of the present' trace the emergence of particular technologies of disciplinary and regulatory power. In his late work he begins to relate particular discursive transformations to the current forms of government in advanced liberal states (Foucault, 1982; Foucault, 1985), work which is later taken up by others (Barry *et al.*, 1996). I am concerned here only with the political conditions of the *emergence* of categories of power. Of course, these two relationships of power/knowledge are inseparable in practice, especially if the political functionality of a category is seen as a condition for its coming into being. Nevertheless, I have found it essential to separate them conceptually in the interests of a manageable piece of research.

The last hole in my Foucauldian credentials is this: I suspect that, according to Foucault's transgressive thinking, the whole notion of a 'Foucauldian Methodology' is a contradiction in terms. Dreyfus and Rabinow (1982) suggest that Foucault's approach to history writing is largely rhetorical. And how could I hope to reproduce the pyrotechnics of his astonishing, playful and persuasive style? Finally though, as he would wish, this is not a problem but a liberation.

1.4 Conclusion

At the beginning of this section on methodology I hinted at some ethical confusion, a lack of certainty about whether my position as a researcher in this field was either overwhelmingly arrogant or, in contrast, pathetically humble, constrained by a realist metaphysic into feeling that, if I cannot make claims to truth, then I really have nothing useful to say. My doubts were exacerbated by the cold reception I was frequently given, when I tried to explain my research approach to questioners who were keen to sympathise with the emotional strain that such work must cause me or to connect it to their own psychological state and memories of childhood. For, as it became clear that I was not a potential technician of human suffering, I seemed to lose all claim to feel compassion – let alone to expertise or to truth. I tried to answer this scepticism by declaring, 'truthfully', that, of course, I feel the utmost sympathy for the subjective reality of individual suffering, be it psychological or physical, but that just was not the point of my research ... But what, then, *is* the point?

The question was answered for me when I found this justification for the genealogical method in the introduction by Nikolas Rose to the second edition of his book, *Governing the Soul*.

> The aim of such genealogies is a kind of destabilisation or de-fatalisation of our present. In describing its contingency, in therefore opening up the possibility that things have been different, could have been different, they try to make it easier to assess that present, in order to make judgments about how to act upon it. If the history of our present is more accidental than we may like to believe, the future of our present is also more open than it sometimes appears (Rose, 1999: xii).

This made sense of putting compassion and truth in brackets and getting on with it. It is a thoroughly political justification of research; research as intervention. Although I may have many reservations about what Rose calls the 'ceaseless confession and solicitude' of therapy (Rose, 1999: xxv), I was taken back to the work I did fifteen years ago. In the way I questioned my clients, it was precisely this 'de-fatalisation' of the present that I was trying to achieve.

2
Invisible wounds

2.1 Introduction

Making the wounded self

This chapter looks at the work that the metaphor of invisible wounds could be said to do in the production of a particular hybrid version of the self in relation to his/her physical and social context. Clearly the uses of this metaphor are many and various, and the imagined picture of the self that such language implies is hard, at first, to figure out. What is it that we see? The object of a horrific and disruptive shock? A life-form disfigured gradually by years of cruelty? The owner of voice seeking empowerment? A medical patient defined by another's expertise? Is this patient pathological or can we still detect glimpses of the normal, healthy space that was there before attack? It is a complex and conflicted view of the inner life that emerges, when the self or the soul is looked at through the prism of psychic harm or wounding. Nevertheless, behind all the variation is one dominant image: that of an individual soul with breachable boundaries, like an individual body, operating defensively in a potentially hostile environment which may cause lesion, shrapnel or foreign bodies lodged in the wound, scarring and long term damage. These wounds are administrable by medical experts in healing, and their relations, but serve and even legitimate the practices of religious solace, the claiming of political rights, social welfare and international aid.

This image of the vulnerable individual seems to be held in place by two major discursive shifts towards the end of the 20th century. The first is the story of the openness of all bounded individuals toward risk or danger in their physical and social environment (Beck *et al.*, 1994) – the risk discourse, discussed in Chapter 1. The second part of the story is a narrative about the increase in psychic vulnerability in late modernity, due to changes in the 'therapeutic self'. The influential work by Philip Reiff, *The Triumph of the Therapeutic: Uses of Faith after Freud*, (Reiff, 1967) has been followed by a number of books describing the development of *Therapeutic Culture* (Furedi, 2004) and *The Therapeutic State* (Nolan, 1998) and exemplified by a current attempt by some psychoanalysts to extend therapeutic thinking into the political domain (Kraemer and Roberts, 1996; Samuels, 2002, for example). Nolan suggests that the self produced by this therapeutic turn no longer exists within the old authoritative moral orders and transcends even the psychoanalytic self, as the latter struggles to adapt to the demands of ever-present social imperatives. This latest self is the product of more humanistic therapies; it exists in a milieu in which it alone is the 'touchstone of cultural judgement' (Bell, 1978: 117); the self and its experience alone is authentic and central to its moral universe: any moral scheme that exists for self regulation is ultimately self-referential. So Nolan finds in his study of political discourse in the USA that the language constantly invokes the goal of individual emotional development, rather than the individual moral growth that used to be seen as the means and end of adaptation to external social mores. As he puts it: 'where once the self was to be surrendered, denied, sacrificed and died to, now the self is to be esteemed, actualised, affirmed and unfettered' (Nolan, 1998: 3). This, then, is our vulnerability. For anyone whose mental welfare requires *all that* must be a little liable to disappointment, or worse!

What sort of entity *is* this vulnerable and demanding self? Nolan, it seems, tends to conflate this morally unfettered, free-floating and reflexive self with the fragmented, decentred self of postmodernity, cognitively aware of its own contingency and reproducing itself by its own operations (Nolan, 1998). But the political language of the therapeutic self posits the soul as a source of emotional control and self regulation, one of the products of normative development, as an individual who is at the centre of its social world, who interacts with it and may be encouraged or harmed by it, but not in some continuous process of social reproduction. This is not a self recreated anew in every social encounter (Gergen and Shotter,1989), but a self held together, integrated by memory and its sense of its own history. In short, it relies for its meaning on a more realist version of personal identity: the authentic, whole, centred individual of humanism.

And the metaphor of the 'invisible wound', in one way, assumes such a self. The concept of psychic harm or thwarted emotional development posits a vulnerable, woundable individual, thus one who is fixed, continuous, there to receive a causal blow. But here the complications begin. This self bifurcates into two, depending on the nature of the harm: first, one whose self-narrative or observable behaviour may be altered by a powerful traumatic event[1] and, second, one for whom the harm is ontogenetic because more subtle and continuously cumulative over time.[2] To complicate matters, this already split self splits again around the distinction between observed behaviour and self-narrative – the visual versus the oral register. The object of observation, carried by the largely medical metaphor, organised around the concepts of trauma, abuse and attachment disorganisation, invokes a linear and positivist psychiatric/psychological model of personal functioning and a conventional doctor/expert–patient relationship. The subject of narrative, on the other hand, is the owner of voice, whose identity develops in some dialogical relationship with her social world, who can claim her rights and for whom therapy is an intersubjective conversation of empowerment. And both these versions may be vulnerable to the two forms of wounding. Moreover, the self-actualising version is often conflated with the medical one, indeed depends on it for legitimation of claims to harm, as do many other uses of the wound metaphor discussed in this chapter. And both are so overlaid by figurative expression and alternative paradigms that 'wound culture' (Das, 2003: 297) seems to abound in ontological confusion.

What is more, if this state of vulnerability is ordinary – what is to be expected – is an invisible wound a normal or a pathological state? Canguilhem pointed out that, within the life sciences, it was through the study of *abnormality* in living form or function, both physical and psychological pathology and developmental deformity, that the understanding of normal, ordinary ways of life at all levels of complexity, was achieved (Canguilhem, 1991; Foucault, 1980a). In the case of invisible wounds, however, we are talking about something different: an understanding of the self arrived at not through a study of its diseases, but through the idea of a severe hurt to the soul or psyche – so severe, in fact, as to result in prolonged psychic distress and disorder. Though the effects of the wound are *as if* the mind itself is diseased, this is, nevertheless, a disorder which, over time, has come to be seen neither as a symptom of an organic condition nor a 'constitutional weakness', neither caused by an illness nor by the predisposing factors which are stochastic features of the landscape in modern, statistical medicine. It is caused by events quite outside the individual which could wound just anybody and from which we are all at risk. This, of course, creates a paradox (one which the Appeal Court Judges struggle with in Chapter 3).

Since the effects of psychic trauma are psychologically debilitating, often attracting medical diagnosis and drug or counselling therapy, the individual sufferer can be said to have a psychiatric condition, but one, on the other hand, which can be said to be normal – a sort of normal pathology.

Besides this, there are other puzzles. For, even in a constrained psychological model of individual interaction with a social environment, it is not clear where the self is located – in the neurological system or in some parallel inner world that might be called consciousness... or in unconsciousness, or in both.[3] At what level is the wound 'invisible'? This raises deeper questions about metaphor itself and the metaphysic in which it sits, described in Chapter 1.

These confusions and complications are touched on in this chapter and they also run right through the book, as it addresses the question of how the metaphor of the invisible wound serves to fix the fragmented, protean, self-reproducing or socially constructed soul of postmodernity or poststructuralism into particular forms. This is not just a matter of language, but also of practice. The metaphor is part of a discourse in which language and practices, in particular those of psy professionals, are inseparable. Later chapters look at the practices of the invisible wound as they evolve in the context of professional journals and other texts. This first chapter is, however, about language and thus more literary, less sociological in content. It traces the implications of the metaphor for particular narrated forms of the self with all their contradictions. It does not attempt to sort out or rationalise the discourse, merely seeing it as reflecting the diversity of social praxis. It picks up examples from a rich, varied usage which has grown over time, migrated across social context and, itself, moves freely between figurative and technical modes of thinking and expression, in both the oral and visual registers.

These examples are taken partly from the psychological literature on trauma – particularly its history – and the biomedical version reviewed more extensively in Chapter 3; this underlies and structures the vernacular usage within a present Anglophone culture which is saturated with 'trauma talk' and which generally covers a wide domain, including identity politics, religion and the more alternative therapies. Some background research was also done in these areas in the process of making sense of the main source of material, which is an ordinary Google search for 'Invisible Wounds' conducted at the beginning of 2006. This search provides, even for this more restricted version of psychological harm, a stunning array of usages across different social contexts, from personal testimony of the psychic costs of chronic physical disease to counselling sites and self-help books offering help for emotional or sexual abuse; from teen magazines discussing racism and bullying or dating violence to religious sites with personal testimony from depressed clergy; or legal or quasi legal sites dealing with sexual harassment at work. There are copious references to a series of zombie films called 'The Living Dead' and, improbably, some interesting visual representations, mostly by German artists, on a site called *fotocommunity.com*. By far the most prevalent context for the use of this metaphor, however, is discussion of the handling and treatment of military personnel, war and 'peace-keeping' veterans – from Vietnam to Iraq through the Holocaust to the former Yugoslavia or Rwanda – and of the indigenous victims of these and other conflagrations and mass injustices around the world, of oppression by cruel dictatorships, of disappearances, torture, mass rape, ethnic cleansing or genocide. And here the metaphor migrates by means of another metaphor; the self becomes, by analogy, the psyche, not just of an individual, but of a group, a nation, the world even; the bearer of the wound and of scars becomes a whole people. Trauma, memory, memorialisation and healing become cultural and political phenomena; 'identity' collective (Ignatieff, 1996).

It is not claimed here that such a search throws up a set of data which is completely representative of the way this metaphor is used across different social contexts, but it does produce examples from a range of sites which do not necessarily use the language of psychological, legal or administrative expertise, which is the subject of later chapters. Indeed, it might be said to give some glimpse of the diaspora of the concept of trauma, as it has become part of what Terry Eagleton calls the 'custom piety, intuition and opinion' that society observes (Eagleton, 1990: 23).

The figurative body

The metaphor of the invisible wound, with its cargo of unreality, emphasises that what it refers to is *not* a wound, at least at a gross physical level. It draws on a linguistic and conceptual distinction between the body and some more interior site, say the soul. But at the same time, the abstract soul is understood through our experience of the frailty, vulnerability and mortality of human flesh. And, as if this were not complex enough, it has to be recognised that the body itself is not free of figurative loading. The bodily metaphor does not only link the soul to obvious physical or corporeal characteristics. The body comes freighted with its own set of metaphors which then, through the serendipity of language, the soul itself acquires. According to examples taken from Emily Martin's anthropological work on immunology (Martin, 1990), the human body has a starring part in the creation of symbolic and social orders in all societies (Durkheim and Mauss, 1963). Particularly relevant here is the metaphor of the body as a nation state. This contains two essential notions; first, the notion of the body as the spatio-temporal, or the cellular (Schindler, 1988, cited in Martin, 1990), basis of individual identity which implies a rigid and absolute boundary between the body (self) and the external world (non-self). Second, 'the identification of the non-self world as foreign and hostile' (Martin, 1990: 411), which implies the notion of boundaries as protective defences against an invasive and dangerous environment. Martin quotes Peter Jaret's florid description of the way the immune system functions:

> Besieged by a vast array of invisible enemies (bacteria etc.), the human body enlists a remarkable complex corps of internal body guards to battle the invaders (Jaret, 1986: 702).

and Lenart Nilsson:

> The organisation of the human immune system is reminiscent of military defence, with regard to both weapon technology and strategy (Nilsson, 1987: 20).

Susan Sontag's work, too, describes the use of a military metaphor in the way we figure cancer and AIDS. In this discourse, the defence of the body extends to the defence of the body politic in its perpetual war against encroaching microorganisms, in the form of disease or mere mortality (Sontag, 1991).

It is argued here that, through the metaphor of the spiritual wound, the soul, itself, acquires this freight of defensive individualism, precluding any notion that it is part of some universal animus, some systemic, all-pervasive mind (Bateson, 1979) or a construct of the social (Gergen and Shotter,1989). This bodily metaphor places the psyche neatly within each individual body-bag. Also, crucially, what it is that lies in the interior of the body is a 'soul-bag', with its own defensive boundaries that can be attacked and pierced by powerful forces from outside – forces outside the body or outside the soul, until, that is, that moment when Freud split the soul into three, so that it could be entirely at war within and with itself.

So the metaphor presents us with two distinctions: first, *within* the individual, between the body and the soul and, second, *between* the individual psyche and the potentially hostile outside world. First, it constructs, through the concept of invisibility, an interior psychic space, problematically related to a physical analogue. But, paradoxically, since it is a bodily metaphor, it somatises the spiritual, suggesting the abstract nature of the 'inner life' as concrete and observable. Second, it individualises the social aspects of the psychological within a linear, causal or interactive model. In this way, third, it creates a particular form of subjectivity and also functions in a subsidiary way to create, by analogy, the possibility of collective identity. Fourth, it medicalises its administration and, lastly, through the concept of interiority, creates a rich discourse about its bringing forth. These functions are discussed here in turn, though there is much overlap between them.

2.2 The mind–body boundary

Body and soul or How interior is inside?

One of the main features of the metaphor of the invisible wound and its variants is that the notion of invisibility leaves open a wide set of options for the wound's location. The wound cannot be seen and we are not told where precisely it is supposed to be. Only a vague notion of interiority is invoked. The following extract from a story in *Sex, Etc.*, the newsletter of the Network for Family Life Education, Rutgers University (Rutgers 1983), is typical of much emotional abuse literature. The story is entitled 'Battered on the inside: Emotional abuse inflicts invisible wounds'.

The heroine, we are assured, had not endured *physical* violence:

She had no broken bones, no bruises that anyone could see.

Nevertheless, she 'was abused. Her wounds were on the inside.' And we are assured that the wounds are 'real' by inference from the subsequent listing of the cruel and 'abusive' acts to which she had been subjected, as the narrative continues with:

The New Jersey teen was a victim of emotional abuse, a form of abuse that many don't regard as real abuse. But it is (Rutgers, 1983).

So the ontological objectivity of the hurt is established from the reality of the hurtful acts and its interior location left tantalisingly unspecified.

Nor do statements like the following from lawyer, Andrew Vachss, clarify the exact whereabouts of inside:

> Emotional abuse scars the heart and damages the soul. Like cancer, it does its most deadly work internally. And, like cancer, it can metastasise if untreated (Vachss, 1994)

But this notion of invisibility creates some complexity in the use of the metaphor, especially in its technical form of trauma. Here the interior wound could be located, first, in the depth of the New Jersey teen's body, at some microphysiological level, not visible to the naked eye or even the cruder techniques of medical detection; second, it could be located in the more arcane reaches of the human psyche, at an abstract psychological, emotional or spiritual level; third, at both levels – seen either as dual systems that run in parallel and reflect each other through mimesis or are connected by some causal mechanism (either way round, depending on perspective) or, finally, fourth, in both systems, combined in the 'individual' in the sort of overarching holistic relationship envisaged currently in DSM-IV[4] and in waves of philosophical and religious thought over the centuries.[5]

In the history of trauma, invisible wounds started off as not a metaphor at all. When it was first used by the neurologist, John Erichsen (Erichsen, 1866), to describe the invisible lesions in the spine which were the consequence of what he called 'nervous shock' engendered in railway accidents, this was not a figurative use. Nervous shock already meant something to neurologists of his generation, because it was the functional equivalent of the phenomenon of 'surgical shock' – a condition, also newly discovered, in which people who sustained wounds, even though very slight, might display a disproportionately serious set of symptoms, which could be attributable to the shock of the accident, which went with the blast of the crash and the shaking up of the railway carriage, rather than the physical injuries themselves. Nervous shock *was* a wound in the spine, so tiny as to be unobservable within the limit of current techniques, but not necessarily in principle.

The wound usage slid into metaphor through the work of successive neurosurgeons and neurologists. By the 1880s, it was accepted among medical men that extreme fear on its own could produce consequences comparable to surgical shock (Jordan, 1880), although they never quite solved the puzzle of how 'fright and fright alone' (Page, 1883: 117) could reproduce the effects of a physical blow or injury. Since they saw the equivalence of symptoms empirically, they just accepted the proposition that fear *is* an assault, as it was held to be in the common law offence of psychic assault from the 18th century onwards. Fear, it seemed, could produce the symptoms of bodily harm through patho-anatomical and physiological pathways (Young, 1995). This is described in Chapter 3 on the development of PTSD – part of the strong neurological strand in medical thinking about psychiatric disorder, also described in the next chapter.

Further, the wound or lesion changed in medical thought over time to become a sort of disorder of memory (Young, 1995), not a wound at all, but something going wrong with the ordinary homeostatic processes by which a human body adapted to changes in its physical and social environment. This was produced by the effect of shock on the neuroendocrine system, in which the event was, as it were, relived by the body. It was no longer a wound but still a bodily harm; not penetrating the skin like a wound, not visible to the naked eye; located at a micro level in the body's interior, but, it is now claimed, accessible to detection through scientific observation of a rigorous empirical nature conducted under laboratory conditions.

Over the same time period as the invisible wound became located in the body's interior, it was also creating an equivalent emotional or cognitive space. It was a short step from the work of these early neurologists with their reliance on instinctive fear as an explanation of physical symptoms to Charcot's insistence on the power of an idea to produce strange bodily 'conversions' in the state of hysteria (Charcot, 1889). In this way, he called on the other strand in medical understanding of disorders of the mind: that of a psychological and, later, after Freud, a psychoanalytic dualism. From this perspective, the traumatic disorder of memory was located in the compulsive recall and forgetting of words and images; that is, in the cognitive and emotional functions of the mind as it related to the social history and cultural context of an individual, which gave them their meaning.

Freud, himself, in his work with Breuer (Breuer *et al.*, 1955 [1893–1895]), saw his patients' narratives and behaviour as embedded in a very complex, somewhat mechanical system of cells and neuronal pathways (Freud, 1966 [1895]). Although he never quite abandoned the hope that the psychic self could ultimately be explained in this way, he was also the inheritor of the 19th-century preoccupation with human phylogenetic and ontogenetic inheritance – an existence *apart* from the purely instinctive reactions of the animal kingdom and interiorised by a growing sense of history as identity in all its complexity. This culminated in his famous and controversial abandonment of the incest theory for the

Oedipus complex and the split he established, by the time he wrote *The Interpretation of Dreams*, between material (or bodily) reality and what he called 'psychical reality... a particular form of existence not to be confused with (the former)' (Freud, 1953 [1900]: 620). For the later Freud and his psychoanalytic inheritors, trauma or invisible wounds are located in a psychical interior, detectable only through the skills of therapists in the confessional context of the clinic (Foucault, 1980b), who are endowed with a professional knowledge which rests solely on metaphor and its theoretical developments.

What developed, historically, were these two locations for the invisible wound, the somatic and the psychic, representing the two approaches to mental disorder in the history of psychiatry (elaborated in the next chapter) and developing side by side. The metaphor is more complex still, however. As in current modernised psychiatry, where the unifying emphasis has been on diagnosis in the Kraepelinian tradition,[6] there are still differences of opinion on the understanding and treatment of such disorders, so there are differences in the approach to psychological harm. It would probably be agreed amongst medical personnel that the body and the mind can, at least, be seen as two analogous systems (van der Kolk *et al.*, 1985: 318), in which change in one is reflected by change in another. Put crudely, this means that a wound might be located in both systems, although there would be disagreement about which way round any causality might run.

Besides this, as already noted, the medical establishment has formulated a version of mind/body holism in DSM-IV (American Psychiatric Association, 1994) – the fourth and alternative location for the invisible wound, inside the 'individual' as opposed to the mind *or* the body or the mind *and* the body. In this approach body and soul are both parts of a recursive system in which their interaction is undifferentiated by any causal, or even bi-causal model – a combination of 'thought bodies' (N. Rose, 2001) and embodied thoughts (Butler, 1993; Grosz, 1994; Nedelsky, 1995). The problem with this model is that it requires a new meta-linguistic in order to be articulated at all, since its understanding is constantly overridden by the dualistic punctuations of our language.

It is argued in Chapter 3 that, in practice, the diverse versions of trauma privilege one side of this duality or the other. It also contends that the social structure of modern medicine privileges the neurological approach to harm over a cognitive/emotional variety. However, in the modern project of clinical psychology the cognitive functions of mind prevail, whilst in psychoanalytic therapies these are conjoined with the emotions in an alternative psychic space. Which system is privileged for intervention and study depends on the diverse beliefs, professional knowledge, organisational constraints and socio-economic conditions of a multitude of professional practitioners worldwide, each with their own local and idiosyncratic considerations.

Moreover, as already argued in this chapter, the technical use of 'trauma' in a context in which its metaphorical status is ambiguous is still predicated on the experience of the human subject, on the expressive language of the vernacular, the figurative language of trauma and a broken heart. Though such personal testimony might concede the possibility of accompanying neurological change (perhaps in the now nearly-defunct language of nerves),[7] in the websites cited by the Google 'Invisible Wounds' search it is generally used to describe the experience of a psychological harm – the psychological sequelae of a deeply unpleasant experience.

A fine example here is the language of the Christian religion which places the wound firmly in a spiritual interior. It is the latter, still significant in the discourse and running alongside the medical or psychological versions of trauma, which offers the most interesting version of this invisibility as a psychic location. The talk is that of spiritual suffering and healing and, especially among the more proselytising or evangelistic versions, about faith and forgiveness as the 'healer of invisible wounds'. An article under this title in the newsletter of *The Catholic Advocate* website runs:

> There is a healing ministry in the Archdiocese of Newark that doesn't have to do with hospital chaplains or the Anointing of the Sick, per se. Rather it involves the spiritual and psychological healing that comes with forgiveness. (*Catholic Advocate*, 2003)

This ministry offers help for those suffering from 'post-abortion trauma', a mental condition, whilst on the website of the United Methodist Church (2006) an article on 'Clergy depression' refers to a 'wounded healer'. On the same website, a bookstore advertises three books for the bereaved, under the sales line 'Faith as Balm for Grief's Tragic Scars'. An article on the Santana High School shooting by the Associate Pastor at a local Baptist Church, also titled 'Invisible wounds', insists that:

> The healing can't be rushed. It's like pulling a scab off. You have the deaths and the injuries, and now you have to have the grieving time. (Santana Baptist church, 2001)

There is no mistaking the psychic location for the invisible wound in the lurking presence of the metaphorical body.

The abstract and its incarnation

This metaphorical relationship is made more complex, however, by the fact that actual physical suffering is associated with the spiritual, not just in analogous parallel systems, as described above, but as manifest physical illness or lesions are used as *expressive*, as a sign or symbol of their spiritual analogue – the body as a walking metaphor for the soul, bringing forth or acting out suffering in a psychic interior, a medium for its *conscious* communication (Young, 2000). (This is unlike psychosomatic suffering, hysterical conversions and the rest, which are defined as unconscious.) An esoteric example is the production of stigmata on the human body by extreme spiritual devotion and mental identification with the passion of Christ, in which it is said that 'the mind wounds the body', though the stigmata are thought not to behave like real wounds, as they do not smell (except, in one case, of roses), become infected or heal (RTE Television, 2004).

The ultimate example of communication through bodily wounds, however, is the Christian account of the crucifixion itself and the wounds of Jesus. The Judaeo-Christian God was an abstract God – a voice, who forbade the making of graven images (Scarry, 1985). His first and only substantiation in the Christian story was his incarnation in the form of the Messiah, Jesus Christ. He put on human flesh in order to suffer and to sacrifice himself for the sins of man. The suggestion is that suffering is a bodily phenomenon, which is puzzling, since we also know that the disembodied souls of the damned can suffer eternal torment in hell. U. A. Fanthorpe makes sense of this in her poem, *Getting it Across* (Fanthorpe, 1989), in which she reflects on God's problem of communication with man, as a somewhat concrete thinker. She calls Doubting Thomas 'Tom, for whom metaphor was anathema'. For when he put his hands in the wounds of Christ, it was to convince himself of the reality of his body and, therefore, of his suffering. As man has remained this concrete thinker, through vast swathes of his history, the bodily wounds of Christ move in and out of the realm of metaphor or symbolism, especially in the form of his wounded and bleeding heart.

The heart, of course, has many confusing dualities; it is the real, physical, emotion-bearing centre of the body and a symbol of sensibility (Godwin, 2002). A wound evokes this dual function of heart as both the bodily organ that reacts most powerfully to changes in the neuroendocrine system and also the heart as the figurative centre of emotional life. Thus its metaphorical status has always been ambiguous. The Elizabethans with their love of paradox played with the physical mobility of the figurative transfixed heart (or 'hart'!).[8] In contrast, the holistic view of mediaeval medicine and religion, to which the anti-rational 19th-century Society of the Sacred Heart of Jesus aspired, made no distinction between the body and the spirit. Christ's spiritual and physical suffering were one in the bleeding heart. When He revealed his wounded heart to the inspirer of the Sacred Heart cult, St Margaret Alacocque, in 1675, it was the real thing (Godwin, 2002: 100–103). It could be said that it is only the rationalistic, enlightenment or psychodynamic dualism, persisting into the 21st century and reinforcing the intuitive punctuations of our language, which make the concept of a spiritual lesion a metaphor and the body a symbol for the soul.

2.3   The individual and the social world

The boundary

If the boundary between body and soul required by the metaphor is not always clear, the boundary between self and external world that it invokes is conceptually simpler, at least on the face of it. The model of psychic harm, which underlies the medical version of traumatic stress and PTSD, as well as the psychoanalytic, implies something semi-permeable, in the sense that the individual exists in and depends on a social world, but is also defensively organised against potential hostility by boundaries which are breachable only by a forcible entry, as if made by a weapon.

The exact nature of this boundary is most discussed and elaborated in psychoanalytic theory. For Freud it was 'the mind's protective shield' (Freud, 1950 [1920]: 31), constituted by a sort of 'fabric' of the inner world (Freud, 1924; cited in Garland, 1998: 10); for W. R. Bion it is the 'psychic envelope'; and for the Object Relations school in general the boundary of the inner world is also the 'container' (Lopez-Corvo, 2003) of a set of histories and beliefs, phantasies and associations which are defensively organised, internally around 'good objects' and their projection onto the external world (Garland, 1998).

Freud's original model of the mind laid out in 'A Project for a Scientific Psychology', was essentially a neurological system open to external stimuli (QE) but programmed to discharge the excitation they produce through motor and psychic activity – a homeostatic, negative-feedback system with a semi-permeable boundary. Self is open to the 'other' and dependent on it as a source of force or energy, but also organised defensively to preclude more than some equilibrium or 'healthy' level of excitation. The defensiveness of the system lay not so much in its external boundary, presumably the skin of the body, but in the structure and function of the individual cells of which it was composed and the way in which Q (the stimulus) was exchanged between them in a series of paths of conduction between each cell and the contact barriers around them (Freud, 1966 [1895]).

Having rather abandoned neurological explanations soon after this exposition, Freud returned to the cell in 1920 in *Beyond the Pleasure Principle*, where the idea of the 'protective shield', surrounding 'the organ of the mind' first arose. For here he used the single cell as a metaphor for the mind, in order to describe how this protective layer is formed, as if a transformation of the contact barrier through its bombardment by external stimuli. He refers to 'a living organism in its most simplified form . . . an undifferentiated vesicle of a substance that is susceptible to stimulation'. As a result of 'the ceaseless impact of external stimuli', a kind of crust is formed around the cell 'which at last would have been so thoroughly baked through by stimulation that it would present the most favourable possible conditions for the reception of stimuli and become incapable of any further modification'. It is at this point that consciousness arises. The shield remains receptive to some level of stimulus necessary to the functioning of the organism, but its primary function remains protective (Freud, 1950 [1920]; cited in Steedman, 1995: 89, 90).

Another, more picturesque, example of the boundary of the soul, as shield, is cited in the health and wellbeing section of a Sunday newspaper. This is the holistic Taoist idea of 'heart protector energy', which forms an 'energetic sheath' surrounding the heart. The sheath is said to support the spirit or 'consciousness' and hold it in the body, there to protect it from 'painful information' (Barefoot Doctor, 2003).

The enemy without . . . and within

It is this 'painful information' that is the enemy in the outside world, potentially hostile or inimical to the wellbeing of the soul. For the early Freud, however, the enemy was not so much information, but, in keeping with the mechanical paradigms of his time, more a sort of physical force (he sometimes called it a 'current'), which produced too much neuronal stimulation of an aversive, unpleasurable kind – too much, in the sense that it could not be processed in the normal way. Normally, it would be defensively 'repressed' and then brought to consciousness by a series of re-registrations at the level of consciousness, until the strength of the negative emotions attached to it was eventually diffused. If there is too much stimulation, the excitation would become stuck at an unconscious level, a piece of shrapnel in the wound that prevents healing (Breuer and Freud, 1956 [1893]; Freud, 1966 [1895]).[9]

For the later Freud of the elaborated unconscious, the enemy lay within the psyche but was projected on to the outside world in order that the soul's defences could be mobilised, *as if* the threat came from its social environment. The move from seeing neuroses as the result of external enemies and dangers to seeing them as the result of internal ones concentrated his theory on a divided inner life (Freud, 1923). In 'A Project', endogenous stimuli only arose from the normal cellular activity of the body; now they arose from another part of the mind, the unconscious, desires and fantasies laid down in early childhood, constantly struggling with the ego. But in an attempt to deal with these 'internal enemies' the vesicle treated them as if they came from outside, so that it might be possible 'to bring the shield...into operation as a means of defence against them' (Freud, 1950 [1920]; cited in Steedman, 1995: 89, 90). So the inside had to be ejected to outside, the self to become other to make use of these defences.

It is claimed that since Freud's move away from the seduction theory, the psychoanalytic movement has been divided in its understanding of trauma between those who emphasise the enemy without and those who are more interested in the enemy within (Brett *et al.*, 1993). Certainly, in the medical history of post-traumatic stress disorder, the first has dominated, thanks to the early influence of Abram Kardiner, and the diagnosis of PTSD itself is predicated on an identifiable external event (Kardiner, 1941). In this thinking, it is the early Freud who is most influential, although his concept of the enemy slightly changed over time. Later, Mardi Horowitz (Horowitz, 1976) developed Freud's mechanical model into a model of an information-processing organism, as cybernetics became a customary way of conceptualising psychological processes, although, far from modern cybernetics, information for him was not a neutral phenomenon, since it held an emotional content which affected the ability of the organism to process it.[10] This work, with its emphasis on explaining the symptom clusters contained within the diagnostic description of PTSD, has formed the basis for further theorising in behavioural and cognitive psychology, described briefly in Chapter 3.

So the external enemy became exogenous bits of information of a shocking and cognitively dissonant nature and the Google search on the metaphor of the invisible wound comes up with an array of examples of these. They range from the witnessing or experience of terrible accidents, violent and brutal warfare torture and rape through to more domestic abuse of a physical, sexual or emotional nature. Articles on 'The Wounds of Spouse Abuse' are particularly eloquent on the destructive power of words, as 'drawn swords' (Psalm 55) (Gospel, 2006). And a women's group discusses 'the many forms that a malicious invisible knight might take' and 'how to battle that which we cannot see' (Diana, 2006). 'Shattered Words' is the title of one article on verbal abuse by Teresa Brouwer, which is followed by another called 'Emotional and Mental Rape,' by the same author (Brouwer, 2006 a and b).

The enemy within meanwhile is seen more as inner conflict which is precipitated by exogenous events. Later interpretations of internal struggles caused by aversive external events from the followers of Melanie Klein and the school of Object Relations turn less on the notion of an internal enemy projected to the outside and more on the idea of a forcible meeting of the inner and outer worlds, causing a massive adaptive failure (Kardiner and Spiegel, 1947).

The breach of the boundary

The above represents an extension of the meaning of trauma, which, as already noted, is, literally, an open injury, caused by cutting, piercing, hitting and similar percussive acts. We have also noted Freud's notions of a breach of the protective shield between self and other. Hence his thought that a delusion is like 'a patch over the place where originally a rent had appeared in the ego's relation to the outside world' (Freud, 1924; cited in Garland, 1998: 10). And this is a language taken up by Caroline Garland, head of the Tavistock Trauma Unit, in her edited book, *Understanding Trauma*, with trauma described as 'a rent in [the mind's] fabric' and 'the catastrophic breach in the protective shield' (Garland, 1998: 10 and 18). Whatever the protective boundary is made of, however – a fabric, a shield, a crust, or Bion's 'envelope' – with trauma it is not just the outer defences that are in disarray. The word represents, for the Object Relations school, an invasion of the inner world by the outer, which leads to the disorganisation and disintegration of the whole personality. Here, for the individual, meaning is also of the essence and not just in the struggle with cognitive dissonance; cognitive schema are here the whole psychic history of an individual and their inner representations of the world, including their deepest fears, the 'objects' lurking behind the protective shield. Lack of fit does not just lead to attempts to rework a terrible memory, but a complete loss of the sense of the outer world and of the purpose of life. The result of what she calls 'a collision between an individual and an event' (Garland, 1998: 18) is an interactive process, as much dependent on the internal world of the victim as on the external world in time and history. This is much like saying, in the metaphor of a physical wound, that the nature of a lesion is not just the work of a powerful, percussive, moving object entering the passive interior of a body, but the result of a complex exchange between object and flesh, blood and bones.

Clearly, although a wound to the body represents a breaching of the physical defences, an intrusion into private space, an invasion of the interior of the self by an alien object, the piercing of the body's protective skin is not a simple notion. Nor is the piercing of the soul. For, as well as invasion, the metaphor of a wound to the body is also accompanied by two other powerful ideas: that of the escape through the breach of something that should be contained and that of penetration. For an example of escape, we go back to Taoism. The Barefoot Doctor writes:

> When the energy of your heart protector becomes momentarily ruptured by trauma and shock, the heart energy itself is effectively weakened and loses control of your consciousness, which moves up out of your body and into your brain, where it gets stuck in a claustrophobic loop of self punishing thoughts. (Barefoot Doctor, 2003)

For the spiritual implication of the notion of bodily penetration, we go to religious symbolism and the iconography of the heart, where both the physical and the spiritual carry a dual implication. For penetration is not just the breach of something that was closed; it is also its opening up, the making of a connection between the outside and the inside to reveal and also make available an interior. In terms of the body, it is significant that a slang word for the female genitalia is a 'gash' or a 'wound', as if the bounded body of the male is transformed by the opening of the body bag into something unbounded, incomplete, penetrable and passive, that is, paradigmatically female (Naffine, 1998; Nedelsky, 1990). But this 'wound', as a passage from the exterior to the inside, also reveals the body's secrets, like the wounds of Shakespeare's Caesar, which could 'ope their ruby lips' to speak the names of his assassins. The labia, as the opening to the birth canal, are the means by which women become the nurturing, female 'mother'. Further, the feminist theologian, Caroline Walker Bynum, has written on the 'feminisation' of Christ's body in the iconography of his wounds and his bleeding heart (Walker Bynum, 1992: chapter 3). She describes representations in the late middle ages, in which 'mother' church herself is born through the wound in his side; the blood from this wound runs down his groin to become like a menstrual flow and he suckles hungry sinners at his breast. And it is what flows from the wounds in his heart and side that, symbolically or not, still feeds his flock at the service of Mass or Holy Communion.

If blood is a sign of suffering but also fertility and feeding, the heart pierced by Cupid's arrow bears a homologous duality; the arrow enters the flesh to pierce the heart, as the seat of sentiment, to open it up to the sight and the sensibility and, also, the cruelty of another, thus to all the pains and pleasures of erotic love. We see this curious conflation of anxiety and ecstasy in the Alexandrian poets, in Elizabethan love poetry, where pleasure predominates, and in the more miserable emphasis of Aphra Bhen's great sonnet on love's cruelty:

> Love in fantastic triumph sate Whilst Bleeding hearts around him flowed....

where the pleasure goes all to her lover, as she inherits the pain (Wain, 1986b).

If this opening up through suffering is a trope in the metaphorical use of bodily wounds, it has also become a figurative aspect of spiritual lesions – the gash in the soul. The media treatment of the life and death of Princess Diana is saturated with a discourse of spiritual wounds, the 'psychological wounds' from her childhood'(Fox News, 1997) 'the wounds opened up by her passing' (*Entertainment Weekly*, 1997) and the consequent flow of emotion to communion with the common man – or more frequently, woman. Far from needing to enter into the body of others to feel their pain, as Adam Smith suggests (Smith, 1976: 9), it seemed necessary, at the turn of this century, only to share their hurtful experiences, albeit mediated by the body, to be opened up to the great community of victims. After all, Diana called herself the 'Queen of Hearts'.

2.4 The wounded identity

So far we have discussed how the metaphor of the invisible wound has created a variable narrative about the vulnerability of the individual psyche to a hostile world of shocks and cruelty, rather as the individual body is seen in the discourse of immunology and invasive disease. As is suggested in the introduction to this chapter, this notion of the vulnerable individual, an individual susceptible to wounds or trauma, is constitutive of a particular form of identity, which also reciprocally creates a particular form of harm. And this is discussed here in conjunction with another narrative which takes the form of a burgeoning critique of the notion of trauma and traumatic identity, both for individuals and, by extension, communities and nations. The critique organises itself around the fact that so called traumatogenic situations might more helpfully be addressed not at an individual psychological level, but at the level of socio-economic, cultural or historical explanations.

'There is no such thing as society'

To start with, and perhaps to state the obvious, the discourse of trauma presents a picture of the world peopled by discrete individuals, separated from others by permeable but defensive boundaries. They are rather like the atomistic individuals of enlightenment philosophy, but different, in the sense that these rational beings were not afflicted by the emotions which this traumatic version of the individual has acquired (Danziger, 1997). Tautologically, the discourse explains the inner state of an individual at a psychological and therefore an individual level. The social world, society, is a collection of individuals. Hence the ease with which the discourse slips from talking of scarred individuals to traumatised nations and wounded worlds.

An example of this slippage is, as Richard Wilson argues in his book, *The Politics of Truth and Reconciliation in South Africa*, the rhetorical creation of a community of suffering by the Truth and Reconciliation Committee in the post-apartheid state, as part of a conscious nation building exercise (Wilson, 2001: 13–16). He quotes Archbishop Tutu's response to a witness complaining of torture in police custody:

> Your pain is our pain. We were tortured, we were harassed, we suffered, we were oppressed. (Wilson, 2001: 111)

Further, he suggests that the TRC was creating a new identity, the 'national victim', whose suffering became symbolic, emblematic, because it was, also, part of the suffering of a whole people. Such a collective of *individual* suffering calls up the idea of the outflow of feeling consequent on the penetration of the soul's protective shield in the metaphor of the wound and the creation of a 'sentimental' community of the traumatised mentioned above. *Patior ergo sumus.*[11]

Whilst it has been argued that this ascription of a psyche to a group or community is improper (Ignatieff, 1996) (and, logically, it is) as a metaphor it is not awkward if the difficulties are only those of quantity and addition.[12] That is, if a community is just a multiplicity of individuals and nothing more – if there is no such thing as society.

History is dead

However, even at the level of the psychological individual, there are problems with the metaphor, especially in the relationship of an individual to his own history, which the discourse of the wound implies is completely organised by the traumatic event. For what defensive individualism omits to address, and what the metaphor of the wound precludes (even in the more florid and complex form presented by the Object Relations school, in which the individual is a more active shaper of her own experience of psychic trauma), is that the world may also be the powerful and constant shaper of the individual and her inner life. There is a ceaseless interchange which does not start or suddenly stop with catastrophe. This is, after all, one event among many, although the individual 'system' may, indeed, be violently 'perturbed' (Maturana and Varela, 1980). The metaphor of the wound (at least in its first, shocking non-ontogenetic form), on the contrary, seems to imply the total transformation of the life trajectory of a previously formed individual by an event which, we will discover later, breaches the limits of what is 'expectable'.

First, the metaphor assumes the definitive nature of the individual laid down by her own narrated social history (for Freud, before the age of three), a continuous entity existing behind some defensively organised, though semi-permeable, boundary, through which new information produces a gradual adjustment, which we sometimes call development or growth, with all its normative implications. This version of personal history has an element of determinism to it, as something contained within normative bounds. For a traumatised individual, the wound interrupts the gradual process of change with a discontinuity, a violent transformation produced by forces from outside (Piper Shafir, 2005). Here is the idea, not only of discontinuity with the past, but the rupture of a sort of preordained future, one that, by implication, was manageable and predictable, more or less more-of-the-same, 'stable' (Piper Shafir, 2005). Trauma, as a discontinuity, not only cancels out the past and its narratives, it violates our expectations; something deeply unnatural has happened, something that was not 'meant to be'.

Isabel Piper Shafir, writing of the discourse of trauma prevalent in Chilean society following the end of the Pinochet regime, argues that this breaking of stability is identified as a 'fracture' that leaves a mark or a scar. Subjects of trauma are not the same again. Even if they heal, they are scarred. Trauma, she says:

> operates as an origin of what we are as a society and of the iden-
> tity of its direct victims... the origin of our major pains (Piper Shafir,
> 2005: 2).

She calls the discourse of trauma 'a rhetoric of marks'.

Second, this sense of normativity in an individual history and its dis-location from an orderly to a disorderly pathway is reflected in the lack of attention to the wider and continuous social context of an individual in the medical model of trauma. For, in all the multiplicity of epidemi-ological and clinical research on traumatic stress and its aftermath, the social context of an individual victim, if it figures at all, is seen as either a reflection of disturbed intrapsychic processes, a symptom of trauma, or merely presents itself as one 'factor' which can influence outcome, statistically adding particular 'resilience' or 'vulnerability' to this reified affliction (Summerfield, 2001).

Long live history!

However, even if more attention is paid to the continuing social his-tory of an individual, this still seems to obscure the wider historical issues which contextualise traumatic events. This is the point of Piper Shafir's critique. As she points out, even attempts by social psycholo-gists to take a less intra-psychic and more interactive perspective still construct the individual as a continuous entity in some sort of causal or bicausal (interactive) relationship to the social world at the level of behaviour and events – and one event in particular.[13] This restricts recognition of the role of wider socio-economic and cultural factors – what she calls 'practices of domination' – in the production of identi-ties (Piper Shafir, 2005).[14] Like the notion of healing and the human rights discourse of reparation in, say, truth and reconciliation commis-sions, it calls on the return to a normal or whole past for the victim. It requires the wiping out of the effects of violence. But these are the effects of a particular piece of history, in this positivist interpretation, a cause located in a past which cannot be changed. The discourse of trauma suggests that the only thing that can be changed is the wound, through healing, and draws attention from what needs to be changed at a structural level, as reflected in current social and political practices and relations. Most importantly, the metaphor of the wound, in fixing a victim identity on individuals and on communities, detracts from their ability to make these major changes, since their defined role in the discourse is to 'work on their healing' (Piper Shafir, 2005: 7, 8; Summerfield, 1999).

Working on healing is a complicated business in both the private and the public, the individual and the collective domain, involving as it does a recovery, not only from a harm, but also, in many cases, from a wrong – a violation not only of some inner psychological space of an individual, but also of some quasi-legal space called 'rights'. For example, on the private level, therapy for incestuous families in the pioneering treatment centre in Great Ormond Street in the early 1980s was incorporated into a sort of legal framework, in which the moral roles of victim, villain and the rest were laid out and had to be acknowledged and adopted by the participants before any reparative scenario could be played out (Bentovim, 1986; Bentovim and Tranter, 1984). Since then, the idea of healing through justice has infused many western legal systems with the spreading practice of Restorative Justice (Braithwaite, 1996). It is accompanied at the discursive level by a widely used formulation of the grief, anger and despair associated with sudden loss through crime or chance, as curable only through the establishment of lines of human accountability and blame for causal events, so that the victims or their families may 'have resolution (or closure) and move on' (Duff, 2006).

This merger of moral/religious, legal and therapeutic models was reproduced at the national/collective level by truth and reconciliation committees in South Africa and South America, which promulgated a combination of a healing, a legal and a religious/redemptive discourse. Here, it is claimed, the concentration on individual trauma, testimony and transgression and the construction of the notion of violence and suffering as the result of 'political intolerance' or 'racism' at a personal level avoided a higher-level, structural critique. This advanced the notion of individual reconciliation and the ANC project of nation-building on the basis of individual healing. Richard Wilson writes:

> Accentuating the normative and moral dimensions of conflict and inequality was crucial to the TRC's nation building mission. This meant that reconciliation could be more of the religious and redemptive variety, where individuals could readily change their attitudes and join the rainbow nation, redeeming both. Explaining violence with reference to the social and political organization of conflict and inequality was more problematical, as this implied a long-term and

contentious programme of socio-economic redistribution and transformation of South African state and societal institutions. (Wilson,
2001: 93)

2.5   The pathologisation of identity

Thus the metaphor of the wound seems to create a particular form
of individual identity in a particular relationship to the social world,
prompting a critique which claims that the discourse of trauma locates
social problems at the level of the individual, militating against social
explanation and possible social solutions. But the metaphor of the
wound goes further – as does the critique – in that the problem it locates
at the individual level is not just a moral or socio-legal one, but primarily
a socio-medical condition, pathologising the individual and requiring
specialist knowledge in its recognition and treatment, therapy or drugs.
Essentially, it cedes power to experts, to their cultural assumptions, their
techniques and the social structures that maintain these – in a phrase,
to their regimes of truth.

It hardly needs saying that PTSD, as the product of a highly sophisticated, modern, evidence-based psychiatric medicine, needs clinical
expertise in its diagnosis and treatment. Even the most mechanistic
and rigid questionnaires such as the much-used Diagnostic Interview
Schedule (DIS) designed technically to be used by anyone to discover
and locate morbidity, have problems both of specificity and sensitivity
(Robins and Heltzer, 1986). These are not solved by less reliable semi-
structured technologies, and only resolved by clinical discretion (Spitzer
et al., 1992). And yet a different sort of expertise is required when the
unconscious, where the traumatic memory is lodged, is Freud's bubbling
cauldron of desire, where time and historical causality have no meaning
until it is elicited by dynamic interaction and interpretation in the therapy room. Foucault, in his famous *History of Sexuality*, (1980b) discusses
the manner in which the terrain of individual sexuality was established
by the psychoanalytic profession as an area only to be accessed by
conscripting the priestly techniques of the confessional to psychiatric
knowledge and power.

This process is seen by critics as reproduced at the level of communities of individuals or nations by the pathologising discourse of invisible
wounds or psychic trauma. In particular Vanessa Pupavac, writing in
2004 about the activities of the western powers in Bosnia, argues that
the therapeutic turn in the construction of war and hunger, does not

just disempower the individual and create dependency. It is the basis for a new international security paradigm, which reproduces, in the name of health and helpfulness, all the political and cultural imperialism of the old (Pupavac, 2004).[15] International agencies with UN legitimation, international aid programmes and charitable activities form a different sort of invasion of a sovereign people, in the name of therapeutic programs for national and individual recovery rather than the rebuilding of economic activity and social infrastructure. Traumatised individuals (or peoples) seem to lose negative freedoms and rights to lack of interference; they acquire medically defined needs (a right to be treated, even!) which appear to be the duty of professional others to meet with a pressing urgency. 'The therapeutic construction of the subject as a vulnerable damaged victim requires third party enablers for self-empowerment' (Pupavac, 2004: 161).

What is more, trauma may be experienced at an individual level, but the number of traumatised people is said to be legion. Trauma of peoples is portrayed in the discourse of international aid agencies as a health crisis of epidemic proportions (Pupavac, 2004). Whilst the Report on Health Security of the UN Advisory Board on Human Security assiduously avoids discussion of mental health issues, a brief look at the material from the Google 'invisible wounds' search suggests that trauma has, indeed, been elevated to a major health problem in western thinking. And this is not only a matter of individual wellbeing; it is also presented as a public health crisis on an international scale, which eclipsed hunger in the 1990s as the issue most flagged up by international aid agencies, UN, WHO and UNESCO (Pupavac, 2004).

The online material is dominated by two sets of claims. The first is about the health needs of soldiers, US veterans of two wars in Iraq, or Canadian peace-keeping veterans of Rwandan genocide. For example, 'Invisible Casualties' (*Daily Press*, 2006), and 'These Unseen Wounds Cut Deep' (Schrader, 2004), both cite numbers of Iraq-based US soldiers needing psychological counselling as about 20 per cent and rising, quoting expectations of the post Vietnam level of over 30 per cent of veterans. They note that more medical resources are needed in Iraq – for US troops! – and that the VA centres in the US will not be able to cope with demand for help. 20 per cent is the Canadian figure, too, for troops returning from Rwanda. A feature in the CBC flagship news programme, the National, on PTSD ('The Unseen Scars'), laments the slowness in the Canadian military to address this problem and the reluctance of soldiers themselves to seek help (CBC, 2005). The second claim, as made by Dr Richard Mollica, Director of the Harvard Program in Refugee Trauma, working in Cambodia and Bosnia and quoted in an article by Maria Vega for Inter Press Service, is that:

> one-sixth of the world's population suffers the psychological consequences of such traumatic phenomena as war, ethnic conflicts, natural disasters, social upheavals, torture, terrorism and landmines, which kill over 15,000 people every year and mutilate many thousands more. (Mollica, quoted in Vega, 2006)

Vega's article goes on to cite civil or guerrilla warfare in El Salvador and Peru, natural disasters in Haiti and their legacy of 'depression, fear and anxiety' widespread in the populations. 'Existing mental health policies are insufficient, because these problems have traditionally been ignored in national health care plans.' (Vega, 2006) And there are other statements about the troubled populations of war-infested zones, about Bosnia (Eager, 2003), about a 'Mental Health Crisis in Afghanistan' (WHO, 2001), about 'Sierra Leone's Invisible Scars,', by Dr Lynne Jones of the International Medical Corps on BBC News (Jones, 2006) and, also, about the effects on Indonesia and Sri Lanka of the tsunami of late 2004 (Harvard, 2005). All claim the desperate need for psycho-social support programmes in these areas.

With the claims outlined above goes the obvious implication that scarce resources are poured into postconflict countries for attending to *visible* wounds and for the rebuilding of infrastructure – called by Mollica the 'blankets, bricks and mortar' approach (Mollica, 2000). This competed for finance with what is implied as the more important task of rebuilding the mental health of nations. While Mollica concedes (2006) that this can be most successfully undertaken in the context of some return to normalcy (school and work) for the afflicted populations, as these assist with psychological recovery (or resilience), he also suggests that this recovery is a crucial, necessary condition for the development of peaceful and economically prosperous societies (Mollica, 2000; Mollica, 2006) – crudely, that war and hunger in the world are some function of mental ill-health.

This is the next development for claims to individual pathology. Not only do these individuals need treating; not only do their numbers constitute a threat to health on an international scale, their unresolved trauma and its consequent pathology passes on to the next generation in the form of helplessness, anger and more major disturbance. Intervention is justified by the paradigm of trauma and therapy on conventional security grounds, because psychological injury is seen as a trigger for future wars, as this extract from a paper produced by the US-based Center for the Study of Mind and Human Intervention suggests:

> Disasters deliberately caused by other groups lead to massive medical/ psychological problems. When the affected group cannot mourn its losses or reverse its feelings of helplessness and humiliation, it obligates subsequent generations to complete these unfinished psychological processes. These transgenerationally-transmitted psychological tasks in turn shape future political/military ideological development/decision making. (Volkan, 2000: 3, cited in Pupavac, 2004)

Thus, the World Health Organisation, for example, invokes a 'vicious cycle' of brutality, 'psycho-social dysfunction, new instability, new vulnerabilities and new hazards' (WHO, 2002: 6). Explanations of war, it is claimed, now sit in human psychology rather than the ritualistic imperatives of revenge, the old socio-economic explanations of tribalism and scarce resources, or the newer inequities of global capitalism.

2.6 The voice of the traumatised subject

So far, it has been argued that the metaphor of the invisible wound has helped to create a version of the self which is vulnerable or injured by events in the social world and in need of professional facilitators to bring it forth; that is, to make it visible, observable, a subject of science or quasi science, or the religious, psychoanalytic or self-help confessional. But in the pronouncements of truth and reconciliation commissions, for example, there appears a discourse which suggests that the individual, private self behind its boundary is not only wounded by the social world but can and must then speak out, give testimony, use the language of the social world to give shape and meaning to its experiences. This relies on the notion that the individual, by giving voice to his suffering, by naming the trauma, by narrating its details in the metaphorical language of the wound, can bring it forth into the social world unaided by science and professional expertise. Further, that this is a process that can create individuals anew, re-author them as subjects with an active rather than a passive voice and bring about the healing of their wounds.

From this stems the South African TRC's rhetoric of 'testifying' as the restoration of dignity to the subject and of the healing power of storytelling – what Fiona Ross identifies as 'the equation of self with voice' (Ross, 2003; Tutu, 1997). 'Revealing is Healing' read the banners at its meetings. This call to testimony was also accompanied by what Ross called its 'construction as an authentically African mode of communication' (Ross, 2003: 328; TRC, 1998)), through the oral tradition and the notion of individual and communal healing and redemption (TRC, Volume I: 112). The approach is also supported by a raft of literature, (Agger and Sorenson, 1990; Gurr and Quiroga, 2001; Herman, 1992, for example). Agger and Sorenson describe testimony as 'a universal ritual of healing' in which the individual becomes whole by reincorporating painful experiences into the self.

The approach has, also, been subjected to major critique, however. The first, by Fiona Ross, accepts the possibility of benefits to the individual from testimony but questions whether these have transpired in the context of the TRC hearings in South Africa.

> Much of the Truth and Reconciliation Commissions work was publicised in terms of giving voice to the voiceless, assuming an unproblematic link between 'voice' and 'dignity' and between 'voice' and 'being heard' .... Transparency of communication and clarity in reception are presumed; the unevenness of social fields and their saturation with power are not (Ross, 2003: 327)

Crudely, her argument is that the format of the TRC proceedings produced formulaic testimonies and, more importantly, the workings of the media, radio television and print served to alienate testifiers from their story, since it became public property and, in some sense, commodified. She also links this process to the problems of interviewing for any academic piece of research, where respondents attempt to operate in fields of power over which they have no control.

The critique operates at another level by questioning whether it is possible to bring forth private suffering in a shared and therefore public language at all. Elaine Scarry's book, *The Body in Pain*, was the seminal text for the examination of the rupturing, fragmenting effects of violence and terror on communities and individuals and the relationship of their experience to time and language. Pain, she says, is 'the unmaking of the world' (Scarry, 1985). Of others written on the same theme, Agamben's book on Holocaust witnessing is the most cited:

> Testimony is the disjunction between two impossibilities of bearing witness... Language, in order to bear witness, must give way to non-language, in order to show the impossibility of bearing witness.

The language of testimony is a language that no longer signifies. (Agamben, 1999: 39)[16]

Writing in *Trauma and the Memory of Politics* on ways of communal memorialisation, Jenny Edkins develops this failure of language in communicating trauma:

There is no language for it. Abuse by the state, the fatherland, like abuse by the father within the family, cannot be spoken in language, since language comes from and belongs to the family and the community.... This is the dilemma survivors face. The only words they have are the words of the very political community that is the source of all their suffering. This is the language of the powerful, the words of the status quo, the words that delimit and define acceptable ways of being human within the community. (Edkins, 2003: 7)

This discourse about both the possibility or the impossibility of bringing forth or making public invisible wounds, not through the visual but the oral register, on one level confirms the picture of individual identity that, it is argued here, the metaphor of the wound creates. First it relies on the idea that personal narrative is a social affair; it takes place within 'fields of intersubjectivity', where in the dialogical process of speaking and being heard we constantly re-author our identity (Jackson, 2005). But what it also assumes is an authentic and continuous private self and an authentic private hurt, existing at a pre-linguistic level (Elaine Scarry's irreducible, incorrigible sense of pain), calling up the concept of the private 'experience lived', as opposed to the public 'experience told', of some feminist research (Ribbens and Edwards, 1995), in which the image of midwifery is hard to escape. There is an implication that trauma is experienced viscerally, bodily, or as if there were a psychic space of pure emotion, of private pain and suffering that is not mediated by thought and, therefore by language; that there is some part of the individual which is not social, lurking, presumably, behind the protective shield and not subject to the constructing and constraining forms of language and relations of power, and that this is a real or lived referent for the metaphor of the wound, as that which words can, or cannot, bring forth.

Lastly, this 'lack of language' can be juxtaposed against a very different version of invisible wounds. This is the post-Lacanian position, in which individual identity, including the unconscious, is thoroughly socially constructed in the flux, the uncertainty and the provisionality of social forms and of language. There is no authentic self (Zizek, 1999). For this social individual the only certainty is the flux, itself, and the impossibility of closure, either at a personal or a socio-political level – what Zizek calls 'the ontological crack in the universe' (Zizek, 1997: 214). It is this cosmic insecurity, this lack of closure, which *is* trauma, the traumatic reality which lurks at the centre of every shifting subjectivity, although we deny it and fantasise its absence. It is this trauma, which is exposed in the context of violence and horror. And it is this trauma which is the one real aspect of the world which all our social fantasies cannot eliminate.

This is a tragic but tempting version of the human condition with which to close. But it should be observed that this account of trauma is the product of a highly esoteric academic elite. In its own terms, it can be seen as the most recent epicycle in the social production of knowledge of the psyche, in which trauma seems to offer to replace sex as the human fundamental. Thus it is yet another way in which the metaphor of the invisible wound creates a psychic space as fact – in this case, it would seem, its only occupant!

2.7   Conclusion

What is argued here is that the metaphor of the wound is not just a bringing forth of a private psychic space but also that which serves to create it. Further, that whatever the claims to locate and identify the real referent of the metaphor of the invisible wound, this concept has been inscribed on an internal space by particular forms of linguistic use and their accompanying practices. I have also argued that this metaphor and its use bring forth a somatic version, or vision, of this space and of the individual's relationship to the social world. The implications of this relationship in reducing social and political problems to one of individual psychology have been examined, and the tension noted between the demands of a traumatic identity and both individual and national recovery. These are partly problems created by pathologising the individual or collective self, which emphasises individual and national healing at the expense of wider socio-economic change. Trauma is a pathology which is also normal, common, (one-sixth of the world's population!) but the pathologisation of normal individuals inherent in the discourse of the wound, so the critics argue, renders them helpless, cuts off their recourse to ordinary community support, or their own resources, and leaves them with the imperialist interventions of 'experts', whom they both need and do not need.

Also, on a more abstract level, what I have traced here (and is developed in Chapter 3) is that, despite its obvious figurative uses, this metaphor of the invisible wound, as transposed into the concept of trauma, has, through the migration and creeping technicalisation of metaphor (Manier, 1980), become reified in medical, psychoanalytic and therapeutic discourses into an observable diagnostic category or an authentic, positive fact about the world and individuals, problematically related to language and voice. No longer a metaphor; in the last version, it is the only real fact about humanity! But, if it is not a metaphor, it presents, in the dualistic context of language, a puzzling contradiction in terms. Consider the concept of a psychic lesion, 'soul murder' (Shengold 1979) or 'spirit murder' (Williams, 1987), for anyone reared in the Judaeo-Christian tradition. This contradiction is solved in two different ways: first, by a thoroughgoing somatisation of those parts of the soul which are thought vulnerable to distress, as I discuss in the next two chapters on the technical medical category of PTSD and its legal form and in Chapter 8 on Attachment Theory. The second alternative is to remain in the linguistic domain – accepting the metaphor, remembering its figurative aspects, which, whilst they depend on this dualistic distinction, also fudge it.

The implication of both solutions is that the secularised, 'scientised' soul of the late 20th century (Hacking, 1995b), far from being everlasting, is mortal, as the flesh is. The bodily metaphor places the human spirit in domains of destruction; the cockpit of war, fields of criminal or accidental violence and, above all, the hospital ward. Just as the regulation of bodies in the military, the law, the criminal justice system and local authority tutelage has come to need the legitimation of the medical profession, so knowledge of the destruction of the human spirit has become a special branch of medicine; the wounded soul is the bearer of a particular sort of illness, in need of expert care and techniques of healing, encompassing the solace or forgiveness of religion, politico-legal rights claiming and social welfare, and ensuring its continual oversight.

3
Suffering from nerves: The management of subjectivity in PTSD

3.1 Introduction

After the overview of the way the metaphor of invisible wounds is used in a variety of social settings, the rest of the book goes on to examine in more detail several specific social contexts in which three different versions of the metaphor are made into fact, acquire form, life and social importance. This chapter and the next look at how the language of nerves and the putative occurrence of an overpowering, negative environmental event is used for the production of two related versions of psychological harm, in which an individual history is said to be overthrown as the result of a sudden trauma. This present chapter addresses the medical concept of psychic trauma and the diagnosis of post-traumatic stress disorder, which came to be enshrined in psychiatric nosology in the 1980 version of DSM-III. (American Psychiatric Association, 1980).[1] It gives what can only be an outline account of the diagnosis, in order to provide an essential context for the next chapter, which looks at the rewriting of this medical concept and diagnosis as the legal category of 'nervous shock' – the name for psychic harm in the English law of tort. The two chapters should be seen as twin studies, set in two different social organisations, first, western psychiatry, especially in the USA, whose powerful research establishment also dominates the medical establishment in the UK, and, second, in the English legal system, in particular within a system of case law in which judgement is based on precedent. They are also studies of two different 'regimes of truth' and how one is exchanged for another, as the Law Lords make clear that while medical positivism is gaining in prestige and respect, even in the 'suspect' area of psychiatry, the truth that prevails in the law is quite different – more of an idealised common sense.

Despite this, the two versions have much in common. As in all that follows, both are made, over time, by 'experts' and the subjective experience of an individual is subordinated to objective, 'scientific' observation (or the gaze of the 'man on the Clapham omnibus', which is the speciality of the law). Both chapters describe versions of psychological harm which elaborate the sort of tensions and contradictions that were identified in the last chapter and which seem to run through all the different forms of the wound metaphor. First, and notably, is the way that the metaphor moves over time from a concept hooked onto a physical reality to something which has a reality of its own, creating new and complex relationships between mind and body. Second, the environmental and therefore potentially universal nature of the wound's cause raises difficult conundrums: are its symptoms a normal reaction to such a cause, or are they symptoms of a pathology and, depending on the answer, how are such harms to be compensated and treated?

Further, two more crucial and related issues, only touched upon in the last chapter, are added in this present chapter on PTSD. They concern, first, this notion of environmental cause, the weapon, the hostile act, the accident or the 'aetiological event', as it is called here. How does this 'external enemy' – something real and observable – which the metaphor of the wound binds together with an interior harm, endow a series of sometimes nebulous, contradictory and invisible symptoms with objective reality and meaning, so that the specification of what counts as this aetiological event vitally affects the inclusiveness of psychological injury as a social problem category? The second issue is the causal theory which relates this event to suffering and abnormal behaviour. This theory was mentioned briefly in Chapter 2, but consideration of the history of PTSD adds a more precise specification. As already described, what developed in late-19th-century psychology and psychiatry was an account of the crucial causal mechanism which links very shocking, horrific events to resulting symptoms of traumatic stress – a mechanism which became known in the literature as 'traumatic memory', a memory so horrific that it has to be repressed below the level of consciousness (Young, 1995).

It was out of the history of this 'traumatic memory' – and of psychiatric medicine and its war time forms – that the diagnostic category of PTSD emerged, claimed by two of its enthusiasts as opening 'a door to the scientific investigation of the nature of human suffering' (van der Kolk and McFarlane, 1996). What is more, the document in which it was written for the first time, DSM-III in 1980, was one which represented the culmination of a modernising project for US psychiatry, which, as ever, influenced its counterparts in the UK and other western countries. The production of the diagnosis was timely – one response to the pressing social and political problem for the US administration caused by disaffected Vietnam veterans and their demand for compensation. The diagnosis allowed legitimate claims to be made.

The process of its production was made complex, however, by the fact that traumatic memory, like psychiatry in general, had, over time, developed along two different tracks: the neurological and the psychological. The psychological version of PTSD was placed in a psychoanalytic interior, which could only be accessed by experts in analysis; attempts to access it by the positivist questioning of modern medicine entailed all sorts of contradictions. So, while both versions are written into the diagnosis, in the recent history of psychiatry, modernisation has been achieved somewhat at the expense of this psychological strand. There has been a reinstatement, after the Freudian revolution, of the somatic understanding of mental illness, which was prevalent in the 19th and early 20th century as the product of hereditary taint or physical disease. Now, a highly elaborated language of neuroendocrinology is used: then, the simpler, now vernacular, language of 'nerves' and 'nervous shock' was important and still plays its part (Shephard, 2002).

The language of nerves, neurasthenia, nervous shock, shell shock, traumatic stress and PTSD have a long and fascinating history, which I can only touch upon here. Much work has been done in this area of medical and military history, including a raft of recent research by Edgar Jones at the Institute of Psychiatry, London.[2] The sources used here are from the psychiatric and psychoanalytic literature, but the work relies heavily on two books for historical details: Ben Shephard's *A War of Nerves* (Shephard, 2002) and Allan Young's *A Harmony of Illusions: Inventing Post-traumatic Stress Disorder* (Young, 1995). For analysis, Ian Hacking's *Rewriting the Soul* (Hacking, 1995b) has been helpful, but Allan Young's book and later work, which presents a rich anthropological version of the making of PTSD – a case study of social construction, within the constraints of a particular symbolic order – has been most used. The medical story told here is essentially a reading of his work.

The history of traumatic memory, as the theory behind PTSD, is briefly summarised in section 3.2, as are the main historical trends in western psychiatry. After this, any historical references here are partial and used in an analysis of the controversial PTSD diagnosis, itself, and its place in the shifting constellations of diagnostic categories which constitute the Diagnostic and Statistical Manuals of the authoritative American Psychiatric Association.

3.2 Trauma and its background history

Traumatic memory

A new version of memory first entered the field of human speculation in the second half of the 19th century, with the most important ramifications for the history of the psy sciences, especially psychoanalysis, and all the proliferation of social agencies and organisations dependent on their knowledge. Not only did it produce, over time, changes in the way that certain forms of invisible wounds were apprehended and sited, but, in the words of the title of Ian Hacking's book on multiple personality, it succeeded in 'rewriting the soul' (Hacking, 1995b). For, in the concept of repression, the old enlightenment version of agency, self knowledge and moral responsibility was challenged[3] and the soul became, not just the *subject* of self reflection and action but an *object* of the nascent science of psychology and psychiatry, producing experts in understanding what is hidden – not just from others, but even from the self (Harris, 1989, cited in Young 1995). The idea of traumatic memory reduces the autonomous subject of enlightenment thinking to an objectifying medical gaze.

Neurological memory

As described in Chapter 2, the phenomenon of 'nervous shock' was first noticed in the victims of railway accidents by a 19th-century neurosurgeon called John Erichsen. Patients with the condition of 'railway spine', as he called it, seemed to display all the symptoms of a physical wound, where none was to be seen and 'compensationitis' or malingering was ruled out[4]. Seen as a functional equivalent of the phenomenon of 'surgical shock' (see Chapter 2), railway spine was as like a wound as it could be without actually being visible within current medical techniques (Erichsen, 1866; 1883). Since anyone, even the strongest and most robust person, is vulnerable to a physical wound (even if invisible) this normalised the condition of nervous shock. So his findings were helpful to plaintiffs seeking compensation from the railway companies. Paradoxically, his contemporary, Herbert Page, another neurosurgeon, who also attributed symptoms to 'morbid changes of the nerve centres which underlie them' (Page, 1883), was hired by the railway companies defending these claims. This, argues Shephard, is because Page's interpretation of nervous shock was more 'psychological' (Shephard, 2002), this word implying, at that date, at least, some kind of susceptibility or weakness of the 'nerves'. Certainly, he saw the affected nervous system as more diffuse and elusive; not just the spine. He thought he was observing changes 'very materially different from the gross pathological changes we are accustomed to see upon the post mortem table, or... [through] the microscope' (Page, 1883: 198–99), suggesting some kind of secondary or parallel nervous system of the type posited by Hughlings Jackson (Jackson, 1931a, b), or Freud himself (Freud, 1966 [1895]). Whilst Erichsen largely put this down to the forces present at the traumatic event, the particular percussive, violent and sudden nature of railway accidents themselves, Page acknowledged certain factors which could be thought of as mental: the desire for compensation and *fear*.

Whether such effects of fear were seen as quite normal is another matter. The lectures of Charcot at the Salpêtrière, his Paris hospital base, suggested otherwise (Charcot, 1889). He, too, saw fear acting to produce symptoms of a hysterical nature, bodily conversions with no organic origin. For him, however, they were produced by *psycho*-neurological pathways (Young, 1995). The effect of fear or extreme shock was to produce a sort of self induced hypnotic state in which the victim is open to autosuggestion from powerful ideas, which presumably remain after the event is over, a sort of memory (Charcot, 1889). But, in contrast to anything previously thought of as memory – a store of ideas in the form of words and images (following Hume) – this memory was converted into physical symptoms (Young, 1995). So, Charcot insisted, the effect of nervous shock was a form of hysteria, which was not just a female malady, in that it presupposed no necessary constitutional susceptibility or vulnerability; its origin was merely fright. And yet he seems never to have abandoned the idea that hysteria was a unitary phenomenon with an underlying physiological aetiology and with heightened suggestibility as one of its symptoms: that is, a conventional mental illness in those biological times (Barossa, 2001; Harris, 1989; Showalter, 1985). Something of this ambivalence is still observable in modern psychiatry.

Despite Charcot's thoughts on the explanatory power of suggestion and therefore of ideas in hysteria (a theme developed by others, including Freud, as discussed below, and W. H. R. Rivers (Rivers, 1920), whose work as Siegfried Sassoon's therapist has recently acquired literary fame quite disproportionate to his contribution to the history of PTSD),[5] the neurological strand and the discourse of nerves still dominated the medicine of World War I and the diagnosis of shell shock. This seems to have resembled 'railway spine' quite closely, at least at the beginning of the war. It required the witnessing or participation in an event, which most people would find horrific, at close quarters, close enough to experience what could only be described as 'shock waves'. Though these could not be shown to have any existence in physics, there was a sense that the diagnosis required the experience of 'commotional'[6] as well as emotional shock. Any psychogenic factors were mostly seen as operating *with* physical factors or as mediating invisible, physical microprocesses (Young, 1995).

Later, after 1916, shell shock just became a generic word for the 'war neuroses' – hysteria, a diagnosis largely given to the ordinary soldier, and neurasthenia, an emblematic disorder for artists among the Edwardian upper middle classes, for the officers (Shephard, 2002; Young, 1995, 1999). For the Royal Army Medical Corps, the war neuroses were called 'neurological disorders' and the doctors who attempted to treat them, 'neurological specialists'. These disorders were also seen as 'functional', in the sense that they reproduced the symptoms of known neurological problems but did not share the same aetiology, which was a puzzle (Young, 1995). However, the specialists, were, on the whole, not too interested in the *aetiology* of shell shock itself, or its exact location, and expended less time on worrying about its cause and refining its classification and more on getting its sufferers back to the front (Shephard, 2002).

Around this time the neurological strand was also developing experimentally and the laboratory research done by US neurologists, George Crile and Walter Cannon on decorticated cats would have been known to at least some medical personnel. These showed the process by which fear reactions,[7] assumed to be normally adaptive stimulus responses and part of everyone's ontogenetic and phylogenetic inheritance, could become pathological (Cannon, 1942, cited in Young, 1995). The deactivating of the cerebral cortex, the part of the brain which damps down the activity of the sympathico-adrenal system, reproduced a continuing state of intense arousal in the cats, as in anger or fear, and this arousal, experienced without cease, seemed to lead eventually to exhaustion of the body and a gradual drop in the animal's blood pressure, until the heart stopped beating (Cannon, 1914; Cannon, 1929, cited in Young, 1995)). Continual but lesser, intermittent shock had, through a process of 'summation', a similar effect. This Cannon graphically illustrated by a study of the workings of fear in the victims of voodoo death (Cannon, 1942, cited in Young, 1995).[8]

This work was taken an important stage further by Pavlov's famous operant conditioning experiments on rats (Pavlov, 1927, cited in Young, 1995), as he showed that the rats, subject to intermittent, inescapable shock, seemed to internalise the source of pain by coming to associate the contiguous conditions of the shock with the shock itself – what he called conditioning – so that these sensory associations acquired a sort of 'mnemonic power' (Young,1995), the power of calling unfailingly on some sort of pathogenic memory of the pain. Since, in Pavlov's thinking, stimulus and response were in no way cognitively mediated, this pathogenic memory was essentially somatic.

Modern neo-Pavlovians such as Bessel van der Kolk and Roger Pitman, taking up Crile and Cannon's basic emphasis on the neurological adaptation of organisms to their physical environment, evolved a further theory in relation to PTSD. It was framed as a description of the neurophysiological analogue of memory, explaining shock victims' compulsion to revisit the event or its associations by their development of an addiction to the endogenous opioids released into the bloodstream in moments of traumatic shock. Whilst the fixed pattern of stimulus response in Pavlov's rats is the source of pathology, lurking as it were in their bodies, exactly like the metaphorical piece of shrapnel in the wound, Van der Kolk and Pitman hypothesised endorphin addiction as something going wrong with a complex and ever-changing process of the neuroendocrinal adaptation of an individual to his equally complex and protean context. It was a disequilibrium – no longer a pathology but a disturbance of function (Pitman *et al.*, 1990; van der Kolk *et al.*, 1985, cited in Young, 1995). Broadly speaking, the work of Crile and Cannon and its Pavlovian offshoots is still the basis of current neurological research on PTSD, albeit at a highly elaborated and technically more sophisticated level.

Psychological memory

Traumatic memory in the more familiar form of an idea, words and visual images, was well developed before Pavlov. Although it started out in a more abnormally pathogenic form, as with its somatic analogue, it also became, by a series of interesting transformations, just a disturbance of the normal processes by which an individual organism regulates its relationship with the outside world. This change can be tracked by the way the notion of the unconscious mind developed among psychiatrists over the late 19th and early 20th century, from Charcot, through Ribot and Janet to Freud. The story, already touched on in Chapter 2, runs, very briefly, as follows.

Charcot was only interested in the unconscious as the place, cut off from conscious processes. The patient knows nothing. Ideas were implanted in the unconscious by hypnotic suggestion and produced a paralysis, not at the time of the terrible event or accident, but 'only after an interval of several days, after an incubation stage of unconscious mental elaboration' (Charcot, 1889: 387, cited in Young, 1995)).

The *content* of these ideas was only of interest in that it determined the form of patients' hysterical conversions (Barossa, 2001; Harris, 1989; Showalter, 1985).

Whilst the French philosopher and psychologist, Theodule Ribot, took up this idea of thoughts 'incubating', concealed and cut off in the subconscious, calling this pathogenic memory 'a parasite' (the psychological equivalent of shrapnel in the wound) (Ribot, 1883: 108–9, cited in Young, 1995), his main contribution to its development in his monograph on *Diseases of Memory: an Essay in Positive Psychology* was threefold: first, he formalised, for the first time, the problem of hypermnesia, remembering too much, which he sees as symmetrical with the well recognised problem of amnesia. Second, as a basis for this adaptive view of forgetfulness, he formulated a twofold version of the self which was to influence the developing theories of the young Freud – the self at the centre of present states of consciousness and the self, over time, subject of its own self narrative. And third, in relation to the unconscious mind, he distinguished between two types of amnesia as concealment: the 'underdeveloped' form associated with 'the victims of somnambulism, natural or induced', and the 'developed' form, which consists of alternating conscious personalities, each with their own self-narratives, which he called 'double consciousness', a state in which one fully developed personality took turns with another, of which she (used advisedly) had no knowledge (Ribot, 1883, cited in Young 1995). It was Pierre Janet, the French psychiatrist, who in 1889 described how, by using techniques of 'distraction', he could talk to more than one such personality at a time,[9] and so made the first suggestion that the mind could be split into parallel and co-existing domains of consciousness: the conscious and the 'subconscious', or 'that which is hidden from the other' (Janet, 1889, cited in Young 1995).

For Janet, this split was pathological, and associated with 'psychological automatisms' of a total or partial variety, which often originate in traumatic experiences (Janet, 1889). Two sorts of secret, pathological remembering and pathological forgetting were both thought of as 'subconscious fixed ideas... [that] grow, [that] install themselves in the field of thought like a parasite' (Janet, 1901: 267, cited in Young, 1995). And the reason why they are thus 'split off' into the subconscious mind is the unassimilability of these memories. They cannot be accommodated in a person's account of himself; they make no sense within his existing cognitive schema and the emotions they stimulate cannot be tolerated. It is the existence of these ideas which is the malady, rather than the symptoms themselves (Janet, 1889: 345, cited in Young, 1995). Therapy helps the patient to discover the 'fixed idea' and by a constant verbal re-recital put it in its proper narrative place (Janet, 1925, cited in Young, 1995).

Initially, there was very little difference between Freud's and Janet's accounts of traumatic memory. Freud's main contribution to the development of this concept and the process of the normalisation of pathology contained in its history was threefold. First, though Janet, according to Freud, attributed to hysterical patients 'a constitutional incapacity for holding together the contents of their minds', for Freud and his collaborator, Breuer, traumatic hysteria, though enhanced by hereditary disposition, could occur in people of the 'greatest character and the highest critical power' (Breuer and Freud, 1955 [1893–1895]: 13). Like PTSD after it, traumatic memory could afflict just about anybody who experienced the right (or, rather, wrong) environment. Second, his notion of the unconscious extended it from Janet's *sub*conscious, the hiding place of pathogenic ideas or 'alters', to the *un*conscious, a permanent part of normal psychic functioning – a universal. Third, he elaborated the ideas of Ribot and Janet on psychic structure and memory into an (almost) coherent equilibrium model of a system, which processed forces or energy fed in from the outside and organised its own defence and regulation in an unstable environment (Freud, 1966 [1895]). Here an excess quantity of excitation of an aversive kind might be impossible to discharge in the usual way and would thus disturb its homeostasis (Young, 1995: 40). Paradoxically, the second achievement could not be complete until he had abandoned the third, namely the psychoneurological basis for the traumatic origin of hysteria and other psychoneuroses. But, in spite of his controversial dropping of the seduction theory of infantile sexuality for the Oedipus complex in *Beyond the Pleasure Principle*, (Freud, 1950 [1920]), much of the basis for his later work on the dynamic and split self, to be found in his concepts of defence or repression and their rationale, was essentially there in the psychoneurological modelling of his early work with Breuer and underlies most of our current understandings of the psychology of memory, even of a non-psychoanalytic variety.

After Freud, there have been as many versions of the traumatic memory as there are psychotherapies, as well as of its neurological analogue. Horowitz's 1976 generic version of modern traumatic memory, as described in Chapter 2, is perhaps the best example, and is still recognisably Freudian. As outlined in Chapter 2, Freud's original model is criticised, even within the psychoanalytic community (Garland, 1998), as being too mechanical and taking no account of the memory's meaning for different individuals.[10] This is rectified by cognitive or cognitive-behavioural versions which use the notion of cognitive dissonance and 'individual fear structures' (Foa and Kozak, 1986; Lang *et al.*, 2001) and by more psychoanalytic accounts, including the English Object Relations school, which see trauma as the 'collision', for an individual, of their inner and their outer worlds (see Garland in Chapter 2).[11]

Trends in 20th-century psychiatry

The first of these trends, as suggested in the introduction, represents the successful project of psychiatry as serious science. In the 19th century, psychiatrists were little more than asylum keepers (Scull, 2005) and even at the International Medical Conference of 1913 the small psychiatric section was considered, by the neurologists at least, not to be serious.[12] While Freud and the psychoanalytic movement brought, after World War I, a whole new inner, psychological dimension to the possibilities for psychiatric treatment by the profession, and were embraced by some part of the intelligentsia, the emblematic psychiatrist of popular culture was still a little tainted by the 19th-century craze of mesmerism – a white haired old man with a couch and alien English; a Svengali-like figure who promised enchantment, but was hardly respectable. By the 1960s, psychoanalysis as a cure for disorder was beginning to be the subject of critique (Wootton, 1959), prompting negative evaluations written up in the 1970s (Luborsky *et al.*, 1975; Strupp and Hadley, 1979). The psychiatric establishment, which had embraced it, was in some disarray. But while the 1960s was its nadir, the 1970s saw a campaign of 'modernisation' by a section of US professionals[13] following 'neo-Kraepelinian' positivism, with its emphasis on the ordering and rationalisation of diagnostic categories, based on symptom clusters alone[14] and, thus, 'theory free'. This culminated in the publication of DSM-III, where PTSD was, in fact, the only exception to the rule, in that the diagnosis included its own aetiology (American Psychiatric Association, 1980). Once the DSM-III method of diagnosis was generally, though by no means universally, accepted,[15] differences in explanatory theories became less threatening to professional unity. Thus the classification of behavioural symptoms alone became the basis for epidemiological and clinical research, which might conform to some accepted norms for statistical reliability and validation (Young, 1995).

The second trend is the grounding of the modernisation movement in the techniques and subject matter of the harder, and therefore hierarchically superior, biological sciences, laboratory research, biostatistics and psychometrics (Young, 1995). This form of modernity was not implied by the diagnostic system itself, although the latter was necessary to it. If the new diagnostic uniformity it brought enabled the start of a more scientific, research based approach to psychiatry, this is not to say that a uniform, biologically based understanding of mental disorder was thereby imposed on the profession. DSM-III left enormous room for professional discretion among psychiatrists, which was well used. Treatments, including the use of pharmaceuticals, varied greatly and psychological therapies did not disappear; on the contrary. Nevertheless, it seems to be a consensus among historians of psychiatry that, after the publication of DSM-IV in 1994, the profession took a more biological turn – *post hoc*, though not necessarily *propter hoc*.

As a matter of fact, over the 1980s, organisational change in the UK NHS, for example, meant that diagnosis and treatment of mental health problems was increasingly accomplished by a multidisciplinary team. More specialisation, as a result of the growing bureaucratic and organ-isational pressure of audit to specify and count exactly what work is performed by whom, resulted in clinical psychologists, social workers and psychiatric nurses taking on different forms of the psychological therapies, whilst medical personnel dealt more and more exclusively with the pharmacopoeia (Horwitz and Wakefield, 2007). Besides this, the 1980s saw a dramatic increase in neurological research, publications and legitimate knowledge for professional consumption and, whilst the language of DSM-IV is holistic (mind and body are one), in fact, most of the psychiatrists working on this document were based in biological medicine (Horwitz and Wakefield, 2007; Rose, 2007). Perhaps, because of this, the diagnostic list increased substantially over that in DSM-III, and its revision in 1987 (American Psychiatric Association, 1987), as the fragmentation and differentiation of categories rose dramatically. As Rose suggests, this was in line with the discovery, a consequence of the growth of neurological research in the 1990s, of a multiplying com-plex of neural circuits, each one of whose chemistry might be targeted by psychotropic drugs of increasing sensitivity and specificity (Rose, 2007).

So, in spite of the developments of psychological studies after Hume,[16] in spite of the Freudian revolution of the early 20th century and the elaboration of a new and timeless emotional interior which contributed so much to the practice of psychiatry, and in spite of the sophisticated vernacular language of psychic harm to be read in self help books and in other media, the old organic tendency in psychiatric medicine seems to have been firmly re-established over the last quarter of the 20th century, although it is presented in a more holistic dress (American Psychiatric Association, 1994: xxi). The current developments in pharmaceuticals, in computer modelling of the brain in cognitive psychology, in brain imaging in neurology and in the breakthroughs in biogenetics, have all contributed to a burgeoning discourse of a subjectivity rooted in the body and bodily processes, no longer in the place within (Young, 1995 and Rose, 2007).

The third broad trend was one which might be called, somewhat paradoxically, 'the normalization of pathology' (Young, 1995). Within this, there were several strands. First, whilst psychoanalysis might be suspect, the Freudian notion of the unconscious as a universal phenomenon, rather than just a hideaway for the pathogenic secrets of the abnormal, was a powerful idea: it was the first coherent theory of human desire; the first suggestion that we all have our own 'neurotic style'. The second, related, strand was that of the inner world of an individual as reactive, not just to internal biological drives, or physical pathogens, hereditary taint, and the like, but to the forces of a social world outside – as a place, out of time, yet shaped in complicated ways by its own history (Steedman, 1995). And, third, in the other 'positivist' project of psychology, emerging after World War II, alongside psychoanalysis and medicine, another case was being made for the psychological mediation of exogenous causes for both the social and the symptomatic bodily behaviour of an individual. The rather primitive notions of Pavlovian operant conditioning gave way to social learning theory (Bandura, 1977) and cognitive behavioural theories (Beck, 1976), which applied to treatment of behavioural problems or psychiatric symptoms, in which people were thought to be the objective observers of their own mental behaviour and strategic generators of their social acts, according to some (tautological) imperative about maximising social rewards. Fourth, was a more sociological point of view. Although the radical critique of psychiatric diagnosis as constructed in social interaction (Scheff, 1966), and psychiatric illness as a myth (Szasz, 1962) or an epistemological error (Laing, 1961, 1964), rather faded after the 1960s, and systems theory has always remained marginal as therapy, the socio-economic correlates of mental illness were recognised in the few but powerful, because large, epidemiological studies conducted on mental illness over the 20th century.[17]

The problem here was always to construct convincing models which relate social factors causally to psychological sequelae, in which the recent development of a species of 'stress' models to explain psychiatric symptoms might be thought of as an unhelpful reification.

Nevertheless, and despite the development of a diagnostic scheme to which cause is irrelevant, the idea that social forces to which we are all vulnerable can trigger the symptoms of pathology persists in pockets of the psy professional populations and beyond. This pathology is seen not necessarily as a sign of psychic abnormality or special vulnerability but just the result of one of the environmental risks that we all face. It is envisaged as a breakdown of normal functioning in the face of an external shock, the loss of equilibrium in the individual, as a homeostatic system, functioning defensively in a potentially hostile environment.

3.3   PTSD: The diagnosis

The process by which the, initially, unique diagnosis of PTSD has been endowed with fact or facticity embodied all the trends in the social history of psychiatric knowledge itemised above: 1) the modernisation according to neo-Kraepelinian symptom-based, 'theory free' diagnoses, 2) the tendency to somatisation and 3) to the normalisation of pathology ... and more. Nevertheless, according to the somewhat triumphalist history of positivist psychiatry, the DSM-III had succeeded in giving a name and a status to something that was always there in the human story (Herman, 1992; Trimble, 1985). Not only was it that the long history of human suffering had been introduced to science; it was that, in this history, a particular symptomatic form could be recognised – as far back as the myth of Gilgamesh – once the symptoms had been collected in a unified diagnostic form and historians of psychiatry knew what they were looking for.

These symptoms are found in many contemporary accounts of the effects of war or major catastrophes, a supposed universal and constant over different histories and cultures (Young, 1995). Iconic figures in our British history are thought to have suffered PTSD: Samuel Pepys, after the great fire; Charles Dickens after a train accident, and so on. In fact, the term embraces all people who are said to have exceeded by far the boundaries of the word 'distressed'; people in a constant state of hyper-arousal, as in intense fear; who relive horrific past events in the present in the form of intrusive thoughts and flashbacks with all their original emotive power, at the same time avoiding, or sometimes, conversely, deliberately seeking similar or associated situations; occasionally amnesiac or dissociated and generally numb and uninterested in social and physical surroundings. And all these symptoms are predicated on the one necessary condition for the diagnosis of PTSD to be given: the occurrence of an objectively verifiable, objectively horrifying event, previous in time to the symptoms, recalled verbally by the individual sufferer, and established clinically to be the disorder's 'aetiological event'.

It is essentially the memory of this event inscribed on the person of the sufferer – lodged in an invisible wound – which is the cause of these symptoms. These are of both a neurological and a psychological kind – this is especially clear in the revised version of DSM-III – representing the two disparate strands of psychiatric thinking, 'psyche' and 'soma' (van der Kolk and McFarlane, 1996). Not only did this diagnosis reflect psychiatry-wide developments by achieving a measure of agreement on the diffuse and somewhat contradictory characteristics of this disorder; the composition of the diagnosis itself embodies the two strands. In this way, though the diagnosis did not avoid a basic causal proposition in terms of the traumatic event, it left room, in accordance with the 'theory free' requirements of DSM-III, for different theoretical understandings of traumatic memory and different explanatory theories for the array of symptoms.

These two strands are held together in the diagnosis by the specification of the essential aetiological event. This unifies and makes sense of the symptoms and also distinguishes them from those of the more conventional and widespread psychiatric diagnoses of depression, generalised anxiety disorder and panic disorder, many of which are indistinguishable from the PTSD constellation – according, at least, to its critics (for example, Field, 1999; Young, 1995). The inclusion of the event in the diagnosis is what accounted for its social and political acceptance. It allowed the claims of the Vietnam veterans to compensation for psychological injury in war. A diagnosis of depression, say, implying individual psychological susceptibility, would have made claiming much more difficult, as the next chapter elucidates. In this context, this special causal form to the diagnosis was helpful, seen as a success and making a unique contribution to modern psychiatry and its more austere and pared down diagnostic processes. In the words of two of its enthusiastic protagonists,

> The PTSD diagnosis has reintroduced the notion that many 'neurotic' symptoms are not the results of some mysterious, well-nigh inexplicable, genetically based irrationality, but of people's inability to come to terms with real experiences which have overwhelmed their capacity to cope... The study of trauma has become the soul of psychiatry. (van der Kolk and McFarlane, 1996: 4)

But, soul or not, the study of trauma encapsulates some major conceptual problems, which all centre on the inclusion in the diagnosis of the aetiological event, discussed below.

First, this inclusion must be the cause of the somewhat puzzling claim in the literature that PTSD is 'naturally occurring' but also 'man-made' (van der Kolk and McFarlane, 1996). It would seem that the symptoms are thought of as ontologically objective – in the world, a universal, free of historical context – but that the diagnosis is 'man-made' in that the symptoms are given their diagnostic status by being linked up to a real happening, the aetiological event within the diagnosis. So the symptoms are, paradoxically, not free of historical context at all, since it is the historic event which gives the symptoms their special meaning.[18] This evokes some of the thinking about invisible wounds in the last chapter, where, in the case of emotional abuse, it was the objective ontological status of the abuser and his/her actions which guaranteed the reality of the psychological harm, the 'battering inside' and its symptoms, and gave them significance. It also, in theory at least, compromises the usefulness of the diagnosis for research into its causal conditions, since its symptoms cannot be identified independently of their aetiology (Horwitz and Wakefield, 2007).

Second, the environmental origin of the PTSD symptoms really complicates the problematic notions of normality and pathology in psychiatry, although it seems initially to solve them for the purposes of awarding compensation. These two notions can so easily be stood on their head. Whilst the development of PTSD can be thought of as part of a process which normalises pathology, in that the diagnostic symptoms depend on an event which could severely affect *anybody*, it could equally be part of a process which pathologises normality, as some other critics maintain (Double, 2002; Summerfield, 1996, 2001, 2004). For example, Horwitz and Wakefield, in their book on the ever-increasing diagnosis of depression, *The Loss of Sadness*, claim that its present over-diagnosis pathologises completely normal reactions to historical events and creates informational noise (Horvitz and Wakefield, 2007). PTSD is, by definition, essentially reactive to an event; the aetiological event is a condition of its status as a diagnosis of pathology. But, if we apply the argument above, it could be thought of as a condition of non-diagnosable normality.

The third, and most important, problem is the contradiction set up in the diagnosis between the symptoms of the causal trauma and the memory of its occurrence. The necessary inclusion, within the diagnosis, of the aetiological event recalled to verbal memory relies on individual testimony. But since this is delivered in the context of a disorder of memory, the content of the psychological strand is somewhat confused and its validity as a causal theory put into question (Young, 1995, 2006). This, it is argued, opens the way to the more objective neurological approach which relies on the visual techniques of neurophysiological measurement and brain mapping (Young, 1995). These developments turn on the complex and contentious nature of traumatic memory and recall of its symptoms' horrific cause, as set out below.

Causality and time

In the workings of medical positivism, cause precedes effect. However, it is one of the main arguments of Allan Young's book, *The Harmony of Illusions*, that the inclusion of the causal event preceding the symptoms in the diagnosis of PTSD 'reverses time', as it is experienced, subjectively, by patients supposedly suffering traumatic memory; it elevates, by implication, the importance of the patient's subjective memory, and thus, the psychological understanding of the symptoms. At the same time, it makes a sort of nonsense of it and, therefore, of its function as a psychological explanation.

This is a complicated argument. The requirement of the DSM-III diagnosis is that the aetiological event is not only something which is objectively horrifying, that is 'horrifying to almost anybody' but, by the 1987 revision DSM-IIIR (American Psychiatric Association, 1987), that it is clearly, and in the mind of the patient, the event from which all his/her symptoms spring. The 're-experiencing', 'the avoidance' of or 'intensification of symptoms after re-exposure to similar situations' are all predicated on the occurrence and, indeed, the memory of the event, if they are to have any diagnostic meaning. This is true even if the patient himself may have forgotten or never consciously remembered the precipitating situation or may never have thought there was one. For, unlike other medical assessments of mental state, which do not necessarily privilege the content of subjective testimony over that of significant others or medical observation, diagnosis relies on a subjective declaration of the patient about an incorrigible mental event in the affirmation of a 'memory', which, of course, assumes something to be remembered. But the psychological version of traumatic memory essentially models a process which could be described as a *disorder* of memory, in which patients are troubled by exactly that which cannot be consciously recalled or verbalised. So the version of cause preceding effect is the opposite of the way in which the aetiological event is often psychologically and subjectively experienced. This was especially relevant in the case of Vietnam Veterans, many of whom were said to have 'late-onset PTSD', possibly years after the so-called aetiological event. Fifty years before this, during World War I, Rivers, for example, was not interested in what may have actually triggered symptoms in his patients. He saw remembered events as merely images on which the men could hook their distress (Young, 1995).

Since the diagnosis of PTSD imposes a framework which makes sense of the patient's troubled and often dissociated subjective state by undermining it, its use in the ordering and measuring of the clinical facts requires intensive work from the PTSD knowledge-makers, from researchers and clinicians dispersed around the western world in widely diverse therapeutic contexts, who, in a sometimes slow and painful negotiation with their patient, reverse time and produce the objectivity of the event – a fact created with hindsight, as in 'recovered memory'.[19] And this process of fact-finding is aided by the discourse of disaster, since much of the clinical and epidemiological work described in the literature has been done in the wake of high profile horrors – as in England, for example, following Lockerbie or the sinking of the *Herald of Free Enterprise*. The tenuous and subjective attachment of the patient to the event, its uncertain memory and meaning, is lost from the story, whilst the objective significance and horror of the occurrence is deemed to have brought their symptoms into being and given them this unique sense (Young, 1995).

With this complication of the psychological strand in the making of PTSD, it goes without saying that the more reliance can be placed on the neurological symptoms and manifestations of this diagnosis, both clinically and epidemiologically, the more easily the aetiological account of the symptoms can be validated, or so it is claimed. As Young writes:

> The neural-hormonal theory offers an...advantage to PTSD researchers, for it provides a solution to the problem...with veterans' verbal accounts of their traumatic memories: the problem of getting time to run consistently in the right direction. The neural–hormonal theory solves the problem by shifting the locus of enquiry downward, from words and meanings to biological states and substances. To obtain facts and findings, researchers now interrogate blood and urine, rather than men. (Young, 1995: 283)

A move from the aural to the visual register potentially establishes PTSD as a fact of nature, the invisible wound firmly established in a biological site. But those who study blood and urine so carefully may use crude, stereotypic psychological stimuli in words and images, assumed to have universal meanings, to promote symptomatic neurological reaction in the laboratory or consulting room, and this might remain another difficulty (Young, 1995).[20]

PTSD: The research

Since its naming in 1980, the phenomenon of PTSD has been the subject of a rapidly growing research effort, which seems to have established it more firmly within the diagnostic firmament. In the medical literature it is celebrated as a success (van der Kolk *et al.*, 1996), the final achievement of a name for something that was always there in the world. The invisible wound has achieved ontological objectivity and, as a name for this fact of nature, PTSD is a sound diagnosis, which has also achieved reliability in the statistical sense. This, in turn, has been the necessary basis for a research programme of quite mammoth proportions – not just clinical and laboratory studies – slanted to establish internal processes, whether psychological or neurological, but also to a burgeoning epidemiology. It is these statistical studies, which have implications for questions about the normality of this particular pathology, about its prevalence and about the size and inclusiveness of this category of internal harm.

The triumphalist version of PTSD is not without its critics, however. In fact, PTSD is presented in more recent literary reviews as 'highly controversial', and a set of 'skeptics' in the research establishment are identified (Brewin, 2003). Whilst these 'skeptics' question the ontology of the PTSD enterprise and others, at a political level, question the value of a psychiatric diagnostic category in helping or healing those who are victimised (Summerfield, 2004), at the level of method, there is the view that these 'fact-making technologies' do not even conform to their own norms of truth. For example, the research literature contains the sort of statistical sleight of hand that many similar bodies of academic literature display. Studies in which hypothesised relationships do not reach the required level of significance are not published, thus creating the impression of unanimity in the literature. If they are published anyway, their caveats are soon forgotten and their results become part of the accepted wisdom, assumed up to the level of facts. Studies with contradictory results[21] also become part of the citation ritual and the negative nature of their findings is conveniently overlooked; indeed, criticism and controversy expand the body of the literature (Young, 1995). Second, the diagnosis may have reliability but it has no independent validity.[22]

More telling for the question about normality and pathology is a critique at the empirical level. This relates to epidemiological findings that throw the original formulation of PTSD into doubt and which have multiplied since Young's book in 1995. McFarlane's study of the psychological effects on firefighters in a major Australian bushfire was one of the first to suggest that the incidence of PTSD among an event-exposed population depended on pre-existing vulnerability factors or risk factors, rather than being 'dose related' – that is, depending, as it were, on the extent of exposure to the aetiological event, or the level of intensity of the event itself (McFarlane, 1986). McFarlane had access to medical records pre-dating the event, but most studies before and since have had no such information and concentrated on exposed populations, in whom what were taken to be symptomatic features of PTSD could easily have been pre-existing risk factors for developing the symptoms associated with this diagnosis (Bowman and Yehuda, 2004). The psychiatric evidence to the Law Commission's Report on Liability for Psychiatric Illness (The Law Commission, 1998: 38–47), especially that from Richard Mayou and Bridget Bryant, question the prevalence of PTSD rather than other psychiatric conditions after major accidents.[23] This raises the whole question of the normality or otherwise of the PTSD symptoms as a reaction to traumatic stress: is it the event which is the pathogen, inducing symptoms in otherwise normal people? Or, are the symptoms the pathological response to an event which by no means induces PTSD symptoms in everybody, or even in the majority of those affected, but only in those 'susceptible' by virtue of pre-existing characteristics of self and/or social environment?

'Conceptual bracket creep':[24] The inclusiveness of the aetiological event in DSMs III, IIIR and IV

As for the inclusiveness of this version of the invisible wound, it crucially depends on what horrific happenings exactly constitute the part of the diagnosis which is the aetiological event. This is, also a matter of some uncertainty, and the rather stringent requirements of Criterion A in DSM-III and DSM-IIIR (that 'the individual has experienced a traumatic event that (1) is outside the range of usual human experience and (2) would be markedly distressing to almost anyone') were relaxed in the formulation of DSM-IV in 1994. These now include, in Criterion A, those who 'experienced, witnessed, or were confronted with an event or events' involving fear for the physical integrity of themselves, but also of others, and not just family members or other close associates; that is, no relational limits are mentioned. To be 'confronted' by such events is vague and might include not just witnessing, but also 'learning about' them, simultaneity not specified, as long as 'the traumatised person's response to these events involved intense fear, helplessness or horror' (American Psychiatric Association, 1994: 424, 427–8). This was some acknowledgement, also, of the individual meaning of experience, which added another paradox to the diagnosis, as observed by Richard McNally, himself a member of the DSM-IV Committee. He points out that, under Criterion C, symptoms of dissociation or numbing, especially prevalent in sexually abused or raped women, are a feature which make nonsense of the *feelings* of horror required by criterion A (McNally, 2004). Most important, DSM-IV significantly enlarged the range of experiences that could officially be regarded as major stressors and so the range of people who could claim to be suffering from PTSD.

The submergence of the subjective in the elevation of an objectively horrifying aetiological event, set out in DSM-III, of course, made PTSD a diagnosis which was eminently suitable for legitimating claims to compensation, because it appeared closely defined, stringent as well as generally accepted. This seems to have been one of the more political motives behind its creation. It was also accepted by the academic medical establishment as a measure with proven reliability, so that it became the subject of a major research programme. Paradoxically, once it was accepted in this way, it seems that a sort of political *volte face* could be achieved. The criteria defining the aetiological event could be relaxed; it could become more inclusive. In this way, the ease with which the diagnosis could be applied and with which not just US Vietnam veterans, but others, could claim compensation, increased, as new wars and disasters came along and social and political circumstances changed. PTSD became, for example, a disorder found in children (Dwivedi, 2000). Allan Young calls the publication of DSM-IV 'the repatriation of PTSD ... bringing it back home from the jungles and highlands of Vietnam' (Young, 1995: 290). He argues that this opened the way to a sort of 'conceptual bracket creep' in the diagnosis, leading to it generally having much greater coverage by the year 2000 (Young, 2006). A revealing epidemiological study of adults in the Detroit Metropolitan Area, undertaken at the turn of the century, showed that, using criterion A in DSM-IV, 89.6 per cent of the population claimed life experiences that could be used to diagnose PTSD (although only 9.2 per cent were actually so diagnosed). Using Criterion A in DSM-IV instead of Criterion A in DSM-III increased the total number of all such experiences by an astonishing 59.2 per cent. (Breslau and Kessler, 2001: 703). As Young writes, some eight years later,

In 1980, the stressor was initially defined as a rare event which always produces severe distress. Today it includes relatively common events that induce serious distress in only a minority of individuals. Thus the repertoire of attributable memories and events has vastly enlarged (McNally, 2004). (Young, 2006: 3)

The possible set of causal events to which a diffuse set of symptoms can be attributed has grown to encompass more experiences, as its definition has become looser and more expansive. PTSD as a social problem category has expanded considerably over time.

3.4   Conclusion

In this chapter I have concentrated on three main questions about the diagnosis of PTSD. First, the uncertain location of trauma in a cognitive/affective space or a biological space or both; second, the problematic relationship of normality to pathology in psychiatry when exogenous causes are mooted and, third, the status of this external environmental cause: the aetiological event. All of these ambiguities, which were each raised and discussed in Chapter 2, beset the diagnostic system of western psychiatry, and they are particularly relevant to a diagnosis such as PTSD, which, unlike the other diagnostic categories of DSM-III, was established in relation to its social or environmental causation.

The dilemmas of PTSD spelt out in this chapter reflect generic difficulties in constructing meaningful operational versions of invisible wounds. The concept of invisibility is not just the essential qualification that makes trauma a metaphor – like a wound, but not a wound – but a genuine challenge to any positivistic explorer of a psychic interior. This is especially true of an interior which was first colonised as a psychoanalytic space, in which the wound lies buried – not just unspeakable, but also unthinkable, as memories of shock and horror are repressed at the level of the unconscious mind.[25] It may be possible, in time, to access these memories aurally, through the interpretive conversations of the confessional, where there is expertise at discovering what is hidden, but *not* through the administration of the DIS, or any schedule whose questions and interview techniques assume away the existence of what cannot be revealed. But, if the explorer attempts to identify a wounded interior through observation of visible behavioural symptoms, how can he/she distinguish the effects of a wound from the signs of other diagnostic categories? If, to solve this problem, a named horrific event is included in the diagnosis, this demands a clear, spoken memory of the trauma – precisely that which is not available! It is not surprising that the newer techniques of neurophysiological mapping and measurement[26] which seem to give direct, non-paradoxical access to a biological interior and a physical wound, albeit at a microbiological level, might be preferred by the medical establishment, especially as it grounds its practitioners in the more prestigious natural sciences, nearer to the fount of funding.

The above is a classic double bind and one found in other situations in which a precise positivistic version of invisible wounds is imposed on this vague literary or psychodynamic idea that functions at the level of metaphor.[27] But such versions are required, not so much for clinical treatment, where the psychological and the neurological forms can coexist, but for medical research, epidemiology and for the legal and administrative imperatives of establishing guilt, accountability and the terms of compensation. Here, not only does an unambiguous pathology have to be established, but also an unambiguous cause, one that unequivocally induces pathology in normal people, where there was none. This is not helped by more neutral investigations of symptoms in recent reviews of the epidemiological research, which show that questions of causality, and normality versus pathology in the individual or the event are not, in fact, answered definitively (Bowman and Yehuda, 2004).

Finally, the specification of the aetiological event decides how many people can be classed as psychologically harmed – whether they are a small exclusive set or whether they are legion. I have argued here that although its dilemmas have laid the diagnosis of PTSD open to increasing criticism, both within and without the profession, it has not obstructed its use, which has grown considerably both within the clinical and the epidemiological community. At first, this growth was predicated on an indication of the objective uniqueness of the sort of event which could induce this psychological harm, producing a diagnosis of great reliability and a basis for successful claiming and statistical research. Then, with acceptance and success within the psychiatric profession and academy, a loosening in the definition of what is to count as a causal event in DSM-IV has greatly increased its inclusiveness, and thus the number of people who can make a medical claim to psychological (or neurological) harm. As the number of wounding events in the environment increase, then more people can claim invisible wounds.

The aetiological event seems to dominate the appraisal of those deemed to be harmed by suffering, much as the tail wags the dog. Not only is the existence and nature of the shocking event used to give meaning to vague symptoms, endowing them with the status of visible signs of an invisible wound, it is as if the shock itself makes a way into the interior; as if the trauma opens up the 'protective shield' to make it available, through the breach, for inspection by explorers from the outside world.

Of course, all three of these questions about invisible wounds – location, normalcy and cause – are much more tightly interrelated in the case of nervous shock in tort law. As we will see in the next chapter, they affect the inclusiveness of any diagnostic or other social problem category. It is the task of managing inclusiveness that makes these three problems a lot more pressing for the Appeal Court judges in their construction of a legal form of traumatic stress, than for psychiatrists or epidemiologists after 1980. Although it goes almost without saying that law and psychiatry in the Anglophone world influence each other and share the same cultural context, nevertheless, we will argue that the English Law Lords were subject to a very different set of social constraints from psychiatrists over the 20th century and certainly felt themselves to be. These constraints were often conflicting, but all related, in different ways, to the size of the category of those who could claim damages for negligence under tort law in cases of nervous shock. The category potentially expanded with the growth and influence of psychiatry but then, quite unlike the diagnosis of PTSD, which, one way and another, has gone on expanding, contracted again by the end of the 20th century.

4
Negligently inflicted psychiatric illness or nervous shock

4.1 Introduction

The last chapter suggested that the history of the medical version of trauma is partly the story of the development of a biological form of knowledge of the self and psychic harm, which has developed alongside the psychological and threatens to supplant it. In the development of trauma studies, the psychoanalytic dualism that predominated in psychiatry towards the middle of the 20th century has been largely sidelined, along with the notion of subjectivity managed by a medical positivism largely based on neurophysiology. This chapter looks at how this medical version of trauma has been used by the English Appeal Courts to legitimate legal decisions about compensation for psychiatric illness due to negligence, as the Law Lords create their own somatic version of psychic harm.

It is not claimed here that these developments have necessarily occurred because they are functional to this or that social group, either within medicine or the law. However, it does seem that the persistence of the language of nerves in medical discourse has allowed the law to incorporate the notion of psychic harm within the broad area of damage to property and, by analogy, to the body, just as the old common law 'psychic assault' is a sub-category of grievous or actual bodily harm as a criminal offence. Thus, an older, more historic form of dualism, legal rather than psychoanalytic, has been maintained (Horder, 1998). By drawing the definition of the aetiological event very tightly, implicitly defining causal shock by its physical rather than mental accompaniments, the law finds its own solutions to the vexed questions of normality versus pathology in the recipient of psychological harm and limits the size of nervous shock as a problem category.

As with medicine, we can see this position as partly dependent on philosophy or forms of knowledge. Cartesian philosophy is still the basis for legal thinking, as much as it was for medical men before Freud. The legal subject is rational, autonomous, morally responsible, and possesses and controls the body, where the passions reside. The idea of a psychic hurt or injury as a harm which is claimable is hard for this legal dualism to accommodate. Granted, the construction of the legal *subject* with its implications for criminal responsibility has changed over time[1] and psychiatry since the late 19th century has played a role in providing evidence on the fitness to plea and the 'dangerousness' of the accused (Foucault, 1978; Smith, 1984), whilst, for example, 'mental distress' has a history as mitigation in criminal proceedings.[2] But the nature of subjectivity, or this interior world, as an *object* of crime or negligent damage is little contemplated in tort law. It raises awkward questions; it challenges a hierarchy of harms implicit in a law based on sovereign rights, with harm to land at the top, then harm to property, then harm to the body (in its cold, mechanistic legal construction as property), beneath which lurks a more sentimental version of the body in pain (Hyde, 1997). The notion of mental distress is hardly considered as a legal harm (Hyde, 1997). Note that the crime of sexual assault is still constructed in law as a harm which is inscribed on property – on the body as metaphorical property whose use is subject to consent.[3] The Lockean precepts underpinning the Anglo-Saxon liberal rule of law envisage the maximum freedom for society's atomistic individuals, preserved by limiting state intervention to a minimum. The idea of a psychic hurt raises the question of whether redress for 'mere mental distress' can be included within this minimum; is such a hurt to count as a harm and, even if it is, is it a harm that is to count? (Hart, 1961; Hyde, 1997) More broadly, how can it be contemplated at all within the Cartesian system of thought? It is simply a contradiction in terms. Psychiatric illness, seen as a physical illness like any other, is a better fit with legal thinking.

This is not a simple matter, however, and for the law, also, not just a question of its dualistic philosophy, but of its social and political context. For the first three-quarters of the 20th century, the problem for the Appeal Court judges appeared to be how to think about and justify commonsense and humanitarian decisions to allow claims for psychological harm, especially where this had obvious physical manifestations. The diagnosis of PTSD, made official in 1980, conveniently legitimated legal decisions in this area of tort, and a *bona fide* psychiatric diagnosis became a necessary condition for successful claiming

(The Law Commission, 1998). After this, the problem seems to have reverted to the central preoccupation of tort law, which is how to allow citizens access to compensation for harm and, at the same time, limit the amount and number of these claims. This dilemma came to a head with the aftermath of the Hillsborough disaster, when the floodgates of litigation were so nearly breached.[4] The judges wrestled with the question: does the 'progress of medical science,' enhancing the authoritative nature of its diagnostic activity, mean that the area of 'mere mental distress', for which no damages are traditionally allowed (Hart, 1961) is an area ripe for colonisation by claimants? At this point, the new-found authority of medical science was discovered to have become a little less certain.

The relationship between psychiatry and the law, it seems, was ever ambivalent. The law's uneasy use of psychiatric expertise in questions of criminal responsibility, dangerousness, risk and so on, has been described elsewhere (Foucault, 1978; Smith, 1984), as has the use of 'welfare science experts' in the practice of law relating to children – in juvenile justice and family law – by Christine Piper and Michael King (King and Piper, 1990). The latter, following Luhmann (Luhmann, 1988) and Teubner (Teubner, 1989) see medicine and the law as two informationally closed, or 'autopoietic' function systems; the law's truth is not scientific truth, the law's notions of rationality and normality bear scant relation to their scientific counterparts. So, they argue, within a legal context, information constructed medically, for example, can only be used if it 'fits' with legal notions of admissibility. In this process of 'fitting', the two systems are said to be in a relationship of structural coupling, in which the medical can do no more than 'perturb' the legal (King and Piper 1990; Luhmann, 1988; Teubner, 1989).

What follows is the story of this relationship in the area of claims to damages for psychic harm, in which the medical diagnosis of PTSD can be said to have 'perturbed' the legal in every sense of the word. But it argues that this is not just an account of the fit – or lack of fit – between two knowledge systems, but of the relationship between two regimes of truth as shaped by their social conditions, their professional imperatives and functions. While this chapter is an examination of the way that the notion of psychiatric illness or nervous shock has been constructed by the judges of the Appeal Court as they have talked their way round these three, now familiar, problems besetting psychiatry and PTSD (the location of the wound, the nature of normality and pathology, and the status and definition of the aetiological event) much of their voluble explanatory dicta is directly taken up with what they see as the social constraints which bear in a conflicting way on their position. They present themselves as steering a difficult course between the rock of natural justice and a hard place manning 'the floodgates of litigation', swept along on the relentless progress of medical science, but always guided by a star that states that mere mental distress cannot be claimed for.

4.2 Tort law in England

The complexity of the English Law Lords' position in the area of 'nervous shock' has to be understood in the context of the complicated nature of tort law in general, of which it is seen as a particularly troublesome sub-category (Harlow, 2005). Tort law is essentially case law in which decisions are based on precedent. It has never been rationalised and codified, like so many other branches of the common law, and various legal philosophers have tried, it would seem in vain, to produce a satisfactory account of its rationale. Tort law cases are actions which exist between private individuals, in which one person sues another for compensation for a loss for which that other is held responsible. The law exists to make the loss whole, in what has been called 'corrective justice'. But this law is just a small complement to a complex of state-run schemes for victim compensation and, as such, is also part of a system of 'redistributive justice', which has become more important in a 'victim culture', where the politics of class have somewhat given way to the politics of injury (Brown, 1995). Its deterrent and punitive aspects also link it to wider policy issues about society-wide risk management and security, and to the ambivalent relationship between lawyers and politicians, especially in matters of political economy.

Historically, tort was a relatively small and confined area of the law in the US and the UK, until a landmark case in 1932 put the tort of negligence on the legal map. After this, tort law grew quickly, culminating in something of an explosion in negligence litigation in the US and then the UK in the 1960s and early 1970s. The US in particular is described as a 'compensation culture', in which litigation for employer and professional negligence (particularly medical) increased dramatically. The sums awarded in certain famous, indeed notorious, class actions reached many billions of pounds, a large proportion of which went to legal expenses (Harlow, 2005: 153–155). Although litigation in the UK has never reached such extremes, and the approach of the judges has become more pragmatic and cautious in the last quarter of the 20th century, the ease of litigation for negligence is still argued by some to deter people embarking on risky but innovative enterprises and socially necessary professions, as the cost of personal or professional insurance in some parts of the economy becomes prohibitive (Harlow, 2005: 164).

Thus the Law Lords' pronouncements on appeals against the judgments of the lower courts in cases of nervous shock in tort, in which they hammer out a version of psychiatric illness or psychological harm, are subjected to all sorts of political and organisational pressures that hardly touch the medical profession. These are not just about keeping state intervention in private life to a minimum, but, given the above, to minimise costs both to the Exchequer and to employers and professional groups, as well as private insurers. This is in contrast to the medical profession, whose Hippocratic imperative to cure and save lives at whatever cost has only recently become susceptible to the bureaucratic needs of budgetary rationalisation and the optimisation of spending on health in the UK. In the USA, the insurance system still perpetuates an extremely expensive service. Psychiatrists, also, have enormous space for professional discretion in decision making, behind the closed doors of the clinic and the therapy room. If the diagnosis of depression is anything to go by, they are not constrained in expanding a diagnostic category. In contrast, the Law Lords make the law in discussing and confirming or overturning what has gone before in a public, transparent and innately conservative process, like a huge, moving committee decision, where there is little room for mavericks. All these pressures on the Law Lords seem to produce a process which is dedicated to limiting the size of this area of litigation to 'reasonable' bounds and a particular anxiety about the containment of the size of a claimable category called 'nervous injury' which, 'once recognised, may extend indefinitely' (Harlow, 2005: 68).

Following this process, which is so constrained by legal, political and economic considerations, we look at how the Law Lords have constructed a closely circumscribed, somatic version of psychiatric illness; how a certain sort of legal dualism has been uncomfortably maintained, and how professional expertise over the nature and applicability of this and other diagnostic categories has been allocated. Overall, the findings of the Appeal Court judges can be read as a strange play of professional rationalities in which these fundamental psychiatric questions are given a distinct, legal interpretation.

As if the status and description of PTSD were not complex enough, English law in the area of nervous shock has its own added complications, the details of which must be gone through before we can get at the underlying legal constructions of psychiatric illness. Before these are discussed, there is a somewhat bald, brief statement of how the law stands now or rather stood in the year 2000 (though there is little difference) and, second, a historical section which gives a survey of how this situation was achieved. For tort is, of course, case law, and the notion of nervous shock has been negotiated in a series of landmark cases over the 20th century. This process of negotiation is described here and the main legal developments drawn out. This is, of course, material which is extensively dealt with in the legal literature on tort.[5] The brief sketch given here is designed to set the scene for what follows, which is a discussion of their Lordships' notions of psychological harm, normality and causality.

4.3   Nervous shock: The law as it stands

What the PTSD diagnosis produced was an affirmation of an injury or a harm – something that could happen to anyone in such violent circumstances – caused by an identifiable event. Perhaps not a physical injury exactly, but as like one in its causes and effects as should make no difference to recoverability. Crucially, the fact that the medical assessment of these may only be minimally dependent on the patient's subjective account, paves the way for a legal assessment which is even less so.

Of course the law adds several more epicycles to the PTSD story of psychiatric illness caused by an event whose experience would be markedly distressing to just about anyone. To start with, 'the patient' becomes 'the plaintiff', who, with the help of his psychiatrist, has managed to remember that a certain accident or threatening happening in his life is the aetiological event which has caused all his debilitating symptoms of psychological harm, for which he can claim monetary compensation at law. The uncertain nature of traumatic memory does not even surface as a problem in this context. Next, another person is introduced into the *dramatis personae* – another person, whose negligence or lack of care results in this event, which is, in law, the 'reasonably foreseeable' cause of the damage to the plaintiff, namely the defendant. Successful claiming for damages in the area of tort liability is organised around the necessity to establish three claims: first, that the defendant owes a duty of care to the plaintiff; second, that the defendant breached this duty of care, and third, that this breach was the cause of a particular sort of actionable damage. In tort, it is mostly damage to property or the person, resulting in economic loss in its widest sense.

The diagnosis of PTSD, which establishes a particular, objectively horrific causal event as part and parcel of a consequent 'recognizable psychiatric illness' (*Hinz v Berry* [1970] 2 QB 40 42, *per* Lord Denning MR) provides for one of two necessary, but by no means sufficient, preconditions for recovery of damages. (Of course, damages have been granted for other 'positive' psychiatric illnesses (*McLoughlin v O'Brian* [1983] 1 AC 410 431, *per* Lord Bridge), which are listed in the Law Commission Report (1998: 47–51), but PTSD has become the diagnosis of preference,[6] because the others present the major difficulties discussed below.) If the first precondition is the establishment, medically, of the illness itself (the actionable damage), then the second precondition is the reasonable foreseeability, by the defendant, of the psychiatric illness of the plaintiff, should he breach his duty of care. Indeed, without this 'reasonable foreseeability', he *has* no duty of care.

In the foreseeability criterion, the law begins to tighten its requirement for its own version of psychiatric illness. First, the event's horrific nature (much less expansive than the DSM-IV definition) has to consist in sudden or shocking fear of injury to self or another, felt by the plaintiff – and, specifically, injury to another who is close in ties of affection, a threat proximate to the plaintiff in time and space and apprehended by him/her directly and not through intermediaries. Second, in case of fear of injury to another, the defendant is entitled to assume, in assessing reasonably foreseeable psychiatric injury, that the plaintiff is a person of reasonable fortitude or 'a normal standard of susceptibility'. Whilst the medical claim for the psychiatric condition of PTSD (questionably supported by the epidemiology) is a disorder which can be sustained by anyone subject to environmental trauma, it does not guarantee lack of susceptibility or zero predisposition to psychiatric illness in all those who are given this diagnosis. Nor can the law, in fact, guarantee that only the non-susceptible can claim. What it can do, in the interest of natural justice to the defendant, is to require, like the diagnosis, that the damage is sustained in conditions in which it would be reasonably foreseeable that even a person of 'customary phlegm' might suffer a recognisable psychiatric illness. The foreseeability criterion, also, lastly, requires that the question of whether a psychiatric illness is foreseeable is considered after the fact; that is, after the event which causes the psychic injury. Otherwise, plaintiffs may claim for genuine harm caused by genuine fear, for self or a proximate other, simply about what *might* happen – an infinite set of possibilities *ex ante*, especially for those of a particularly anxious and imaginative disposition, and in no way reasonably foreseeable by the defendant.

4.4   Nervous shock: The case history

Dulieu v White and *Sons* [1901] 2 KB 669, is constantly cited as the case which established nervous shock in the English law of tort. A pregnant barmaid was made ill when a brewer's dray was driven into the pub where she was working. She feared for her life and the baby was born prematurely, 'an idiot'. Here, Kennedy J. established that the only shock that can be claimed for is 'one which arises from a fear of immediate personal injury to oneself' ([1901] 2 KB 669 675). The issue at debate was: could mental states count as part of a 'natural' causal sequence in the infliction of physical damage, to someone 'ill in body by negligent driving which does not break his ribs but affects his nerves'. Phillimore J. was of the opinion that 'the fact of one link in the chain of causation being mental only makes no difference' ([1901] 2 KB 669 682). For the first time, damages were allowed for physical illness (miscarriage) caused by 'fear and fear alone'. Here we can see the influence of Page, if not Charcot, although whether fear, which might be thought of as an emotion (and, therefore, in legal philosophy as a bodily state), also had a cognitive component was a moot point, as seen below.

In the history of tort it has been said that, in *Hambrook v Stokes Bros* [1925], 1 KB 141, the 'impact theory' – nervous shock is the result of a reasonable fear of impact to oneself – was challenged by a more general 'shock theory,' in which, for example, the fear might conceivably be for impact and injury to another. This was a move which in the official DSM-diagnostic category of PTSD did not happen until 1994, clearly reflecting the difference in the sort of cases to which it was applied. Here – and a far call from Vietnam veterans – the estate of an erstwhile pregnant mother of three claimed for damages for nervous shock, caused by the woman's reasonable fear, not that she would be hurt, but that her *children* would be hurt by a lorry she saw careering down the hill without a driver. One child was, in fact, killed and the mother became ill, miscarried and died. Again, there was much discussion of the relation of mental states to physical hurt and the nature of shock, but the shock theory was never put to the test, because the claim was allowed on the grounds of a very narrow extension of the duty of care. The defendant did have a duty of care – not just to the children but to the *mothers* of endangered children, who witnessed all the relevant events. How could the judges allow a mother in such circumstances to claim, if she (selfishly, it was implied) feared for her own life, but not if she feared for her children?

Bourhill v Young [1943], House of Lords 92, was a further test of which theory was to apply – impact theory or shock theory. A woman, again eight months pregnant, heard a motor cycle collision with a car, although she did not observe it because there was a bus in between her and the accident. As she said, she 'came over a pack of nerves' and her baby was stillborn. As a 'pursuer' only, the plaintiff was not near enough to the accident to be in fear of physical injury to herself through impact. The issue was: could she claim for mental shock which was actionable under other circumstances (thus turning over the point of law established by Judge Kennedy in *Dulieu v White and Sons)*, rather than just extending it to mothers? This was discussed at length, including the highly pertinent question of whether it was relevant to the concept of nervous shock and its effect on the victim, that the mental state of the plaintiff, as one step in a causal chain, contained particular beliefs or fears. As the plaintiff described her mental state, she seemed to have none: her mind was a blank. Thus Wright L. J. plumped for a thoroughly mechanical approach:

> Modern medicine may, perhaps, show that nervous shock is not necessarily associated with any particular mental ideas. The worst nervous shock may for the moment paralyse the mind. (*Bourhill v Young* [1943] 1 AC 92 110)

This interesting question, still not solved by the medical experts, was never decided, as the appeal was not allowed on the grounds that the defendant (now dead in the accident) did not owe the appellant a duty of care. She was too remote from the accident, so that her injuries were not 'reasonably foreseeable' by virtue of her lack of physical proximity. The defendant could expect 'customary phlegm' and 'a normal standard of susceptibility' ([1943] AC 92 117, *per* Lord Porter and 110, *per* Lord Wright) from someone in this position, a requirement which, as Lord Hoffman, in *White v Chief Constable of South Yorkshire* [1999], pointed out, reflected 'a robust wartime attitude' (1 ALL ER 1 40).

By the time of the next significant case, *McLoughlin v O'Brian* [1983] 1 House of Lords 410, the diagnostic category of PTSD had been established in DSM-III and the notion of psychiatric illness as an illness of the mind, but an illness like any other, had gained more currency in medicine and the wider world. The House of Lords allowed the plaintiff's appeal for damages for this 'psychiatric illness' although she also had physiological symptoms. Her husband and children were injured in car crash. She heard of it from a neighbour and arrived at hospital a while after her family, finding them all covered in blood and oil, in shock and her youngest daughter dead. The issue was, would this claim satisfy the foreseeability criterion, as she was not physically close to the accident? In allowing it, this criterion was stretched to its utmost and the so-called 'aftermath principle' established, in that experiencing the direct aftermath of a bloody accident might be as shocking as witnessing it oneself.

The case is considered to mark the height of the expansion of tort liability and to have finally established the more general 'shock', rather than 'impact', criterion for the application of the foreseeability principle. The dicta support a wide theory of liability for claims for psychiatric injury in principle. But it is noted that, although so far in the history of nervous shock the floodgates argument had proved inapplicable, the embracing of the shock criteria might encourage increased pressure of litigation. There was much discussion about the need for limitations on the extension of the foreseeability criterion as a matter of policy. And Lord Wilberforce first enunciates the principle of policy limitations to claims, on the basis of close relationship to the victim physically endangered, proximity to the accident in time and space and the learning of it by direct apprehension, rather than communication by a third party. These so-called 'control mechanisms' limit the reasonable foreseeability of psychiatric illness but also, by limiting the process by which claimable harm can be sustained, implicitly limits the *type* of damage which is recoverable ([1982] 2 ALL ER 298–303).

The famous case of *Alcock v Chief Constable of South Yorkshire* [1991] 1 House of Lords 310 saw this policy principle of limits to recovery put into practice. This was a case stemming from the Hillsborough disaster of 1987, where 95 football spectators were crushed to death and over 400 injured in the most horrific circumstances. A failure of policing was held responsible. The plaintiffs in this case, who all had relatives and friends among persons killed or injured, saw events in the stadium or on live television or heard a live radio broadcast, with seemingly devastating results to their health. They were all diagnosed with PTSD – the first time this diagnosis was so uniformly used – and incorrectly, according to the strict criteria of DSM-III which then applied. The defendant admitted negligence, but the question of his duty of care to the plaintiffs remained. Were they sufficiently proximate in relationship to those for whom they feared? Is proximity of time and place to the event provided by a television broadcast? The judges ruled in the negative to both questions and the appeals were not allowed. What had to be reasonably foreseeable was not just any psychiatric illness but a psychiatric illness produced under certain conditions; implicitly, the type of harm had to be of a certain sort.

This was made more explicit by the judges adding a further epicycle to the conditions of proximity, which is known as the 'shock requirement'. This stated that a claimable psychiatric illness had to be the result of shock – in the sense of 'a sudden assault on the nervous system' which could only be produced by direct sight or hearing of the event, or its near aftermath. The aetiological event was all important. From this it followed that mere fear or grief, 'mere mental distress', however much it produced the symptoms of a psychiatric disorder, was not sufficient to recover. It was a vital and contentious distinction (discussed below). In fact, this case became a *cause celèbre*, a cause of outrage among the general public and some legal experts, who argued that these limits to recovery were arbitrary and imposed by policy quite against the dictates of natural justice (Handford, 2006). One academic even went as far as arguing that nervous shock as a part of tort law should be abolished altogether, because it had fallen into such disrepute (Stapleton, 1994: 87).

Walker v Northumberland County Council [1996] Queen's Bench Division 2 was something of an exception to the usual cases in not obeying the shock requirements. A social work manager 'brought down by the impact of the work on his personality' was allowed to claim for 'stress at work' ([1995] 1 All ER 737). The other major cases in this field centred, as discussed above, round the question of how tightly these limiting conditions to recovery could be drawn. In *Page v Smith* [1996] House of Lords 155, a plaintiff claimed for damages for psychiatric illness resulting from a car crash in which he was involved but physically uninjured, although his existing chronic fatigue syndrome was exacerbated. His appeal was allowed by means of a newly drawn distinction between primary and secondary victims. Primary victims were those at risk of physical injury; secondary victims, those merely close in time place and relationship to those physically endangered. For primary victims, of whom Page was one, the foreseeability of physical injury was held to be a sufficient condition for claiming for psychiatric injury on grounds of a duty of care. Both physical and psychiatric injuries are personal injuries and not 'different kinds of damage'. So the requirement of the foreseeability of psychiatric injury for 'reasonable fortitude' (which Page's claim would not have met) were dropped for primary victims. By the same token, in the case of secondary victims, the need for 'control mechanisms' as they were then called, was clearly recognised and asserted. These limits were again confirmed when in *White v Chief Constable of South Yorkshire* [1998] the House of Lords reversed the findings of *Frost v Chief Constable of South Yorkshire* (1997). This had allowed police and rescuers in the aftermath of Hillsborough to claim, although the families of victims had been denied damages in *Alcock*. It was ruled in *White* that rescuers are not a special case of secondary victim and that the restrictions on the claims of these secondary claimants should apply on the grounds of distributive equity. The claims of natural justice (always a flexible concept) were, it seems, subtly rewritten here. No longer did they dictate arguments for meeting the claims of secondary victims, however pressing. Distributional equity dictated confining these claims to an absolute minimum, otherwise any lines drawn further out would seem arbitrary and unfair.

4.5 Discussion

In 1861, Lord Wensleydale in *Lynch v Knight* [1861] 9 HLC 577 590, described mental pain or anxiety as 'something which the law does not value and does not pretend to redress'. One hundred and twenty years later, in his authoritative *Casebook on Torts* 7th edition, Weir gives the following account of nervous shock, in which he almost agrees:

> There is...no doubt that the public...draws a distinction between the neurotic and the cripple, between the man who loses his concentration and the man who loses his leg. It is widely felt that being frightened is less than being struck, that trauma to the mind is less than lesion to the body. Many people would consequently say that the duty to avoid injuring strangers is greater than the duty not to upset them. The law has reflected this distinction, as one would expect, not only by refusing damages for grief altogether, but by granting recovery for other psychical harm only late and grudgingly, and then only in very clear cases. In tort, clear means close – close to the victim, close to the accident, close to the defendant. (Weir, 1992: 88)

This is a comment *ex post* from a historian of 'Black Letter Law', for whom there is a distinction between observable physical harm to property or body and 'mere mental distress' or 'psychical' harm. Not only is this distinction clear, it is supported by public opinion, which embodies a natural hierarchy of importance for these two harms, physical injury and 'being upset.' The late and grudging allowance of claims for psychic harm are seen as the exception which generally proves the rule; that you can claim for the first but not the second. This may be an accurate summary of where this particular section of the law of tort ended up by the turn of the century, but, it is argued here, it does not reflect the moral reasoning of the appeal court judges, whose dicta and decisions formed the concept of nervous shock and its ambivalent history over the whole of the 20th century.

As already suggested, there are at least four major interdependent themes which can be read into the discourse of the Appeal Court judges, which naturally changed over this time – though, perhaps, not as much as might be expected. The first two themes feature strongly in the report of the Law Commission on psychiatric illness, published well after the Hillsborough disaster, in 1998. In fact, the Commission seems haunted by two major sources of anxiety, mentioned on nearly every page. The first is, predictably enough, the old fear of the opening of 'the floodgates of litigation', if what counts as a claimable harm is too inclusive. The second object of concern, and the potential cause of the first, is the march of medical science, particularly after 1980. This second narrative refers to events detailed in the last chapter: the profession's expertise is credible and useful in legitimating certain legal moves and the whole notion of psychiatric illness is more acceptable, more normal even, and has the weight of authenticated academic research behind it. This of course has its downside in potentially enlarging the numbers of those claiming for nervous shock; the 'floodgates' threaten to open, because of the expanding knowledge base and respectability of psychiatry – a somewhat surprising story given the uncomfortable nature of the old relationship between medicine and the law.

The third narrative centres on concepts of natural justice: the judges are humane and liberal men – and they *are* men – determined to show that there is no intrinsic reason to distinguish between physical and mental illness. They recognise that psychiatric illness can cause as much damage and disruption to lives as physical illness – more even! Medical science tells us so. Even mere mental distress can have appalling and debilitating effects on people's lives. There is no intrinsic hierarchy in these different forms of harm. This expansive narrative was at its widest in the early 1980s, at the time of *McLoughlin v O'Brian* [1982] but this was also the time when a fourth narrative came into play: that of the dictates of policy. It was also clearly recognised by Lord Wilberforce that, if there was no intrinsic hierarchy of harm, one might have to be created as a matter of policy for 'floodgate' reasons, as well as natural justice to the defendant ([1982 2 All ER 298 303 *per* Wilberforce L. J.). There was much discussion in *McLoughlin* among other judges (notably Lords Scarman, Bridge and Edmund Davies) about whether it was the responsibility of the judiciary to include public policy matters in their deliberations. The question was whether these are 'justiciable' or should hold no relevance for legal decisions and are better left to the legislature. Still, this case gave a very different account of the 'control mechanisms' from that of Weir, above.

What we seem to be seeing here is the management of the old legal imperatives in a social context in which, as described in the last chapter, mental distress or harm has gradually come to be taken more seriously as a genuine affliction, This affliction is literally embodied in a branch of medicine rapidly improving its scientific credentials. It is an accepted cause for suffering and therefore complaint. Further, it is a context in which, in the search for legal as well as unofficial solutions to social wrongs, the voice of victims is increasingly heard. There is no way in which this is an easy tension to manage. The judges argue at length for embracing psychological harm as a cause for damages, talking themselves volubly into a position which potentially flies in the face of the English public school culture[7] in which they were socialised, which devalues the emotions, suspects the neurotic and elevates the traditional British virtues of fortitude and phlegm. (It is no accident that the first three claimants in landmark cases were pregnant women and the fourth a prolific mother.)

And yet what Weir describes is indeed the state of the law of nervous shock at this time. The rulings after Hillsborough still outrage a section of public and legal opinion, which appeals to natural justice for shocked and bereaved families and rescue workers who have suffered since without compensation. So what happened? And why did the expansive narrative of the judges in the end become so confined? To invoke the floodgates argument and the powerful legal imperative to maintain Weir's hierarchical distinction between physical and mental harm gives only part of the answer. Another part at least must lie in the way the judges constructed the notion of psychological or psychiatric illness as a certain sort of harm for which damages can be claimed, particularly in the way they used what was relevant from medical knowledge and its social status to both expand and then contract the category.

This is not to claim causal power or status for an idea, but rather it could be said to be permissive, a flexible concept which was functional to the judges in arguing the way that legal and organisational imperatives pushed them, as these sometimes cancelled out the dictates of natural justice to claimants. It could be said that the driver in the case of *Dulieu v White and Sons* took a coach and horses through Weir's clear distinction between physical illness or injury and mental distress. What emerged from this case and those subsequent was a mediating concept – something between the two, later called psychiatric illness, which fudged the distinction and which, variously defined, belonged in either camp, both, or neither. The rest of this chapter is about the way that the legal version of a psychiatric illness due to traumatic stress, and called nervous shock, is made in the discourse of the judges. It describes how this version changes over its history, and how it differs from its medical counterpart. The process is viewed through its changing boundaries, first, with the concept of physical illness or injury, on the one hand, and, second, with mere mental distress on the other. A reading of the judgments for both of these distinctions can be divided into the three historical phases: 1) the impact phase, 2) the shock phase and 3) the policy phase.

The physical/psychological illness distinction

The impact phase

In this first phase, the judges predicated this expansive acknowledgement of the devastating nature of psychic harm on the indisputable claimability of physical harm, where there is a duty of care. They hooked psychic harm to the notion of bodily injury – just as bodily harm is hooked to the notion of damage to land and property. In their pronouncements, it was, in fact, just another version of physical harm and, as such, was clearly distinct from mere mental distress. The pronouncements in *Dulieu v White and Sons*, about 'fright with consequent physical damage' sounds much like those of the neurologist Page, mentioned in the last chapter, whose work would have been well known in legal circles. Fear is inscribed on the nervous system, a trigger of bodily reaction and 'gross' physical symptoms. Phillimore J. was of the opinion that 'a bystander may have an action for physical damage, though the medium through which it is inflicted is the mind. ([1901] All ER Rep 353 366). The means of infliction may be mental but the harm is physical. As noted, the three claimants in the main cases of the first phase were all pregnant women who lost their babies, or who suffered premature delivery, following the shock of a threatening incident.

Not surprisingly, there are still puzzles, partly due to the ambiguities of the English language, in which expressions like 'injury' or 'abuse', refer to the act as well as its results. For example, Kennedy J. plays with the question of whether nervous shock which causes serious physical illness, is *accompanied* by a physical injury as well or *is* itself a physical injury, or whether physical injury is merely its consequence:

> For my own part, I would not like to assume it would be scientifically true that a nervous shock which causes serious bodily illness is not actually accompanied by physical injury, although it may be impossible, or at least difficult, to detect the injury at the time of the living subject. I should not be surprised if the surgeon or the physiologist told us that nervous shock *is* or may be in itself an injurious affection of the physical organism...

but he decides, anyway, that it does not matter.

> Let it be assumed, however, that the physical injury follows the shock... as its direct and natural effect. Is there any legal reason for saying that the damage is less proximate in the legal sense than damage which arises contemporaneously? ([1901] All ER Rep 353 362)

Presumably damage would arise contemporaneously if the shock *were* the physical injury.

Sargeant L.J. in *Hambrook v Stokes Bros* takes up the question of how an event which only threatens forceful impact to the body of the plaintiff, but does not produce it, could produce a physical injury. This is just, simply, the forceful effect of shock on the nervous system – 'such an immediate threat of impact on the plaintiff as to produce physical injury to him, or her, through the nervous system'. There seemed to him 'no magic in actual personal contact. A threatened contact producing physical results should be equivalent' and analogous with a threatened battery which may justify damages for assault.

> In the case of a threat of imminent danger to a plaintiff resulting in illness through nervous shock, there is... as real and direct an interference with the personality of the plaintiff as if the illness had been caused by actual physical contact with him. ([1924] All ER Rep 110 113)

The shock is the assault equivalent.

If Kennedy J. had been unsure of the exact position of science in all this, later Appeal Court judges had no hesitation in invoking their own versions of it. Lord Atkin, in *Hambrook v Stokes Bros* ([1924] All ER Rep 110 114/5), recalled that there has been a theory:

> that damages at Law could not be proved in respect of personal injuries unless there were some injury that was called 'bodily' or 'physical', but which necessarily excluded an injury which was only 'mental'. There could be no doubt at the present day that this theory is wrong...

He suggests that it was based on a 'false analogy between the action of negligence and the action of trespass to the person, involving some sort of impact to the person' and 'a belated psychology which falsely removed mental phenomena from the world of physical phenomena'. (Is he referring to psychoanalysis?) His stance is supported later by Lord Macmillan in *Bourhill v Young*, who stated firmly that 'the distinction between mental shock and bodily injury was never a scientific one' ([1942] 2 All ER 396 402). In short, the latter produces gross damage and the former, neurological damage of a much finer kind, which may then manifest itself in more or less visible or gross physical symptoms. There is no distinction in science. Nervous shock is or produces bodily injury.

The shock phase

This phase starts after World War II and coincides with a period where psychoanalysis, and then other psychological therapies, achieved more of an influence medically and culturally in thinking about psychological illnesses or problems. It culminates in the case of *McLoughlin v O'Brian* [1982], which effectively establishes the 'shock principle', proposed by *Hambrook* but never really decided upon by a landmark case up to this point, since there was no decision on this matter in *Bourhill*. By 1982, nervous shock has become not a physical illness or injury whose origin was a causal event in the form of shock, but a 'psychiatric' one, pure and simple. In *McLoughlin*, Lord Wilberforce states:

> Although we continue to use the hallowed expression 'nervous shock', English law and common understanding, have moved some distance since recognition was given to this symptom as a basis for liability. Whatever is unknown about the mind–body relationship (and the area of ignorance seems to expand with that of knowledge) it is now accepted by medical science that recognisable and severe physical damage to the human body and system may be caused by

the impact, through the senses, of external events on the mind. There may thus be produced what is as an identifiable an illness as any that may be caused by direct physical impact. ([1982] 2 All ER 298 301)

But, according to Lord Bridge, another judge in this case, this identifiable illness is not a physical one produced by a mental event. It is 'a psychiatric illness' – an entity in its own right and, by implication, a state of mind, since it may or may not have 'psychosomatic symptoms' ([1982] 2 All ER 298 301). The plaintiff is described by Lord Wilberforce as suffering from 'severe shock, organic depression and a change of personality'. He adds that 'numerous symptoms of a physiological character are said to have been manifested', but these seem to be symptoms of a psychiatric illness as distinct from a physical one ([1982] 2 All ER 298 301).

At this point, although there is still a legal tradition that follows much medicine in grounding psychiatric illnesses in the physical – note the attribution of 'organic' depression to the plaintiff, though all the circumstances point to it being 'reactive' – it is clear that psychiatric illnesses do not need to be 'physical illnesses' to have claimable status. The plaintiff's state is claimable by applying 'the ordinary criterion of reasonable foreseeability to the facts, with an eye enlightened by the progressive awareness of mental illness' ([1982] 2 All ER 298 311/12 *per* Lord Bridge). As later confirmed in *Page*, psychiatric illnesses are another form of personal injury, equal in claimability for primary victims as physical injury – medically a different kind of damage, but not legally ([1995] 2 All ER 736 759). Even for those called secondary victims in *Page*, later clarified in *White* as suffering from 'pure psychiatric harm', the final demise of impact theory establishes that claimants do not need the threat of physical injury to themselves to claim.

So the category of psychiatric illness threatens to unhook itself from its pairing with physical injury and, as it were, float free. The category of those claiming for psychiatric illness due to shock becomes potentially boundaryless and not necessarily contained by the foreseeability criterion. This is one problem, as already noted, much discussed in *McLoughlin*. The other, more pressing problem, as this pairing drifts apart, is that the distinction it maintained between psychiatric illness and mere mental distress becomes a lot less clear than when 'illness' was physical and 'distress' was mental. Although this was not discussed in *McLoughlin*, the horrific circumstances of Hillsborough, which involved so many in such distressing experiences, meant that the floodgates really threaten to open in this section of tort litigation for the first time.

The policy phase

This phase is marked by the reaction to Hillsborough and particularly by *Alcock*. With a reaffirmation of the control mechanisms and the specification of the nature of shock, as opposed to other causes of psychiatric illness, 'the shock principle', the language of nerves that characterised the first phase and largely disappeared in the second, is back. With the reaffirmation of the shock principle, so the language of assault, damage and injury (see *Page*) becomes interchangeable with illness. Psychiatric illness is hooked up to physical illness again. Nevertheless, there is notably a subtle change in the argument. In the impact phase, nervous shock was claimable as a version of physical illness or injury, set in a cultural context which more or less took for granted Victorian neurology and the discourse of nerves still prevailing in World War I. In this policy phase, nervous shock becomes a psychiatric illness, whose status to claimability is supported by the advance in medical science, freeing itself from psychoanalysis and supported by the strong neurological, organic base of modern psychiatry. As Lord Lloyd said in *Page v Smith*:

> In an age when medical knowledge is expanding fast, and psychiatric knowledge with it, it would not be sensible to commit the law to a distinction between physical and psychiatric injury, which may already seem somewhat artificial, and may soon be altogether outmoded. ([1996] All ER 736 759)

This is confirmed by Lord Goff in *White v Chief Constable of South Yorkshire Police*. 'Psychiatric advances,' he says, 'are revealing that psychiatric illnesses may have a physical base.' ([1999] 1 All ER 1 16.)

Somewhat puzzlingly, the story of the first phase seems to have been turned on its head. Having established first that a mental state can mediate physical illness and then, by appeal to the progress of psychiatric knowledge, that psychiatric illness is a claimable entity in its own right of equal status with physical injury, their Lordships next use the relentless progress of medical science to legitimate this process by arguing afresh for the grounding this illness in bodily function. But it is puzzling only until it is remembered that these shifts track the changing relationship of neurology to psychiatry in general, shown, in particular, in the history of PTSD.

The psychiatric illness/mental distress distinction

If, in managing the boundary between psychiatric and physical illness or injury and keeping the two phenomena close together, the progress and reliability of psychiatry is continually called upon in one way or another; in the management of the boundary between mental distress and illness, it is the *inexactness* and lack of progress of psychiatry which is appealed to.

The impact phase

In phase 1, mental distress features prominently in the discourse of the judges as 'that which cannot be claimed for' – rather as sex features in the discourse of Victorian England as 'that which cannot be talked about'.

The shock phase

The importance and the difficulty of distinguishing mental distress from psychiatric illness gets its first outing in the shock phase in *McLoughlin*. Lord Bridge, again, is acutely aware that his version, at least, of psychiatric illness begins to challenge this distinction.

> The common law gives no damages for the emotional distress which any normal person experiences, when someone he loves is killed or injured. Anxiety and depression are normal human emotions. Yet an anxiety neurosis or a reactive depression may be a recognisable psychiatric illness, with or without psychosomatic symptoms. So the first hurdle which a plaintiff claiming damages of the kind in question must surmount is to establish that he is suffering, not merely grief, distress or any other normal emotion, but a positive psychiatric illness. ([1982] 2 All ER 298 311)

Here Lord Bridge establishes a normal/abnormal distinction, which on first reading seems plain enough. And yet relatives suffering from extreme reactions to Hillsborough and diagnosed with a psychiatric disorder, who could, presumably, be classed as displaying abnormal behaviour, were refused claims on the grounds of the proximity criterion.

The policy phase

Further discussion of this distinction in *White* suggests that this is a problem which could run and run, as the policy phase extends itself. Lord Justice Steyn gives this somewhat confusing summary of the position:

> There are those who did not suffer any physical injuries but sustained mental suffering. For the present purposes this category must

be subdivided into two groups. First, there are those who suffered from extreme grief. This category may include cases where the condition of the sufferer is debilitating. Secondly there are those whose suffering amounts to a recognisable psychiatric illness. Diagnosing a case as falling within the first or the second category is often difficult. The symptoms can be substantially similar and equally severe. The difference is a matter of aetiology... Yet the law denies redress in the former case: (see *Hinz v Berry* [1970], but compare the observation of Thorpe L.J. in *Vernon v Bosely* [1997] that grief, constituting pathological grief disorder, is a recognisable psychiatric illness and is recoverable). Where the line is to be drawn is a matter for expert psychiatric evidence... ([1999] 1 All ER 1 32)

Or is it? Lord Hoffman, in the same case, casts some doubt on the helpfulness of psychiatry in determining this issue:

> The courts have developed sufficient confidence in medical expertise to be willing to award damages for mental disturbances which manifest themselves in bodily symptoms (such as miscarriage) or in a 'recognised psychiatric illness'. The latter is distinguished from shock, fear, anxiety or grief, which are regarded as normal consequences of a distressing event and for which damages are not awarded. Current medical opinion suggests that this may be a somewhat arbitrary distinction; the limits of normal reaction to stressful events are wide and debatable, while feelings of terror and grief may have as devastating an effect on people's lives as the 'pain and suffering' consequent upon physical injury for which damages are regularly awarded. ([1999] 1 All ER 1 40)

In the management of this distinction, the success of psychiatry-as-science has produced great complications with the proliferation of diagnostic categories around the emotions of everyday life, in which distinctions are quantitative rather than qualitative and, as Lord Hoffman says, lines drawn may be arbitrary. From the point of view of the Lord Justices trying to maintain a tight line between psychiatric illness and mental distress, the project of modernising psychiatry, at least in terms of its production of unquestionable illness categories, had better be seen as less successful after all. The Law Commission report for example refers frequently to DSM definitions of mental disorders and diagnostic categories, but quotes the DSM-IV document, itself, as stating categorically that these diagnoses have been drawn up for clinical and medical research purposes. This 'should not imply that these conditions meet legal or other non-medical criteria for what constitutes mental disorder' (The Law Commission, 1998: 52).

The normal/abnormal distinction

So, somewhat surprisingly, given their celebration of psychiatric advances, there seems to be a legal consensus that psychiatrists cannot be called upon to manage the distinction between the normal and the abnormal in this branch of litigation. There is a *legal* category called psychiatric disorder organised around the notion of claimability. Mental distress is excluded by definition, as not being a psychiatric diagnosis and second any claims for excessive or abnormal distress, which might otherwise attract a diagnosis, are not reasonably foreseeable, as the defendant is entitled to expect a normal standard of susceptibility in the plaintiff. Now, it might be thought that psychiatrists whose distinction between normality and pathology and views on aetiology are, in modern medicine, supposed at least to be strictly statistical, might supply the best evidence to a judge 'as to the degree of probability that a particular cause would have a particular effect' (*McLoughlin v O'Brian* [1982] 2 All ER 298 312, per Lord Bridge). But what is *reasonable* in legal discourse appears not to be that of science, presumably based on statistics, fact, *ex post*, and the laws of logic and inference. There is almost instant slippage in legal 'rationality' talk from what is reasonable to what is average or customary or even just intuitively obvious. The legal distinction between the normal and the abnormal is normative and *ex ante*. In considering reasonable foreseeability, 'the route usually taken and the route to be preferred,' according to Lord Bridge, is that the Judge,

> Relying on his own opinion of the operation of cause and effect in psychiatric medicine, as fairly representative of that of the average layman, should treat himself as the reasonable man and form his own view from the primary facts as to whether the proven chain of cause and effect was reasonably foreseeable. ([1982] 2 All ER 298 312)

In other words, the legal distinction between mental illness, which is pathological, and mental distress, which is normal, is based on what a group of highly educated upper-class men *think* that the man on the Clapham omnibus would think would be the medical view of the likely aetiology of certain behaviours and the degree of their pathology.

So a view of the legal construction of psychiatric illness which is a slightly strange one from a lay or medical point of view emerges.

There is a hint of paradox about the way certain cases are described in the Law Reviews. In *Hunter v The British Coal Corporation and Another*, for instance, the plaintiff suffered 'nervous shock and depression' from hearing of a friend's death in an accident that happened at about thirty yards' distance from him. His claim, as a secondary victim, was not allowed, because his illness was 'an *abnormal* reaction to the news of [his friend's] death, triggered off by an *irrational* feeling of responsibility and not a foreseeable consequence of the defendant's breach of a duty of care' ([1998] 2 All ER 97). It is as if the foreseeability criterion constructs a legal version of mental illness in which only the normal can be held to be mad and the abnormal must be held to be sane. Of course, once traumatic time is introduced here then the paradox unravels. It is the aetiological event which is crucial, as Lord Steyn, already quoted in *White*, averred. The legal notion of mental illness here constructed depends crucially not just on the reaction to the event attracting a psychiatric diagnosis, but on *which* psychiatric diagnosis, and attracting the right sort of diagnosis depends on the aetiological event itself being horrific in a way which is beyond everyday experience. So, psychiatric illnesses such as depression and anxiety, which are abnormal extensions of mental distress, are pathological reactions to everyday events such as losing loved ones, seeing gruesome accidents and dead bodies strewn about the place, which those of 'customary phlegm' take in their stride. In other words, they are *abnormal* reactions to *normal* events. The psychiatric illness of PTSD, on the other hand, is a *normal* reaction to *extremely abnormal* events and the quality which defines the abnormality of this event is what it produces in the way of *shock*.

Shock

Brennan J. in *Jaensch v Coffey* (1984) 155 CLR 549 587, quoted by Lord Ackner in *Alcock v Chief Constable of South Yorkshire Police* [1992] 1 AC 310. 401, defines 'shock' as 'the sudden sensory perception – that is by hearing or seeing or touching – of a person, thing or event, which is so distressing that the perception of the phenomenon affronts or insults the plaintiff's mind and causes a recognisable psychiatric illness'. This definition suggests that shock, in legal discourse, is, literally, the relationship of three factors: (1) a uniquely horrifying event, (2) its proximate, immediate and therefore forceful perception and (3) its consequent effect on the plaintiff's health and functioning – and any or all of these three. All are features in the legal usage of this very slippery concept. Shock (1) an event, appears in the Law Commission Report (1998) as 'a sudden occurrence', or, according to Judge White, as 'effectively one event' (*Tredget v Bexley Health Authority* [1994] 5 Med LR 178 (CC)). Shock (2) is a perception, and, according to Ackner L.J. (in *Alcock*: 401) 'the sudden apprehension by sight or sound of a horrifying event which violently agitates the mind,' which is, in turn, the trigger to a neurological reaction. Or it is 'a sudden assault on the nervous system' (Keith L.J. in *Alcock*: 398) which produces shock (3), a 'shock-induced injury' (*Young v Charles Church (Southern) Ltd*, *The Times* 1 May 1997; Transcript No QBENF 96/0920/C), 'a shock-induced psychiatric illness' (*Hegarty v EE Caledonia Ltd* [1997] 2 Lloyd's Rep 259, 266 *per* Lord Brooke) or 'nervous shock.'

It is the nature of definition (2), or shock as a perception, which remains problematic in these pronouncements. A perception is usually thought of as a mental event, a cognitive process which may trigger an emotional one. But a shock or a fright can be and is, also, thought of as operating at an emotional level only – an instinct; our flight/freeze/fight responses programmed by our phylogenetic inheritance. We see the opinion that the neurological reaction to a horrific event is not necessarily mediated by any particular thoughts discussed in *Bourhill*, where the plaintiff 'came over a pack of nerves'. Unlike grief, which is always described as 'a mental state', and relies by definition on certain subjective and therefore incorrigible thoughts (Scarry, 1985), shock is a word that slips around. Some of its connotations are of physical forces like electricity, reminiscent of Freud's early physiological explanations of 'trauma'. It is the logic of the control mechanisms established in *Alcock* that shock (2) does not need to be verified by any thoughts stated by the plaintiff, but by its mechanical processes or effects. It could be subjected to the same criticism that Freud's theory received from the psychoanalytic community, that the essence of nervous shock lies not in how the event is perceived in terms of its meaning to the plaintiff, but in how, in the sense of *by what means*, the plaintiff apprehends it: the suddenness, the forcefulness, the violence of the agitation, that is only produced by a physically proximate experience. This is emphasised, in particular, by the judgment in *Alcock* that words and images were not sufficiently forceful to convey the full horror of an experience recoverably shocking. In other words, their Lordships seem to be talking about shock and its effect on the individual organism *not* as an information-processing model, but rather some model of physical forces, 'commotional as well as emotional shock' and those palpable shock waves, unknown to physics, yet the cause of shell shock in World War I.

In this discourse, not only does 'the nervous system' stand proxy for the complex interaction between mind and body in a way which is no more worked out than in the time of Rivers and Freud, but this branch of the law has travelled even less far than the psychiatric profession away from 'Railway Spine'. It is not quite back with *Dulieu v White and Sons*, where their lordships barely held the claimability of psychological illness caused by fear of impact on the person. But it has reproduced the opinion of the neurologist, Page, in which fear *is* the impact.[8]

4.6 Conclusion

It has been argued here that the internal wound or trauma, constructed by the discourse of the Appeal Court judges in processing claims for compensation for psychiatric illness in the area of nervous shock in English tort law, is, at the end of the 20th century, much as it was at the beginning. And thus, it is suggested, a traditional form of legal dualism[9] has been maintained. This has been achieved not only by an insistence on a physical location for the wound and its symptoms, but by the visceral unmediated nature of the shock administered by the aetiological event, arising from the tight definition of the 'foreseeability criteria', which determine a duty of care for the plaintiff. First, the Appeal Court judges have been very much less open than the psychiatric profession to any consideration of the psychological mechanisms underlying the sustaining of an invisible wound. Not seen by the naked eye, it lies in the microcosmic level of the neurological system, which is visible in principle. Second, since mind or mental states are more or less eliminated from the symptoms and their cause, there is no taint of mental abnormality or weakness; this wound is only to be reasonably expected even in someone of normal or 'customary phlegm', given the enormity of the fear and shock which are its cause. Third, the policy conditions dictate that this shock is mechanical; it involves such proximity to its source for the plaintiff' as would be necessary for the infliction of an assault by physical forces. The wound produced by the judges is as near to an observable physical wound as possible, without actually being one, and the causal assault, in the experience of the body assailed and the consequences it bears, as much like a physical assault as possible without actually being one.

It is also argued that this is somewhat different from the position of psychiatrists in relation to administering the diagnosis of PTSD. It has been suggested that the law and psychiatry shared three philosophically problematic areas, at least in this area of case law: first, the relationship between mind and brain or the psychological versus the neurological strand; second, the 'normality' of psychiatric disorder, and third, what was to count as an aetiological or causal event in the environmental induction of this condition. It has also been shown that the advance of medical science was accorded a significant influence in the development of this area of tort law. However, the diagnosis it developed offers a far more inclusive category than that of nervous shock in legal terms. Despite the rise and rise of the biomedical sciences in the 20th century and a positivist science of psychiatry which has all but taken over from the more psychoanalytic approaches of the mid-century, the psychological strand in the history of PTSD still exists, even if in much-attenuated form. The contradictions and criticism around PTSD are managed within the profession and even add to the impressive size of its body of literature. If the internal locus of the wound in PTSD is ambiguous or shifting, the causal happening that the diagnosis of PTSD allows is also now far more subjective. The definition allows thoughts as well as bodily instincts in the apprehension of events; it leaves little holes through which cultural meaning and interpretations, new forms of relationships and informational media can seep. Fear is not just a bodily assault. This difference in the way the two professions solved these problems seems closely related to the divergent organisational imperatives and social conditions to which the two disciplines were subjected over the course of a century.

4.7 Postscript

I have been discussing two very different socially produced versions of psychological harm and nothing points up the effects of social pressures on their organisational form more than their continued divergence since the millennium. Whilst there have been no new landmark cases in the area of nervous shock in English tort law, and the criticisms over the Hillsborough-related findings are still being voiced, the use of the diagnosis of PTSD continues to grow in clinical practice in both psychiatry and psychology and in psychiatric epidemiology. It is particularly here, in this last site, that new forms and sub-types are continually being thrown up, as academics do not, it seems, feel the need to adhere to the DSM manual for the identification of what they are studying. For instance, already, by the turn of the century, there were the beginnings of a raft of work on 'partial PTSD' – a sub-type of the diagnostic category, where not all the symptoms are present, but which is deemed to be equally debilitating and potentially claimable for US health insurance purposes (Stein *et al.*, 1997, cited in Young, 2006).

Initially, these epidemiological studies were concentrated on Vietnam and Gulf War veterans and sexually abused respondents, but, by the end of 2001, history had provided a whole new set of research subjects at the epicentre of an event of truly mammoth and unpredictable proportions. There was no happening in the history of the USA which had more potential as an aetiological event for PTSD than the destruction of the Twin Towers in September 2001. The US authorities moved to protect the privacy of anyone actually involved, personally or through close relationship, with the fallout of the attack. Thus the PTSD researchers, who seemed determined not to lose the opportunity provided by this unique event to measure its effects on the nation's psyche (Behrens *et al.*, 2007; Yehuda *et al.*, 2005; cited in Young, 2006), turned to those millions of Americans who had watched the events, repeatedly, on television. Their symptoms, of which there were many, were identified in telephone interviews (rather than the clinic) and formulated into the epidemiological category of 'Virtual PTSD' – PTSD at a distance, in which the criteria of 'confrontation' defining the relationship of the patient with the aetiological event seem, literally, to have been relaxed out of sight. Certainly, it would not have been recognised by the uncompensated claimants of the Hillsborough disaster, for whom harm from repeated televisual images of a disaster to strangers violated all the legal conditions of 'closeness'. In this new disaster, television images of collapsing twin towers were deemed, epidemiologically at least, to be an assault equivalent. Although found to be individually 'dose related' (Ahern *et al.*, 2004), they could also be seen as producing symptoms *en masse*, as the discourse turned from individual psychiatric illness to the reaction of a nation to the threat of international terror, and the containment of a mass expression of ontological insecurity – the collective wound discussed in Chapter 2. As Young concludes, the production of this new virtual version of PTSD was not just 'bracket creep', but an example of how new social circumstances, breeding different purposes and practices, may give rise to different and quite 'new forms of life' (Young, 2006: 10,11) and to different and quite new versions of invisible wounds and their causes and consequences.

5
The emotional abuse of children: An inward turn

5.1 Introduction

Overview

Emotional abuse is an expanding category in everyday language as well as in the administrative discourse of the child protection system, through which the predicament of UK children is policed. It features increasingly in accounts of unhappiness in adult relationships and their attributions of blame. It is part of a growing self- help literature and of the obsessive unpacking of remembered family life so popular in the media. Moreover, whilst it draws on the iconography of the broken heart, a sort of cruelty behind closed doors, it also invokes a more technical, public discourse about psychic trauma, emotional needs, rights and responsibilities. It has become part of the politics of injury, and of the great socially sanctioned battle for the unimpeded burgeoning of the self. But if this concept of emotional abuse has become part of the 'moral fabric' of our society and of a well-developed commonsense language of psychic harm, which can be used about adults and children alike, it was the growth trajectory of the narrower social problem category of emotional abuse as a risk to children that propelled it into this position and still gives it meaning. This chapter and the next concentrate on the history of this narrower concept as it emerged as a separate entity from the much more widely discussed, official category of child abuse in general, of how it grew as such and of how it became claimed as the most important category of all – 'the core of all abuse'.

The last two chapters about the medical and legal versions of psychiatric illness due to traumatic stress looked at the way the fundamental problems endemic to notions of environmental harm to the psyche (its varying location, normality and cause) were managed in these two

different regimes of truth. Also, the notion of 'bracket creep' was introduced and the idea that categories may bifurcate, or throw up new and
divergent forms, as the medical/clinical threw up the medical/statistical.
This chapter and the next, on the emotional abuse of children, are about
a social problem category, which is in some ways similar to the medical
and the legal versions of post-traumatic shock, in that it, too, comprises
three distinct forms of life: the clinical, the statistical and the adminis-
trative/legal. There are two differences here, however. The first is that,
in these chapters, the medical/clinical takes the form of child welfare
and paediatric knowledge, as well as psychiatry, the statistical version is
more psychological than medical and, in terms of the legal, courtroom
action gives way to the workings of a statutorily constituted administrative system for Child Protection.[1] The second difference is that PTSD and
nervous shock are the products of two separate regimes of truth, which
existed side by side over the 20th century. In contrast, the medical and
the administrative versions of emotional abuse arose almost simultaneously and formed a single, hybrid version, which expanded by 'bracket
creep', until a statistical form broke off to make a life of its own, mostly
in the USA. The clinical and administrative forms are still closely tied,
however, causing tensions and confusions within the child protection
systems, where they are found.

   Conceptually, whilst the idea of traumatic stress is rather simple, albeit
complex in its elaboration and development, even the idea of emotional abuse is very complicated. To start with, unlike PTSD, where the
injury inheres in the victim, there is the obvious ambiguity that this
form of abuse can refer to a destructive act, the cause of an invisible
wound, as well as the wound itself. This cause is non-specific, multidi-
mensional and is most likely to be a cumulation of small events over a
lifetime. Further, the concept can be said to describe an intimate human
relationship, and, as a relationship, it may defy the metaphor of the
wound, which is one-sided, intransitive, characterised by the wounder,
the weapon and the wounded in a rigid pattern. With emotional abuse,
the wound's cause, the wounder's behaviour, as well as its effects, may be
developmental, ontogenetic, part of an interpersonal or systemic process
in which identities are created over time.

   Despite this complexity, the requirements of the administrative and
legal system which is Child Protection demands a positive identification of the source of a child's distress or deviance. And this difficulty
is not solved by any direct access to an emotional interior. It is not
that psychoanalytic explorers have laid repressed memory there, as in
the dilemmas of PTSD, or that a social context is unsympathetic to

disclosure, or even that language itself is insufficient because the words of the powerful cannot encapsulate the horror of the oppressed, as discussed in Chapter 1. This wounded inner life is that of a child, which has been formed over time by abusive circumstance; the 'abuse' cannot be recognised and told by a victim, who has known no other life. So, in terms of the three major considerations that dog the idea of environmental harm (its location, normalcy and cause), questions about the wound's location in some psychological, analytic or neurophysiological interior are hardly asked. The academic and professional literature does not contain much complex theorisation of an inner life; indeed, the harm is defined by its obvious differences from visible bodily harm of child physical abuse or the visible or narratable trauma of sexual abuse. Its nature is assumed rather than explored. Whilst this invisible wound is located in increasing numbers of children by the child protection process, it is only in the statistical work of psy academics that some version is accessed and measured – and this in representative samples of adults by retrospective questionnaire.

Also, questions about the 'normality' of the symptoms of emotional abuse, so important in the last two chapters, are put in the background. Emotional abuse is not seen as a pathology in itself; it does not feature in any official medical diagnostic system – as do the other forms of child abuse.[2] The focus of the emotional abuse literature appears to be the third problematic: the relationship between the wound's cause and its effects, mostly long term and developmental. This is either discussed statistically, as described in section 6.2, or it is looked at in terms of the definition and application of the category in a welfare system, which is the product and basis of medical and administrative action, as described in section 6.4. Thus, it is the specification of emotional abuse and how it has changed over time and context that forms the subject matter of these two chapters. As ever, the inclusiveness of this invisible wound category and the space it occupies depends, tautologically, on the varying set of hypothesised dimensions of what is claimed to constitute causal, emotionally abusive acts.

The shifting terrain of child abuse

Child abuse in the USA and the UK has been an ever-expanding, fragmenting and transforming category from the early 1960s onwards. It named a phenomenon which was cast as one of the major social problems of our time, whose wide, detailed and emotive coverage by the media, professional and campaigning groups was characterised by Hacking, in 1995, as 'the most important piece of consciousness raising in the past three decades' (Hacking, 1995b: 66). This was a campaign that hit a nerve. It was about children, whose iconic potency in our culture has not changed since the 19th century. It was also part of an expanding discourse about individual rights and their endangerment (Douglas, 1992), in which the diptych of child villain and child victim was much invoked. It is claimed that over the last half of the 20th century, western societies have come to view the world no longer through the rose coloured spectacles of progress and utility, but through a complex calculus of risk (Beck, 1992). The safety of children has become a particular preoccupation in this 'risk society'.

The emotional abuse of children is a special case of this abuse phenomenon – intriguing, as a problem category, because something of an exception. Unlike the other forms of child abuse, emotional abuse has not been the subject of major displays of public outrage and, presumably for this reason, has not been on any public political agenda, either here in the UK, or in the USA. It was as physical abuse that child abuse first burst upon the world in Denver, Colorado, USA, as a serious and dramatic social problem, 'an issue leader' (Nelson, 1984). It was as a medical category, more precisely a phenomenon of paediatric radiology; 'The Battered Baby Syndrome', (Kempe *et al.*, 1962) in which the media assisted with a recital of horrors and the visual presentations of the wounding and emaciation of the frail, small bodies of children. It was later, during the 1980s, after ten years of feminist campaigning and mounting public scandals about incest, that child abuse became synonymous with sexual assault (Hacking, 1999). As such, it was cast less as a diagnostic, more as a forensic phenomenon; the thrust of professional activity became more a matter of investigation of criminal adults, in which medical evidence became secondary to the child's own story as the main evidence (Parton, 1991). Either way, the newsworthy and publicly revealed aspect of child abuse was, and is, that of assault on a child's body; the symptoms of a syndrome, the physical evidence of molestation or the narratives of survivors. The category of emotional abuse, in contrast, is a cruelty which does not touch the body – a 'non-physical variation' (Hacking, 1999: 138) – and, it seems, cannot be encapsulated in a child's narrative. It emerged without public notice, almost as an afterthought to the medical and feminist furore – appropriately voiceless and invisible.

Yet the use of this voiceless and invisible category has grown enormously – albeit silently and out of the public gaze. Although it would be possible to trace its multiple genealogies from child welfare, psychiatry, trauma studies and the law, emotional abuse entered statutory language in the UK as a narrow, small administrative and legal category under which children are registered by their Local Authority Personal Social Services Department (LASSD) as likely to suffer harm from a carer, unless some remedial action is taken. It was slipped, unpublicised, into official usage by a Department of Health and Social Services (DHSS) amendment to statutory guidance to the Local Authorities in 1980 (DHSS, 1980), lagging similar additions to Child Abuse Reporting Laws in the USA by a few years (Nelson,1984). Initially, it was not much used as a registration category, with only 4 per cent of the total until the early 1990s, when it increased rapidly to 17 per cent (DOH, 1999) overtaking the size of child sexual abuse (CSA) at 15 per cent. It reached 23 per cent in 2007, a much larger percentage than CSA at 7 per cent of the total and, in 2005, overtaking even the category of child physical abuse (CPA) (DfES, 2005).[3]

Though its official definition (DHSS, 1980) has not much changed, the category has clearly become a great deal more inclusive. What is more, there are increasing claims by therapeutic and welfare professionals that, despite the tendency of the medical and legal professions to somatise psychic hurt, *all* forms of abuse, physical and sexual assault, as well as harsh and threatening words, are inscribed, not just on the body, but more deeply and lastingly on the soul itself, or some modern version called 'identity' (Glaser and Prior, 1997; Iwaniec, 1995, for example). In the case of voiceless children, this inscription cannot be spoken and is recognised by disordered behaviour and developmental delay.

The growth of this category's application and its changing place within an official taxonomy of harm can be seen as part of a cultural shift or social change within the child protection arena or the field of child welfare, reflecting all the other contexts in which the gaze of professionals has gradually turned inwards from the physical to the psychological, and psychic trauma and emotional harm have become much-used currencies. This is not to endow a discursive shift with causal status, however, but rather to suggest the story of the emergence of the concept of emotional abuse as part of this 'inward turn'. This is partly in the working-out of child welfare policies at governmental level, which is covered in this chapter, and partly in the work of academics who have presented this category of abuse as under-used, under-researched and under-estimated in its prevalence and damaging consequences, which they claim reflects difficulties in the interprofessional politics of the UK child protection system (see next chapter).

The tensions here should not be underestimated. This is a multi-professional system, which comprises statutory, administrative, therapeutic and legal activity. Emotional abuse, like other forms of child abuse, is the object of specialist, professional and/or 'scientific,' as opposed to lay knowledges. Decision taking in this area is accomplished within a dense discursive context, which includes the complex interplay of different organisational interests and practices. For instance, as an administrative concept, it is formally, at least, coded in the language of risk. As a legal concept under the Children Act, 1989, considerations of child welfare are, in theory, paramount, although the doctrine of rights, both parents' and children's, tends to dominate practice. However, the traditional knowledge of welfare professionalism, which is grounded in medicine – paediatric, psychological and psychiatric expertise – is still used to treat, and also to legitimate, the legal processing of extreme cases. Moreover, all this activity occurs in a context in which the official application of this category, as with other forms of abuse, has enormous effects on the lives of the increasing numbers of those whose relationship is so classified. This is either directly through the power of the state acting through the courts, or within the court's gaze, which does not go uncontested, or, indirectly, through the subtle, recursive effects of labelling; the 'looping back' through which people are made up (Hacking, 1995a); and the 'iatrogenic' effects on the behaviour of those who have 'caseness' thrust upon them.

Chapter structure

With such a protean context, the space into which this concept emerged was not a clearly bounded one, but constantly shifting over time. One can identify several, not entirely distinct dimensions to such a genesis – first, *developmental*: gestation, and birth, growth etc. to its mature form; second, *textual*: its different locations in professional or academic literatures, in legislation and social praxis; and third, *spatial*: its migration or spread across different sections of society and between societies or cultures. There is no room here to take all these dimensions separately (let alone all their combinations) and what follows in this chapter and the next is an account in four parts only:

1. A summary of emotional abuse's gestation and birth up to 1980, in both the US and UK, where the first can be seen as influencing the second (and not just on a 'post hoc, ergo propter hoc' basis). In this phase, the academic literature, legislation and institutional practice are closely interrelated and organised around a primarily medical/clinical concept, which expanded to incorporate social and administrative aspects.

2. A description of the UK policy context between 1980 and 2003, in which the registration category of emotional abuse grew steadily amid a mounting chorus of claims that its (initially) small size in no way represented the underlying situation in the UK, in which this form of abuse was much more prevalent and much more destructive than its physical equivalents.

3. The next chapter, based on the academic literature from 1980 to 2006, starts with the US version, which seems after 1980 to take on a flourishing life of its own – the product of research programmes run from psy university departments, for which any definition of the concept of emotional abuse is made for the purposes of positivistic research. This is an approach which no longer identifies abuse with a 'disease', as did earlier, clinical research (Parton, 1985) but which, with its explicit use of a calculus of risk, is more appropriate to modern statistical medicine, epidemiology and psychometrics. More importantly, without the constraint of the treatment or administration of clients, these academic psychologists develop a technique for locating and measuring invisible wounds, through the direct interrogation of adults and their memories of childhood, which are taken to be quite uncomplicated by fantasy or repression.

4. This forms a vital prelude to the second theme of Chapter 6, which describes and maps the more clinical or practical output of UK writers (1980–2006), which is not only professionally based, often in conferences, but for which the definition of the category used in the research has been made for the purposes of writing about either treatment or administrative intervention. This writing presents a picture of the uneasy relationship between the clinical/welfarist version of emotional abuse and the administrative/legal one, to which the UK policy context is vital. Also, just as UK administrative and legal developments in child protection followed closely their US equivalent, it appears that nothing which purports to be academically respectable is written on child abuse in the UK without much citing of the US research literature. For these three different forms of the concept of emotional abuse – the medical/clinical, the psy/statistical and the administrative/legal – which started life as one, still depend on each other, not just for legitimation, but also for meaning.

5.2   Gestation and birth of a concept: 1960–1980

The concept of emotional abuse was born on the back of baby battery or physical abuse, of which it was seen as a rare variant. What is traced here is the gradual expansion of the concept of child abuse from the narrow medical category of baby battering to physical abuse as a socio-medical category and one which was eventually flexible enough to expand, by 'bracket creep', to include other forms of abuse and neglect.

The political acceptance of abuse as an 'issue'

The social construction or political journey of child battery and non-accidental physical injury in the US has been very well documented, particularly by Jan Pfohl (Pfohl, 1977), Barbara Nelson (Nelson, 1984) and Ian Hacking (Hacking, 1999). Nigel Parton has linked this story with the UK politics of child abuse (Parton, 1985), in particular emphasising the influence in the UK of Henry Kempe, author of the original 'Battered Baby Syndrome' paper, given to the American Association of Paediatrics in 1961 and later published by the prestigious American Medical Association (Kempe *et al.*, 1962). Kempe's is an almost emblematic career in child protection: Director of the National Center for the Investigation and Treatment of Child Abuse and Neglect, in Denver, Colorado, where he was a paediatrician; founder of the International Society for the Prevention of Child Abuse and Neglect, which ran a series of large international congresses for professionals and academics, the first one in Geneva in 1976; first editor of the *Journal of Child Abuse and Neglect* (first edition 1977) and co-author, with Ray Helfer, of the child abuse classic, *The Battered Child*, which runs to five editions currently. Both men are described by Anna Freud's collaborator, Albert J. Solnit, in the Foreword to the third edition, as 'international leaders in (the) crusade' (Solnit in Helfer and Kempe, 1980: ix). Parton sees Kempe and Joan Court (Director of the NSPCC[4] Battered Child Research Unit in the UK) as highly influential in the promotion of this concept as a social problem category in their respective countries. Certainly, the NSPCC followed Kempe's lead, seeing the issue of abuse as a way of finding a new direction for an organisation which was being increasingly sidelined, as the state took on a bigger role in child welfare (Parton, 1985). Court and other NSPCC officials spent time training with Kempe in the US and the new child abuse treatment centre set up by the organisation in London was called Denver House (Parton, 1985).

Barbara Nelson also emphasises that the efforts of these individuals found a favourable ecological niche in the economic and social conditions of early 1960s America and UK. Both were prosperous, somewhat concerned with equality, willing to spend on child welfare and beginning to be concerned about violence as a social problem. On the other hand, any more conservative resistance to spending – and this grew in the mid-seventies after the first world oil crisis – was pre-empted by the fact that child physical abuse was a narrow tight version of abuse: 'baby battery', a medical phenomenon, which was caused by individual pathology in parents. The backgrounding, at this time, of any social dimension, meant that it was not politically threatening, as, for example, talk of neglect might have been at this stage, raising, as it does, the spectre of child poverty (Nelson, 1984). US politicians, unmindful of any major resource implications, rushed with unprecedented haste to pass reporting legislation for the physical abuse of children in all the states of the union by 1968,[5] seeing this as a cheap way of establishing their moral worth before the next election – their public image much assisted by an intensive media campaign (Nelson, 1984).

UK politicians were a little less responsive to the campaigning of the NSPCC, even though this was supported by the medical establishment (the British Medical Association and its journal, the *British Medical Journal* (BMJ) for example). Joan Court's prolific writings on physical abuse in various welfare journals was not matched by any local authority social work writing on the same subject[6] and, even though the DHSS produced its first official publication for Local Authority Social Services Departments (LASSDs), called *The Battered Baby*, in 1970 (DHSS, 1970), officials there waited until 1974 (by which time Joan Court had moved to the DHSS to join them) before producing their first official LASSDs guidance, *Non Accidental Injury to Children* (DHSS, 1974a). This was a year after the establishment of a paediatrician-led campaigning group of professionals, called the Tunbridge Wells Study Group, at an inaugural conference on non-accidental injury to children.[7] It was also the year that the Maria Colwell enquiry became a political *cause celebre* (DHSS, 1974b). It was only after this landmark case that child physical abuse gained the momentum of public interest in the UK.[8]

Interprofessional aspects of child abuse

This narrow, tightly defined, medical version of abuse, the serious physical injury of babies, which was politically acceptable as a campaigning issue and seen as scientifically researchable, had met with a conjuncture of favourable circumstances in both countries, which had propelled it into the position of a social problem category. What happened after Denver in the USA and Colwell in the UK was a more aggressive state intervention in family life, and, also, the gradual widening of the definitional frame. The victim category changed to include older children; the effect of the abuse was not just the wound; the longer-term sequelae were seen as effects on behaviour and development. This said, normative child development remained the terrain of the psychology department, and it was not until the beginning of the 1980s that the first study relating adverse developmental outcomes to actual abuse in a sample of maltreated children was embarked upon (Aber *et al.*,1989)

Not surprisingly, interprofessional relationships were dominated by this concurrent politicisation and medicalisation of child abuse in 1961 – the defining moment of the period – but this period from 1960 to the early 1980s saw a gradual shift from the initial medical dominance of the problem category to a stretching of the medical frame to include psychological and social variables, and social workers, in the diagnosis and treatment of abuse.

In both post-Denver USA and post-Colwell Britain, administrative reporting systems were set up. Statutory responsibility to investigate abuse and to intervene in family life lay with the LASSDS in the UK, and with the States' child welfare services in the USA, invoking existing children's law if necessary. For paediatricians wanting to maintain their ownership of this concept, the problem was to accommodate to the inevitable multi-professional co-operation this would involve. It was not so hard maintaining a hierarchically superior and distant relationship with the police and lawyers. In the UK, at least, these were relatively low profile in the interprofessional processes of the Child Protection System until the run-up to the Children Act, 1989, and the Cleveland crisis.[9] Just as baby battery was seen as affecting a child's health and wellbeing, rather than his or her legal rights, so the invocation of the law was seen (even by child care lawyers, it would seem), as an addition to the main thrust of therapeutic or curative intervention. It was the state's nastiest medicine rather than the final weapon in its armoury or punishment for the guilty (Parton, 1985). So the main problem for continued medical hegemony in this area was with the question of medical accommodation to the social: to both social explanations and social workers.

Initially, social explanations of abuse by parents were excluded by the paediatric recruitment of psychiatric knowledge. Abusive acts by parents were not seen as part of some social or even interactional phenomenon, but as acts mechanically produced by a combination of personal, historical and psychiatric predisposing, and precipitating factors. The aetiology was intra-psychic pathology, 'unmet dependency needs' and the like, rather than social or moral causes. The bid by sociologists (Gelles, 1979a; Straus *et al.*, 1981) in the late 1970s for the inclusion of socio-economic stress as one of the main factors in the causal story was controversial. In an opening address to the influential Second International Congress on

Child Abuse and Neglect in 1978, Kempe insisted that the high rate of abuse in army families, who were nevertheless financially secure, was a conclusive counter example (Kempe, 1979: xiii).

While there was a sense, however, in which this category widening was enlarging the medical empire, that is, paediatricians embracing the social and psychological within their own ambit, the social at least was fighting back. There was a strong strand of social work opinion – and social work in the UK, for instance, was at its most radical around 1980, at the time of the Barclay Report (Barclay/NISW, 1982) – which resisted the pathologising medical tendency, as it borrowed its individualising explanations from psychiatry. Some highly critical accounts of the psychiatric research were published (for example Gelles, 1979b). Opposing accounts in the UK invoked 'different childrearing standards' and a 'culture of poverty' (Dingwall *et al.*, 1983).[10] While it was the medical profession, paediatrics and child psychiatry, who kept control of the multidisciplinary committees which guided the administration of child abuse procedures, it was front-line health visitors and social workers, in their formal investigations of paediatric referrals, and also the magistrates courts in their legal handling, who had the power to limit the extensiveness of the category of abuse, which was being much more rigorously applied from a paediatric point of view (Dingwall *et al.*, 1983).

Though it is not the case that any profession could be said to have achieved ownership of the concept of child abuse by 1980, from the point of view of the emergence of emotional abuse as a problem category in its own right, this emergence could be mapped onto the declining influence of a purely medical version of abuse. As the local welfare services, in both countries, became involved in child abuse administration, it was the influence of social workers, psychodynamically trained as the technicians of family life, which set the initial medical understandings of the causes of physical abuse into a complex web of intra-familial relationships. This was the context in which socio-economic or purely material circumstances were psychologically or emotionally mediated. Gradually, these psychic or emotional factors, rather than the socio-economic ones, came to dominate accounts of the relational networks. And this did not just occur in the causal story, but also in the analyses of consequences – professional understandings of how abuse, of any kind, could have such profound effects on children.

The emergence of emotional abuse

It has been suggested that emotional abuse as a problem category came into the world in 1961 in the slipstream of the concept of baby battering.

This social problem was like a noisy and showy sibling who grabbed all the attention of the world, whilst, silent and invisible, emotional abuse lurked shyly in the nest, making only fleeting outings with its siblings. In the literature it gets the odd showing, but, since, as Hacking suggests, the concept of child abuse, as it emerged then as a social problem category, *was* physical abuse (Hacking, 1999), the idea of emotional abuse, and by the same token, emotional neglect, with its psychological qualifier, was still a metaphor – as in the psychic wound – with Ryle's message, '*not* abuse', '*not* neglect', attached.[11]

Though emotional abuse and neglect may have had only metaphorical status, it was not the case, that professionals, paediatricians, social workers and welfare administrators were unacquainted with talk and writings that mentioned forms of abuse other than physical (although there was very little in any form until after 1962). They were particularly familiar with the concept of neglect, which was an old word in the world of the charitable organisations associated with child welfare. Indeed, it was a review of the incidence of and services for 'child abuse and neglect' by the American Humane Society (the US equivalent of the NSPCC in the UK) in 1954, which gave rise to a report by J. Mulford of the Denver Branch (appropriately enough) called *Emotional Neglect* (Mulford, 1958). This was, possibly, the first publication in the literature of professional child welfare in the USA that associated, in its title, some form of an inner life with direct harm from parents, be it neglectful or abusive.[12]

As suggested above, during the 1970s thinking about child abuse, family relationships and professional intervention did begin to broaden from the narrow version of the early days of physical abuse. It is possible to trace ways in which the ground was being prepared for the outing of emotional abuse into the world by its recognition and adoption as a social problem category in its own right. The first way (i) was via the change in how this concept of neglect was applied to families. All the other ways (ii–iv) are reminiscent of the conceptual pathways in which psychic harm, trauma or shell shock in WWI emerged from the fact or notion of physical injury or harm (see Chapter 3) – (ii) producing physical harm or the risk of it, as in nervous shock, (iii) acting in concert with it or amplifying it, as in surgical shock or (iv), finally, producing psychic harm unmediated.

Below, the emergence of emotional abuse is related to each of these developments in turn, as they are traced in the early days of the child abuse literature, legislation and conference speeches – in particular the Second International Congress on Child Abuse and Neglect, which took place in London in 1978. This was attended by a large set of multinational delegates, claimed by its two founders to be 1000 people from 35 different countries (Helfer and Kempe, 1980: 431). It seems to have been a key event in the history of early multi-professional responses to child abuse. Most of the papers were given by professionals from the USA or UK and many of the players in the future development of emotional abuse in the UK were there, though none gave papers on that subject. The conference was introduced by Henry Kempe and summarised at the end by Dr Alfred White Franklin, a UK paediatrician and leader of the influential Tunbridge Wells Study Group, close to the DHSS (Franklin, 1979; Kempe, 1979).

i) Emotional neglect

Neglect is a significant concept in the long history in child welfare, and was originally thought of mostly in terms of the physical wellbeing of the child. But, by the mid-1970s, it seems to have included, by consensus, some notion of emotional as well as physical deprivation. Chapters 7 and 8 of this book describe a history of concern with the emotional life of children, centred in the child-psychoanalytic movement, which informed the practices of child guidance clinics, even before World War II. If, in its early stages, this concern was organised by childhood as the cradle of the adult psyche, after the war the causation was reversed, in the sense that childhood wellbeing was seen more as a function of maternal actions, presence and emotional responsiveness. This socio-biological model of the family, often associated with 'Bowlbyism',[13] was more generally organised around an idea of the emotional needs of children, expounded in the USA by Mia Kellmer Pringle, a child psychotherapist (Pringle and DHSS, 1975), and likewise Vera Fahlberg, who wrote some influential pamphlets for UK childcare practitioners, including some for the British Association of Adoption and Fostering in the early 1980s (Fahlberg, 1981a, 1981b). It was in this area of childcare social work that the main concern about children's emotional needs was felt – and still is.

The growth of the fostering and adoption field in childcare was due mostly to a shift in the political and economic circumstances in both the US and the UK in the early 1970s. Tight State and Local Authority budgets combined with a crusading commitment to tackling child physical abuse as a psychological problem of parents, rather than a problem of poverty, meant a more interventionist policy stance, less in favour of prevention and more targeted on 'child rescue' in cases of abuse. The academic and professional literature was, consequently, much more bound up with the pros and cons of the state as psychological parent and the question of how a child's 'attachment' could be transferred from a natural to a foster parent with least damage (Fahlberg, 1981a). It therefore focussed on the emotional as well as the material needs of children. The correlate of this focus was a greater interest in cases where these emotional needs were thwarted. These were cases of emotional neglect, which were no longer seen as 'not real neglect', but as a bona fide form – just as serious, or more so – than its physical equivalent.[14]

By this time the category of neglect had not only expanded to include emotional deprivation, but the neglect of 'child abuse and neglect' – the subject, by now, of numerous organisations' publications and conferences – had acquired a somewhat different meaning. It would be fair to say that before 1962, neglect was a condition of parents: what they did, or rather failed to do to children. These were not acts for which parents would be prosecuted or children removed. This was the passive accompaniment of extreme poverty, drunkenness or aban-donment. It was dealt with by welfare workers, both charitable and government social caseworkers, by hopeful support of the mother with material goods or psychodynamic casework – a process which Kempe described, rather disparagingly, as the 'trickle down' approach to child welfare, in his opening speech to the Second International Congress on Child Abuse and Neglect in 1978 (Kempe, 1979: xi).

By this stage, for Kempe, neglect had become the *effects* of neglect, a state of deprivation and a medical and treatable condition of the child, an attitude which chimed well with the comparatively new rhetoric of children' rights, which he also used. (The next year, 1979, was to be the first International Year of the Child.) Though neglect had hardly featured in his first edition of *The Battered Child* (Helfer and Kempe, 1968), which was exclusively about physical injury, as were the first round of the reporting laws of all the state legislatures in the US (Helfer and Kempe, 1968: Appendix C: 237), by the next volume, published in 1974, Kempe was writing of 'child abuse and neglect' (Helfer and Kempe, 1974) and neglect had made it into the reporting laws of most states, though only one, Kentucky, mentions 'emotional neglect' specifically (Helfer and Kempe, 1974: 212). Neglect had become legally actionable and in the 1980 (third) edition of *The Battered Child* there were even two pages attempting to define the concept of emotional neglect for lawyers (Cantwell, 1980: 192–194). So emotional neglect as an accepted part of neglect hardened to become, in theory at least, an actionable condition in the child. And the line between emotional deprivation and emotional abuse, unlike the relatively clear distinction between physical abuse and neglect, has always been a fuzzy one, as Chapter 6 on definitions discusses.

ii) Failure to thrive (FTT), or the somatic consequences of mental states

In the world of child welfare, the most easily identifiable result of emotional neglect was called non-organic failure to thrive (FTT). This is a medical diagnostic category, a condition in the child, in which failure to grow appears to have no organic, that is, physical reason; it is thought of as due not to 'lack of calories' but to 'lack of love' (Franklin, 1979: xvii). Known to paediatricians for centuries (Iwaniec, 1995) and brought out by Spitz's famous studies of babies in German hospitals at the end of World War II (Spitz, 1945),[15] it relates events at the level of perception to a physical state, as its other names, 'deprivation dwarfism' (Franklin, 1979: xvii) and psychosocial dwarfism (Kavanagh, 1982) make clear. The non-assaulting behaviour of parents leads to a physical state of the child which can be construed as an illness category and therefore as a harm. As such, with its physical, tangible and measurable presence, in the form of paediatric growth scales, it is easier to pin down than the more general 'emotional neglect', both medically and legally. It accords well with the medical construction of abuse as a condition of the child, as in 'non-accidental injury'. What is more, any monitoring of the child or intervention in the family hardly needs a legal justification. For, as it is largely concerned with the condition of neonates, it is treatable on medical grounds alone. And these are also the basis for any psychosocial intervention with parents who produce this syndrome, who are 'treated' on the unquestioned assumption that this is all part of the package in any good public health perinatal service (Kempe, 1979: xiv).

As a medical category, FTT is a natural extension of the tight narrow category of physical abuse, and the two paediatricians who introduce and summarise the Second International Congress in London in 1978 are very interested in it. There are several papers at this conference on the condition, though only one on emotional abuse (see below). Kempe, who has stuck very closely to the narrow physical interpretation of child abuse in the first edition of *The Battered Child* (1968) and of physical child abuse and neglect in the second edition (1974), announces here that he has come to the conclusion that there are, indeed, progressive steps in a society's acceptance of child abuse: stage 1, denial; stage 2, concentration on horrific injuries and gross neglect; stage 3, recognition of more run-of-the-mill injuries and failure to thrive, 'an example of passive abuse' and, only after this stage is gone through comes stage 4, a recognition of emotional abuse and neglect. (Stage 5 is attention to child sexual abuse and stage 6 is attention to the needs of all children) (Kempe, 1979: x, xi). So Kempe, himself, having constructed a developmental story, thought that the acceptance of the FTT syndrome, as a social problem, was a vital stepping stone to seeing emotional abuse as such.

FTT was included by some states of the Union in the second round of the reporting legislation, in place by 1973, without emotional abuse. When emotional abuse was first introduced as a registration category in the UK in the LASSL (80) circular two years later, though clearly differentiated from FTT it was presented in tandem with it, almost as if it derived some legitimation from this proper diagnostic category (DHSS, 1980).

iii) Psychological risk factors for physical harm

Thanks to the influence of Kempe and Court, the professional response to the new social problem of baby battery in both the charitable and the governmental sector was a wish to take this problem on, not by wresting children from their parents but by preventing its recurrence through intensive treatment of children and families. So, after 1962, a series of child abuse prevention and treatment centres were established on the lines of Kempe's National Centre in Denver, both in the US and the UK. In the latter, some, like Denver House in London were run by the NSPCC, others were specialist NHS centres, like Great Ormond Street Hospital for Children, in London, and the Park Hospital, in Oxford. These contained family centres, where the child was certainly treated, but where abusive parents were also subjected, often on a residential basis, to intense psychotherapy, usually of a psychodynamic sort, combined with more behavioural modelling of good parenting and the encouragement and supervision of play with their children. A good example of this is the work of the Park Hospital in an account by Lynch *et al.*, 1975.[16]

Here was much talk of post war Bowlbyesque notions of poor attachments, bonding problems, or, worse, failure (Lynch and Roberts, 1977b). The same problems had been for decades the stuff of family life seen by social workers and Child Guidance clinics. But now these were subjected to a much more intensive intervention which was 'preventative' in a new way. In the 'trickle down' era, all forms of what we now think of as abuse of children (as well as spouses and elders) were part of a general pattern of behaviour in 'chaotic families' with 'inadequate parents', symptoms of poverty, addiction and a generally tenuous hold on material existence. After 1962 and the concentration of social focus on child battery, there was a flurry of research studies relating, statistically, the incidence of physical abuse with characteristics of family interaction, child and parent, but mostly parent. These largely social-psychological characteristics were no longer just the symptoms of general chaos; they were now the predisposing or precipitating factors, the weak or strong risk factors, for physical abuse.[17] The Park researchers ran one programme trying to identify risk factors in the perinatal period that might be predictive of later child battery (Lynch, 1976; Lynch and Roberts, 1977a, 1982; Lynch, 1978). This was not very successful from any rigorous point of view (Dingwall, 1987) but the practice of screening mothers of neonates for risk factors for child physical abuse became an institution in at least one maternity unit in Oxford.[18]

As Bill Jordan, the radical UK social work academic, rather disconsolately suggested, children who were 'at risk' used to be children who were 'at risk' of coming into care, but by the mid-1970s they were seen as 'at risk' from their parents. For uppermost in the articles emanating from these centres during the 1960s and 1970s was the assumption that these poor family relationships, in which parents, pathologically unable to give the nurturance to their children which their own childhood had lacked (due to their consequent 'unmet dependency needs' or just sheer ignorance of how it was done) and in which children, especially babies, failed to elicit the right emotional response from their parents, were a major cause of, and one of the strongest risk factors for, the physical abuse of children. This was certainly found in the research publications of the consultants at the Park Hospital (Ounsted *et al.*, 1974), where Dr Ounsted would quote, at ward rounds, his favourite lines from Horace:

> Smile at your mother, little boy, Because your life depends upon it.
> (Personal communication)

iv) Psychological accompaniments and effects of physical acts of abuse

It is not surprising that, with its new concentration on the condition of the child, professionals working in this preventative area should become aware that events at the psycho-social or emotional level were not just *risk factors* for child battery, but that they were also one of its *effects*. As Franklin said in his summing up at the Second International Congress:

> Several strands run through the congress, perhaps the most important being the effects of abuse and neglect on child development, shown in delayed acquisition of language skills, in delayed emotional maturation, and, most strikingly in deprivation dwarfism...

'The end result', he continues, linking emotional factors as causes with emotional factors as effects, 'may be abuse and neglect in the next generation' (Franklin, 1979: xvii).

These psycho-social circumstances also accompany physical injury, acting with it, possibly amplifying it. And they act with it to produce not just physical harm, but also effects of a psychic kind. Franklin continues:

> We are agreed that physical abuse is always accompanied by emotional deprivation, and that, of the two, emotional damage lasts longer, brain damage, blindness and death excepted (Franklin, 1979: xvii).

This is a common claim in the emotional abuse literature, though the last words are a chilling reminder of the less probable but, arguably, much worse, and certainly more arresting outcomes attached to child battery.

v) Emotional abuse unmediated

From this position it was a small step to seeing the effects of these emotionally negative relationships between children and parents not just as neglectful, or as predictive of, or amplifying, physical abuse, but as abusive in their own right. Judith Trowell, while Child and Family Psychiatrist at the Tavistock Clinic, described the thinking in the following way. Working as a young consultant at the NSPCC centre, Denver House, she began to notice that, though the intense preventative approach could indeed stop the physical abuse of children, these same children did not necessarily 'do well' after the intervention – far from it. Of course, she could have attributed this to the long-term sequelae of physical abuse, or to the sort of longer-term emotional and psychological consequences of the deprivations that go with physical injury, suggested by Franklin. Her view was that, in the families she was seeing, persistently difficult parent–child relationships were still actively harmful to the child, producing effects that had serious developmental consequences. These were not just the causes, consequences or accompaniment of physical abuse, but since their consequences were just as serious, they constituted an abuse in their own right and thus could occur without the mediation of physical injury. She did not write this up until after 1980, but her article, entitled 'The emotional abuse of children', published in 1983 in *The Health Visitor*, was the first on the subject in the UK (Trowell, 1983 and Personal Communication).

An abuse in its own right

Thus, difficulty on a psychological and emotional level, from being the context in which physical abuse was embedded, became an abuse in its own right. And, clearly, Trowell was not alone in making this conceptual move. By the late 1970s, in the US literature, the concept of emotional abuse itself made a few lone appearances. First, a single paper at the Second Annual Conference on Child Abuse and Neglect in 1977 by Lourie and Stephano, sponsored by the US Department of Health, Education and Welfare (Lourie and Stephano, 1978) sets the tone for a clump of further articles on the concept's definition: James Garbarino's, 'The elusive "crime" of emotional abuse', written just at the same time and later published in Kempe's journal; *Child Abuse and Neglect* (Garbarino, 1978) was followed by four other articles.[19] The International Congress, too, had a single paper on emotional abuse (McCarthy, 1979), and in his opening address, as already described, Kempe announced the broadening of the abuse category to include a version, which he defined as 'seen in a child who is rejected, scapegoated, unloved and so emotionally deprived as to significantly interfere with the normal physical, intellectual and emotional growth and development' (Cantwell, 1980; Kempe, 1979: xi). Later, in the third (1980) edition of *The Battered Child*, and perhaps due to the influence of the more medically oriented Helfer, emotional abuse gets two single page references in the index – the same as the first edition.

This ambivalence towards emotional abuse is also reflected in the US state reporting laws. By 1980, emotional abuse had crept into some states' laws, most with custodial provision for protection of the child, but few legislative directions involving law enforcement agencies. (Hence Garbarino's use of inverted commas around the word 'crime'.) In a 1997 survey of state laws (Hamarman *et al.*, 2002) these still only numbered 20 states of the 50, or 51 with DC.

Meanwhile, in the UK, emotional abuse was gaining more political recognition, due, in part, to this country's more homogeneous political structure and due also, somewhat counter-intuitively, to the House of Commons Select Committee on Violence in the Family. This was convened originally in 1975 to consider 'violence in marriage' and then reconvened in 1976, with its wider remit. Its first report called *Violence to Children*, published in mid-1977, with much corroborating research, states significantly that 'violence against children is only part of a much larger problem of child abuse and neglect and how children should be brought up' (House of Commons, 1977, quoted in Parton, 1985: 110).

It emphasised the diversity of social causes of child abuse, including 'stress, isolation, lack of bonding and unwanted pregnancies' (Parton, 1985: 110) and the importance of prevention at every level, including that of the community.

By mid-1978, the government had responded with a White Paper seemingly accepting the Select Committee's framing of child abuse as a wider and more general problem than physical injury alone and of their broadly preventative approach. The paper produced the caveat of budget constraints and hoped (vainly) that better prediction could concentrate preventative resources on a smaller group of children (House-of-Commons, 1978, quoted in Parton, 1985: 111). The DHSS was clearly influenced by the Select Committee and also by the movement towards a wider definition of child abuse apparent in the US literature (and its smaller UK equivalent). It produced a draft circular to the Local Authorities, by the end of 1978, followed by the revised circular, LASSL (80), two years later. This, though it centrally addressed the question of rationalising the system of Child Abuse Registers across different local authorities, also recommended an enlarged abuse category in the following terms:

> Previous guidance stressed the importance of multidisciplinary management of cases of non-accidental injury, that is, physical injury and extremes of deprivation and neglect. However, it is increasingly being recognised that the same requirements should be applied to children who suffer mental or emotional abuse. (DHSS, 1980: para 1.1)

And these were minimum requirements of the local authorities in this modification of government guidance to statutory children's law.

The publication of the LASSL(80) circular did not create a huge public stir, and even the social work weekly, *Social Work Today*, though it lead with the story by its staff reporter, Margaret Fogarty, spent only one short paragraph announcing that 'emotionally battered children' would now be included in the local authority child abuse registers. The rest of the article discussed the pressing question of the pros and cons of these controversial registers (Fogarty, 1980). Emotional abuse had arrived as an official social problem category in the UK, but this was hardly a fanfare.

World passing within

The making of emotional abuse as this, as yet, tiny social problem category, was a process which involved not only politicians, but the changing vision of their clinical and academic advisers on the social problem of child abuse, as they gradually shifted the locus of its consequences from the body, exclusively, to include some version of an internal territory to be explored. This change can be seen reflected in the movement of the DHSS publications on child maltreatment over the seventies, which went from *The Battered Baby* (DHSS, 1970), to *Non Accidental Injury* (DHSS, 1974a), to the broader 'child abuse', which included other forms, including emotional abuse (DHSS, 1980).

The shift in thinking was more complicated than this sounds, however, for it seemed to involve the loss of any influence that radical sociologists and social workers might have had on the general understanding of abuse. The House of Commons Select committee, in its investigation of violence in families, like Kempe and his collaborators who advised on the US federal legislation, became gradually aware that this physical violence sat in a whole complex of interpersonal difficulties. As Parton argues, the politicians saw violence as a social issue (Parton, 1985), as the result of stress, social isolation and unwanted pregnancies, rather than one of individual or even family pathology. Nevertheless, in the delicate economic situation at that time, neither they nor the DHSS had any traction on lack of social support, poverty, demographic or distributional factors. So they concentrated on observable social interaction which was psychologically mediated, as in 'bonding failure'. As Kempe gradually *expanded* his consideration of the intrapsychic characteristics of abusers to include the interpersonal context, so the committee members, and the DHSS officials who responded to their report, *reduced* the social context to the social-psychological. And the gaze of both groups consequently turned inwards, not just to the hypothesised pathology of abusive parents, but to a psychological relationship and an abusive harm done to the inner life of the child.

What the politicians and civil servants saw in this internal space is not quite clear. But the committee was well served by experts, as were the subsequent publications of the DHSS. The second part of this chapter is an account of how some of these 'experts' and bureaucrats in the UK social policy arena continued and encouraged this 'inward turn' amongst psy practitioners after 1980, so that the size of emotional abuse increased from about 4 per cent of the annual total of children registered in the early 90s to 17 per cent in 1999 and to 23 per cent by 2007. This story is set in the complex history of child protection policy over this period.

5.3 Growth of a category: 1980–2003

Child Protection in the UK: 1980–1989

There should be no doubt that, after the mid-1980s, this child protection system was completely dominated at all levels – political and professional – by the issue of child sexual abuse: in the academic, practitioner and self help literature; in DOH documents, and in awareness-raising and treatment training courses all across the professions. Although, by 1999, emotional abuse, as a registration category, overtook the size of sexual abuse as a proportion of the whole, the latter still dominates the airwaves. The academic and professional literature on physical and sexual abuse produced in the UK, and even more in the USA, by far exceeds that on emotional abuse, which, in comparison, is minute. Its small size confirms one of its prevailing narratives, which is that the emotional abuse of children is a far more pressing social problem than is generally believed or recognised by public and practitioners alike – an assertion, of course, belied by the actual number of children registered – at least in the UK.

Since the drama of the Maria Colwell Enquiry in 1973, which put child abuse on a public and political agenda in the UK and increased Emergency Protection Orders by over 300 per cent in a year (Parton, 1985), the state had become more interventionist as far as the safety of children was concerned. Furthermore, the promotion of CSA over the 1980, by feminists, survivor groups and then by government agencies, as a social problem of massive prevalence and importance not only marked a further widening and fragmentation of the abuse category, it also promoted this shift of multi-professional resources and organisation on to the forensic investigation of abuse, rather than on 'working with problem families', or what was later called 'family support'.

This marked discursive shift from a socio-medical to a socio-legal approach to child protection (Parton, 1991), occurred in a period dominated by the Jasmine Beckford Inquiry (Dingwall, 1986), the Cleveland crisis (Butler-Sloss, 1988; Campbell, 1988), and the preparation and passing of the new Children Act, 1989. It was accompanied by the decline in the social policy of paternalistic welfarism and a rise in the language of individual rights and risk – all features of the wider, New Right ideological context. Freedom for individual responsibility and enterprise in the private and civil spheres was to be maintained by vigilant and forceful policing at the boundaries. This strong law and order imperative was applied to those who assaulted or molested children – theirs or somebody else's.

Child Welfare politics in the 1980s were also taken up with the run-up to the Children Act, 1989, in a period of hard campaigning by many disparate groups (Parton, 1991: Chapter 2). These included the broadly socio-medical advisers to the preceding Short Report (House of Commons (HC 360), Social Services Committee, 1984). This was a review of child welfare in the UK which was supported by a raft of DHSS-funded research by social work academics (DHSS, 1985). It espoused traditional child welfare considerations, criticising the unplanned, inconsistent and sometimes arbitrary nature of social work child-care decisions and lamenting the departure from the preventative position of the Seebohm Report (1968), which established the LASSDs as the last plank of the postwar Welfare State. There was also strong representation from pressure groups for parents' rights, as well as the rights of children both to autonomy and protection.[20]

The resulting Act can be seen as a fudge of different interests or, alternatively, as cleverly designed to have broad appeal. It can also be seen as the last throw of a sort of crypto-paternalism within the DOH. For what was written into the act was an ideal of child welfare that could not be met at the time of the Act's construction. Under the Thatcher government, officials from the Child Care Division and the Social Services Inspectorate of the DHSS 'were not allowed to write about poverty' nor publicly address their concerns about the emergence of an underclass. Rather, they had 'secret meetings' (Ex Senior DOH official, personal communication).

The Children Act 1989 was widely seen and described as a piece of legislation which not only pulled together and unified a set of disparate and fragmented pieces of legislation in the area of child welfare, in both public and private law, but which was also designed to clarify and shift fundamentally the relationship between the child, the family and the state. (Aldgate and Hill, 1996; DOH, 1989a). Basically, the welfare of the child was made paramount and his 'wishes and feelings' were to be taken into account (according to age) in any decision made about his future. Apart from some dramatic changes in family law, the Act made two major provisions. First, the responsibility of the LASSDs for protecting children was enshrined in the Act in Section 47, though, in a way, much of the accompanying regulations to the Act concentrated on reducing the 'abusive' and intrusive nature of the Child Protection procedures. Children were seen as having rights to protection from an overweening state, as well as from abusive adults (Parton,1991).

The second crucial provision of the Act was to enshrine in a coherent legislative form provision for ensuring the welfare of children and the recommendations of the Short Report. Part 3 of the Act was devoted to making LASSDs statutorily responsible for the provision of services to 'children in need' – who were defined, somewhat tautologically, as 'in need of local authority services'. These services were seen as voluntary and therefore 'non-stigmatising.' They were intended to cover a spectrum of children, from those who required protection at one end, to those who were disabled or in hospital at the other. Since Child Protection services were hardly voluntary or non stigmatising for parents, the Act, in effect, established a conceptual dichotomy between, first, those children who were 'likely to suffer significant harm' and, second, those who were 'likely to suffer significant impairment if their needs were not met' – that is, those who were 'at risk' and those who were 'in need'. From a purely welfarist point of view, there was not much difference in effect between significant harm and significant impairment (Brandon *et al.*, 1996). Legally, the difference was an attribution to the actions of carers in the first case but not in the second. Thus, the first group of children was in the Child Protection system and the second was not.

An actual dichotomy was established by the economic circumstances under which the Act was designed and passed. The Act was 'budget neutral' and, since the local authorities were by no means doing their duty by welfare cases under the old legislation, there was no way in which they were going to manage new duties in this area. Most of the LASSDs' scarce funds were earmarked for child protection. An already expensive system of procedures was elaborated and enlarged after the Act, acquiring all the characteristics of a formal risk management system, bureaucratically managed, with layers of surveillance from the Social Services Inspectorate at the top, to the child and family below. A rigidly technical discourse about sampling, monitoring and risk differentials was applied to a world which was as turbulent as ever, and where psychopathy had just been added to poverty as the defining characteristic of its inhabitants. Professional survival for social workers and resources for clients meant reframing them as dangerous or at risk.

Child Protection in the UK: 1990–2003

Child Protection during this period saw the regrouping of the traditional socio-medical/welfare lobby, as the 1990s were dominated by an examination of the initial workings of the Children Act as well as by even more tightening Social Services budgets. The results of a raft of DOH-funded research on social services' decision-making under the new Act was published in 1995 (DOH, 1995).[21] Not surprisingly, given the financial difficulties of LASSDs, the traditional welfarist leanings of the largely social-work academics who conducted this research and its ideological nature (examining sets of decisions and procedures against some largely inexplicit notion of good practice), this work was highly critical of the child protection system. Rather puzzlingly, social services departments were criticised for investigating too many cases in proportion to the number of children registered (Gibbons *et al.*, 1995) and of putting too much emphasis on the actual registration of children and not enough on service follow up (Farmer and Owen, 1995). Also, it was found that, either *de facto* or intentionally, the system seemed to have evolved in a way that required registration as a trigger for any services at all. The only 'children in need' being served, apart from the physically disabled and those with extreme learning difficulties, were those children 'in need of Child Protection services': that is, those children 'at risk' (DOH, 1995).

The child welfare rhetoric amongst the knowledge makers and advisers to the DOH was that the system had to change (Aldgate and Tunstill, 1995). This was a difficult act for Social Services managers, since the dependence of services on registration was a self-fulfilling cycle, which, one would think, could only be broken with more funding. In the end, in response to pressure from central government, directives went out from County Hall to area offices requiring Children and Families Teams to reduce the number of children registered by substantial amounts. A system of financial incentives to support this form of management was installed. The threshold for registration was thus presumably raised, as numbers on the register dropped by the end of the decade.[22] This was seen as a cynical management ploy by those who had thought that the registration of a child was recognition of the fact that they were being abused. It was also a somewhat paradoxical result of what could originally be seen as a propaganda move of the welfarist lobby. It suggested that abuse was not something that could be recognised in the world, but was the movable result of local authority finances and administrative procedures.

Along with this, however, in 1999 came 'Quality Protects', a five year plan to re-emphasise and develop family support services to children, with, at last, the funding to go with it – nearly £900 million over five years, initially (DOH, 1998). This was twinned with the *Framework for the Assessment of Children in Need* (DOH, 2000) which instructed local authorities to change their initial and 'core' assessment procedures to relate to need rather than risk, the latter being just a sub-category. Following this, the discourse of Child Protection was to become less forensic and recoup its socio-medical leanings, as it homed in on the long-term consequences for child welfare and development of all types of abuse.

By 2003 the result of this was not clear. The new, resource-consuming assessment procedures were still bedding down in some LASSDs. There was considerable high-level organisational change, including the setting up of Integrated Children's Services in the Local Authorities (DOH, 2004), under the Department for Education and Skills and the Government Green Paper, *Every Child Matters* (Her Majesty's Government, 2003). This introduced the rhetoric of a more universal preventative approach to child welfare services and Local Authority responsibilities.[23] Nevertheless, the government response to the Laming Report on the death of Victoria Climbie (Lord Laming, 2003), published in the same year in the form of *Keeping Children Safe* (DOH; HO; DfES, 2003), still concentrated on the child protection system.[24] It is argued that the conceptual dichotomy between child welfare in the form of 'family support' and Child Protection, though deplored, was kept alive by the 1995 research and reactions to its message (Fawcett *et al.*, 2004). Furthermore, the organisational dichotomy may be just as enshrined in the local authority bureaucracy as it ever was.[25]

The growth of emotional abuse

Amid all this interprofessional complexity and tension, emotional abuse as a registration category has grown rapidly, at least proportionately – and is growing still. The preoccupation of all services about how to respond to CSA has subsided and panic has on the whole been replaced with more measured responses. But the prophecy of some who envisaged the 1990s as 'the decade of emotional abuse' did not come true. It grew quietly, as a problem category, whilst the media responded to scandals about organisational abuse,[26] and to paedophilia in all its real and virtual manifestations. Still, it did increase substantially in relation to other categories, and the way in which the invisible wound of emotional abuse replaced the external bodily wounds of physical and sexual abuse as a major source of social concern in the UK registration of children at risk seems to reflect the processes already described in section 5.2 above.

It has been suggested elsewhere (Cawson *et al.*, 2000), that this change may have happened, in part, because of the increased prominence given to emotional abuse, or poor emotional development, by DOH publications, in which it is identified as an area of potential maltreatment along several different dimensions. Typical was a much-used DOH guide to family assessment, published in 1988 to accompany the 1989 Act and called *The Comprehensive Assessment*, (DOH, 1988). Similarly, the DOH summary of the 1995 research studies identifies a core problem of families 'low on warmth and high on criticism' as 'a risk factor for adverse childhood experience' (DOH, 1995: 54), whilst the *Framework for the Assessment of Children in Need* (DOH, 2000) goes further in identifying the importance to child development of an emotionally warm and secure home environment, and the dire consequences of its negative. However, these direct injunctions to social workers clearly found a very receptive audience and, since there was no great educational effort by the DOH on the subject of emotional abuse itself (Training Officer, Oxfordshire Social Services. Personal communication), it could be argued that there was a more subtle process in play.

The 1988 guide, nicknamed 'The Orange Book', was to be used by social workers in assessing the social circumstance of children who were the subject of a child protection case conference. It was indeed 'comprehensive' and set the investigation of any likely abuse into a welter of questions eliciting the most intimate details of family life, with more emphasis on the psycho-social dimensions than the material ones. The family was cast as the crucible of psychological problems, both for the potential abuser and the abused (DOH, 1988). This was reinforced by the re-emergence of a more welfarist slant to DOH preoccupations, with the programme of research published in 1995. In the 1990s, the advisers to the DOH were still socialised in the sort of postwar 'therapeutic familialism' that went with a largely psychodynamic education for social workers (Rose, 1999). Their welfarism may have included a concern for poverty and inequality, but since there was little they could do about that, their models for change, or at least for services, were centred on family tutelage and the management of psychological relationships. We should note here the resurgence of the popularity of attachment theory (discussed in Chapters 7 and 8).

The 'family' of 'family support' services to children 'in need' was being (re)created after the postwar model,[27] as a psychological, not a sociological, entity and although the 'support' might be sometimes material or practical, it was certainly not financial. This point is underlined by a study by Ruth Sinclair (DOH, 2001b) of the ways in which social workers account for the needs of children in their caseload. Of a sample asked to choose the main causal category of childhood difficulties, 40 per cent voted for 'unstable family' and not one ticked the 'poverty and social disadvantage' box – and this against a 20 per cent to 4 per cent differential on a similar piece of research commissioned by the DOH only four years earlier (Sinclair and Carr-Hill, 1997). Abuse, as a cause of need, in both studies, came out at about 13 per cent (DOH, 2001b).

So, it is something of the same story as the first half of this chapter. All forms of abuse are seen more and more within the context of a complex of 'maladaptive' psycho-social relationships from which the social is gradually lost. What remains is interpersonal and intrapsychic. From seeing these factors as the *causes* of physical forms of abuse, it is a small step to identifying psychological *consequences* of psychological causes and hypothesising a harm in some interior site. In a way, social workers had less far to travel along this road than paediatricians, used to working on the body, or politicians, who saw violence as the product of sociopathy. Social workers have always had their eyes half-turned on some inner territory, though the skills they have to explore it are a little second-hand. But, whereas earlier they might have seen only sadness, anxiety and confusion there, in the 1990s they began to see more clearly the definite and actionable outline of a wound.

What is more, this story seems to suggest that the consequent growth of emotional abuse, as a registration category for children at risk of significant harm, has been a somewhat paradoxical result of the re-valorisation of welfarism in the DOH. It has played its part in an ongoing debate on the proper role of social services, or more specialist child welfare experts, in child protection, and on the place of child protection procedures in the overall social policy for children and families. For the concept of emotional abuse sits, uncomfortably, in a site where two orthogonal systems overlap: first, a much promoted governmental policy to relieve children in need, (including those experiencing the psychological consequences of all forms of abuse for child wellbeing and development), and, second, a system for managing risk which is largely legalistic and administrative and remains so, even if its terminology continually changes over time.

5.4 Conclusion

What has been described here in this bipartite presentation is, first, the emergence of the registration category of emotional abuse from the tumultuous history of child physical abuse as a social problem category. This calls on, and has the characteristics of, traditional social constructionist work, which looks at the making of a social problem category within the context of a politico-professional milieu of claims making by pressure groups and professional and research institutions, all within the constraints of particular socio-economic systems and political organisations, including local government. It presents emotional abuse as a very minor socio-political phenomenon, a break-away from a larger category, both having, at that time, a predominantly medical/welfarist and administrative/legal base.

What this social history also documents is how the gaze of child abuse experts gradually turned inwards in both periods. As the physical wounds on the body of the child became well-documented and disseminated, and physical abuse was accepted as a political, administrative as well as clinical problem, then this hidden, and so more complex and challenging, area seemed to offer opportunities for exploration. For, as the social context of physical abuse came under examination, and broader social considerations were eliminated from the inquiry, so did the negative relationships that drove it and were its results. What other effects did these relationships have on a child, especially on that vital area called development? What were the internal harms that drove poor growth, unhappiness and antisocial behaviour? With the revalorisation of therapeutic familialism and the psychological aspects of family life after the policy emphasis on child rescue during the 1980s, attention gradually shifted, slowly over the 1990s, from the body at risk to the vulnerability of this invisible space and to a harm which, it was claimed, was just as serious – and potentially more so – than that which could be seen, or told. A new set of exploratory activities, new techniques and some new technicians addressed themselves to this inner world of the child, although who it was who could claim the skills for this work was a moot point.

6
The heart of all harm: The emotional abuse literature, 1980–2006

6.1 Introduction

The last chapter discussed the inward turn in the way that abuse is construed within the context of the US and then the UK social policy conjuncture – how the category of emotional abuse moved from being a rare variant of physical abuse into having a flourishing life of its own, at least in the UK, where it became a registration category in 1980 and grew dramatically from the middle of the 1990s onwards, though this growth was not repeated in the USA.[1]

This chapter tracks the concept in both the US and the UK emotional abuse literatures as they developed since 1980; it discusses how the idea was defined and, in particular, the prevailing narratives, in both literatures, about the vagueness and difficulty of definition and the consequent under-diagnosis and lack of seriousness attributed to what is claimed in both as the most serious of injuries. These claims were a feature of the UK literature even after the growth in registration (Glaser, 2002). Not only that, both literatures entertain another, even more expansive narrative: the increasing claim that emotional maltreatment, is not only as important or more so than other forms of maltreatment, but that it encompasses all of them, because they are all set in a psychological matrix, and that it therefore lies at the heart of all abusive harm.

Whilst these literatures have much in common, it was suggested at the start of the last chapter that the category of emotional abuse bifurcated around the year 1980 and that the version of the wound produced by the US literature can be seen as a new form, which is not defined by administrative or clinical processes, but constructed in an academic environment where funding is an issue. Its career has to be seen as part of the booming psy literature phenomenon in the USA. This boom was less a product of clinical research and more of epidemiology and psy-statistics, in which inner wounds are identified for psychometric purposes, whose techniques are then used to study them. The hidden interior world of the child is teased out and the wound measured and scored, not by analytic, clinical, administrative or even common-sense conversations, but by interview schedule and adult recall.

Not only that. As its technicians search for new angles with new collaborators, the invisible wound begins to fragment. Its different causes are identified. With different organisational imperatives, it expands and presents new opportunities for exploration and measurement and, free of administrative definitions, it accords to those with the appropriate techniques of visualisation its multifactorial relationships with other forms of abuse. It shifts between subtle forms of denigration, fear from violence or watching loved ones in danger, and, at its margins, the category of emotional abuse is reunited with the concept of trauma, just as it begins to be seen, not just as a consequence of psychological aggression or distancing, but also the main and more serious result of bodily assault and injury, the core of all abuse.

The category constructed by the UK professional and academic literature on emotional abuse over the 1980s and 1990s represents the other half of this bifurcation. In the discourse of this (small) set of articles and books, 'abuse' is a registration category, or a clinical concept – that which ought to be registered or recognised as a source of need – a hybrid, with normative medico-welfarist origins and legal implications. Here, the exploration of a wounded interior is scarcely attended to. Rather, its presence is assumed. Its invisibility and lack of specific symptoms or cause drive the experts to concentrate on the problems of its description, for the purposes of recognition and appropriate medical and bureaucratic processing. Nevertheless, it still reflects the US literature in advocating for the category still wider and more powerful application.

Crucially, most of the important contributions to this UK literature were written in the mid-1990s, before the dramatic increase in the proportion of children on the register under the category of emotional abuse, and so it principally forms a discussion of the slowness or failure of the child protection system to recognise this harm and the reasons for it. It reflects (and reflects on) all the tensions that dogged the child protection procedures then (and probably still do) and which make the eventual growth of the category all the more marked and surprising. It was suggested in the last chapter that this growth owed something to the change in policy emphasis emanating from the DOH. It would be hard to establish any clear causal link with the exhortations in this literature, especially in light of a general view in this field that social workers do not read the academic and professional literature relating to their work. No time! However, unlike the bulk of the US literature on emotional abuse, this UK work does address the dilemmas of practitioners and though there is little enough of it, the writers were and are extremely influential figures in the child protection field. The literature is taken here as a comment on the system, possibly contributing to the inward turn in the view of its practitioners.

6.2   The emotional abuse literature stateside

The US academic and professional literature on emotional abuse must be more profuse by a factor of fifty than its UK equivalent. It is also more technical in its language and approach, more embedded in mainstream psy professional and scientific journals, like the *American Journal of Orthopsychiatry*, than in such specialist child protection journals as *Child Abuse and Neglect* (scion of Denver, Colorado). Likewise, in specialist books, like Kempe and Helfer's, *The Battered Child*, emotional abuse only achieves a whole chapter for itself in its 5th edition (Helfer *et al.*, 1997). After 1980, emotional abuse became a more general object of scientific study. And, although it is part of an academic exercise which is predicated on the, admittedly political, events in 1962 and their aftermath, with their consequences for the availability of research funding, research on emotional abuse as a socio-medical category has, also, to be seen in the context of a broader psychological and psychiatric literature which has grown exponentially since the mid-1960s – a field of endeavour driven by the medicalisation of interpersonal relationships and the scientisation of the soul (Hacking, 1995b), social panics about deviancy, professional projects and (lately) the forging of personal careers under academic audit and competition for research monies.

In the comprehensive Psychinfo database the references appear in sections of roughly equal size. The first section of academic psy literature, mostly from the UK and USA covers the period 1872 to 1966; the next section the following eleven years; by the mid-1990s, one section covers three years but, after 2000, can only cover half a year. An emotional abuse search of the same database (also using the terms psychological abuse and psychological maltreatment, which seem to be used interchangeably in the US literature) not surprisingly, shows most of the characteristics of this broader context; in the first long section the book in German published in 1934 sits alone; and there is nothing more till after the USA reporting legislation, when the series of articles on definition, already mentioned in section 5.3, appear around 1980. Although these efforts did not really make the concept much less elusive the attempt at definition was the necessary basis for the start of a positivistic research project and the literature then increased at about the rate of other literatures in the psychological field.

This burgeoning literature in the database reveals the painful excavation by statistical instruments of more and more pathology in the world, more and more environmental causes (and, sadly, little corresponding increase in effective treatments). Information on all forms of abuse proliferated from the early 1980s, in line with the number of knowledge workers involved, and the concept fragmented so that the number of different forms increased. For example, the concept of 'elder abuse' which had been written into US reporting laws in 1978, soon after emotional abuse, broke up into the same forms as child abuse itself: physical, sexual and psychological and neglect, with the special addition of 'financial/possession abuse'.[2] Spouse or partner abuse also took the same basic multiplicity of forms (except neglect, which implies relationships of dependency) and further articles attempted to relate each of these adult variants, for victim or perpetrator, to each of the childhood forms – with the causality running both ways round – in the ceaseless search for intergenerational cycles of violence or abuse, which seems to characterise the maltreatment literature.

Exploration and measurement

Much of the earlier clinical research on causes and consequences of child abuse was being savaged in the literature (for a good summary, see Sheppard, 1982), and the 1980s saw attempts at a more sophisticated research design and methodology, mostly from academic psychology departments. With research on emotional abuse of children, the problem was to identify abused populations, in order to mine the data for causal factors, as well as to study it as, itself, a risk factor for adult disorder. With certain exceptions (for example, Claussen and Crittenden, 1991), there are few studies of groups of abused children. They are difficult to locate for ethical reasons, and even harder to study over a period of time. In practice, these are confined to a few large cohorts of children and families organised, at some expense, by major universities, with diverse funding, including grants from government agencies, the National Institute of Mental Health (NIMH) and the National Centre on Child Abuse and Neglect (set up by CAPTA). However, most of the research effort (especially for those, studying for research degrees, with limited resources) has centred on adult recall of abuse in childhood in more easily available research populations – generally, groups of adults in some way socially monitored. Apart from the self replenishing pool of college students, whose 'dating behaviour' is so much studied, subjects tend to be people on treatment or community programmes as well as those more completely institutionalised; that is small, usually racially defined groups of the poor, the criminal, the addicted, the sick or the insane.

In the quest to operationalise this adult recall of childhood abuse, new scales, questionnaires, indices and inventories – and their acronyms – have been devised and, in the intricate world of family relationships and intra-psychic dynamics, everything is measured that can be measured. Here is just a small selection: the Childhood Maltreatment Questionnaire (CMQ) and its Psychological Maltreatment (PMT) subcategory (Demare, 2001), the Comprehensive Child Maltreatment Scale (Higgins and McCabe, 2000), Record of Maltreatment Experiences (ROME) (McGee *et al.*, 1995), the Subtle and Overt Scale of Psychological Abuse (Jones *et al.*, 2005), the Childhood Trauma Questionnaire, (Bernstein *et al.*, 1994), the clinician-administered PTSD Scale – Child and Adolescent version (CAPS–CA), the Paediatric Emotional Distress Scale (Spilsbury *et al.*, 2005), the Childhood Stress Inventory (Marcil, 1996) and the Verbal Aggression and Violence Scales of the Conflict Tactics scale (J. Archer, 1999).

Once measurements were established in the literature (that is, repeatedly used and cited, even if, psychometrically, their reliability over different research populations did not turn out to be very high), it was possible to argue that research studies showed that emotional abuse or psychological maltreatment (PMT) had as much negative effect on a victim's future as other forms of abuse – more, even (Kaplan *et al.*, 1999; McGee *et al.*, 1997; Mullen *et al.*, 1996; Vissing *et al.*, 1991). By the turn of this century, emotional abuse in childhood, rather like disorders of attachment, had been claimed as a risk factor for almost all pathologies and social problems, depending on the research population chosen: addiction and delinquency (Fraser, 2002; Moran *et al.*, 2004), sexual problems (Ace *et al.*, 2007), depression (Ali, 2000; Maciejewski and Mazure, 2006; Stuewig and McCloskey, 2005) and other forms of 'negative affect' (Chirichella-Besemer and Motta, 2008; Harper and Arias, 2004), trait aggression (Garno *et al.*, 2008) and general neuroticism

(Karesh, 1996), personality pathology (Bernstein *et al.*, 1998), 'erosion of identity' (Hirigoyen, 2000), dyslexia (Anyanwu and Campbell,
2001) and dissociative disorder (Sar *et al.*, 2006), PTSD (Veach, 1996),
anorexia and bulimia (Hodson *et al.*, 2006; Mazzeo and Espelage, 2002;
Witkiewitz and Dodge-Reyome, 2001), and schizophrenia (Schäfer *et al.*,
2006). In addition, cycles of abuse also feature, as for example in a
study of adult offspring of Holocaust Survivors, where PTSD and emotional abuse are seen as transmitted across the generations (Yehuda *et al.*,
2001).

Besides this, over time, as researchers reach for new angles, the limited set of available research populations are mined for more and more
improbable dependent variables and their correlates. For instance, in the
field of emotional abuse itself, it was possible to read in 1980, in an article entitled 'Aggression against cats, dogs and people', that – in a group
of male psychiatric patients referred for cruelty to animals – paternal
emotional unavailability was a strong risk factor for this behaviour
(Felthous, 1980); whilst, by 2002, research on a population of incar-
cerated sex offenders suggested that emotional abuse, along with other
forms of maltreatment in childhood, was a strong predictor of bestiality
(Fleming *et al.*, 2002). Further, in the same year, a population of female
methadone maintenance treatment programme (MMTP) dropouts had
their claims to emotional abuse in childhood – as measured on some version of the Childhood Maltreatment Questionnaire (CMQ) – regressed
against their current 'HIV risk behaviour' (Kang *et al.*, 2002).

Lastly, by the millennium, a new problem has been discovered for psychometrics in the field of child abuse: the phenomenon of multiple type
maltreatment (MTM) (Bryant and Range, 1996; Higgins and McCabe,
2001; Kinard, 1994; McGee *et al.*, 1997; Rossman and Rosenberg, 1998),
where respondents report more than one type of maltreatment as children. Whilst MTM was a phenomenon which did not show up so
much on the few samples that there were of maltreated children (where
they were classified administratively, mostly under single categories), an
interrogation of childhood memories by questionnaire allowed for all
sorts of variations and combinations. The problem that this raised could
be characterised as follows: unless effects are type specific, how can we
know what are the consequences and causes of what? Further, the effects
of each type may interact and be cumulative. We know that multi-type
maltreatment is associated strongly with poor adjustment in adults, so
this is likely. We cannot be sure, however, unless effects are isolated and
interaction studied. It may even be that 'poor adjustment in adults is
the result of a third variable (for example, 'family dysfunction or other

childhood stressors' [sic] (Higgins and McCabe, 2000: 17)). MTM is a challenge which calls for a redoubling of effort and more research.

Trauma, violence and abuse[3]

MTM may have presented a challenge for psychometrics but it was an acronym for a situation which any welfare professional would have recognised – and one of the many in which the neat categories of psychologists are hard to map onto the chaos of human relationships. However, as a result of psychologists' attempts to do just that, the categories of abuse shifted somewhat over this period. Not only did emotional abuse or PMT grow in seriousness and claimed prevalence, but the category itself was suspected to be much more inclusive. But the crowning claim, already mentioned, was that PMT, far from being an 'also ran', or even just an accompaniment to other forms of abuse, was integral to all forms and, indeed, lay at their very heart. This came about in two ways, exemplified by the two major research teams in the US that directly and consistently address, over a long period, the issues of emotional abuse or psychological maltreatment.

The team of Stuart Hart and Marla Brassard secured a federal government grant at the beginning of the 1980s from the US Department of Health and Human Services and National Centre on Child Abuse and Neglect, for 'developing and validating operationally defined measures of emotional maltreatment' (Hart and Brassard, 1986), though these measures were not uncontroversial (Barnett *et al.*, 1991; McGee and Wolfe, 1991a).[4] This work supported the First International Conference on the Psychological Abuse of Children and Youth, whose proceedings were later published as an edited book (Brassard *et al.*, 1987); it furnished the substance of articles published later in the decade, also into the 1990s, and inevitably formed the basis for the development of a rating scale, the PMRS (Brassard *et al.*, 1993). During the 1990s, Hart and Brassard became the official lexicographers of the concept; no edited book on child abuse, of which there are many, has appeared without a chapter by them on PMT. They provided the PMT contribution to Volume 5 of *The Battered Child* (Brassard *et al.*, 1997; Helfer *et al.*, 1997), and to *The APSAC* (American Professional Society on the Abuse of Children) *Handbook on Child Maltreatment* (Hart *et al.*, 1996, 2002). They have also inaugurated the first volume of a new journal, *Emotional Abuse*, with the leading article (Hart *et al*, 1998).

It is not surprising that it is Hart and Brassard whose research has received an official imprimatur. Their work is in the psychological mainstream, still seeing abuse as a problem of individual pathology, and PMT as one hitherto neglected form of it. It is a diagnostic category to be mined from intrapsychic and intrafamilial behaviour, always included in a swathe of abuse literature as the third or fourth type – the poor relation. Even after all their educational efforts, they are still describing emotional abuse or PMT as a 'little known' and 'underused' category in 2002 (Hart *et al.*, 2002: 79) – although, according to a burgeoning epidemiological story, more potent in its effects than was originally thought. These two psychologists acknowledge the problem of MTM, but are not crudely mechanistic; they accept some interaction between these different abuse forms (Hart and Brassard, 1991). Indeed, by the same year, they were so impressed by the epidemiologically revealed fact that PMT, in many instances, can accompany physical or sexual abuse, that they made another step in subscribing to the widely made claim (for example, Navarre, 1987) that, though it is little known and underused, 'psychological maltreatment lies at the core of all abuse' (Hart *et al.*, 2002: 79).

Whilst the progress of Hart and Brassard towards this grand claim was somewhat linear, developing from the original perception of the paediatricians of physical abuse, set in a psycho-social matrix, the same claim was precisely the message of Garbarino's first article on emotional abuse (Garbarino, 1978) and the constant theme through all his work. He is of a systemic or ecological persuasion, therefore concerned with child identities constructed by the social environment. His book, with its play on Helfe and Kempe's title,[5] established that it is the *psychological* effects of adverse environments that are important – and not only the *effects*. Adverse environments have effects through psychological *means* also, through what they communicate (the social system is a communications system), and can therefore be seen as forms of psychological maltreatment.

Before the book, the most serious adversity for Garbarino seemed to be poverty. After the book, with new collaborators, it seems that violence rather than poverty began to define a psychologically adverse environment at all levels of context. Violent communities are 'The American War Zone,' (Garbarino, 1995) or 'The War Close to Home' (Kostelny and Garbarino, 2001) and, in 1995, Garbarino introduced a new metaphor with his article, 'Growing up in a Socially Toxic Environment', which medicalised the problem as a version of PTSD with developmental consequences.

So psychological abuse, set in a matrix of warfare – interpersonal, intercommunity and international, was used as the basic concept in a strong social critique: emotional abuse, no longer as a concept of positivist knowledge, but a legitimater of powerful political claims about the traumatic, psychologically destructive nature of violence in all its forms. In this, invisible wounds are not just the consequences of harsh words, but also of hostilities that include physical and sexual assault.[6] And this time they are not just seen as psychological accompaniments to physical abuse or violence, but as the main, the more serious, the more lasting of its operations and effects – the psychological as the heart of all harm.

6.3 Describing the UK literature

This last claim is not just confined to the US research literature, but much exercised the UK professional writers whose work is mapped in this section. The challenge of the US emotional abuse literature, however, of grand talk about violence and of political points swathed in military metaphor, has not been taken up in the UK equivalent. Garbarino, being first off the mark with writing on this form of abuse is ritually cited, but more citations go to Stewart Hart and his collaborators, whose work is more congruent with the 'individual pathology model' which prevails – and, given its organisation, *has* to prevail – in UK child protection. The model, in this UK context, does not produce the raft of statistical research which is generated by well-funded US university departments – even though, by the late 1990s, this research was more frequently referenced in DOH guidance and its other sundry publications, whose writers were aspiring to become more 'evidence based.' On the contrary, the UK literature is rooted in professional practice and, even for the medical diagnosticians and therapists, within the multi-professional world of child protection decision-taking. As a result, it is a commentary on the workings of institutions other than the academic: national government and statute, local government, NHS treatment centres, now Child and Adolescent Mental Health Services (CAMHS) and, increasingly, more non-governmental child and adolescent-centred services. It suggests a version of emotional abuse which indeed reflects the professional and institutional context in which it is produced. As a category, it is primarily organised by the registration process in child protection, a bureaucratic risk-management system. But it is a hybrid, which, apart from its figurative freight, encapsulates both a welfarist, medically based strand, which primarily refers to the effects of abuse on child wellbeing, combined with a notion of what is healthy in developmental terms, and a more legalistic strand, which refers to the cruel actions of parents or other adults, seen against a standard of what is socially acceptable.

With its limited personnel, the progress of this category in the UK child emotional abuse literature is easily traced and put into its political, social and discursive context. This section presents a short account of the literature, and section 6.4 a mapping of the concept as it emerges in this body of work, over the course of the 1990s – the period of the category's maximum rate of growth – to 2006. First, in this mapping, various definitions of emotional abuse are teased out, involving much quoting of the US literature by UK writers in their attempts to pin down this elusive concept. Then, the even more hazy question of the claims to its under-diagnosis in the child as opposed to the general population are looked at in the light of the difficulties of definition and the uncertain processes by which such statistics are made. Third, the making of child protection statistics in particular are examined: how do these relate to competing claims to the category's definition, ownership of its administration or treatment and how do these claims contribute to the inclusiveness of the concept? As with other versions of invisible wounds, like PTSD and nervous shock, the size of the category varies with what is included in accounts of the wound's cause.

The UK emotional abuse literature: 1980–2006

Apart from Judith Trowell's lone article, (Trowell, 1983), there is virtually no UK publication on emotional abuse from the 1980s through to the early 1990s, although there are some on failure to thrive (see below). Arnon Bentovim, the Great Ormond Street Hospital (GOSH) Child Psychiatrist, who is well known for his work on the identification and treatment of child sexual abuse, did write a paper on emotional abuse for the Third International Congress on Child Abuse and Neglect in 1980, but regrets not having published it in article form (personal communication). No doubt this omission was explained by the fact that his writing on child sexual abuse at this time was extensive, and with the help of his colleague, child psychiatrist, Danya Glaser, GOSH was fast being established as a national centre of expertise in this area and, for social workers with difficult cases, the referral of choice.

In fact, it was Danya Glaser, from GOSH, who became the 'moral entrepreneur' for emotional abuse in the 1990s, the promoter of 'children's emotional safety' – the title of a paper she gave in a conference on neglect in 1997 in Ballymena, Northern Ireland. She is practised at such promotion, having worked in this high-profile way with sexual abuse and will take up other causes, including the training presentation of attachment theory for practitioners, especially its neurological aspects (see Chapter 7), having an ability to disentangle complicated ideas and write succinctly and simply for non-specialists. She published her first work on emotional abuse in 1993, in a book on clinical paediatrics, edited by Hobbes and Wynne, the Leeds paediatricians who achieved prominence in the Cleveland crisis (Glaser, 1993). Subsequently, she and two long-time collaborators, Margaret Lynch, ex-Park Hospital and now a consultant at Guy's Hospital, and Vivien Prior, a researcher with Glaser at University College London, were funded by the DOH to carry out a study for them on the registration process for emotional abuse in four Local Authorities in the South East of England (Glaser *et al.*, 2001). This study was originally unpublished, although made available through the British Association for the Study and Prevention of Child Abuse and Neglect (BASPCAN). (This is the British version of ISPCAN and certainly the most important organisation of its kind in the country, its yearly conferences being the main meeting place for leading players in the field.) Later, in 1997, its official journal, *Child Abuse Review*, one of whose editors happened to be Margaret Lynch, called for papers on emotional abuse for a special edition, whose first piece was by Glaser and Prior, describing their research (Glaser and Prior, 1997).

This was the only special journal issue on the subject of emotional abuse in the UK literature (Browne and Lynch, 1997) and the various professional and intellectual strands are, not surprisingly, well represented by the composition of the contributors' list. Apart from Glaser, there is also Judith Trowell, by this time at the Tavistock Clinic, London, representing child psychoanalytic psychiatry and writing of the work of a family centre and the question of case description and registration (Trowell *et al.*, 1997). There is another paediatric strand, that of failure to thrive, represented by Dorota Iwaniec, an academic in the Social Work Department at Queen's University in Belfast (Iwaniec, 1997), who worked on FTT with Martin Herbert (see Chapter 7) and produced her own PhD thesis on the subject at Leicester University in 1983 (Iwaniec, 1983). She placed this diagnosis in its emotional abuse context in the early 1990s, producing the second UK monograph on this subject in 1995, *The Emotionally Abused and Neglected Child: Identification, Assessment and Intervention* (Iwaniec, 1995).

The social work or child welfare strand of emotional abuse is represented in the 1997 volume of *Child Abuse Review* by June Thoburn's research team, which again focuses on the registration process (Wilding and Thoburn, 1997). Thoburn represents the traditional quantitative research approach of the DHSS and DOH to Local Authority Child Protection processes, having contributed to both of the major government-funded research efforts of the 1980s and 1990s, respectively. She has, however, not been much involved with the progress of the concept of emotional abuse and it was her fellow social work academic, Olive Stevenson, who wrote a contribution to the first volume of a new journal, *Child and Family Social Work*, entitled, 'Emotional abuse and neglect: time for a reappraisal', (Stevenson, 1996). Stevenson, who trained at the LSE when Clare Winnicot was teaching for the social work programme, is a standard-bearer of the traditional social work casework skills to be found in the pre-Seebohm Children and Families' departments of the local authority personal social services. She is also a champion of social workers against increasing criticisms and attacks for incompetence in government enquiries (she herself was on the Maria Colwell Committee of Inquiry, writing a minority report), and was primarily concerned with emotional abuse through her interest in neglect and her sense that it was not given enough attention in child protection. The latter was stirred by her experiences on the Stephanie Fox Inquiry, the only official examination of the death of a child where extreme neglect was an issue. She finally published a book on the subject in 1998 (Stevenson, 1998).

Apart from Celia Doyle, another social work academic, who contributed a study on the prevalence of emotional abuse to the 1997 special issue of *Child Abuse Review* (Doyle, 1997a), the only other social work contribution to the development of the concept of emotional abuse is that of Kevin O'Hagan, a colleague of Iwaniec at Queen's University, Belfast, who, curiously, mixes a great concern with its taxonomy with many years as a practitioner and a rich knowledge of relevant case material. In his book, *Emotional and Psychological Abuse of Children* published in 1993, he is determined to pin down the difference between these two phenomena (O'Hagan, 1993) He contributes a paper pursuing this difference to an ISPCAN European conference in Oslo in 1995, where Stevenson and Glaser, among others, debate the question vigorously (O'Hagan, 1995).

Generally, emotional abuse has not had a high profile at multi-professional conferences. Some papers on the subject at a BASPCAN conference in 1994 influenced the setting up of a multi-professional project to identify, study and treat cases of emotional abuse in Nottinghamshire (Boulton and Hindle, 2000). A paper at the 2003 BASPCAN conference, written by an Australian social work academic, based on an earlier book (Sheehan, 2001) was later published in the UK journal, *Child*

Abuse and Neglect, on a study of the fate of cases in the Victoria family courts where emotional abuse was registered (Sheehan, 2006).[7] However, since the special issue, the literature has remained sparse and spotty. There is further work on prevalence by an NSPCC team (Cawson *et al*., 2000); an article by Cheryl Dance and Alan Rushton on the very poor outcomes for children in the care system whom they take to be 'emotionally abused' (Dance *et al*., 2002); another article by Glaser in 2002; a community approach to emotional abuse intervention by a health visitor (Hancock, 1998); 'The emotional abuse of elite child athletes by their coaches' (Gervis and Dunn, 2004) and three or four articles by psychologists, more in the US style.

The level of discussion of this form of child abuse at both conferences and in the UK professional and academic literature has by no means kept pace with its proportionate growth as a registration category in child protection, and Glaser's 2002 article still describes the problem as 'under-recognised' (Glaser, 2002). Perhaps this is because, as the next section will show, it is a concept which those who write about it claim to be elusive and hard to define.

6.4 Mapping the territory

Definitions of emotional abuse: Finding the grid reference

For these UK writers, academics and professional practitioners, the terrain around the emotional abuse of children is a very muddy field. The problem is where to find it. The term stands for a basketful of others, spreading out over the eclectic area of professional childcare talk, between which there are no clear boundaries: 'emotional neglect', 'psychological deprivation', 'emotional withdrawal', 'psychological unavailability', 'emotional disturbance', 'mental injury', 'psychological torture or terror' and 'psychological maltreatment'. These are all examples given by Kevin O'Hagan in his book, mentioned above. His was the first UK monograph on this subject written after a decade in which the registration category of emotional abuse remained very small – under-used, he suggests, because practitioners find it hard to recognise. It is a 'difficult, diffuse concept' (Calam and Franchi, 1989: 75, cited in O'Hagan, 1993: 20), or 'nebulous, because the outward signs are hazy, indistinct and obscure' (Morgan, 1987: cited in O'Hagan, 1993: 20). O'Hagan himself makes a heroic attempt to bring clarity to the field by pinning emotional abuse down to its adverse effect on child development. After this, he resorts to a multiplicity of case examples, as do all the other authors of monographs in this field (O' Hagan, 1993).

This process of defining by pointing to examples is not necessarily an invalid procedure or a sign of defeat, however. Ian Hacking (1995) has suggested that most often when we try to define classes or concepts, or names for things, we proceed by way of finding prototypes for the thing in question. We do not, for instance, tease out the essential 'birdness' of a bird, but rather use an example, like a sparrow or an eagle, which is seen as typical; literally, a fine example of its kind. We place the eagle at the centre of a definitional field, in which some other, more deviant, kind, like an ostrich, would be placed at the extreme periphery, distinguished mostly by its obvious difference from the prototypes. If this is a useful procedure in the defining of natural kinds, how much more useful might it be in defining seemingly vague ideas in the social world. Nevertheless, the literature about emotional abuse is 'scientific' and so proceeds relentlessly the other way about. Every research or clinical paper on the subject is prefaced by an attempt at a stipulative (or persuasive) definition, usually lining up a whole range of preceding attempts and opting for the one which, with embellishments, seems most appropriate to the preoccupations of the writer. Thus, in exposition, the case studies are merely illustrations of what has already been decided upon, although they may have contributed implicitly to the decision.

Nevertheless, in taking (literally) a more 'bird's eye view' of the terrain of UK emotional abuse literature, the idea of the prototype is very useful in extracting from the literature the place of emotional abuse within the wider category of abuse as a whole. Here, as Hacking has suggested, physical abuse and sexual abuse have been, and are, taken as the definitional prototypes of child abuse in general. In terms of his avian example, emotional abuse appears at first, at least, and in relation to the other two, to be rather like the flightless ostrich. As it displays the negative aspects of a metaphor, it is easier to say what it does not resemble in the prototypes than what it essentially is: easier to define the boundaries of the space it occupies than to describe its detailed topography. But in exploring what it does resemble in the prototypes, it is possible to piece together a picture of its internal consistencies and contradictions. Using the attempts at definition in the 1997 special issue of *Child Abuse and Neglect*, in which the US literature is much quoted, this process reveals three different domains of usage in the building of a defining picture. The first is the figurative language of the vernacular with its emotive and persuasive definitions, which was addressed in Chapter 2 and not further investigated here. The second is the positivistic language of welfare science, which tries to locate this problem, through its indicators, in the real world of problems, technically defined (although, like all relatives of medical science concerned with health and wellbeing, it is entirely normative). The third acknowledges the socio-legal aspects of abuse and its relationship to varying legal and quasi-legal standards and administrative procedures.

i) The figurative domain

One reason why emotional abuse is so hard to pin down is that it refers to injury in an area of human identity which is largely understood in terms of metaphor and, particularly, figurative tropes of the body, as already described. It occupies a space bounded on one side by assault of a physical and or sexual nature, leaving visible bodily signs or wounds, and on the other by more subtle seduction and misuse of power which is revealed in the telling. As Judith Trowell argues, in emotional abuse, 'victims are unable or do not speak of the abuse; 'symptoms' are non-specific and there are no pathognomic findings on examination' (Trowell *et al.*, 1997: 358). If emotional abuse leaves a wound, it is invisible, inscribed on some site that we might call the inner life. Any non-specific behavioural symptoms could be read as an outward expression of this wounded inner state.

ii) The domain of welfare science

Battery, murder and abuse may all refer to both a deviant action and its effects. But in the official DOH lexicon of abuse definitions, on one side of the border, child physical abuse is defined as the wound, the physical effects of abuse; on the other side, child sexual abuse is defined by the deviant acts of a perpetrator. This is probably due to their origins, the first in paediatrics and radiology and the second in the more abstract power-based discourse of feminism. So the abuse prototypes, in their official definitions at least, fall either side of the ambiguous space that emotional abuse occupies. Child emotional abuse is officially defined as both effect and action; the wound inscribed on behaviour and development, rather than the body as such and the abusive behaviour defined, somewhat tautologically, as is appropriate to a legal document, in terms of its effects, as:

> The actual or likely adverse effect on behaviour and emotional development ... caused by persistent or severe emotional ill-treatment or rejection (DOH, 1989b: 49).

This is not just an official partial-truism. Whilst authors in the research and clinical literature agree that the DOH definition is unhelpful, ambivalence about whether emotional abuse refers to a behaviour or its effects persists across this body of work. This may be partly due to competing traditions of research in which psychiatry has a long history of assessing 'dangerousness' in the perpetrators of crime, whereas the traditions of paediatrics, and then developmental psychology, are more obviously concerned with symptoms and growth patterns in its object – the child. While some writers give a set of definitions that focus on parental behaviour alone (Bailey and Bailey, 1986; McGee and Wolfe, 1991a, b), others (Iwaniec, 1995; Skuse, 1989, for example), as is appropriate to experts on failure to thrive, focus on the effects of parental behaviour on the child. Kavanagh (1982) focuses specifically on its physical effects in psycho-social dwarfism. However, these one-sided definitions create technical problems, since neither the parental behaviours nor their effects on children are highly predictive of or specific to emotional abuse (Aber and Zigler, 1981; Trowell *et al.*, 1997). Therefore, emotional abuse cannot be reliably inferred from either set of indicators. Just as in the diagnosis of PTSD, the symptoms are made sense of by the aetiological event(s), so effects have to be linked to acts to gain specificity. Thus Garbarino and his colleagues produced a much quoted combination of these two as 'a concerted attack on a child's development of self and social competence'. This takes five forms – 'rejecting... isolating... terrorising... ignoring... corrupting' (Garbarino *et al.*, 1986).

This list is somewhat similar to that of Hart and his colleagues (Brassard *et al.*, 1987), which is used by Doyle and extended by Glaser (Doyle, 1997a; Glaser, 2002; Glaser and Prior, 1997).

These parental acts in emotional abuse definitions also distinguish themselves from those in the large boundary category of neglect, that is, essentially, acts of omission, and from those in its binary category of deliberate acts of cruelty, most clearly seen in the socio-legal category of sexual abuse. Again, emotional abuse is seen by most writers cited as comprising both. In this welfarist definition, for example, emotional abuse consists of:

> parental acts that thwart children's basic emotional needs such as psychological safety, the need for a family environment free of extensive hostility and violence, the need for a stable and available caregiver and the need for self esteem (Barnett *et al.*, 1991: 19).

'Thwarting' needs is stronger than 'not meeting' them, but still neutral as to whether it is a hostile or neglectful act. Questions of criminal responsibility and intentionality are not relevant to welfare considerations, in so far as it pronounces on effects only – matters of damage to health and development.

At the socio-legal level, it is partly *because* of their relation to the criminal justice system that physical abuse and sexual abuse are defined officially, at least, as one-off acts, and are certainly investigated and thought about in relation to events which have already occurred. In contrast, Iwaniec and Glaser, for instance, insist that these emotionally abusive acts of parents should persist over time for them to be judged abusive (Glaser and Prior, 1997; Iwaniec, 1997). Otherwise, the definition is too inclusive of the odd lapse in parenting standards that may happen in the best of families. Such lapses are not allowed in perpetrators of physical injury and *any*, even remotely, sexual act with a minor may be processed as abusive. Emotional abuse is assumed to be much more a matter of degree. Though Belsky questions the ethics of this, there seems to be a consensus in the literature that the negative nature of emotional abuse is in some sense cumulative and should be defined in relation to its long-term consequences (Belsky, 1991).

Unlike physical or sexual abuse, which may be constituted by the one-off act discussed above – 'an event' (Glaser and Prior, 1997), the infliction of an injury, a molestation, or even the taking of a photograph – Glaser and Prior insist that emotional abuse refers to

> A relationship rather than an event. Such relationships constitute an heterogeneous collection of psychologically undesirable interactions or forms of ill treatment which are pervasive or characteristic of the parent-child relationship. The relationship may be actually or potentially harmful to the child (Glaser and Prior, 1997: 315).

Trowell, in the same volume, supports this view and emphasises the role of emotionally abused children's 'developmentally damaged' behaviour in eliciting from parents, who might initially have been merely neglectful, negative and overtly hostile reactions. Thus, emotional abuse can be seen as not only cumulative but, potentially, growing exponentially, a system subject to positive feedback (Trowell *et al.*, 1997). This more interactional approach towards abuse reflects similar descriptions of parent–child interaction by attachment theorists such as Crittenden and Ainsworth (Crittenden and Ainsworth, 1989; Crittenden *et al.*, 1991). However, although these describe a relationship, they place responsibility for abuse firmly on poor parenting inscribed on a *tabula rasa*, the face of childhood innocence. It is the parents who are responsible for the relationship and not the child. And this is the responsibility, Doyle (out of Hart and colleagues) reminds us, of all 'parent figures, who are in a position of differential power that renders the child vulnerable' (Doyle, 1997a: 331).

Finally, we have noted that emotional abuse, unlike sexual abuse and many cases of physical abuse, is seldom, if ever, indicated by a single event and can be seen as the result of a relationship over time. What constitutes abuse is a quantitative rather than a qualitative matter. In this, it is much like physical *neglect*, which it also resembles in the way that parental acts are not necessarily deliberately destructive but are to be judged by the effect that they have on the welfare of the child. In both cases, the problem, both practically and theoretically, is where to draw the line; where does poor or inadequate parenting end and abuse begin?

iii) The socio-legal domain

Unlike severe physical abuse and sexual abuse, which are criminal acts and are partly, at least, investigated and assessed forensically (though of course acts of excessive physical punishment are more socially contentious), the drawing of the line in emotional abuse implies 'tutelary' intervention in families rather than criminal prosecution (Donzelot, 1979) and is a judgement based, presumably, on the knowledge of welfare or child-care professionals. This knowledge is not only factual but normative, being not only expertise in child development and what is statistically normal, but also in what is normal because healthy and therefore 'acceptable'. The crucial question remains: 'acceptable' to whom?

According to Doyle (1997), emotionally abusive behaviour consists of:

> Acts of omission and commission which are judged on the basis of a combination of community standards and professional expertise to be psychologically damaging. Such acts damage immediately or ultimately the behavioural, cognitive, affective, social and psychological functioning of the child (Doyle, 1997a: 331).

This suggests two sorts of judgments – the one, clinical, based on notions of health, in this case mental health, and the second, moral or evaluative, based on 'community standards' and more socio-legal considerations. It is not clear whether these standards relate to the acts *per se*, to unacceptable levels of damage or to their likelihood. However, this definition of emotional abuse is one of the few in this literature that acknowledges that some notion of social values and therefore contingency is implied in the term 'abuse'.

Further, it is claimed by Glaser and Prior that the word abuse implies action – not just an expression of values but a particular type of process:

> The abuse threshold is reached when the continued viability of the parent–child relationship is regarded as unacceptable without attempted intervention (Glaser and Prior, 1997: 315–316).

Crucially, a poor relationship becomes abusive at the point at which it cannot be allowed to go on without this 'intervention', which in a clinical context means treatment and, in the multi-professional world of child protection, means administrative and occasionally legal action as well. As we will see, however, Glaser is not entirely sure of its desirability in all cases.

Size matters: The prevalence of emotional abuse in the UK

The above delineates three distinct sources of difficulty in definition. The first concerns the precise applicability of figurative understandings; the second the task of recognising emotional abuse when you see it, because of the vagueness of the behavioural indicators and their embeddedness in the interactional patterns of a relationship over time. The third acknowledges the cultural context in which terms like abuse are used, which suggests that different meanings and, indeed, different professional practices attach themselves to the clinical and the administrative versions, although often, in the definitions offered, the assumed cultural context is not made clear.

In such presentations of a social problem category, attempts at definition are usually followed by estimates of prevalence. But with such a slippery concept, open to various interpretations, it would not be surprising that different claims are made about the spread of this phenomenon over the general population: to how many people this concept can be applied; what its location is in particular sections or classes; and its seriousness and importance as a social problem category. What is surprising is the level of unanimity on its under-representation in the official figures, when how it is to be recognised, and by whom, is so contentious.

Of course, as with any social behaviour which is a feature of the 'private' or family sphere, and certainly with all forms of abuse, there is a public rhetoric about 'the dark figures' – those instances that will not be picked up by official administrative procedures, nor be revealed in answer to prevalence-study questionnaires; a suspicion that there is more of it about than meets the eye and a call for more professional vigilance, more knowledge and, of course, more research (O'Hagan, 1993). Iwaniec writes about 'a growing consensus among professionals that emotional maltreatment is more prevalent than was realised' (Iwaniec, 1997: 370). Certainly, the only two UK prevalence studies of emotional abuse available to date show a greater proportional identification of this category in the general population than in the child protection statistics (Cawson *et al.*, 2000; Doyle, 1997a, b). In these classifications emotional abuse has always, until the turn of the century, been the smallest – far from being the largest category, or one of them, as suggested in the prevalence studies. The fact that it is emotional abuse that is so widely recalled but not so widely registered seems to require explanation. Technical aspects of the way that the child protection figures are collected may account for a small but not a major part of the discrepancy.

Of course, not even the most naïve realist would think that a prevalence study set against official data was comparing like with like, though these differences might be thought to operate for all categories of abuse claims. It is not just that recall is unreliable compared to some present assessment, or that self-report may be more extravagant in these times of increasing interest in victimhood. On the contrary, all the research evidence suggests that professionals are more likely to classify certain behaviours as abusive than victims or the general population (McGee, 1995). But first there is the important issue of saliency which causes major, though often unacknowledged, problems with any questionnaire data and also with its subsequent validation by professionals; these issues are recognised in an artificial way, because they are put high up on the agenda of respondents and experts alike by the research context and the well established volatility of the emotional abuse data supports this (Friedrich *et al.*, 1997). These considerations would be even more influential for an experience which, like emotional abuse, does not relate to an objectively verifiable event. Much more telling for the argument from uncertainty, however, is the thought that putting someone in a category for research purposes only has consequences for the research; the discourse is scientific, as in the US literature described. The classification by registration of children and their families in the context of a multi-professional case conference in child protection, however, is an administrative and legal process which has enormous, powerful and potentially negative consequences for all the actors involved. The process of its negotiation is hardly scientific, but rather, it is claimed by some (Parton *et al.*, 1997; Thorpe, 1994; Wattam, 1992), primarily political – an activity which has little to do with the filling in of a questionnaire.

The making of child protection statistics

The making of child protection statistics over the 1990s is a multi-professional process, although the Personal Social Services Department of the local authority is statutorily *responsible* for receiving and investigating concerns about the wellbeing of any child in its area and, indeed for the whole child protection process. When a child is referred to social services, he or she becomes an eponymous case file which will start on a journey. This journey can be seen from different perspectives and is mapped in several distinct ways in the child protection literature. Generally, it is seen as a series of alternative pathways and gateways at certain decision nodes which will relate to questions of investigation, registration, a protection plan, monitoring and care proceedings. This is framed to present a bureaucratic model of the 'if, then' kind: if certain conditions are fulfilled, the child goes into a particular category and certain procedures are triggered. What is implicit in this rendering are categories of risk and, after 2000, increasingly, categories of need.

Much research on the Child Protection process (usually financed by DOH) is, as already noted, an evaluation along this approach to decision making, against an implicit model of 'good practice'. But the framework of gateways and pathways may also tell an entirely different, more sociological story about the making of a 'child protection career'. This becomes an interactional process, negotiated between child, family and professionals, whose case talk, writing and meetings can be seen as a process of situated reasoning, in which the moral worth of parents is continually assessed (Dingwall *et al.*, 1983; Parton *et al.*, 1997; Thorpe, 1994; Wattam, 1992). Rittner and Wodarski claim that the complexity of abusive situations in families requires an ecological approach to its assessment, occurring, as it does 'within a milieu of family dysfunction, environmental stress and societal values relating to child rearing' (Rittner and Wodarski, 1995: 45). But the logic of an ecological approach is that the assessors too are part of a complex ecology[8] within which child protection statistics do not just describe or misdescribe the world, however complex. They are also made by it and make it; they are part of an intricate social process that has its own 'rationality' (Perrow, 1984).

Pushing the boundaries: The statistics and child emotional abuse as an official problem category

The child protection statistics for emotional abuse can be seen to embody all the complexity of their administration. Whilst they clearly grew over the 1990s, which might be taken as some indication of a cultural shift, either within social services, or the society at large, or both, the predominant narrative in the professional and academic literature on this subject – what little there is of it – is that there is still a mismatch between the problem's prevalence and its size as a registration category. The story is that emotional abuse as a social problem is under-represented in the Child Protection statistics in comparison with other categories and that this is the fault of the administrative procedures and the decision-making process when applied cases of suspected emotional abuse.

The first part of the narrative is the positivistic one about all the difficulties with definition noted above, which means that social workers and other professionals (but mainly social workers) cannot recognise emotional abuse when they see it (Kaplan *et al.*, 1999; O'Hagan, 1993). Next, a development of this account, more legalistic in flavour, is that since all the behavioural indicators are non-specific, even if 'the emotional abuse inherent in the situation' is not 'missed' (Trowell *et al.*, 1997: 338), it is extremely hard to prove that developmental delays in children are 'caused' by particular parental behaviours, singly or in combination. This is the proof that will have to be shown if 'significant harm' is to be established in court. Lack of proof might presumably prevent a case conference from putting an official imprimatur on a suspected case – although registration as a trigger to services is a counter-argument here.

The third, more prevalent narrative is that social workers or the case conference may recognise the characteristics of emotional abuse in a case under discussion, but not appreciate its seriously damaging nature in comparison with other forms of abuse and, therefore, not feel the necessity to register. This applies to emotional abuse when it exists on its own, or also where it co-exists with other forms for one child. Child physical abuse and child sexual abuse and even neglect are registered in preference. Circumstantial evidence for this is given in Trowell's analysis of a group of children referred to a north London family centre for treatment, where few are registered for emotional abuse but the level of concern, expressed by referrers and staff of the centre alike, is about the emotional and developmental state of the sample children (Trowell *et al.*, 1997). Glaser and Prior (1997), in their DOH-sponsored study of the registration process in four local authorities in south-east England, note a significant delay in the registration of their sample children for emotional abuse, 96 per cent of them previously known to social services, which, they claim is only explained by some reluctance on the part of the case conference/ social services to register. They observe that in contrast to those cases of abuse which, definitionally, depend on the occurrence of a particular sort of 'event', where registration is prompt, the registration of emotional abuse seems to depend on a slow build up of, probably, non-specific concern. This contrasts interestingly with registration for neglect, a process in which it has been noticed that a long term symbiotic relationship between social services and these traditional 'revolving door' clients is precipitated, catastrophe like, into a more coercive interaction by 'an incident' – an event involving actual physical or sexual injury to the child, or indicating, at least, a high level of its probability (Allsopp and Stevenson, 1995; Stevenson, 1998).

What is apparent in the case accounts of a large sample of social workers, interviewed in 1994, is an implicit hierarchy in the administrative response to different forms of abuse, explicitly recognised in this statement by a social services manager:

> If we looked for emotional abuse we'd have half the country up Social Services. [So we look to see if children are] clean, well dressed, well fed, robust... the outward and visible sign of inward spiritual grace, if you like.... If the same children were to appear with runny noses and muddy ears, with wet underwear and dirty clothes and not having had breakfast etc. etc., it starts to be a different ballgame [neglect]. But even then we sort of hang on in there. But if they've got a lump missing from the side of their head, or Mum's boyfriend touched their bottom or something.... It's that bit which is very, very important' (Allsopp and Stevenson, 1995: 42).

It is this hierarchy which is implicitly recognised in the emotional abuse literature, in the constant injunction that emotional abuse should be allotted more importance in our concerns about the wellbeing of children. The claim is that emotional abuse and its effects are 'as serious' as (Glaser and Prior, 1997: 316) indeed 'more damaging' than (Iwaniec, 1995: 370; Trowell *et al.*, 1997: 358) those of other forms of abuse.

What is being asserted here? Is it just that physical, outward harm is more easy to prove (Trowell *et al.*, 1997) and so more children are registered under this label; or is it that members of case conferences genuinely think that the harmful effects of emotional abuse on children are so much less than that of other forms? What may also be implied, though not explicitly spelled out in the literature, is the important issue of time in the decision-making process. This process is coded in the language of risk – an approach heavily criticised in the child protection literature since the mid-1990s. A commonplace of the DOH research on the decision-making process (DOH,1995) is that most of the time is taken up with establishing whether a particular event has occurred, in order to identify abuse, rather than, more desirably, discussing future plans for ensuring the welfare of the child (Farmer and Owen, 1995). This preoccupation may be for legal reasons, but it is also because an incident of physical or sexual abuse is the best predictor of another occurrence, without intervention. It may also be seen as an indicator of what may be escalating violence or a build-up of stress as the 'critical path' models have it (Lynch, 1976). Given the characterisation of emotional abuse as a long-term relationship, the point in time of the intervention is not so crucial. As Glaser and Prior point out in their 1997 paper, unless the intervention involves removing a child from her caretakers, any therapeutic plan can only be expected to make a difference to a child and family over the long haul. The situation does not threaten to deteriorate, catastrophe-like, in the near future. It is the nearness of this future which may also be crucial to the different decisions taken for each form of abuse. According to the assumptions of welfare economics,[9] however objectively equal the damage to the child in the different forms of abuse, the disutility of an event or outcome in the far future would generally be smaller than that attached to an event which may be imminent – even if the process were entirely dominated by objective welfare considerations. But this is a system of risk management, in which the layers of surveillance and monitoring extend from the child and family, through social services management to the Social Services Inspectorate. With high levels of anxiety, accountability, and frequent turnover of jobs, it would be hardly surprising if the more imminent forms of harm had more saliency in the outcomes under consideration and the more predictable forms of abuse took precedence in the registration process.

Category confusion

There is something strange about the logic of the claims of these academics and practitioners in the child welfare field, which extends across the medical, psychological and social work professions. In claiming the inadequacy of the registration process in recognising the extent of emotional abuse as compared with a, presumably, more accurate response to other forms of abuse, they are recognising that the production of this data is an entirely contingent process. Yet it is, at least partly, both on the basis of this data stream, and the concept of emotional abuse encapsulated in the government guidance of 1980, the ontologically subjective product of a human and highly fallible process, that much of their scientific, or social scientific research is based. Moreover, it is this research, through its enumeration of various behavioural indicators and family characteristics, or the way that self report questionnaires build up a threshold of 'seriousness', which is used to identify emotional abuse as a problem in the real world which has an objective existence, independent of the official Child Protection category.

Perhaps this is the confusion that underlies the assertion of the highly influential Child Psychiatrist, Danya Glaser, when she writes about the difficulties surrounding the interventions of the administrative processes in the psychiatric treatment approach to a case of emotional abuse:

> This paper... while advocating an early response to concerns suggesting emotional abuse,... raises questions about the appropriateness of the immediate use of Child Protection procedures in the investigation and assessment of suspected emotional abuse. Alternative approaches are suggested which may not need to include police and Social Services in the early stages. The response to recognition of emotional abuse is more appropriately considered as working towards protection (Glaser and Prior, 1997: 315).

She follows the old medical line that registration and possibly court proceedings should be used as a last resort, its threat a therapeutic lever on the families she is treating – nasty medicine rather than a punishment. This approach is inimical to many social workers, who see the use of registration-as-a-threat as, indeed, punitive. At the same time, they see it in bureaucratic mode and feel that registration is essentially descriptive; it should be used to register concern when abuse has been established; it is not there to be used strategically (Glaser and Prior, 1997: 324). They might also see in her stance shades of the old child protection problem of doctors wishing to retain medical confidentiality.

They might, nevertheless, agree that emotional abuse is not appropriately processed by social services, as the social work manager quoted above. He envisaged a complete flooding of the system, which does not seem to have happened. This could be attributed to a common attitude among social services managers and has been attributed by the medical sector, including Glaser, to the requirements of the procedures themselves, which prevent official recognition. Thus, Glaser arrives at a contradictory position, or at least at a position of wanting it both ways. She suggests that the administrative category is not inclusive enough, that social workers or case conferences are not sensitive enough to recognise the medical fact of emotional abuse when they see it, but that if they were to recognise it, it should remain a medical category, otherwise it would trigger all the procedures that she finds so unproductive. Either way, this looks like a bid for expansion: to keep the definition and management of emotional abuse, at least initially, out of the child protection system and in the hands of medical personnel, where the only limit on its growth as a medical category would be NHS rationing.

In contrast, Olive Stevenson, characterised in Section 6.3 as a distinguished social work academic and one of the traditional welfarists described above, also makes an expansionist claim in her keynote article in the first volume of a new journal, *Child and Family Social Work*, (Stevenson, 1996). Her opinion is that since the sequelae of all forms of abuse is emotional damage and developmental delay, techniques for managing emotional abuse should become the main feature of all child protection work. Such techniques should be informed by the sort of quasi-medical knowledge about children and families and their relationships which should be a major part of the knowledge base for social workers, since it is presumably they whom she envisages as doing the work.

Yet, while the child psychiatrist and the welfarist social work academic are making widely different claims about the proper ownership of this category, they are not disagreeing about the definition. Glaser lumps child protection social workers with the police in the context of the child protection procedures, whilst Stevenson claims wider concerns and skills for social workers, (who are not just bureaucrats and can therefore recognise problems of abuse independently of whether they do or should invoke the procedures). Such skills relating to child welfare can still be used and indeed are necessary to a proper use of the procedures themselves. Stevenson supports the notion that the concept of emotional abuse, even for social workers, should be something other than an administrative category (Glaser and Prior, 1997; Stevenson, 1996).

Category inflation

However, Stevenson, here, is also making another sort of expansionist claim in the bids of emotional abuse academics for an equal or higher place in a hierarchy of 'seriousness' for emotional abuse, as distinct from other forms. Her claim that the management of emotional abuse is the basis of *all* child protection work, because it is the consequence of all forms of abuse, amounts to the sort of curious 'categorical imperialism' (*pace* Kant) that we saw was present in the US emotional abuse literature (from Garbarino, 1978, onwards). It seems to be the consensus, in the professional research and clinical literature of those disciplines which assess and treat abused children, that 'whether the abuse of a child involves neglect, physical or sexual abuse, it is the emotional and psychological damage that generally leads to long term difficulties.' Trowell, who reproduces here the message of Franklin twenty years earlier, also supports Stevenson when she continues, 'increasingly the emotional and psychological sequelae of other types of abuse are recognised as the target for work' (Trowell *et al.*, 1997: 357). Iwaniec, in the same journal, goes further in establishing, as Trowell did in 1983, that these sequelae *are* in fact emotional abuse in their own right, but, in the contorted logic of the following piece of prose, it is also possible to detect that she is claiming something more:

> There is now a growing consensus among professionals that emotional maltreatment is more prevalent than was realised; it is at the core of all major forms of abuse; its impact is usually more damaging than the effects of physical and sexual abuse; and it requires special attention to disentangle emotional from physical acts of maltreatment (Iwaniec, 1997: 370).

There is a subtle shift of definition here from emotional abuse or maltreatment as a category of abuse which comprises certain parental acts, which relate more specifically to certain developmental outcomes for the child, to one which refers more generally to 'damage' to some inner life, whatever the nature of the abusive actions. The sequelae of all forms of abuse, emotional abuse becomes the 'core' of all abuse, following Hart. Although, at the same time, physical acts of maltreatment can still be 'disentangled' from the emotional, for the administrative purposes of registration say, they have also become emotional acts of maltreatment. Thus the set of all environmental causes of emotional harm is considerably widened, enlarging the category by many times. If emotional abuse is a concept which primarily refers to all 'emotional and psychological damage' inflicted by another, whether by physical or psychic assault, then it becomes a category which encompasses all other abuses, since they all have psychological sequelae.

This extended category also helps to confirm emotional abuse's ontological status in the objective world of welfare science, requiring the 'special attention' of experts in its recognition and treatment, because, however the wounds have been inflicted, the resulting harms are *the* 'target of work'. It is a larger, more important and serious proposition, it is claimed, than the category of the emotional abuse of children in the Child Protection registration process, which, in contrast, is a mere construct of administrative and legal processes and their participants' obsession with proof and 'incidents'.

6.5 Conclusion

These two chapters on the growth of emotional abuse as a registration category in child protection have much in common with the two preceding ones on PTSD and the law. There three different forms of life were identified: the medical-statistical; the medical-clinical and the administrative-legal. In these two chapters, other, similar forms are described. First, the emergence in the context of USA and UK social policy of a problem category which had a primarily medical or socio-medical base, child physical abuse and emotional abuse as a rare variant; then the growth of this form of the category in the legislative and organisational context of the UK after 1980. Noted here was the shift of emphasis in the processing and understanding of abuse from a socio-medical, diagnostic, to a socio-legal, more forensic, formula and then possibly a re-emergence of the first, in a constant dialectic between a system ideal based on the administration of risk and one based on the administration of welfare.

This present chapter has featured the burgeoning of a statistical, research-based version of this phenomenon in the USA, using different forms of definition and identification, but still referred to as a source of knowledge by professionals and practitioners applying an operational rather than a statistical category. It was partly due to this research base of adult recollections of childhood, that psychological abuse began to be seen as such a pervasive and serious category of abuse and a core part of all forms of maltreatment.

This theme has also become part of the equivalent UK literature, where the confusing nature of the concept's profuse definitions in the emotional abuse literature has been identified, with conflicting claims to its correct application, as the category covers two different domains – the socio-medical and the socio-legal. It is argued that confusion arises at their interface, because the two systems for identifying and understanding this social problem not only exist side by side, not only legitimate each other, but depend on each other for meaning – existence even.

Out of this confusion and multi-professional difference, the category of the emotional abuse of children has grown enormously, in the process of which it seems to have gone through certain phases: 1) as non-existent or only metaphorically abusive; 2) as an also ran to physical and sexual abuse, a cause or a consequence, part of the psycho-social context and still half metaphor, as described in Chapter 5; 3) as another, much less prevalent form of abuse than physical or sexual abuse, used for registration and existing along-side these other two; 4) as an increasingly registered, larger category than the latter; 5) as a more prevalent, just as serious, or more serious form of abuse than physical or sexual maltreatment and lastly, 6) claimed to be prototypical of abuse in all its forms. With these claims, it moves from the periphery to the centre of the definitional field, where Garbarino always put it. Such an inclusive category is no longer the last of the litter. And no longer an ostrich, but an eagle.

There is a difficulty here, however. This categorical eagle – emotional abuse as the long term developmental consequence of all forms of abuse – came into life and grew as a small legalistic registration category and grew quietly as such, though some claimed it as a class of damage to which the normal legal and administrative processes are not necessarily appropriate, since the welfare consequences of being 'in need' or 'at risk of emotional abuse and neglect' are not greatly different. It can be argued that the growth of social work interest in acting to promote the emotional wellbeing and development of children, including all those that are abused, owed much to the efforts of the DOH to shift the LASSDs after 1995 towards putting more scarce resources into long term child welfare. On the other hand, this 'action' seems to have taken the form of registering more and more children in the UK under the child protection category of emotional abuse, still an administrative form of life, generating an ever-increasing consumption of resources under a sovereign compulsory regime for the state's intervention in family life, rather than any form of voluntary tutelage. This is something of a paradox and, perhaps, not what the welfarist authors of the Children Act intended. This eagle may be ready to fly, but it is still caged by a framework of legislation and a rigid, bureaucratic taxonomy of harm, which divides the mind from the body parts of children.

7
Attachment: An 'internalised something' and the natural world

7.1 Introduction

When reactive attachment disorder (RAD) was written into DSM-IV in 1994, it joined a mounting number of other diagnoses of childhood in the canons of psychiatric medicine, including autism; attention deficit disorder (ADD) and attention deficit hyperactive disorder (ADHD); then, most recently, bipolar disorder; and, of course, the depression being found in children in increasing quantity – much more of it about than was thought (Horwitz and Wakefield, 2007)! As a diagnostic category, RAD itself is barely distinguishable from these other childhood conditions, since none have a specific set of symptoms (WHO, 2009). It is a diagnosis given to a small but resource-consuming group of children, whose seemingly intractable and troubled behaviour presages high levels of deviance in adolescent and adult populations. These may be delinquency, mental illness or substance abuse and the more extreme and dangerous disorders of personality. It is the subject of books whose titles speak for themselves. Here are some examples from the bibliography of the IACD, the Institute for Attachment and Child Development, Evergreen Colorado, Director Forrest Lien, ('Saving Children, Saving Families, Saving Lives'): *Broken Hearts; Wounded Minds* (Randolph, 2001), *Broken Spirits – Lost Souls* (Ryan, 2009), *First Steps in Parenting the Child Who Hurts* (C. Archer, 1999), and, most fundamentally, *The Primal Wound* (Verrier, 1993). These titles give us a clue to what distinguishes this disorder of childhood from others. It is a question of cause or origins. Their symptoms cannot be attributed to a genetic/organic disorder, as with the others. These children are wounded. They have suffered invisible wounds – emotional harm inflicted by a hostile environment in infancy. Just as in PTSD, it is the environmental aetiology which distinguishes this category from those with similar symptomatology but possibly organic origins. But this environment is not a physical warzone, nor is it social in its broadest sense; it is the close and intimate environment created by the people who are the infants' main carers, who in most cases are their mothers. The wound is the internal effect of a poor relationship between mother and child.

It might be thought that attachment disorders or difficulties are a less dramatic, widespread and media-targeted social problems than these other pathologies of childhood, and certainly the language of attachment in its technical psychological sense has not entered into the vernacular in the way that descriptions like 'depressive', 'manic', 'autistic' and 'hyperactive' have. Nevertheless, attachment problems have become part of the general diagnostic repertoire of the medical profession,[1] for example. Although categories in attachment theory, other than RAD, do not map easily on to official psychiatric nosology, and the diagnosis is less widely used in the UK than in the United States, attachment is increasingly becoming part of the language of expertise among psy professionals in this country, and especially the technicians of the family. Not surprisingly, attachment theory is seen as particularly relevant to the troubles of childhood and their treatment, the subject of myriad multi-professional conferences and training days, especially in the area of fostering and adoption, and part now of the language of the UK family courts, the Department of Health and the DfES in their statuary requirements for the assessment of children and families in 'safeguarding' procedures – children 'at risk' and children 'in need'. Attachment theory is used to inform a huge state- and charity-funded preventative initiative aimed at improving childcare in the early years, from the perinatal period onwards, in both the USA and the UK. It is the subject of a large network of informative and hortatory websites, encouraging mothers to do better and spelling out the dire consequences of failure. Lastly, it is used as a basis for therapy in a host of treatment organisations of varying degrees of orthodoxy. Anyone doubting the influence of attachment theory in the realm of therapy should note that the relatively well established Institute of Attachment and Child Development in the USA reveals on its website that, in its own town of Evergreen, Colorado (population 9216 in the 2000 census), there are at least six clinics offering attachment therapy (IACD, 2006).

The concept of attachment has been chosen as the subject of this chapter and the next partly because of this increasingly commanding position among professionals as a theory of psychic harm within the family, and partly because, as such, it is the most coherent and well-researched theorisation of emotional abuse or emotional neglect that exists. It maps onto this category of child abuse in three different ways. First, it theorises a harm done mostly by the unnatural backsliding of mothers rather than 'the sins of the father', which Hacking notes are the attributions of the sexual abuse narrative (Hacking, 1999); second, the way that the harm is done is ambiguous: it may be due to dangerous behaviour by the carer, often deliberate but not necessarily. It may also be due to inattention and emotional unavailability which results in a systematic failure to protect the child from a threatening environment. Essentially, it arises from a relationship in which fear is not managed. Third, although the theory was originally predicated on studies of sudden traumatic loss to the child of his main carer – often called 'maternal deprivation', the wound of attachment theory is less likely to be the result of any sudden occurrence. Rather, it is the result of cumulative events over time, as in Freud's original summative version of trauma – the subtle distortion of individual growth and development towards a state of mature self regulation, in which the complexities and dangers of the outside world can be faced with impunity. It is the spoiling of this developmental process, which underlies all thinking about the sequelae of emotional as well as other forms of abuse, and it is this that is theorised in the working out and adjustment of attachment theory over time. For the theory, though starting from an engagement with sad and delinquent children and their developmental psychopathology, has also become the dominant psychological theory of normal child development – with all its tropes of desirability and goals of attainment

So, whilst the last two chapters have outlined the career of emotional abuse largely as an administrative category, looking at its social context, connotations and consequences and not at its denotation or referent, the nature of the harm, these next two chapters describe one particular journey into the interior. For they are the story of how, in a hypothesised inner life, a particular cognitive and affective site called attachment was created and established by a metaphor – within the American and British academies, the world of psy professionals, of parents and of governments. Furthermore, in line with the thesis of this book, it is an account of how this attachment space was initially carved out not as a psychic generator of normal healthy behaviour but as that which is associated with pathology and deviancy; and of how, even with its emergence as a standard for psychological health, it remained a space in danger of growing malformed or spoilt and leading to developmental deformation. For, as Nikolas Rose reminds us in his book, *Governing the Soul* (Rose, 1999), the development of attachment theory was part of a process in which normality in family relationships, though described as 'natural', was made to look fragile and easily lost – hence the need for constant maternal self-appraisal and expert scrutiny if the worst is not to happen.[2] And, if it does happen, so the story goes, the resulting wound, whether due to carelessness, sadness or malevolence, can only be healed by professionals, whose ministrations call up the image of the 'sensitive mother' and what she would have done, if she had behaved as nature intended and prevented all this.

Thus the exploration of emotional abuse turns from the issues of the definitions and inclusiveness of a category, looked at in the last four chapters, back to an investigation of one explanatory theory, attachment theory. This raises the old questions about the exact interior location and observability of psychological harms, together with the normality or pathology of those afflicted. Thus, these chapters are a threefold enquiry – a study of the theoretical development of a particular slice of inner life: first, seen through its questionable location and therefore its relationship to the ways it is made visible and knowable; second, viewed through the tension between statistical and clinical knowledge and, third, through the assumptions of the latter, which problematically relate what is abnormal to what is unnatural. It is the explicit engagement of invisible wounds with the natural world which comes more into play in this narrative.

This chapter and the next are about the history of this theory from its birth in the UK at the end of World War II to 2006, over a period when its professional status and popularity as a way of construing psychopathology and psychological harm to children in families waxed and waned with changes in social policy towards both families and academics. The story is divided very roughly into three periods, though, for narrative ease, some of the literature and references have been allowed to stray over the borders somewhat. The first period covers the ascendancy of the postwar welfare state, which can be said to start to decline in the early 1970s; the second stretches from the late 1970s until the late 1990s, during which time New Right thinking controlled policy; the state rolled back its frontiers; market disciplines were imposed by audit on academics (and many other public services) and policy aimed at the welfare of children became swamped by concerns about child abuse. These two periods are the subject matter of this present chapter. The next chapter, covering the final period of unprecedented policy activism towards children and families by New Labour, takes us to 2006. Under this regime, as described in Chapter 5 on emotional abuse, notions of risk and need became more psychological, as did its crucial ideology of children as social capital, and attachment theory flourished in the psy professions and in the language of government regulations.

What is presented here is an account of the various inscriptions on this interior site called attachment, in an attempt to capture the fluctuations, the setbacks and the final flourishing of the theory which holds this abstract concept in place. This history also borrows something from the evolutionary tropes of its subject matter. It traces the developmental adaptation of attachment theory to social policy as its wider ecological environment and, within that, the niche of the American and, to a lesser extent, the British academies and their professional offshoots.[3] This adaptive development makes for a theory of great complexity, methodological disputes and critiques which generate an ever increasing body of literature, to which it is impossible to do justice here. For clarity, the major intellectual innovations are incorporated into the narrative with a brief explanation of the theoretical and empirical issues involved, which is expanded in the endnotes.

7.2   Attachment, period I, 1945–1978: Falling between two stools

Maternal deprivation

As every account of attachment theory has pointed out, it was born in Britain in World War II out of a marriage of psychoanalytic theory and ethology and developed under the transatlantic, intellectual partnership of John Bowlby, an English aristocrat, and Mary Ainsworth, his Canadian-born, US-based collaborator. Politically, at this time, the perennial problems of law and order and distributional inequity were mixed with wartime and postwar concern with the psychological health and morale of the nation. It was also a time when this interest in psychological health was transforming the way that the socialisation of its citizens was thought of. The 'maladjusted' child of the old prewar child guidance clinics, whom the moralising project of socialisation had failed to reach, was giving way to the 'maladaptive' child, diagnosed as psychologically rather than morally unfitting (though the symptoms might look just the same), who might benefit from therapy rather than punishment. Juvenile justice, for example, began to take on a more reformative, rehabilitative stance, according to the best psychological principles. In this reframing, the moral character of children was superseded by their psychological welfare as an object of policy and their health needs were seen as relating not just to their growing bodies or moral sense, but to the development of some inner set of emotions and capacities (Rose, 1999).

With this rewriting of children's needs as psychological went a reframing of the family and its forms of regulation. It was still to be the agency of social reproduction and continuity, urged on by the new paternalistic welfare state, which was there to support parents and protect the welfare of its citizens from the worst excesses of the capitalist market.[4] Prewar forms of family tutelage were still provided by the courts and the education system, plus charity workers and the beginnings of the social work profession (Donzelot, 1979), but now, also, there was a more exclusively psychological perception of the family creeping into the therapeutic repertoire of the psy professionals; the family was being transformed from a moralising institution into a set of psychological relationships, which, if right and healthy, produced psychologically well adjusted children, but which also needed the constant vigilance and support of psy professionals in the form of a sort of 'therapeutic familialism' (Donzelot, 1979; Rose, 1999).

In the UK, this therapeutic approach to families took hold among some of the social workers in the newly professionalised Children and Families Departments of the local authorities, who were being trained in a technique called psychodynamic casework. Further, psychiatric social workers and psychiatrists, mostly of an analytic persuasion, presided in the ubiquitous child guidance clinics and public mental health services. Here, a somewhat more relations-based psychoanalytic philosophy than the original Freudian and Kleinian orthodoxy was appearing – reflecting the influence of American theorists and, of course, John Bowlby. Attachment-based advice and interventions were, for over two decades after the war, part of this therapeutic familialism.

In this gradual and crucial reframing of the way the child and family was thought of in public policy, the immediate social problem of the host of refugee children, who were living in war nurseries or were troublesome and failing to thrive in their new foster homes, provided a vital catalyst. The individual child had been subjected to a philanthropic and scientific (medical and psychological) scrutiny since the late 19th century, under which he or she had been reinvented by techniques making measurable and visible their growth and change. Children had also been the subject of the disciplinary gaze of the state through schooling and the Juvenile Courts, but this was the first time that the individual child suffering distress and loss had been subjected to systematic psychoanalytic observation outside the pathologising context of the child guidance clinic. It was the first time that the inner life of otherwise normal children – no mental illness or hereditary taint – was perceived to bear the marks of a negative emotion which affected their behaviour (Rose, 1999), producing the sort of 'normal pathology' discussed in Chapter 2 and 3. The immediate cause seemed obvious and undeniable: it was separation from their families and, most especially, the person who cared for them most – separation from their mother.

John Bowlby, trained as a psychiatrist and analyst and with earlier voluntary experience working in schools for maladjusted children, followed by employment in ordinary child guidance clinics, had, by the end of the war, already come to the conclusion that it was early childhood experiences provided by parents, particularly their early loss to the child through death or separation, which were crucial in the development of neuroses and delinquency (Bowlby, 1940, 1946). This was confirmed for him by his experience of observing refugee children[5] and later, with his assistants, those separated from parents by hospital admission. It began to be clear to him that the psychological wellbeing of children depended (naturally) on the continuity of a crucial, primary relationship with mothers or mother surrogates (Bowlby, 1953b). In this postwar context, however, attachment theory did not start by presenting an account of the behaviour of mothers as the basis for healthy normative psychological pro-social development. Bowlby was still a (heterodox) member of the psychoanalytic community and, as a version of psychoanalysis then in the ascendancy, his attachment theory provided an explanation of the devastating psychological effects of maternal deprivation. It gained some currency in the 1950s and 1960s, especially in the UK, where it formed much of the basis for the spate of popular professional advice to mothers of young children,[6] especially about the importance of constant maternal presence in children's lives. This was at a time when, correlatively but not necessarily causally, women were moving from the war-time factories back into the home and were subjected to a barrage of pro-natalist propaganda, as well as exhortations about the proper conduct of motherhood, and warnings about deviation from the path (Riley, 1983).[7]

As such, it also gained a foothold in criminology where the family role in socialisation was being added to physiological and individual psychological explanations of criminality by such as Edward Glover, the Freudian founder of the *British Journal of Criminology* in 1950 and later by Travis Hirschi, the US sociologist (Hirschi, 1969). It was influential in Social Work and Probation Officer training, where certain key ethological texts like Konrad Lorenz's accounts of imprinting in birds (Lorenz, 1958) and descriptions of Harlow's monkey experiments (Harlow, 1961;

Harlow and Zimmermann, 1958) were used to reinforce the human message. This message, couched in the language of attachment and security, though the theory was complex, had broad intuitive appeal. In the newly professional Local Authority Child Care Departments, it was used to reinforce traditional social casework practice under the injunction that families in trouble should be kept together at all costs.[8] Later, after child abuse hit the political agenda in the 1970s in the UK,[9] and social policy towards children 'at risk' became more interventionist, theories about the effects of maternal deprivation seemed to give at least some leverage on the awesome problem of taking a child out of its family of origin and supervising its future care in the fostering and adoption system or an institution. At worst, they illuminated the difficulties (Fahlberg, 1981a, b).

War in the Interior

Whilst his initial theory about maternal loss was still influential in the applied psy professions, Bowlby's own interest moved naturally from the consequences of this loss of an attachment figure to the nature and importance of the attachment relationship itself. From this, his detailed, many-layered and complex theory of normal attachment began to evolve, although the first volume of his trilogy (*Attachment and Loss*) was not published until 1969. Also, the progress of this normative theory of ontogeny within the broad, complex and heterogeneous field of child psychological development and its knowledge workers was less rapid than his loss theory of delinquency and psychopathology among psy professionals. Bowlby was exploring an inner terrain which was already overrun by competing colonists. Educationalists, such as Cyril Burt, argued with Behaviourists; the British Psychoanalytic Association was split down the middle between Kleinians and Freudians – and Bowlby was caught in the crossfire.

These disputes were not just about the nature of the landscape of the child's internal world, they were also about how to get there. The right route was fought over by the research-based approach of the psychological sciences (either behaviourist observation or statistical survey and analysis), producing potentially universal and verifiable, because measurable, truths, versus the practice based/clinical and individual insights of psychoanalysis, where behaviour was subject to elaborate theoretical interpretations, which were not necessarily verifiable and even, some thought, self fulfilling (King and Steiner, 1944). Given different techniques of approach, accounts of what they found there were inevitably very different. Cyril Burt saw permanent and observable features of the landscape of characteristic types – he called them 'traits' – constantly formed by the internal energy source of biological drives. The Kleinians and the Freudians both found a stratified terrain, in which the hydraulic power of instincts had been repressed and diverted into a seething underground lake, from which neuroses constantly bubbled up. The ground above it was a layer of ego rock impacted under the force of a final super-ordinate laval crust. The two schools could never agree on how this crust was made and how long it took. For Kleinians, it was formed entirely by internal convulsions from the primordial moment of birth, in which love, hate, destructive phantasies, guilt, anxiety, desire and despair, all converging on the mother object, gradually resulted in instinctual repression and a rudimentary ego and superego. For Freudians, it was a slower process, more congruent with actual neurological maturation and cognition, in which the stratified formations are made by the external pressure of a patriarchal society and the social and cultural conditions of dependency on the libidinous instincts of the child. The behaviourists just attacked the explorers en route and did not visit the inner territory at all.

Such conditions were not especially favourable to the staking out of an inner space called attachment, though in different ways it overlapped with these others and mediated some of their disputed polarities. It seemed to offer something for everybody, which is probably why, initially, it pleased nobody very much in either parent intellectual community – psychoanalysis or science – and the theory has always sat a little uncomfortably between the two. John Bowlby was accused of apostasy by certain members of the psychoanalytic establishment for several reasons. First the 'environmentalism' of his theory was somewhat revolutionary in the context of British psychoanalytic community at the time,[10] dominated as it was by Anna Freud and Melanie Klein and a theory of object relations, in which the intrapsychic conflicts and representations of the infant were a great deal more important to its behaviour than actual experience (Klein, 1932). Bowlby wrote defiantly:

> Psychoanalysts, like the nurseryman, should study intensively, rigorously, and at first hand, the nature of the organism, the properties of the soil, and the interaction of the two (Bowlby, 1940: 2).

It was, perhaps, a reflection of his own analysis with Joan Rivière, a friend of Melanie Klein, that Bowlby assumed that the 'soil' in which the childish organism grew was the intersubjective context of mother and child – the Kleinian couple, rather than the Freudian threesome of the Oedipus Complex.

Second, and as a consequence, the actual inner space of the child in Bowlby's theories was, some claim, surprisingly non-psychoanalytic in appearance, as much influenced by Piaget as Klein (Fonagy, 2001), although others (Bretherton *et al.*, 1991, for example) maintain that it was influenced by Fairbairn and the Object Relations school (Fairbairn, 1952). In fact, attachment theory was fundamentally systemic – based on the identification of a two-person behavioural and motivational system, which did not need a psychoanalytic theory of internal drives to explain it. Its explanation was teleological; its goal an (initially) spatial, dyadic relationship, best described as the proximity of an infant to its main carer, under conditions of perceived danger. This represented further a complex infantile state in which fearful arousal is not only resolved by this proximity, but in which a positive position of felt security is achieved as a basis for exploration and learning. In the face of exogenous danger to the mother–child system, the infant's reflex-like attachment behaviours are triggered. The mother's response determines how these behaviours develop, and so how the growing attachment, or affective bond, between mother and child, is felt, displayed and gradually conceptualised by the infant, as her cognitive faculties mature.

What was built up internally in the attachment space, on the basis of the child's attachment experience – and therefore the behaviour of the mother – was a *learnt* set of cognitions, a 'working model' of the attachment relationship. How it *would* work was based on how it was *perceived* to have worked, plus templates, scripts, narratives and all the soft furnishings of a cognitive space (Bowlby, 1953a: 62). This Internal Working Model (IWM) was seen as developing at the time when infantile memory progressed from the representational to the semantic (about the age of two years), when the left side of the brain begins its developmental spurt. The IWM acted as a series of expectational filters to information from the outside world about the behaviour of attachment objects and it was also accompanied by a reciprocal model of the self as the expected object of responsive parental behaviours. This, Bowlby thought, generalised later to an evaluative model of the social world and the child's own place within it (Bowlby, 1969, 1973, 1980). Of course, the processing of interpersonal information also invoked affective and motivational states within this inner space. These might include fantasies and desires not necessarily based on experience, as later attachment theorists pointed out. (Bretherton and Waters, 1985; Sroufe and Waters, 1977a).

Third, although the theory, at least in its broadest sense, reproduced Freud's intuition that the initial relationship between mother and child is the developmental prototype for all further love relationships, unlike much psychoanalytic thinking about human development as a process of individuation from parents and growing autonomy, attachment theory presented an essential paradox: that exploration, hence learning, cognitive growth and a sense of self in relation to the social and physical world, depend on the child's sense of a 'secure base' (Ainsworth, 1969; Bowlby, 1988) with the parent. And, further, that secure, affective relationships throughout the rest of life are the basis for a well developed adaptive sense of self efficacy and independence. This had critical implications for attachment-based psychotherapy.

Fourth, the theory that Bowlby came up with to support his observations was most controversial. He turned to ethology or animal behaviourism for an explanatory hypothesis which rooted infant–parent relationships in a period of evolutionary adaptedness for the reproductive survival of the species. There, proximity seeking infantile behaviour was selected for because it was functional for this survival. This was not only anathema to psychoanalysts such as Winnicot, who saw it as intolerably mechanistic and crude, but it also did not please the psychological community, since ethological explanations of human behaviour seemed an alien and somewhat circular approach. On the scientific side, having seemingly rejected the individual clinical insights of psychoanalysis, Bowlby did not choose the statistical approaches employed in academic psychology at that time. He retained his clinical assumptions about what is healthy development, but located them at the distal evolutionary level – healthiness equals natural adaptedness. – and he approached the inner life of the child through the strictest methods of naturalistic observation, borrowed from animal behaviourism and incorporating the latest techniques of film and photography. Attachment theory was grounded in an ontology of the natural.

A strange situation

It was Mary Ainsworth who helped greatly to develop Bowlby's theories, as well as these ethological techniques. Together with others of Bowlby's collaborators at his research department in the Tavistock Clinic, she began a lifetime of rigorous empirical research by studying the effects of separation from their parents on hospitalized infants (Robertson, 1953a, b). However, like Bowlby, she turned from studying maternal deprivation to a study of a normal sample of Ugandan mothers and babies, when her husband's work took her to that country in the 1960s (Ainsworth, 1967). She later established herself in a major US university, moving as a Professor of Psychology to Johns Hopkins, to undertake the famous Baltimore Study in the 1970s. This was her home study, intended as a pilot, of mother–baby behaviour over a sample of 26 mother–child dyads, with a sub-set also observed under laboratory-like conditions.

Ainsworth also worked within the postulates of evolutionary biology, identifying and recording a range of infantile 'attachment behaviours', which she described as 'a repertoire of reflex-like behaviours' (Ainsworth and Bell, 1970), seemingly triggered by fear and hypothesised as 'genetically programmed' and, 'species characteristic' (Ainsworth *et al.*, 1974: 100–101). She also elaborated what was known at this period of mother–child interactions (when looking at developmental child psychology within an interpersonal context was in its relative infancy),[11] hypothesising that:

> Adults generally, despite a massive overlay of learned behaviours – are biased to respond to the species-characteristic signals of an infant in ways that are also species-characteristic, ... that infant attachment behaviours are adapted to reciprocal maternal behaviours, that a mother responsive to infant signals is a salient feature of the environment of evolutionary adaptedness, and that unresponsive mothers may be viewed as the product of developmental anomalies and likely themselves to foster anomalous development in their infants. (Ainsworth *et al.*, 1974: 101)

Her attempt to pin down empirically and, indeed, more precisely, the varying patterns of attachment behaviour that she observed in the homes of her sample resulted in her famous 'Strange Situation' test, in which a sub-set of her Baltimore child sample were subjected to the increased and artificially produced stress of being put into a room with a stranger, with, and then without, their mothers. The mother–child reunions were observed and the resulting behaviours classified into three types of attachment behaviours (Ainsworth *et al.*, 1978). 'B' children, classified as 'Secure', greeted their mother, often tearfully, on reunion, but were soon comforted and settled down to play again. 'A' children, classified as 'Insecure Avoidant', took little notice of their mother's departure or return and were thought to precociously downplay affective arousal; 'C' children, classified as 'Insecure Ambivalent', were highly aroused, hard to comfort, alternately seeking soothing and then rejecting their mother's advances. There was a fourth category, which contained children who were deemed unclassifiable.

It was in her explanation of these observed behaviours, as well as her pursuit of the concept of 'anomalous development' that Mary

Ainsworth herself fell foul of the scientific community and was, after the Baltimore study, never funded again by any government or private research organisation, despite repeated applications (Main, 1999b). The first difficulty was her formulation of attachment as an internal psychodynamic, rather than a behavioural phenomenon. Like Bowlby, she theorised behaviours seemingly triggered by fear as displays of an 'attachment' – an affectional tie which one person forms between himself and a specific other; a tie which forms an early spatial relationship between them, endures over time and is the secure basis for the exploratory system to come into play – another hypothesised evolutionary necessity (Ainsworth and Bell, 1970; Bowlby, 1958, 1969). Reflecting on her intellectual influences, Ainsworth wrote in her book on Ugandan mothers and babies:

> Attachment is manifested through specific patterns of behaviour, but the patterns themselves do not constitute the attachment. *Attachment is internal. This internalized something that we call attachment has aspects of feelings, memories, wishes, expectancies, and intentions, all of which ... serve as a kind of filter for the reception and interpretation of inter personal experience and as a kind of template, shaping the nature of outwardly observable response.*(My italics) (Ainsworth, 1967: 429–430).

'A something' inscribed on an inner space: she thought she had avoided the reifying tendencies of behavioural models or diagnostic processes by hypothesising an explanatory psychological construct which was essentially psychodynamic. Bowlby was, after all, still part of the psychoanalytic community and Ainsworth herself spent some years in psychoanalysis (Main, 1999b). Not surprisingly, she found herself, on the one hand, out of step with the growing fashion for behaviourism in academic psychology, in which behaviours were all a response to context and 'the mind' remained an unexplored black box and, on the other hand, differing radically from trait theory, in which unchanging internal characteristics were inferred from particular sets of index behaviours, whereas attachment behaviours might vary greatly over stage of development and social context.

Her attachment construct was also the basis for the way she saw and developed the notion of 'anomalous development', which, with her clinical training, was as interesting to her as normal development. Not only did attachment persist over time and, by implication, influence how future social interactions were experienced, but the variable responses of mothers did not alter it quantitatively (or in the number of particular behaviours it seemed to generate) but rather qualitatively. In other words, attachment behaviour was not extinguished by an unresponsive mother, but rather, different forms of adaptive behaviour were generated, depending on maternal response. Nor was this to be seen only along the dimension of security to insecurity. It was Ainsworth's major work to classify the differences in the individual attachment behaviours in infants of eighteen months or so and, by implication this, 'anomalous development' into this set of three different forms. If group B were secure responses, then A and C were very different forms of insecurity (Ainsworth *et al.*, 1978).

This method of classification of her sample was the second major difficulty with Ainsworth's work, although the Strange Situation Test remains fundamental to the whole attachment project. There were obvious criticisms: the smallness of the laboratory sample; the assumption of the stability of these classifications for an individual over time (although some longer-term follow-up of the infant respondent groups suggests that this was reliable)[12] and the relative simplicity of the psychological assumptions behind the experiment, which preclude any notion of normal conflictual patterns of behaviour in the children involved (Mahler, 1967).[13] However, the most fundamental and telling feature of Ainsworth's approach – as of Bowlby's – is the assumption of the universality of mother–child behaviour and the ignoring of cultural specificity (Burman, 2008). This applies not only across different societies, but also across social groups and different socio-economic conditions, across individual families and even individual idiosyncrasies. Research along the same lines in different countries did, in fact, give some strange results (Grossmann *et al.*, 1981, 2005),[14] which would not have been a problem if the origins of attachment theory in the observation of pathology had not imposed a normative typology.

The majority of children in the Baltimore study fell into the B category: that is, the B category was the statistical norm. However, Ainsworth also assumed it was the psychologically healthy outcome for all children because seemingly most adaptive under stress or in danger. Types A and C children may have adapted their behaviour to different versions of maternal response, but this was also seen as *mal*adaptive in a wider social context, generating high levels of anxiety, overt in the case of C children and defensively suppressed in the case of the As. Crucially, as Main has pointed out (Main, 1999b), Ainsworth was not just interested in the statistical norm and a theory which explained the patterns of normal development implied. Her approach was clinical and also a bow to psychoanalysis's emphasis on individual difference. She wanted to explain the behaviour of every child classified in her sample. This was seen as eccentric by other psychologists (Main, 1999b) and even Bowlby, on first hearing Ainsworth's paper on the Strange Situation results, thought her theory lacked parsimony (Main, 1999b), although he later retracted.

However, it was not just at the level of psychological explanation, in which the clinical clashed with the statistical, that the normativity of Ainsworth's individual difference theory foundered. A further undermining of attachment's clinical approach came with a questioning of the imposition of a mental health paradigm on an evolutionary theory (Lamb *et al.*, 1984). Ainsworth had based her normative classifications on this evolutionary underlay – that is on an assumption that the healthy interaction between type B mothers and children was also evolutionarily favoured or selected for and, therefore, that a particular environment of evolutionary adaptedness had prevailed at a crucial time in our phylogenetic history. In a way, Bowlby and Ainsworth could be seen to be trying to preserve the clinical assumptions of psychoanalysis, by grounding them in what seemed, on the face of it, a surer and more self-evident evolutionary science. Unfortunately, they made an assumption at the distal evolutionary level which was no more (or less) proven than their clinical assumptions at the level of individual ontogeny. For five years before the publication of the first volume of Bowlby's *Attachment and Loss* trilogy, the theory of evolution (which had developed little since the days of Darwin) changed dramatically with the publication of a single paper by the biologist, William Hamilton, although its implications took time to work out (Hamilton, 1964). Bowlby was unaware of the dramatic change when he published.

This paper attacked the hypothesised goal of attachment behaviour as species survival, strongly suggesting, on the basis of games theory, that evolution works at the level of the individual, not the species and, moreover, at the level of the individual gene. Consequently, it is not about species or individual survival, but about genetic replication as the ultimate target of natural selection (Hamilton, 1964). This 'selfish gene' type of imperative[15] might generate different optimal patterns of behaviour, not just in the infant, but also in the mother and the mating youth. An argument could seemingly be made out that all three of Ainsworth's classifications might be adaptive at the phylogenetic level to particular different environments of evolutionary adaptedness (EEAs). This also suggests that the internal space called attachment might not be understood in terms of its cognitive/affective *content*, models and the like, either normally secure or 'anomalous', but in terms of an adaptive capacity to generate ecologically appropriate attachment models, and their behavioural correlates, in response to the mother's behaviour, which would be determined by a particular EEA and its socio-economic conditions (Belsky, 1999b; Belsky *et al.*, 1991; Simpson, 1999).

Whilst Bowlby recanted in the second version of the first volume of his trilogy (Bowlby, 1982), neither he nor Ainsworth or most of their intellectual heirs seem ever to have got to grips with what this meant for Ainsworth's theory of individual difference, of the normativity of the 'secure paradigm', of the responsive mother as a salient feature of the EEA and of secure infantile attachment as 'nature's state of grace' (Belsky, 1999b: 144).[16] Curiously, this development did not seem to be seen at the time, or since, as a major source of concern to attachment theorists.

Whilst Jay Belsky later attacked founders of the theory and their followers for intertwining 'evolutionary theory and mental health theory ... in a way that violated the former while reifying the latter' (Belsky, 1999b), it was, in fact, an attack on Ainsworth's work at the psychological level, back in the 1970s, which the consensus in the literature seemed to feel as a heavier blow, historically marking the nadir of attachment theory. This was a critique by behaviourists (Maccoby and Feldman, 1972; Masters and Wellman, 1974, for example), who argued that that they could find no stability over time or context in the index behaviours of the different forms of infantile attachment. Besides this, the more simplistic, maternal deprivation version of Bowlbyism was dealt a blow by an exhaustive empirical examination of the evidence by a UK psychiatrist and epidemiologist, Michael Rutter, in a book called *Maternal Deprivation Revisited* (Rutter, 1972). This academic setback occurred at much the same time as the place of attachment theory in the field of 'therapeutic familialism' was becoming more precarious, in response to several other factors. First, the importance of its sister psychoanalysis declined in psychiatry[17] and was under attack as a form of intervention in the personal social services, as being time-consuming, expensive and with dubious outcomes (Wootton, 1959). Second, social learning theory burgeoned as a theory of development and socialisation (Bandura, 1963, 1977) academically and in the training of the psy professions and, third, behaviourism, or brief, task-centred, quasi-contractual work, became, at least in the textbooks (Reid and Epstein, 1972, 1977; Reid and Shyne, 1969), the intervention of choice in both probation and social work – congruent as it was with a growing managerialism and Taylorisation of work in the helping professions (Cohen, 1985; Howe, 1992; Sheldon, 1978). From another angle, feminism, too, mounted a fierce critique of

Bowlby's theory and methods,[18] whilst radical social work increasingly emphasised the wider socio-economic and community, rather than close interpersonal, context, of their clients' family problems.

At this point attachment's career as an internal site on which a wound could be inscribed looked a little bleak. Its two essential requirements, an internal space as an expression of a metaphor turned theoretical construct and a normal/abnormal dichotomy to define the presence of harm, both seemed problematic. Despite these setbacks, however, it was as an academic, mid-level theory of individual ontogeny, in which this cognitive/affective phenomenon called attachment is inscribed on an inner life, that this theory survived and eventually flourished, although the evolutionary basis of its mental health assumptions has never been very sure. Further, it was Ainsworth's work on individual difference, this two-pronged approach, this 'clinical' interest in understanding not just the development of the normal or 'secure' child, but also the mal-adaptive or 'insecure' forms of behaviour in the infant in the strange situation, which, although it was regarded with suspicion by many contemporary psychologists, formed much of the basis for the growth of the theory in the second period.

Looking ahead in time, the nature of attachment as an internal site was to be established and the concept greatly elaborated and, second, a crucial development at an empirical level was to enhance its contribution to mental health theory, so that the uncertain evolutionary basis for its normative assumptions seemed not to matter. Ainsworth's work was an elaboration and systematisation of Bowlby's original work, which of course started as an explanation of the pathological at the ontological level. It was to become the dominant theory of normal child development, flourishing in the psychology departments of North America, but, as a mental health paradigm, it also gained a foothold in departments of psychiatry, as the other side of the coin, attachment as part of a theory of developmental psychopathology, held its own alongside.

7.3 Attachment, period 2, 1978–1999: An academic work in progress

Background

The 1970s were a decade of complex and contradictory change in the UK, shadowing earlier movements in the USA. Contractionary responses to the first oil crisis across the capitalist world effectively ended the post-war, Keynesian, full-employment consensus, creating a large army of the 'structurally' unemployed and changing gendered employment patterns into the future as effectively as feminism. It was this latter movement, starting in the UK at the beginning of the decade, which was the first to substantially question inequity based on biological assumptions of difference. Others followed, creating what have been called 'new political movements' together with the politics of injury as a new form of radicalism, which paradoxically relied on the idea of a state with strong legal powers to right these inequities (Brown, 1995). At the same time, the traditional anti-authoritarianism of the left passed to the radical right with the rise of the New Right movement over the 1970s. Emanating from the USA, where writers such as Charles Murray greatly influenced UK thinkers in the Conservative party and beyond,[19] it culminated in the political success of Thatcherism in 1979 and the near dismantling of the traditional British Welfare State. Welfare dependency was out. Individual rights and responsibilities were in, and the family of public policy was yet again reconstructed. A newly responsible, autonomous family was to be the bastion of privacy between the individual and the state.

Of course, the corollary of this large area of private responsibility was a powerful law and order initiative in the policing of its boundaries. In relation to the family, this came in the form of monitoring and intervention in cases of suspected child abuse. For the UK, this discovery of child abuse as a social problem of supreme importance also occurred in the 1970s, and dealt an equally powerful blow to therapeutic family work. Problematic children and families were increasingly scanned for risk, not for welfare considerations, and therapeutic resources were diverted to the investigation of allegations and the ensuring of physical safety. Any therapeutic work was justified as 'preventative'.

Whilst elements of attachment theory were surely present in the newly 'responsibilised', self-regulating desires of parents – images of the sensitive and responsive mother and the secure child abound in the child-care advice of the period[20] – the late 1970s and 1980s marked a low point for attachment both in the academic literature and as a basis for any clinical work which was done on both sides of the Atlantic. The story of its survival and eventual turnaround is located in the USA, and not in the realm of professional practice but in a series of university psychology departments across the country. Here it was established by its followers as a viable part of a growing scientific enterprise which was also adaptive to the prevailing policy discourses, as it was to the more immediate demands of the psy knowledge industry. What is suggested here is that the latter produced a momentum for theory development which enabled attachment academics simultaneously to produce an increasingly well-researched account of normative development, and also to theorise the psychological effects of abuse and adapt to the pre-vailing language of risk. Progress was made both in policy arenas and in statistical medicine or developmental psychopathology, the last of which came to dominate the attachment literature in the third period.

Samples from the World of Science database show an astonishing growth in attachment-based publications, a near threefold increase from 1975 to 1978, (the year of Ainsworth's book on her research), then an increase of 1000 per cent to 1999, (the year of another milestone publication).[21] To some degree this was because, as with any psycholog-ical subject, it was part of the vast and exponentially growing literature for psy professionals and academics and an explosion of interest in child development and state funding for research to go with it. But even within a general growth in psychological and psychiatric liter-ature, it also seemed to acquire more than proportionate importance and acceptance as a basis for the study of child development ('the dominant paradigm') and for intervention in individual and family lives. It acquired its own eponymous journal, *Attachment and Human Development*, in 1999. Major psychological, psychiatric, psychoanalytic journals (and a social work journal in the third period) have all pro-duced special issues on attachment theory as a way of understanding this development and its disorders and generating, it is claimed, effec-tive psychotherapeutic interventions.[22] Of course, this may reflect the perceived inadequacies of its rivals, as behaviourism failed to address intrapsychic and developmental processes. It was also the result of the work of a dedicated and close group of (mostly) US-based researchers which grew massively over time. They pushed the implications of the initial work of Bowlby and Ainsworth, with their encouragement, from a study of maternal deprivation to a study of normal infant/mother inter-action. The thrust of the group's research was to establish the empirical basis for a theory of development over the whole life-cycle in which the early attachment bond is seen as the prototype for all subsequent close, affective as well as romantic relationships, including the relation-ship between therapist and patient. Further, in the maladaptive version, insecure attachments are seen as a risk factor, at least, for all subsequent interpersonal difficulties and psychopathologies (Belsky, 1999a; Sroufe *et al.*, 1999).

A family and its theory

What was the immediate academic ecology to which attachment the-ory had to adapt? It has to be said that in the USA, social conditions in the 1980s and 1990s, in the form of academic and state interest in the child and family, growth in psychology departments and state funding for research – especially scientific research – all favoured its flourishing. Here, the original, egalitarian ideals of the Kennedy era, producing the war on poverty and the Headstart program, also extended to the founding of the National Institute for Child Health and Development (NICHD) by the president's sister. Although this 'elite liberalism' was replaced by a more conservative contraction of welfare spending in the 1970s, it was also accompanied by a political determination to tackle child abuse or maltreatment and to provide a continued investment in mitigating the developmental consequences of poor parenting. The same institutions persisted, and the study of child development remained a funded endeavour in all subsequent administrations, with psychologists becoming more involved in politics in the 1990s (Phillips and Styfco, 2007).

Not only were conditions favourable for research in attachment and child development, but the nature of the theory itself and the social organisation of its knowledge workers within the academic community contributed to its survival – and reproductive fitness. As stated, the theory, as first conceived and constantly worked on by Bowlby, was a marriage of different approaches to the development of behaviour patterns in different individuals. It combined an explanation at the level of ultimate cause, in terms of their phylogenetic origins and evolutionary history, middle-range causal accounts of ontology and the development of particular attachment styles and empirical studies of the proximal environmental conditions that trigger the attachment system. Thus, it is seen as a unique theory, one of broad coverage, as well as flexibility, with a potential for illuminating many different fields of academic endeavour, amongst which are evolutionary biology, developmental biology and ethology, developmental, cognitive, personality and social psychology, psychiatry, developmental psychopathology, neurophysiology and neuropsychiatry and, lastly, several different forms of psychotherapy. Whilst it was suggested earlier that one reason for the theory's decline is that its multifaceted nature pleased nobody at first, as the academic conjuncture changed, and administrative pressure on academics to keep up publication rates increased, it is possible that it became deeply attractive to many different mates.

What is more, the relative success of attachment theory in thinking about the normal and pathological development of children cannot be separated from the efforts of the academic entrepreneurs who advanced the theory and its position in this area. One could say that not only did the theory survive and flourish in an increasingly favourable ecological niche, but that the agents of its reproduction displayed all the mutually supportive network and reproductive co-operation of a family. Looking at the academic attachment community from the outside, one sees, as with any such, a labyrinthine network of connections, but, since they all seem to stem from the intellectual collaboration of two people, the network has a decidedly dynastic appearance, with intellectual exogamy (and some real endogamy!), as well as rivalrous splits in the second and third generations. This structure provided its members with the sense of continuity and belonging furnished by any family.

As is appropriate, the various memoirs and tributes to Mary Ainsworth on her death in 1998 paint a picture of her as the perfectly responsive, nurturing mother to her group of graduate students, as Bowlby was their intellectual father on the other side of the Atlantic. The two wrote and exchanged ideas and articles frequently. Bowlby's letters, written in a fine hand in green ink, were read out by Ainsworth to her assembled students and they would send him papers for his generous comments (Main, 1999b). Ainsworth herself, on retirement from her professorship at the University of West Virginia, abandoned her own research and spent the rest of her considerable working life encouraging and supporting her own students and others in the development of her theories. They, with all the independence and resilience of the securely attached, went forth and peopled the psychology departments of North America, keeping in touch long distance (Main 1999b). Karl and Karin Grossman of Regensburg University, who became Ainsworth's academic foster-children, recall pleasurable family reunions at the yearly Society for Research in Child Development meetings in the USA (Grossman and Grossman, 1999).[23]

These children were upwardly mobile in terms of the hierarchies of the academic establishment and, from the beginning, had no trouble attracting research funding from the NICHD or directly from NIMH, where they sometimes started their postdoctoral career as fellows. The collection of their work (with one or two notable exceptions, and some significant additions) in the monumental *Handbook of Attachment*, edited by Jude Cassidy and Phil Shaver (Cassidy and Shaver, 1999), has something of the size and authority of a family bible. It is a testimony to the volume, breadth and depth of the output of Ainsworth's original psychology students and their collaborators in developmental psychology and to how the theory was expanded – first, to make it relevant to others in neighbouring fields and ensure its continued academic reproduction, and, second, to re-establish its relevance to the changing policy conjuncture.

In this task, the original theories of Bowlby and Ainsworth gave this new generation several problems. First was the power of the behaviourist attack, which questioned the existence of this inner space on the basis of index behaviours. Second, was the problem of how this space could be observed and described clearly and its stability over time and dyadic context established empirically, when displayed within all the complex maturational, intergenerational and social processes that development allowed. Certainly, the research data did not conclusively support this stability either within a lifetime, between generations or over different relationships (Fonagy, 2001). Third, the clinical distinction between normality and pathology of the A, B and C classifications of the Strange Situation were a little controversial and blurred. The solutions found to these difficulties resulted in some important changes to how the inner space of attachment was understood and accessed, as described below.

Attachment as an organisational construct

It was Everett Waters who saved the attachment construct from the attack of the behaviourists. There is a consensus in the attachment literature that one of his most important papers was an answer to the critique of Ainsworth's work. Written with Alan Sroufe, his doctoral supervisor, this restored attachment theory to academic respectability, taking on the so-called misunderstandings and misapplications of the theory by trait and social learning theorists, current at the time (Maccoby and Feldman, 1972; Sroufe and Walters, 1977a). The critique reduced attachment to certain index behaviours, and, when these were not intercorrelated or stable over time, dismissed them as useless. Answering it was no easy task, given the complexity of infant–caregiver behaviours which are not specific to the attachment system. These could change over social context and over time with changing capacities, an equally complex learning process and the intervention of many other social variables, including what is often referred to as 'the ecology of the family.'[24]

Sroufe and Waters re-emphasised Bowlby's conception of attachment as a behavioural control system with informational inputs, following Ainsworth in moving the emphasis of the goal of the system from proximity towards exploration and therefore felt security. Thus, the affective aspects of the attachment tie were said to mediate the informational inputs to the system, explaining the infant's preferences for her caregiver under stress and accounting for the cumulative effects of repeated or long-term separation. They reaffirmed attachment as an organisational principle, embedded in a piece of social interaction, which was also embedded in its wider social context (Sroufe and Walters, 1977a).

Thus they restated that what Ainsworth knew she had observed and classified in her Baltimore sample was the qualitative functioning of the attachment system, which is 'normatively integrative and flexibly adaptive', rather than a quantitative behavioural phenomenon, which measured the strength of a drive or a trait (Ainsworth *et al.*, 1978).

Strange situations and the importance of naturalistic observation

Of all Ainsworth's students, Waters was the one whose work seems most concerned with the respectability of attachment theory as science, with impeccable statistical method and methodology, the clarification of the theoretical constructs and the linking of theory to empirical observation (or validity). He did his best to keep the tradition of mother–infant observation alive with his Attachment Q-Sort research (Posada *et al.*, 1995; Vaughn and Waters, 1990; Waters and Deane, 1985), emphasising in a later paper that the observation, presumably over time, of 'secure base behaviour' in the naturalistic setting of the home was the 'gold standard' to which all other observational or questionnaire data in attachment research had to be tied (Waters, 2002). The trouble was that, in establishing stability over time and relationship, naturalistic observation had its limits.

The fundamental task of Ainsworth's students in restoring the credentials of attachment theory in the scientific community had been to confirm its empirical basis by replicating the (pilot) Baltimore study results on other, larger samples. They established its stability by extending the studies of mother–child interaction to an older age group. Mary Main set up new large-scale study and a flourishing centre for attachment research on the Berkeley campus of the University of California, where she revisited her sample and established a positive relationship between infantile attachment classifications and those at the age of six (Main and Cassidy, 1988). Her partner in this, Jude Cassidy, worked similarly on a five-way classification of strange situation reunions for a sample of kindergarten children in West Virginia with Bob Marvin (Cassidy and Marvin, 1992); and the Grossmans (mentioned above) replicated the Baltimore study in Bielefeld in Germany, though finding less stability over time (Grossmann *et al.*, 1981). But, for obvious reasons, there was a limit to what observation could show with older age groups, even if this was at all practical.

A further difficulty was the inconvenient fact that research based on the 'gold standard' over all ages gave highly variable results and would continue to do so. As Peter Fonagy put it at the turn of the century, 'observation alone has not yielded convincing results for a factor which mediates security over time and relationship.' (Fonagy, 2001) Moreover, if Ainsworth's experimental evocation of this inner space failed to generate consistent results, this implied one of three responses – or all. Either the means of accessing it via its effects should be changed, or the inner space, the theoretical construct itself, needed to be modified or, finally, the original empirical results needed to be carefully reworked.

The adult attachment interview

The way forward on a change of access was the first of Mary Main's two major contributions to attachment theory, which took the theory back, nearer to psychoanalysis, as well as forward to its life-cycle and inter-generational possibilities.[25] In the empirical work on the mother–child dyad, there was a problem with showing a strong correlation between mothers' observed responsiveness and the infants' Strange Situation status. Also, establishing the attachment basis of this responsiveness in the mother by interview seemed impossible, as adult recall of attachment experiences in childhood is not necessarily stable or reliable. Main made a methodological move, in the title of her 1985 article with Nancy Kaplan and Jude Cassidy, 'to the level of representation'. The move was, indeed, to the use of an interview schedule, but it was one with a difference. She did elicit an account of each mother's own childhood (Main *et al.*, 1985). However, this she interpreted and scored, not simplistically by its content, but by how this content related to its narrative style and, above all, its coherence, flexibility and the ability it revealed to reflect on the feelings and motives of self and others. She also noted the respondent's co-operation with the interview process. She called this schedule the 'Adult Attachment Interview' (AAI) (George *et al.*, 1985; Main, 1995). What she thought she had found access to was not the mother's attachment status as such, but to her 'state of mind with respect to attachment' (Main, 1996: 240).

Like Ainsworth, Main used a three/four way typology to classify her results, which Ainsworth was the first to notice mapped almost perfectly, both conceptually and empirically, onto her own Strange Situation classification of infant behaviour (Grossman and Grossman, 1999).[26] Of course, the AAI was still grounded in Waters' 'gold standard' of mother–child observation and there seemed to be some correlation between the maternal 'state of mind with respect to attachment', as revealed by Main's interpretation of the interview, and the observed responsiveness of the mothers in her sample. This pinpointed some of Ainsworth's 'developmental anomalies' that produced 'unresponsive mothers;' the connection was not sufficiently strong, however, to explain the powerful, almost dramatic association Main found between maternal AAI score and the attachment classification of the infant, even when the AAI was assessed before its birth – nor has it been shown to be stronger by further research (Hesse, 1999; Pederson *et al.*, 1998). The AAI itself has proved to be robust over time and independent of the obvious mediating variables, such as IQ and discursive style. Its strongly, quite unusually predictive, results, in terms of the Strange Situation behaviour of the infant, had been reproduced in at least fourteen other studies by 1995 (Van Ijzendoorn, 1995).

This impressive predictive power of the AAI ensured its success as a measure. It was extended to teenagers and even down to articulate six year olds in the Child Attachment Interview (Target *et al.*, 2003). What is more, it joined the Strange Situation classification as the main plank of attachment research and enabled it to branch out from mother–child observation in a number of ways. Crucially, attachment theory joined most other heavily researched versions of psychological difficulty, psychopathology, abuse, violence and the rest, as having a life-cycle and intergenerational aspect, making it a powerful framework for thinking about social policy towards the family. Since connections or causality across the dyad and across time remained something of a mystery, this was even more fertile ground for the growth of funded psychological research, in both developmental, affective and cognitive psychology (Fonagy, 2001).

'From your mother's arms to your lover's arms'[27]

The discourse analysis of the AAI might be seen as an even more methodologically dubious venture than the interpretation of the Strange Situation test, from a strictly scientific point of view – Main called it her attempt to 'surprise the unconscious' (George *et al.*, 1985; Main, 1991: 141), to come across the inner life by stealth – open as it is to the subjectivity of a meaning giving and appraising observer, and to the ins and outs of an elaborate cognitive/affective theory of mind, set out in her key article on metacognition (Main, 1991). And perhaps as a reflection on the reliability of the AAI method and its interpretive nature, all researchers who employ it have to undergo an expensive training from a strictly controlled list of licensed trainers. The schedules and procedures were and are still kept in the form of unpublished papers in the Berkeley campus of the University of California (George *et al.*, 1984, 1985, 1996).

However, this move to the interrogation of adults opened the way for another methodological addition to the techniques used to explore the attachment space, this time in the form of a straightforward Adult Attachment Style (AAS) self-report questionnaire which elicited information, not on the past but on the respondents' current romantic relationships. Of course the AAS and the AAI clearly occupy separate methodological domains; they measure different things and they refer to different behavioural systems or attachment orientations, between which, despite initial claims (Hazan and Shaver, 1987), the 'source and degree of overlap…remains controversial', according to Chris Fraley (Fraley, 2006). The AAS is more in line with a schedule from positivistic psychology than the AAI and was imported from the study of adult relationships in personality and social psychology, where Phil Shaver was one of the first and most prolific psychologists to apply attachment theory to 'adult pair bonding'. His acceptance into the attachment family was crowned with joint authorship of the mammoth *Attachment Handbook*, mentioned earlier (Cassidy and Shaver, 1999) and proved to be another significant step in the development of attachment theory, its applications and attractiveness as an area of enquiry.

Shaver's methodological contribution to the field was most appealing to research students and to epidemiologists. Studies in the area of adult attachments could float free of Water's 'gold standard' of naturalistic secure-base observation,[28] or the AAI interview which was still validated by the latter. Questionnaire data of a self-report variety was possibly not more reliable, but a great deal easier to administer and interpret. The AAS provides attachment scoring on two dimensions, instead of categorisation, at both the adult and the infant level; a more usable, statistical version of the old system of classification and the schedules are straightforward and available to all (Brennan *et al.*, 1998).[29] That slice of inner life called attachment was no longer an area of complex affective and cognitive processes only amenable to technicians of the dynamic and their trainees; it was now amenable to study by anyone through a simple questionnaire. What is more, this change seems to have been accepted by the specialists. Despite the strict control of AAI use, Mary Main herself, in an epilogue to the Handbook, looked forward to the possibility of merging the different adult attachment schedules, or at least to the use of both together in a coordinated form (Main, 1999a).

From content to capacity: The internal working model

Main's move to metacognition also opened the way to dealing with the modification of another crucial piece of the theory: Bowlby's Internal Working Model (IWM). This cognitive model was seen to structure the attachment control system, and perhaps to account for the persistence of the secure-base phenomenon for any dyad over time and between generations, as well as the possibility of its generalisation by an individual to other important affective relationships. Such a model is obviously open to endless elaboration and reformulation, especially about the way that affect and arousal mediate the availability of attachment information, as well as being part of it. It has, indeed, been criticised as a theory of such generality that it can explain anything (Belsky and Cassidy, 1994; Hinde and Rutter, 1988; Rutter and O'Connor, 1999; Thompson and Raikes 2003). The reformulation of this model required by disappointing empirical research data was also tackled by Ainsworth's students and their collaborators (Bretherton *et al.*, 1991; Bretherton and Munholland, 1999; Main, 1991; Main *et al.*, 1985; Sroufe, 1996). It is seen, in its revised metacognitive form, as in the domain of the AAI, not as cognitive or affective *content* of the mind – templates narratives, scripts and the like – but as the *capacity* for coherence of discourse, reflexivity and empathetic evocation for the thoughts and feelings of others. Using this revised version of an inner space, current research seems to indicate a positive connection between infantile security and its adult forms and between maternal security and the attachment classification of infants.[30]

The emphasis on mental capacities, privileged structural models of psychological functioning and, thus, opened the way for two further lines of development in the third period. First was a re-engagement with psychoanalysis, which is Peter Fonagy's project (Fonagy, 2001), and second, an increasing interest in the way such models are mirrored in neurophysiology by structural models of brain development, in which neural connections of increasing complexity are made and maintained in interpersonal communication (Siegel, 2001).

Attachment and psychopathology: Or D is for Danger

It is in the epidemiology of psychopathology that Main's work in Berkeley had one more crucial developmental outcome for attachment theory, also built on its life-cycle implications, and bringing it right into line with the mainstream policy preoccupation with child abuse, its intergenerational predictors and consequences. She re-examined the classification of children in Ainsworth's original Strange Situation test. As in Baltimore, roughly 13 per cent of her Berkeley study sample did not fit Ainsworth's three-way classification and fell into the dustbin category that was called 'unclassifiable' in the earlier study (Ainsworth *et al.*, 1978b). Main and collaborators pushed Ainsworth's clinical interest in individual difference further, by studying these unclassified children in detail, following their sample up at the age of 6 years and finding the category size stable. They classified these children as Type D: their behaviour in their natural surroundings and in the Strange Situation test was described as disorganised, unpredictable and signifying confusion and disorientation (Main and Solomon, 1986). At first, they interpreted their mothers' AAIs as tending to show 'unresolved' mourning for an attachment figure, 'or some other traumatic experience' (Main and Solomon, 1990). Later, in a key article in 1990, Main and Eric Hesse famously linked disorganised attachments in infants to 'frightened or frightening caregiving,' in which children, in the second case, were faced with the dilemma of fearing the figure whom they wished to approach for comfort in times of distress, or worse, saw the attachment figure as the cause of the distress (Main and :Hesse, 1990).

Subsequently, the emphasis of attachment research shifted from child observation to the implications of the theory for child and adult psychopathology. There is some suggestion in the literature that the Type A classification is associated with internalised problems – anorexia, depression, 'disorders of inhibition or compulsion' – and Type C with 'acting out' problems, acute anxiety, behaviour disorders, obsessional behaviour and the like (Crittenden, 2000: 244). Further, Pat Crittenden has now produced a 'Dynamic Maturational Model' of attachment based behaviour in adults which encompasses all forms of psychopathology within the original three-way classification (Crittenden, 2000). However, it is, crucially, the Type D classification, rather than the two other insecure categories, avoidant and resistant, that was shown over a series of epidemiological studies in the 1990s robustly to predict psychopathology in later childhood and adulthood (Carlson, 1998; Lyons-Ruth and Block, 1996; Lyons-Ruth and Jacobvitz, 1999; Lyons-Ruth *et al.*, 1991, 1996, 1999; Ogawa *et al.*, 1997).[31] Disorganisation in childhood is especially associated with the diagnosis of attachment disorder, as described in the children we met at the start of this chapter. It is also predictive of psychosis (Dozier *et al.*, 1999), dissociation (Liotti, 1992; Main and Morgan, 1996), and severe personality disorder in adults (Fonagy *et al.*, 2000). Empirically, it provides much stronger continuity over time, generation, and dyadic relations, than other attachment classifications. Not only has it increasingly become the focus for attachment research, it dominates treatment-oriented thinking about attachment also (Holmes, 2001), for it strongly predicts the most problematic diagnostic categories, socially, in the regulation of the dangerous and the criminally insane.

With this development, attachment theory began to spread from the psychology departments of North America and Britain and into the psychiatric and psychotherapeutic clinics, to be described in the next chapter. What is more, Type D classification has become almost uniquely applied to those whose attachment figures were not only unresponsive to the danger of their children, but its actual source, that is, to the subjects of parental maltreatment. It consequently spread further to welfare services in the USA and the UK, especially those dealing with the fostering and adoption of children whose infancy had been blighted by parental abuse or mental illness. A type D attachment, generating disorganised behaviour, is, par excellence, the psychological and invisible site of a wound, whether there are also outer wounds or not.

Further, attachment theorising has been taken over, in this area, by the culturally dominant language of danger and risk, of which Pat Crittenden is a prime user. She writes of her 'Dynamic Maturational Model of Attachment, tied to risk assessment and treatment,' as 'particularly relevant to individuals who are in at-risk situations, have been exposed to danger, display disturbed or mal-adaptive behaviour, or are diagnosed as having a psychiatric disorder' (Crittenden, 2009). The theory that it employs is based on the maturational development of 'individual strategies for dealing with endangerment' and the therapy this implies enhances the quality of life for 'endangered, endangering, and vulnerable humans.'

Besides this, these 'internal somethings' called attachments are reified in DOH publications, as they became 'faulty' or 'damaged' (Cleaver *et al.*, 1999: 58, 76 and 65). Also, the language is further ratcheted up, during the 1990s, by a strand of psychiatric and neuropsychiatric literature on the effects of maltreatment on the neuroendocrine system: diurnally early high levels of cortisol found in type D children are thought to have a destructive effect on the body's stress regulatory system.[32] Thus, Bruce Perry's article on the effects of maltreatment on the brain is entitled 'Incubated in Terror' (Perry, 1997) and Allan Schore writes of 'traumatic relations' and 'traumatic attachments' (Schore, 2001b). In the discovery of Type D, trauma and attachment join forces, as did violence and emotional abuse in Chapter 6, as an attachment seems to take on the characteristics of its threatening or destructive environment. Psychological harm is thought to be caused to the infant, not just, as in trauma, because of excessive fear itself, not just, as in the original attachment theory, because of the unavailability or unresponsiveness of the mother in the face of an exogenous threat to the mother–child system but – worse than that – by a threat from the very person the child would go to for protection; an endogenous hazard – an abusive mother – danger in the very heart of the family.

The rats of NIMH: A postscript[33]

This theoretical elaboration of an internal psychological space called attachment as a response to attacks by behaviourists, and the necessity to validate empirical results, dominated mainstream attachment research during this period. It had its critics, who deplored this drift from Bowlby's so-called environmentalism towards a more psychoanalytic psychologism, and a small space was allowed in the Handbook (Cassidy and Shaver, 1999) for an even more extreme critique of attachment as primarily a psychological construct. The challenge was based on a more detailed examination of animal behaviour, appealing to the biologism of attachment theory, which had, in its inception, been based on evolutionary explanations of cross species instinctive behaviour and not much examined at that time (Polan and Hofer, 1999; Suomi, 1999). The concept of attachment was not the monopoly of the psychological department.

The work in ethology or developmental biology over the 1990s, particularly by Myron Hofer and Steve Suomi, whose subjects are rats and rhesus monkeys respectively, not only confirmed cross-species continuity of attachment behaviour, which was just assumed by Bowlby. In studying and elaborating it, they also challenged the 'circular' notion of attachment as a theoretical concept, used as a psychoanalytic or organisational construct to explain certain universal forms of behaviour – from which it is also inferred. This concept, they claimed, is merely a metaphor. Alternatively, they located attachment deep in the sensory experiences of its mother for the foetus and neonate in the relevant species. For example, it was through tactile, auditory, olfactory, gustatory and visual experiences that the fundamental physiological regulation of the rat pup was achieved (Kraemer, 1992; Hofer, 1995). The distress of the pup at the loss of its mother was not an invisible wound but the physical discomfort caused by the loss of these regulatory processes, rather than any process which is symbolically mediated (Hofer, 1996; Polan and Hofer, 1999).

Attachment as a physiological regulator enlarged its scope from being confined to a protective system for the management of fearful arousal to other aspects of the mother–child relationship. As Main pointed out in her epilogue to the Handbook (Main, 1999a), this work indicates that Bowlby had actually underestimated the ultimate importance of mother–infant interactions, in the sense that they are not only effective in protecting the infant from external dangers ('the outer ring', as it were), but in actually promoting life. They also regulate independent internal homeostatic systems, temperature, hunger etc., as well as arousal, even prenatally. She quotes a recent review of neurophysiological experiments on monkeys (Amini *et al.*, 1996):

> The nervous system of social mammals is constituted by a number of open homeostatic loops which require external input from other social mammals for internal homeostasis to be maintained. The manner in which this input is achieved is through social contact and bio-behavioural synchrony attained with attachment figures... In this view, then, the attachment relationship is postulated to be a crucial organising regulator of normal neurophysiology for social mammals (cited in Main, 1999a: 866–867).

In defence of her own work, however, Main is also careful to note, incontrovertibly, that what actually constitutes 'attachment' is 'a matter of semantics' (1999: 866). She might have added that the equation of 'social' with 'ventral' contact between mother and child – human or rat – might also have its semantic problems (Burman, 2008). Peter Fonagy has argued that this move is not necessarily reductionistic, however; it elaborates and extends the biological basis of sociality that Bowlby and Ainsworth had always assumed. He points out that Hofer's work on the cross-species basis for attachment does not preclude the development, in the human case, of the highly complex, flexible and reflexive mental life of the new IWM, described above. Indeed, it is the basis for its dyadic creation (Fonagy, 2001). Consequently, the loss of this relationship is not just damage to an inner space, which is reactive to extreme distress or fear, however prolonged, as in the disorganisation and psychopathology literature. It is, also, the loss of a homeostatic regulator with the consequent dislocation of the infant from the pathway of emotional and cognitive development it supports. It is the loss of the opportunity for human sociality, as it was meant to be.

7.4   Conclusion

This chapter has offered an account of the way in which one theoretical construct, a metaphor for a close dyadic relationship, was inscribed on the inner life of an infant and seen to organise his behaviour in a way which would affect his negotiation of social relationships far into the future. It was a theory of how this 'internalised something' might be shaped by a mother figure into producing adaptive or maladaptive behaviour which might presage healthy-normal, or unhealthy-abnormal outcomes for the child in adulthood. The emergence of the theory has been set briefly in its historical, policy, academic, social and even interpersonal environment, which was divided into two periods. The first covers the postwar work of John Bowlby, the birth of the theory out of a cross between psychoanalysis and evolutionary theory, and its development by Mary Ainsworth. The second covers the work of Ainsworth's students in establishing the theory within the North American academy.

This history, in both periods, has been dominated by three different themes. The first is the slightly uncertain relationship of this hypothesised inner space, called attachment, to the various ways in which it can be observed or measured, and how its nature has been adjusted over time accordingly, as the stringency or complexity of the measurement requirements have been heightened and then relaxed. The second theme is the theory's clinical assumptions. It is noted that a strong theory of normative development and secure attachment behaviour arose from an initial study of conditions determining pathology, or the wounding or dislocation of this inner state. This normal space is still envisaged by its difference from the pathological, however. And these two theories, of the normal and the pathological, therefore developed side by side, although by the end of the time frame of this chapter, the pathological had outstripped the normative in one of the most powerful developments of attachment theory. This was the theorisation of the psychological and thus developmental consequences of all forms of child maltreatment – in the words of the book title with which this chapter started, 'The Primal Wound.'

The third theme is the problematic grounding of the theory's clinical assumptions about infantile behaviour and its inner correlates in a theory of evolutionary adaptedness, so that what is normal and desirable becomes 'natural' and what is pathological is maladaptive. In the first period, this seemed to sit uncomfortably with developments in evolutionary theory, but was developed in the second period in an examination of cross species attachment behaviour in which the attachment concept is extended to describe physiological regulation in nursing dyads, as its biological base. This signals forward to developments described in Chapter 8 in which the neurophysiological basis of infant sociality is increasingly emphasised in academic and professional research and therapy, as 'the social' seems to acquire a whole new meaning.

8
Risk and resilience: Attachment at the turn of the century

8.1 Introduction

The development of attachment as a theorisation of abuse and neglect and its psychopathological consequences has meant a dramatic revival in its fortunes. The previous chapter showed how Bowlby and Ainsworth's original concept was elaborated by the latter's students in US university psychology departments over the 1980s and 1990s, and how this and other transformations were achieved. By the turn of the century, however, attachment was also subject to a promotional diaspora across an array of organisations throughout the Anglophone world, Israel, Spain and South America. These were aimed at parents; at professionals working with children and at governments administering their welfare. What is more, it seemed that this theorising was not just addressing abusive parenting, which seemed to fit with current social preoccupations and government agendas: it was also addressing the way in which normal parenting had been talked up as being predictive, with a high level of certainty, of emotionally well regulated individuals who were in some way protected from temptations to deviancy and the debilitating stress of risk society.

Besides this, the protection against socio-economic stressors or deviant tendencies were more and more seen as emergent from complex statistical models, where correlations were privileged over intricate causal connections located in a psychological space. Whilst these causal theories developed in complexity over the second period, in this third period, up to 2006, they can be seen to decline in importance and what was increasingly developed in the programmatic rhetoric of certain writers on attachment were hypotheses, not so much at a psychological level, but at the level of the brain and the neuroendocrine system – inscribed in a biological as well as a psychological space. This space was increasingly theorised over the 1990s in the heavily funded academic research project of neurophysiology. Attachment theory was only marginally involved in this growth, but it was a development to which its ideology of natural healthiness was eminently adapted and for which enthusiasm among parents and professionals was marked. Thus, in this period, attachment theory is more complicated and multifaceted than ever.

What is more, the policy conjuncture around this third phase of attachment theory's history was complicated by the UK Labour government's attempt at a 'third way' between postwar paternalism and the seeming realities of the global market, to which the New Right had exposed the national socio-economic system. The decline of Thatcherism and the electoral victory of the Labour party in 1997 saw so much legislation and organisational change directed towards the agencies of childcare and education, both private and public, that the results continue to be somewhat confusing. There were, however, certain clear, broad changes. First, this was the most extreme level of policy activism towards children by any UK government and, while much of the New Right rhetoric about the limits of the state, and about individualism and the strengthening civil society, remained, this seemed to have involved, paradoxically, a dramatic spread in the disciplinary role of the state under a rationale of partnership, the mixed economy of care and its audit and regulation. The second change is that, whilst children have always been of social interest as adults-in-the-making – as 'becomings' rather than 'beings' – no government before has made this 'social investment' attitude to children so explicit in policy terms (Esping-Andersen, 2002; Giddens, 1998).

Third, in its Third Way ideology, the New Labour government produced something of a contrast to the social policy behind the postwar welfare state. The consensus in the social policy literature is that, while the optimistic narrative of the postwar Labour government was about protecting individuals and families from the inevitable inequities of a market system of increasing international connectedness, the discourse of New Labour was about the affordances of the market, supporting individuals to integrate flexibly into its processes and opportunities. It was in this way, supporting people in work and in enterprise, that it tried to fight poverty, rather than by straightforward redistribution of income. It was the potential of children as economic participants, as well as citizens, which was to be protected, nurtured and realised – both by parents and other socialising institutions, in partnership with the state.

Moreover, this was especially true for those groups of children selectively targeted by policy as being at risk of economic or social exclusion. These were young offenders; poor children on sink estates; the 'looked after' or the abused, those whose excluded state constituted most risk to economic production as well as social reproduction. Such an ambitious project required an intense programme of both tutelage for wayward parents and training for children in transferable social and IT skills and, most important, in the necessary condition for success – the robust capacity for emotional self management.

Fourth, and as a consequence, mental illness was cast, subsequently, as a mounting social problem or crisis both in the USA and in the UK, and not only in its knock-on effects on delinquency and dangerousness. As the diagnosis of depression was undergoing a meteoric career of expansion, it was the effects, in social as well as economic costs, of perennial unhappiness on parenting, employment and 'quality of life' in general (and on childhood in particular) that caused concern. In the language of the new economics of positive thinking (for example, Layard, 2008), individual happiness had become not just a capital good for the investment state, but also a consumption good for its citizens.

A fifth aspect of social policy under New Labour, according to John Clarke (2004), was that, in spite of the new political movements, which still provide a countervailing impetus in the form of identity politics, the old biologisms of postwar social policy seemed to have persisted into the turn of the century. Difference was still largely perceived as having a natural rather than social basis or construction, which meant that many hierarchies based on race, gender or sex were still implicit in social policy as *naturae rerum*. Individuals and families were still implicitly treated as the biological, atomistic units of consumption and enterprise in a market which was as much a feature of the natural world as the Great Lakes. Families, in their composition, were also, like individuals, implicitly psychobiological phenomena, private arrangements, shielding their members from wider socio-cultural structures, in whose politics they did not partake –'havens in a heartless world'.

Clarke also suggests a new biologism for the turn of the century, 'practising under the sign of the gene' (Clarke, 2004: 63). Whilst there is, as yet, little sign of this new biologism, in the form of the genome project, in the discourse of social policy makers, the structural effects at the academic level are profoundly felt in the funding and growth of the biological and human sciences compared to the social sciences. This is certainly felt in the relatively confined world of attachment theory and child development in the form of new knowledge and expertise at the level of the brain and the neuroendocrine system. Equally influential is policy interest in psychological explanations of delinquency,[1] disturbance in the population, and in the optimal emotional development of children, all of which ultimately relate to the goal of integration into the global market for all citizens. It was suggested in the last chapter that it was the complexity and flexibility of attachment as an academic theory which allowed its flourishing in the US psychological academy. In this chapter, it is suggested that it was this same flexibility which allowed its flourishing in the protean policy environment created by New Labour in the UK at the turn of the century.

What follows is a sketch of attachment-based literature up to 2006, and its application in the world of psy professionals, based on the issues suggested above: the first part comprises attachment as a theory of developmental psychopathology; the second looks at attachment as a theory of therapeutic intervention, when prevention fails. The third relates to attachment as a theory of stress mediation and its possibilities for self-regulation and resilience in the developing individual; the fourth surveys the use of attachment theory in the vast preventative efforts of the state and non-state organisations and, finally, the fifth looks at the relationship of attachment theory to the burgeoning of biological science as a research enterprise of wealth and power. In the case of attachment theory, this new biologism is confined to the development of the neurophysiology of the emotions in the 1990s, 'the decade of the brain' – an enormous subject of great complexity which can only be touched on here. This discussion in five parts is prefaced, below, by a brief description of the organisational structure of the attachment world.

8.2   Attachment research and its application

Organisational growth

After the burst of attachment research activity in the 1980s and 90s, by 2006 the basic work of Ainsworth's students and their associates had been continued and widened by the next generation into the new areas already touched upon. A summary of the attachment literature, produced in this same year by a search of the World Of Science (WOS) database, gives some indication of the way the range of application of the theory broadened.[2] The provenance of the articles in the sample shows an even spread of university psychology departments, right across the USA (and a scattering from the UK), as Ainsworth's trainees from the Universities of Maryland and West Virginia have colonised other academic locations and produced their own trainees or enthused co-workers with the attachment message. Typically, in the States these clusters of attachment theorists form 'Attachment Laboratories', as at the University of New York, Stonybrook (SUNY); or the Adult Attachment Laboratories at Davis and the University of Massachusetts; and the Attachment, Personality and Emotion Lab at the University of Illinois. Each has its own collaborators and research staff working on joint research projects.[3] More important for the spread of attachment theory beyond academic bounds is the recent proselytising work of some of the major departments which have set up organisations to liaise with and train psy professionals interested in the relevance of attachment theory to intervention with children, families and adults. For example, there is The New York Attachment Consortium, a project of an independent charity, The Center for Mental Health Promotion, which brings together the work of four New York-based universities including SUNY and the Yale Child Study Centre.

Emanating from all these centres, on both sides of the Atlantic, internet information seems to be an endless source of attachment material, not just on the theory but on attachment-based advice to parents and on the availability of treatment, should the worst happen. Furthermore, attachment-based therapy centres, many of a private nature, have sprung up, mostly across the USA. These variable websites, although they invariably claim to be 'evidence based', show a broad spectrum of ways in which attachment theory is presented, from those close to the academic source of the theory who present themselves as strictly in the 'Bowlby and Ainsworth tradition' (henceforth known as the BAT) and those which are more demotic and proselytising. For example, the institutions range from the International Attachment Network (IAN) – part of the BAT, originally founded in the UK, with offices now in London, Barcelona and Washington and publisher of the already mentioned journal, *Attachment and Human Development*, to the Buenos Aires based website of the Attachment Research Centre, to the US based *personalityresearch.org/attachment.html* 'Great Ideas in Personality,' to the Kansas Attachment Center... which seems to have a staff of one (Cross, 2007).

Therapeutic approaches vary accordingly, from relations-based psychoanalytic therapy, in which attachment theory is used to inform principles and practice, as in the very respectable IAN member; the Bowlby Centre in Spitalfields, London; or the more recently founded Centre for Child Mental Health, also in London, which offers 'integrative therapy' for children;[4] from middle ground of therapies for children and families with diagnoses, like the Dyadic Developmental

Therapy purveyed by Daniel Hughes in the USA, to Attachment Therapy and those organisations devoted to training and treating by its more radical principles – most abundant in the USA.

However, attachment-based therapy and training is not just a feature of private health provision on either side of the Atlantic. In Britain, the use of attachment theory in the NHS may be a highly variable phenomenon, dependent on professional discretion[5] but it is now well established as part of a State legitimated and promoted knowledge base about children and families, which is to be used by all professionals when assessing them for service provision (see below). It is therefore not surprising that it is also entrenched in handbooks, such as the series produced by the British Psychological Society (Herbert, 1996)) and in training courses for social workers at all levels of specialisation. Typical would be those provided by the Centre for Research on the Child and Family at UEA, where David Howe, for many years its director and author of several books on the subject, has observed social workers' enthusiasm for this approach and hunger for a coherent framework to underpin their work (Personal communication). Attachment is one of the few theories that seem to provide a framework for intervention in childcare issues (Daniel *et al.*, 1997).

Besides official social work education and training, there are a plethora of lecture programmes and conference papers on attachment theory and therapeutic practice, provided by individuals affiliated to or bought in by non-governmental organisations and subscribed to by an array of different psy professionals. Their success is no doubt assisted by the fact that the whole attachment field is populated by charismatic speakers on both sides of the Atlantic, the USA providing a series of 'roadshows' which visit Britain.[6] However, perhaps the major promoter of attachment theory is Sir Richard Bowlby, son of John Bowlby, who, after working for thirty years in the UK as a scientific photographer, retired in 1999 and has taken to studying and lecturing on his father's work. He has already written a biography of Bowlby Senior and made a teaching video on attachment theory and its application. Not surprisingly, he chairs major attachment organisations and features as keynote speaker at conferences and training days on this subject, an emblematic reminder of its origins.

Attachment as a theory of developmental psychopathology

Compared to the vibrant world of professional attachment therapy and training, the academic attachment scene has faded a little. It is not that the literature is waning in quantity. On the contrary, it is multiplying exponentially. But one glance at the World of Science [WOS] sample, mentioned above, gives an eloquent picture of how attachment theory has changed. There are very few articles in this sample developing the theoretical nature of the internal psychological attachment construct or its life-cycle implications; these seem to be well accepted, as is the use of self-report questionnaire data. Moreover, with this methodological tool well established in the field, studies of the effects of attachment styles, particularly in adults, are pushed into new areas. At the same time, the original technical evolutionary definition of the term, as relating to a particular set of behavioural systems, primarily in infancy, is becoming somewhat diluted.

By far the majority of the articles are concerned with the development of individual psychopathology and/or delinquency in relation to attachment insecurity or disorganisation, and are those most in tune with the perennial law and order concerns of government. However, the more totalising, theoretical accounts of attachment insecurity as the developmental source of all psychiatric diagnoses (for example Crittenden, 2000) are missing – and the literature is criticised for this lack of theory (Raikes and Thompson, 2005). What prevails is the language of epidemiology, in which questionnaire-based assessments of attachment status for captive samples, of all age cohorts, are correlated with a series of outcomes. Low attachment score, seen as a psycho-social variable, has become a risk factor for whatever disastrous outcome of an individual or social nature the researcher is investigating. It is not surprising that insecure attachment styles, as a measure of dyadic and, also, individual affect regulation, are discovered to be predisposing factors for both 'internalising' as well as 'externalising' psychiatric problems (Moss *et al.*, 2006; Ronnlund and Karlsson, 2006). These include depression (Eberhart and Hammen, 2006; Murray *et al.*, 2006), anxiety (Bogels and Brechman-Toussaint, 2006; van Brakel *et al.*, 2006), anorexia (Troisi *et al.*, 2006; Zachrisson and Kulbotten, 2006), bulimia (Elgin and Pritchard, 2006; Ferguson, 2006), obsessive compulsive disorder (Aaronson *et al.*, 2006; Nuckolls, 2006), psychosis (Berry *et al.*, 2006; Onnis *et al.*, 2006) and, most significantly, borderline personality disorder (Chessick, 2006; Minzenberg *et al.*, 2006), as well as more general behavioural problems such as bullying and violence amongst adolescents (Banyard *et al.*, 2006; Marini *et al.*, 2006) or substance abuse (Brook, 2006; Kotov, 2006).

In this way, attachment theory has become part of the growing discipline of developmental psychopathology, the eponymous journal of which was founded in the early 1990s and edited by Dante Cicchetti of Rochester University, a major academic in this field. The journal generally features a systems model of development towards psychopathy in which human intrapsychic processes at different levels of analysis interact, within the constraints of gene expression, with environmental variables, also at different levels (family *v*. wider culture etc.), and all with multiple feedback loops. The developmental nature of the model brings an added complication as it incorporates the notion of developmental pathways, dynamic processes in which development at time *t* is dependent on development at time $t - 1$, so that if the model is to be fully specified, it needs to capture the drivers of change over time, that is, 'course and cause' (Cicchetti and Sroufe, 2000: 259). In such a model, which arose out of earlier epidemiological studies of the relationship of schizophrenia to various hypothesised causes (Rutter and Quinton, 1984; Sameroff and Fiese, 2000), individual variables such as attachment score are subject to 'multifinality', or being a risk factor for many pathological outcomes, as well as 'equifinality', in which several different risk factors may increase the likelihood of one outcome (Rutter and Sroufe, 2000). Thus a low attachment score as a consequence of abuse and neglect and representative of some inner cognitive/affective state becomes just one vulnerability factor for an array of poor outcomes (Cicchetti, 2007: 168).

In this way, attachment theory itself is an explanation for development in which the attachment construct is no longer *the* driver for behaviour and behaviour change. Attachment has become a highly probabilistic paradigm.

As a research approach which uses a model designed to reflect the complexities of actual human development in statistical form, much writing in this area is programmatic as well as descriptive of pieces of current research. Although these latter each add to the general picture as informational inputs to the model, they are, in sum and at present, inadequate to reflect the systemic nature of a process in which everything is seen to depend on everything else – let alone one which can be so punctuated and the small parts so dissected that the causal mechanisms over time underlying each relationship are known and their effects measured.

Attachment and psychotherapy

Cicchetti, Toth and Lynch wrote, as early as 1995, a long article called "Bowlby's dream comes full circle", in which they celebrated the fact that Bowlby's original attachment theory, as an account of the causes of psychopathology, had been revived, after attachment had become for some time predominantly an account of normative child development

(Cicchetti *et al.*, 1995). But Bowlby was a clinician, with a clinical theory, and might have found the *Developmental Psychopathology* programme a little disappointing. He may have thought, as some others, that the theoretical development of this internal space called attachment has been attended to, recently, a lot less than the refinement of statistical method (Pollak, 2005). For this produces a general systems model whose relationships may be suggestive in terms of preventative state policy but is certainly not directly helpful therapeutically. Here, some sort of relatively simple guiding theory of the mechanisms of development and change is necessary, which cannot necessarily wait for the statistical elaboration of a highly complex approach to pathology.

However, another glance at the WOS sample shows other sources for the necessary clinical theory. It is, paradoxically, provided by attachment as normative development and a basis for the affective content of human relationships over all ages and social environments (and extended to place as well as to people, as a burgeoning geographical, planning literature theorises (Alegre and Juaneda, 2006; Molcar, 2006; Sivaramakrishnan and Vaccaro, 2006). Most important for intervention, as an account of affect, it is also seen as a way of enlightening the relationship between psychotherapist and patient: a reframing of the traditional psychodynamics of transference and counter-transference, with more emphasis on nurturance and the containment by the therapist, as attachment figure, of the most disturbed excesses of her client (Shine, 2006; Shorey and Snyder, 2006; Steckley, 2006).[7] Crucially, it is presented as a more hopeful means of engaging those with severe personality disorders (notoriously difficult) in the process of treatment (Fonagy and Bateman, 2006; Levy *et al.*, 2006; Wang and Tian, 2006). For what attachment's theorising of affect development suggests, both neurophysiologically and psychologically, is a form of therapy that is different from the pharmacology of conventional psychiatry or the psychoanalytic talking cure, although it may have piqued the curiosity of psychoanalytic practitioners. Here, images of the right sort of sensitive mother and theories about the vital developmental importance of the emotional right brain and its implicit non-verbal communication function come into play, in an approach to therapy in which the nature of the emotional relationship between therapist and patient – a fresh enactment of the mother–child relationship at a profound emotional level – is paramount. Further, it is claimed, this can form the basis for a later coherence in a patient's formerly confused and disorganised accounts of attachment experiences, without ever addressing these at all (Holmes, 2001).

It is not surprising that this form of attachment theory suggests a similarly non-verbal affective type of therapy for children, sometimes based on play, as in the 'Theraplay' method, aimed at helping family relations through 'attachment-based play'.[8] For whilst it is evident that attachment theory has much to say about the ontogenesis of the depressive personality as the insecure resistant infant, as well as the developmental aetiology of some of the more extreme and dangerous disorders of personality in adulthood as the result of attachment disorganisation, it is on childhood that much popular, professional and governmental concern and effort is concentrated, especially on the policy-targeted group of 'Looked After Children' (Howe, 2006a; Steele *et al.*, 2006). It appears that many of these children with extreme difficulties seem to have acquired the psychiatric diagnosis of AD or RAD (as described in the introduction to Chapter 7), and amongst these, children who are fostered and adopted are highly over represented, as are specialist organisations like The Post-Adoption Centre in the UK, the Adoptive Family Counseling Center or the Parents' Network for the Post-Institutionalised Child, in the USA.

The area around AD and attachment therapy seems a confusing one from the output of attachment websites. This disorder is sometimes described as rare, compared with other psychiatric disorders, at approximately 3–4 per cent of the population (Rygaard, 2007) or sometimes as prevalent at 'over 60 per cent of children in foster care and adoption' (Cross, 2007). It seems it is also a disorder which needs highly expert diagnosis (APSAC, 2006), so as not to confuse the RAD child with the ADD and/or the ADHD child or the autistic child. Above all, it must be distinguished from 'the bipolar child' – a phenomenon which, it is claimed in a book for parents, is much more common than ever imagined (Papolos, 2002). It is claimed, in the promotional literature of a course run by the Post Adoption Centre 2004/5 (called 'Working with severe attachment difficulties (AD)'), that these disorders 'present very specific issues which require very specific intervention and parenting' (Post Adoption Centre, 2005). But this intervention seems like an almost impossible task when the specificity of AD is so elusive. The Cascade Centre for Family Growth, Orem Utah, for example, treats all the problems listed under its client group of 'children with severe behavioural disorders and issues' with 'attachment therapy' – which is simply defined as 'helping children and parents develop strong attachments and bonds'.[9]

It would appear, however that this process of help is, also, far from simple. The Attachment and Child Development website describes this therapy as 'a unique synthesis of many different techniques' (IACD, 2006). It lists individual psychotherapy; body work; family therapy; biofeedback; neurotherapy; quantitative EEG; massage; movement therapies; alpha theta training and acupressure – the whole gamut. What is more, this synthesis appears to be specific to the idiosyncrasies of the particular institution involved. A compendium of methods from a UK-run organisation called Keys,[10] claiming to practice attachment therapy, differed markedly from the above. It advertised the practices of regression and 'physical holding' (Keys' quotation marks) and 'alongside holding, psychodynamic play and art therapy, drama, sand tray work and creative arts therapies that include time lines, memory journeys and life story work, clinical hypnotherapy, counselling, psychotherapy and EMDR (Eye Movement Desensitisation Reprocessing)' (Fearnley, 2006).

One practice that these different versions of attachment therapy do have in common, is encouraging parents to hold their child, sometimes for long periods, sometimes against their will, sometimes under a blanket in a process of 'rebirthing'. Most mainstream psychiatric and psychotherapy professionals are careful to dissociate themselves from this approach to therapy, after the horrible death from suffocation of ten-year-year old Candace Newmaker in a clinic in Evergreen, Colorado, USA, under such therapeutic ministrations. The case became a cause célèbre in the US and the subject of an APSAC investigation and report (APSAC, 2006), as well as the trigger for practice guidelines laid out by the American Academy of Child and Adolescent Psychiatry in 2005.

'Security in an insecure world'

The statistical approach of much of the attachment literature in the 2006 WOS sample also addresses the second concern of government identified here. It takes us directly into the probabilistic world of risk and risk management, where it not only uses the concept of risk factors for a particular harmful outcome, but also throws up the idea of 'anti-risk factors' which can mediate favourably the effect of adversity, creating what has come to be known as 'resilience' in this literature. This is the other aspect of attachment theory which is important to social policy. For attachment has also become a theory of stress mediation, as a significant group of the 2006 sample shows. Attachment security mediates coping in general (Fivush and Sales, 2006), maternal adjustment to childbirth, including postnatal depression (McMahon *et al.*, 2006), the care of a disabled child (Howe, 2006b; Steinberg *et al.*, 2006), including blindness (Adenzato *et al.*, 2006), the progression of dementia in old age (Browne and Shlosberg, 2006; Dupart, 2006), the effects of diabetes (Ciechanowski and Katon, 2006; Ciechanowski *et al.*, 2006) and other somatoform problems including cancer (Farge, 2006; Hamama-Raz and Solomon, 2006) and acute and chronic pain (McWilliams, 2006; Meredith *et al.*, 2006a; Meredith *et al.*, 2006b). Most importantly for our current social preoccupations, it seems to mediate the effects on the individual of trauma and 'terror' plus the severity of PTSD. (For instance, 'Attachment and psychological adaptation in high exposure survivors of the September 11th attack on the World Trade Centre' (Fraley et al., 2006) and 'PTSD reactions among children with learning disabilities, exposed to terror attacks' (Finzi-Dottan et al., 2006).

As such, this is a theory which can inform political policy in relation to both children and their adult selves, of a preventative and protective kind. For not only is there an ontogenetic risk from having the wrong sort of mother – the likelihood of developing as a psycho-social deviant directly because of the inadequacy or worse of your most intimate social (and biological) relationship – there is also a risk due to a failure of this relationship to minimise vulnerability to wider socio-economic adversity, which might have very much the same result – a risk of a lack of psychological protection.

Raising the standard

The risks highlighted by attachment theory are not confined to the individual, however. There is another sort of risk which the former implies, namely risk to society in the form of resource consuming antisocial behaviour – distress or deviancy, the newer problems of poor economic performance and political discontent, and the perennial problem of internal law and order are much as they ever were from the 19th century onwards. Take the websites of two attachment-based preventative parent support organisations, the UK Parents in Partnership – Parent Infant Network (PIPPIN) and the US Marycliff institute in Maryland, linked to Surestart and Headstart respectively, and definitely in the BAT: The British version, PIPPIN, emphasises 'the heavy cost attached to children who are not securely attached, both in human and financial terms, to their families, social services, schools, healthcare and sometimes the prison service' (Pippin, 2007). The USA-based Circle of Security is more floridly explicit: in an article on its Spokane website, entitled 'Changing history one baby at a time. Therapists attempt to resurrect parents' ancient wisdom', Larry Shook writes: 'Mounting evidence clearly implicates inadequate early care-giving as a root cause of exploding prison populations, teenage pregnancy, runaway divorce rates, drug abuse. . . .'

(Shook, 2001: 1). Apart from paedophilia and gun crime, he gives us a complete compendium of our social fears.

All these grave risks and threats underlie the enormous government and non-governmental programme aimed at prevention via the advising and encouragement of parents in the art or 'science' of child-rearing. Here attachment comes into its own as a theory of normal child development in a model of healthy affective and physiological homeostasis. The homologies between affective, physiological and political regulation do not need to be pointed out and neither do the links between psychological and state security. The message of these much-used parent-support organisations and their websites, parent-training programmes and parent-support groups is implicitly setting up a standard for parenting, guiding all the anxieties and aspirations which attend this state into a desire for the attributes of responsiveness, sensitivity, 'mind mindedness' and much more, which attachment theory promotes. This is a standard to be maintained against the threat of the worst, if there is too much slippage.

The Spokane website's atavistic appeal to parents' 'ancient wisdom' nostalgically evokes behaviour presumably thought to have developed in a period of evolutionary adaptedness. Other websites straightforwardly appeal to a simpler utopian state in which parents just do what comes naturally, evoking a close, private and tactile way of life a little suggestive of Hofer's rats in their nest. The Association of Infant Massage, for example, sponsored by Richard Bowlby (Bowlby's son), is part of a flourishing infant massage movement. There are many others: Attachment Parenting International (motto, 'Peaceful parenting for a peaceful world') is a very popular site, decidedly not given the IAN stamp of approval for its much more extreme invocation of nature in the parenting process. Apart from the high level of parental availability and emotional responsiveness, to be expected from any attachment based programme, this organisation, with its network of parenting support groups, recommends the importance of 'nurturing touch', skin-to-skin contact between parent and child; 'baby wearing' and the 'Tummy-2-Tummy' carrying of infants, as well as the controversial practice of co-sleeping and night-time breastfeeding (naturally!) in bed. To facilitate all this, there is a website link to Bella Baby, a commercial seller of baby care and nursing products, for mail order of the Nurse-N-Glow pillow, winner of the 2005 Juvenile Products Manufacturers Association Innovation Award. Ancient wisdom, new technology...and clearly, ancient wisdom, let alone natural instincts, are not quite enough, as the website offers a formidable bibliography of self-help books, videos and DVDs for parents, leaders, professionals and group libraries (API, 2007).

Attachment-based parenting as a standard is not only sold on a myriad private, although often partially state-funded, sponsored or regulated websites. It is promoted further by the official regulatory writings of government agencies, if not in legislation itself. In the UK, for example, the authors of the introductory chapter to the DOH manual, *Assessing Children in Need and Their Families* (DOH, 2000a), started with the importance to such assessment of 'paying attention to attachment for all children, irrespective of their age'. Indeed, 'attachment to caregiver' is scheduled as the first of four 'developmental tasks' for the preschool infant (DOH, 2000a). The accompanying *Framework for the Assessment of Children in Need and their Families* (DOH, 2000b) does little in spelling out how this is to be done (Reder and Duncan, 2001), however, and its successor, the *Common Assessment Framework* (DOH, DfES, 2006) is just as vague. But the training for professionals to accompany these assessment frameworks, bought in by the DOH and then the DfES from a private organisation run by Arnon Bentovim, the distinguished child psychiatrist from GOSH,[11] does have a programme that addresses some qualitative rating of a child's attachments as one of many dimensions of observation and questionnaire recording. It has also, lately, introduced into its services another training programme for the administration of a new 'evidence based', 'research derived interview' to refine assessment of the attachment style of prospective foster and adoptive parents for SW practitioners, or guardians etc (the ASI-AF).[12] The DfES is a good customer for the output of attachment-based research.

A spin off of this official adoption of attachment as an assessment dimension is that the language of attachment is also now universally used in the English Family Courts – part of a standard against which the suitability of parents to care for their children is measured, although there is some doubt as to whether this is a technically accurate or rather a devalued language, with a 'loss of specificity.' For example, Reder and Duncan, suggest that when family solicitors request an assessment of a child's attachment to a parent from a professional expert, they are more interested in the overall parent/child relationship, its emotional warmth, and the child's trust and sense of security, which depends as much on current parental practices, as on the past (Reder and Duncan, 2001). Writing in the same year, Bacon and Richardson thought that the courts looked on attachment 'simplistically, as a protective factor' when judging the appropriateness of parental care, but that, thanks to 'expert witnesses', 'the courts are now coming to recognise that abuse by attachment figures can be particularly damaging. The rationale and methodology for assessing attachment has therefore assumed increasing significance' (Bacon and Richardson, 2001: 382).

The Emotional right brain

The old biologisms permeate much of this more recent literature, in the sense that the assumption of a protective private interpersonal relationship still remains. It is a natural limit which is not permeated by the social and political forces from outside, especially in the idea underlying papers on attachment security as a buffer against stress. In terms of the new biologisms, there are surprisingly few papers in our WOS sample on the neurophysiology of the emotions and the physiological ways of understanding the attachment process. Such a gap reflects the state of play at the end of the 1990s, (dubbed by President George Bush senior as 'the decade of the brain'), when the *Attachment Handbook* contained a negligible number of articles of this type.[13] However, Mary Main's epilogue on the ways forward for attachment theory tentatively acknowledges the contribution of neurophysiology and brain science to the study of attachment, and thinks it may possibly have future potential. Indeed, this rapidly developing field is referred to, if only briefly and with careful caveats (but also with increasing frequency), in most current attachment based articles. It is seen as, potentially, providing empirical back-up and hard scientific legitimation of the theorised mother–child interaction at the level of the brain and the neuroendocrine system, which is further claimed by some as the origin and site of what is metaphorically called the attachment bond (Polan and Hofer, 1999; Hofer, 1995).

This new 'scientific' support is held to contribute greatly to the elaboration of the questionable connection made by Bowlby and Ainsworth between what is psychologically normal and healthy with what is natural. Before, they invoked nature at a distal evolutionary level to account for the assumed genetic programming behind the development of secure/insecure infantile attachment behaviour, the immediate causal mechanisms being seen as psychological. Now, in the new marriage of attachment theory with neurophysiology, biology accounts for behaviour at the same level as the psychological, also manifest in an experimental context, through neurophysiological measurement rather than behavioural observation. The pressing question is: Is biology, or should biology be, privileged as an account of the causal mechanisms whereby an intimate environment can create the developmental trajectory for a child, with effects that last over a lifetime?

There was always a tension between the ethological and psychodynamic origins of attachment, and this question highlights the difficulty of the theory with the status of the inner space on which the different forms of attachment are inscribed. The interesting consideration is, first, whether this new neurological angle on attachment has caused the internal and essentially psychodynamic or affective/cognitive site called attachment to revert to a metaphor or an epiphenomenon on a biological base, which is now open to more direct, more scientific observation. Or, second, is the study of neurophysiological processes simply a new way of envisaging activity in this internal space, supplementing the old methods of 'gold standard' behavioural observation and the self-report on cognitive and emotional behaviour summoned by questionnaire? Has the 'gold standard' moved to careful observation of just another form of behaviour – what the brain does – this time written into myriad neural networks, in which a version of an inner life can be read and its wounds registered?

This is a question which the denizens of the US and UK developmental psychology departments seem to be approaching with some caution. All would agree that the approach has certain seemingly incontrovertible foundations based on the great strides made in brain science over the 1990s, and driven by advances in techniques of psychophysiological measurement and functional mapping of the brain – EEG, PET and fMRI.[14] In particular, in the discourse of attachment writers, certain incontrovertible 'findings,' which strongly link neurophysiology to attachment theory, are acknowledged. The first is the development of a brain science which allows for a theory of human behaviour as driven by an emotional as well as a cognitive space. This was the emergence in the academy of a subject called affective neuroscience, the title of whose landmark book by Antony Damasio, published in 1994, *Descartes' Error*, speaks for itself (Damasio, 1994). The aim of its practitioners, notably Damasio himself, Jan Panksepp in the USA, and Mark Solms, in the UK and South Africa, is to reverse the bias of neuroscience toward cognition or linguistic brain activity (seen as largely left hemisphere) by mapping the emotional brain (right hemisphere) and also by investigating the unconscious functioning of the mammalian brain (the limbic system and the brain stem) and their relationship to the later acquired (human) cortical regions. All this has reversed the 'corticocentric' nature of neuroscience, and emphasised the importance of the early years of infancy which witness the rapid maturation of the right brain (Panksepp, 1998; Solms and Turnbull, 2002).

The second finding is the empirically established plasticity of the brain, which allows for the relational development of the maturing neurophysiological system, called epigenesis. Such knowledge changes the old perception that development is an interaction between a fully formed genetically programmed brain (biology) and its relational environment (society). As in attachment theory, the biological and the social (interpreted a certain way) are seen as becoming indistinguishable. The development of brain structure, functioning and organisation not only affects, but is affected by, experience, which produces changes in patterns of neuronal and synaptic connections. So, the partially random nature of gene expression in experience-independent maturational processes (Rutter and Sroufe, 2000) is modified by experience-expectant processes of neural pruning within specific maturational period (as in the first 18 months of life, or in early adolescence). Equally, experience-dependent processes of synaptogenesis respond to new environmental information, in which the individual brain is seen as self organising in a unique fashion (Cicchetti and Curtis, 2006). All of these processes are thought to interact and differentially affect how each individual develops. Thus, for example, the cytoarchitecture of the cerebral cortex is shaped by genetics and the environment, in a process in which corticogenesis should be seen as a process of self-organisation guided by self-regulatory mechanisms (Cicchetti and Curtis, 2006).

Third, most research to date has been conducted on animals, for obvious reasons, and on people with already established brain damage or neuronal malfunction. More valuable to the studies of neuroplasticity, the population of abused but otherwise normal children has presented itself as a perfect source of subjects for a growing number of research studies which suggest that early experience of maltreatment or trauma has particular neurological effects, especially on the neuroendocrine system. These are said to cause disruptions in basic homeostatic and regulatory processes essential to the maintenance of optimal physical and mental health. Specifically, variations in maternal care have been found to alter the expression of genes whose function is to regulate behavioural and endocrine responses to stress and to modify synaptogenesis in the hippocampus, as well as to influence the responsivity of the hypothalamic-pituitary-adrenal (HPA) axis to later life stressors (Levine, 1994; Meaney, 2001) cited in (Cicchetti, 2007: 169). It seems to be accepted that the wounds inflicted by maltreatment can be observed experimentally, through neuro-imaging or physiological measurement.

Based on this foundation, the discipline of developmental psychopathology has opted for the first alternative in answer to our question about the status of neurophysiology as the basis of observed behaviour. Not surprisingly, it has embraced a neurological approach to human psychological problems as part of its interdisciplinary approach to risk and resilience in child and adult development. Lip-service is paid to systems theory, in which, Cicchetti writes, 'ideally, investigations must direct their energies toward an examination of multiple levels of analysis within the same individual [sic]' (Cicchetti and Posner, 2005: 570). These 'multiple levels' are, in theory, all variables in a complex cybernetic model of development, in which social, cognitive, affective and neurological processes all co-evolve in some sort of holistic relationship. Nevertheless, the language of later articles and special editions of *Developmental Psychopathology* (for example, Cicchetti and Cohen, 2006; Cicchetti and Posner, 2005) on the contribution of affective neuroscience to its academic and policy project subtly changes. The psychological level joins the social in becoming 'psychological and social experience'; that which mediates external information and transforms it into experiential input into the self organising brain (Cicchetti and Curtis, 2006). The brain is the biological base, the driver of behaviour and behavioural change, which in its environmental adaptedness provides the explanatory or causal mechanism through which this experience is internalised and structured into persistent, programmed responses to external stimulus over time (Cicchetti and Curtis, 2006; Pollak, 2005). So any internal psychological space merely mediates the brain's co-evolution with its environment and, in this construction, the basic organising locus of attachment behaviour has moved to a biological site.

Perhaps this is why mainstream attachment theorists seem not to have embraced neurological insights wholeheartedly – and this, despite Hofer's work, described in the last chapter, as well as Alan Sroufe's reconfiguration of attachment theory as a theory of (initially dyadic) affect regulation (Sroufe, 1996), which opened up the subject to neurophysiological inputs (mostly, as above, from animal research) as well as their socio-behavioural or psychological correlates (Cassidy and Shaver, 1999). For, in such works, the neurochemistry of arousal and its regulation seems fairly uncontroversial, even if measurement is not without its set of methodological problems.[15] Significantly, Mary Main in her epilogue to the *Handbook* has cautiously opted for our second version of the relationship of neurophysiology to attachment theory as just one more means of observing the effects of a form of inner life, which may, or may not, yield interesting new information (Main, 1999a).

In this article, what Main was specifically interested in accessing and observing was the workings of the dynamic unconscious, just as she had been in the construction and interpretation of the AAI, years earlier. The question was, with this new source of information could she examine what appeared to be the dynamic mechanisms of defence and repression? This concerned the behaviour in the individual difference tests that she and her colleagues had interpreted psychodynamically as forming a defence behaviour avoidant of emotional expression in the Strange Situation test (what Bowlby called 'repression in the making' (Bowlby, 1969)) – and, also, an inability to recall or unwillingness to address (by implication) negative events in childhood in AAI interviews. Could such behaviour be shown, by dissonant measurements of emotional arousal or brain functioning, to be indeed repression? Alternatively, in the latter case at least, could they be shown to be due to failures of memory because of impaired neural function – in other words, perhaps not repression at all? Likewise, could such impairments be correlated with the interview scripts of those of a disorganised classification, showing narrative incoherence and confusion?

The answers she finds in the research data are not altogether clear (Main, 1999a, b). Experiments using readings of Strange Situation infants' cortisol levels show only that those infants that appear stressed in this situation – distressed, confused, and so on, as in the group of disorganised children – have higher post session cortisol readings. Since cortisol is known as the 'stress hormone' it would be hardly surprising. Avoidant children (in some experiments) appear to have the lowest cortisol levels, although raised heart rate (Sroufe and Walters, 1977b), so the assumption has to be that they do precociously down-regulate arousal – although whether this should strictly be defined as defence is another matter. In the case of the AAI and memory difficulties, the latter were shown by existing research to be more likely, also, in disorganized (D) respondents, often those who have been abused (Nelson and Carver, 1998). For example, loss of working memory may be due to damage to the prefrontal region because of long term stress and raised cortisol levels.

Main also wonders whether differential asymmetry in the activity of brain hemispheres, found in infants and also adult respondents tested with EEG for temperamental difference, map onto the dismissive versus the preoccupied AAI script as left versus right dominant. Whilst abjuring the 'dichotomania' of the past, she notes research which suggests that 'the left side of the brain typically subserves positive emotions' and the right side their negative. (Main, 1999a: 674; Springer and Deutsch, 1997). She also cites evidence that might suggest poorer memory retrieval in a left dominant, dismissive AAI script rather than dynamic defence (Wheeler *et al.*, 1997).

All this is speculative however, and may, according to Main:

> yield no more than an interesting instance of cartography... That is, finding neurological correlates to already mapped behavioural and discourse patterns may or may not provide additional insights into mechanisms and leverage points for clinical intervention. (Main, 1999a: 856)

Certainly, given the agreed plasticity of the brain and the 'use it or lose it' rule for brain growth and development, there are some chicken and egg problems with causality here.

Main may have been wise in saying in 1999 that, as yet, neuroscience may contribute no more to attachment theory than can be gleaned from psychological techniques of observation and interview schedules. Allan Schore, however, a leading and prolific proponent of the neurological approach to psychological health and wellbeing seems to have no such doubts. He is the academic who has done most to connect affective neuroscience to attachment theory and to communicate his approach to therapeutic practitioners (though his part in the BAT is questionable). Not only does he make connections between the researchers and the professional players but also, in a way, mediates the distinction between the first and second versions of attachment's relationship to neurobiology and the status of the inner life. As a UCLA based psychotherapist, he still identifies with the psychoanalytic world, but, less cautious than Mary Main, he simply equates the Freudian inner world of the split self, id, ego and super ego, with the structure of the brain. In Schore's writing and lectures, the Freudian unconscious simply *is* what he calls the emotional right brain, as both function the same way in laying down the child's earliest experiences of his environment in an unconscious form which will influence all his subsequent psychology and behaviour. The Freudian unconscious can be mapped, it seems, and its dysfunctional aspects made visible. What is more, the life-span effects of the stored attachment experiences seem to signal a return to a form of determinism (Schore, 1994, 2000, 2005).

Besides this, Schore produces a curious reversal of the roles and status of the conscious ego, which negotiates with the external social world of the individual and is amenable to psychological study through observation and self report, and the unconscious id, which is only to be glimpsed in the esoteric interpretations of the psychoanalytic couch. If the right brain is the id, then the left brain is cast as the ego in a process in which not only does 'dichotomania' seem to have re-emerged, but the totemic language of left brain/right brain seems structured on a set of highly evaluative binary oppositions. Panksepp himself talks about 'the emotionally deeper, more sincere right brain' and the following list, gleaned from Schore's writings, gives the feeling that Descartes' error has been somewhat overcorrected:

Good	Bad
Right brain	Left brain
More connected to the body	Less connected to the body
Deeper	Higher control
Animal brain	Human brain
Ancient	More evolved
Emotional	Rational
Non-linear	Linear
Non-verbal	Semantic
Implicit	Explicit
Sincere	Insincere
Authentic	Inauthentic
Spiritual	Temporal

and so on (Schore, 1994, 2001a). There is something deeply puzzling about this line-up. It is as if his elision of mind and brain creates a set of paradoxes. It seems to suggest, for example that the left brain, associated with conscious knowledge, language and therefore culture, is not to be trusted as an object of scientific observation. Meanwhile, the emotional right brain is more natural, more real and more authentic, less contaminated by the tricky enlightenment world of language and reason and is, therefore, more amenable to observation and study by a natural science, whose epistemology is totally alien to it.

What is more, an upside-down version of the super-ego also seems to emerge in Schore's work. His most powerful, attachment related point is that in the first two or three years of life, when the right brain experiences an exceptional growth spurt, 'reciprocal affective transactions within the mother–infant dyadic system are influential in its emerging structure' (Schore, 1999: 51). This is incontrovertible; no developmental biologist or neuroscientist would disagree. But having emphasised the deepness, sincerity and authenticity of a right brain unencumbered by language and culture, he goes on to claim that interactive affect-regulating events, 'right hemisphere to right hemisphere affective transactions between mother and infant' (Schore 1994), act as a mechanism for the '*social* construction of the human brain' (my italics).

This reference to the social is puzzling until it is made clear that, again, the social is just interactive, and not even person on person, but 'a relationship with another self, another brain' (Schore, 1999: 51).

What begins to be suggested is that out of the neural connections and hormonal systems which subserve affective ties between people, a new version of the social and indeed, the spiritual and the moral, is emerging. Decidedly not Freud's version of the super-ego, not culture-specific but universal, not reflecting socio-economic structures, complex social codes, or moral imperatives, but grounded in the biological need of the individual for emotional congress with others.

This is reflected in the new position in social policy that neurobiology is tentatively acquiring. The right brain to right brain emotional ties of mother and child are being expanded. This new message about community and thence society is emerging from the communications between the neurobiological research academy and the wider world of therapeutic professionals and organisations of social and political influence. For example, we learn from an interview given by Dr Dan Siegel soon after the publication of his latest book, *The Developing Mind: Toward a Neurobiology of Interpersonal Experience*, in 2007, that neurobiology has been 'of interest to and utilised by a number of organisations, including the Council on Technology and the Individual, the Sundance Institute, numerous psychiatry departments worldwide, the US Department of Justice and the Vatican' (Siegel, 2007). Alan Schore, himself was a driving force in the production of the 2003 report of the Commission on Children at Risk (produced by 33 research scientists and jointly sponsored by the Dartmouth Medical School, the Institute for American Values and the YMCA of the USA). It goes by the title, *Hardwired to Connect: The New Scientific Case for Authoritative Communities* (American Values, 2003; Will, 2003). The thrust of the report is a recognition of the mounting crisis of poor child mental health, to alleviate which drugs may be 'necessary' but insufficient. Here, by implication, families are also deemed inadequate, so that the wider social environment has to be more favourable to mental health and healing. The child is biologically primed to make affective relationships with others: 'our brains are physically wired to develop in tandem with another's' (Will, 2003: 1). The biochemistry of connection, in the production of the hormone oxytocin in moments of physical and emotional intimacy, promotes bonding in females and lowers male testosterone production, enhancing co-operative as opposed to violent behaviour. What is more, in a startlingly associative leap, this biological need for emotional connection is taken to imply a 'natural need for moral and spiritual meaning' only to be afforded by a supportive and containing community (Will, 2003:2). The biological relationship of the nursing dyad can be extended to infinity. Mother's milk is the new Coca Cola!

Of course there are a whole range of questions in this area which remain to be answered – if they ever could be. For example, how research on animal brains can be applied to human brains (especially in the context of a theory of *evolution!*) How are animals, let alone humans, isolated from the experimental context? How do the not uncontroversial techniques and methodological problems of rendering brain activity into visual information intervene between what is being studied and what is read? This is a particularly difficult question, given the much vaunted complexity of the brain and the imperative emphasised by Jaak Panksepp to avoid 'the neo-phrenological slip' of considering selected regions as providers of large scale functions (Panksepp, 2008). Moreover, how the study of brain relates to mind and to consciousness, how subcortical or unconscious brain activity relate to Freud's dynamic unconscious, whether emotional neuroscience can ever be a continuation of Freud's original neuroscientific project are all matters of lively and sometimes acrimonious debate in a new field called neuropsychoanalysis, where psychoanalysis and brain science meet in a sort of monistic version of self, seen from two different perspectives, subject and object (Solms and Lechevalier, 2002). This is already institutionalised in a series of conferences and a learned journal, established at the turn of the 21st century (NPSA, 2006).

It should be noted that although attachment academics may proceed with some caution in incorporating the contributions of brain science in their work, this has not damped a growing enthusiasm for neurophysiological explanations of attachment behaviour. They inform an increasingly large part of advice to parents and professional training days – hence Alan Schore's successful lectures. For example, Quolkids (2007), a flourishing Australian internet site for information on childcare (20,000 hits every month) has produced a summary of the key findings of 'Infant Brain Research' for parents. In the parental guidance rubric, two influential texts have been adopted by other sites: the first is an unpretentious paperback called *Love Matters: How Affection shapes a Baby's Brain* (Gerhardt, 2004); the second a large glossy manual called *The Science of Parenting*, well illustrated with colourful cerebral mappings and chapter headings such as, 'Parenting your Child's Brain'. The latter, a BMA prize-winning book, is by Margot Sunderland, founder of the Centre for Child Mental Health in London, who has been mentored by Jaak Panksepp over a number of years (Sunderland, 2008).

She is also influential in giving and organising training in this field – significantly, for professionals and parents in the fostering and adoption system, where many of the severely disordered children already mentioned can be found. What is more, after the Tavistock Clinic's annual Fostering and Adoption Conference in November 2006 (for both professionals and parents), interest in the subject was such that the US speaker on the findings from brain development research for the aftermath of abuse and neglect was invited back, by popular request, to give a further workshop.

Like Main, we might puzzle about what this new neurophysiological layer of information adds to our knowledge about these severely disordered children, whom we met in the introduction to Chapter 7. What might it tell those who care for them that they do not know already? An obvious speculation, at a functional or therapeutic level, would be that the invoking of psychopathology or wounds that are invisible often shades into questions of desire, will and moral accountability. On the other hand, psychological harm that is visible, so unambiguously ensconced in medical discourse, legitimates behaviour as symptoms of illness and liberates the players from the problem of blame. But then why does the evidence from psychological and much psychiatric medicine no longer seem quite scientific enough to explain our wounds and their treatment? Why does *bio*-medical information seem so much more convincing as we think about ourselves and our suffering? Can it be that the evidence of the confessional is entirely devalued; that expertise in interpretation is suspicious, and that even the authentic voice is somehow deceptive, as in the work of Alan Schore, cited above? Is it the case that, more and more, direct vision is the preferred register once again; that the use of metaphor has slipped away, and that the making of our wounds visible is the only way to understand them – and ourselves?

8.3 Conclusion

We have examined here the history of one form of harm to an inner life; the variable ways in which this inner space has been thought to be made manifest, and, in particular, its hypothesised relationship to the natural world. This chapter has looked at the more statistical, less theoretical elaboration of the theory in which the discourse of risk and resilience has become predominant and the nature of the theoretical construct of attachment more or less taken for granted, until challenged by the further development of ethology and affective neuroscience.

It has further been suggested that this history has an evolutionary flavour, as the theory which holds this harm in place has developed, adapted to the ecology of the academic and professional environments, and to the prevailing social policy conjuncture.

What has been described here is the advancement of a theory in terms of publications (implying university posts and preferment for its promulgators) and its promotion in non-academic, preventative and therapeutic circles. This is partly a development of a set of ideas, first, within the dialectic of a disputatious but also strategically co-operative academic context and, second, within a wider culture which has become imbued with questions about developmental psychology and psychopathology, the developmental sequelae of child abuse and, above all, about the self in therapy. At the same time, the state and its agencies have become increasingly willing to fund research and preventative public interventions in this area.

In this chapter, it is further argued that the flexible nature of the theory and its hydra-like aspect as a theory of normative and pathological development fitted well with the complicated policies of New Labour. Specifically, it has been argued that 1) attachment theory accommodated to current concerns about risk, security and the regulation of dangerous individuals. 2), alternatively, it accommodated to the needs of neoliberal political organisation for the development of individual citizens as self regulating entities, able to work flexibly in the context of an unrestrained global capitalism; mental health is therefore deemed to be of paramount importance to performance and contentment, itself a necessary base for political stability. 3) All these issues have been approached statistically rather than theoretically, in line with the direction of academic research effort, and money has been directed towards theories and professional interventions which have empirically testable outcomes, distinguishing attachment theory from more conventional psychoanalytic approaches to child development. 4) This approach has led to the rapid development of the techniques of the neurosciences in which the burgeoning neurological version of the theory might be said to have emphasised its tendency to determinism and its construction of motherhood, and, by extension, of community, co-operation and social life in general, as the expression of a force of nature.

This latter seems destined to replace evolutionary biology as the theory directly underpinning attachment's clinical assumptions. What is more, whilst evolutionary biology was used by Bowlby and Ainsworth to complement their dynamic, cognitive affective construct, this new biologism seems to merge with it (or take it over?). For the clear line between the biological and the social, nature and culture, is disappearing. There is a case being made for the invisible wounds of insecure and disorganised attachment becoming, at least in principle, completely visible. There will be no more problems with their interiority, their inaccessibility, their lack of definition and subjectivity. The affective life of the human 'interior' melds with the life of the emotional and mammalian brain and is amenable to the observational techniques of a heavily funded biological science.

9
Conclusion

These chapters have been an exercise in what Foucault called 'historical ontology'. They have tracked the development over time of the idea of an invisible wound into the massive academic professional and administrative apparatus of the psy, operating variously in different countries and in different regimes of truth. They have looked at some of the ways in which a psychic interior has been explored, and at the emerging knowledges that have brought this problem category of psychic harm into being; that have made it culturally prevalent in the Anglophone world at the turn of the century and a powerful legitimation of claims to injury.

The presentation of these narratives of internal exploration and their implications has attempted a neutral and distanced stance. This has not been a social critique. Of course, we are all products of our historical circumstances and some prejudices may have crept into the writing unintentionally: a strong sympathy with the critique of psychological individualism presented in Chapter 1, for example; perhaps some deep misgivings at the therapeutic turn our lives have taken or the belief that the more a form of knowledge of subjects reaches into individual memory and desire, the more it is constitutive of identity, and so the more oppressive it is. But this work set out with a Foucauldian brief, so these prejudices have to be dismissed. They conjure up some enlightenment individual who has negative rights to privacy, freedom from interference and the rest – a scion of western liberalism and, therefore, just another constituted identity. Besides, no-one is interfering with our liberally defined freedom here. The new subjectivities of the psychological, the therapeutic and the affective turn, though convenient to self government in a neoliberal state, have not been imposed on us. How could they be? They are the ways we choose to see ourselves. And the discourse of the wound with its rhetoric of psychic damage, scarring, developmental dislocation and healing is just part of the construction of selves at the start of the 21st century.

Not a social critique, the method here has been genealogical, mapping the discursive, social and political conditions which gave rise to this wound category. As a writing of a history of the present, it traces the ancestors of this idea and presents it as dependent on what went before, arising from historical conditions. In this way, it suggests a time when such ideas were not prevalent or even thought and, so, the possibility that they might never have come into existence. In the words of Nikolas Rose, quoted at the end of Chapter 1, it 'destabilises' or 'de-fatalises' the present (Rose, 1999). As a method which only investigates the ancestors of a particular present, it does not consider all the other presents that are, or might have been, and all their would-be progenitors. It presents neither a full picture of our present nor our past. Nor is it meant to. It is a method designed to challenge or question claims to truth in the world – not in the usual way, by using the rules and methods of the discourse in progress, but by establishing their historical nature, or contingency.

This history or genealogy has been conducted almost entirely at the level of discourse – bodies of knowledge which organise academic, professional, legal and policy texts and their accompanying practices, in which the different versions of psychological harm are inscribed. The three basic versions that I have described, trauma, emotional abuse and attachment disorder, each have different discursive origins and histories. Although, as I have argued, the concept of trauma has migrated across many discursive sites and so links all three and they each support the same regimes of truth: the medical/clinical, the epidemiological/statistical and the administrative/legal, I would not conclude that they have become part of one larger overarching discourse. While such grand epochal claims are tempting, one can recognise an important and undeniable cultural shift towards psychological individualism in the last quarter of the 20th century and yet see the discursive sites of these wound categories as still local and distinct.

What these categories of harm do have in common is that they are embodied in techniques and assessments that have real consequences for self and society. For, amidst all the variations, and the ambiguities and controversies caused by the wound's subjectivity, these different versions are all items of knowledge which are also units of power in 'the making up of people' (Hacking, 1995). They are formulae which can change the lives of individuals to whom they are applied. In other words, what I have described here is the historical development of ways of knowing which have real, though variable, consequences for ways of being. Although this second half of a recursive loop is not something could be pursued here, as stated in Chapter 1, it is assumed, on the basis of an extensive literature in the social sciences, that socially constructed categories do have complex consequences for labelling and identity formation.

Also assumed here is that these categories of knowledge play a part in the making of programmes and strategies of government, in its broadest sense. In Chapters 1 and 8, there is an account of the way that risk of psychological harm and its consequences has played a part in recent governmental preoccupations in the UK. This was intended partly to set out the political conditions for the emergence of these wound categories, partly to establish its present cultural prevalence. As stated in Chapter 1, this account is also suggestive of the particular configurations of power, in the Foucauldian sense, that such versions of knowledge allow or will allow, but a full speculation here would be the subject matter of another book.[1] Nevertheless, as these categories figure in the making up of people and the creation of certain subjectivities rather than others, so they are undoubtedly elements in current formations of power; in the regulation and self regulation of souls in all social spheres and in both the coercive and non-coercive activities of the state.

The genealogy of these concepts is a story set in the dialectic between body and soul as a location for invisible wounds. This was a theme that dominated the study from the start, as the movement from engagement with physical wounds to interest in psychical wounds seemed to reflect Freud's move from the neurological to a psychoanalytic understanding of shock and trauma – achieved, literally, through the use of metaphor and associative thinking, though backed up by a complex theorisation of the internal wound as repressed memory. The major discursive shift from somatic threat to psychic threat, discussed in Chapters 1 and 2, presented itself almost as a linguistic phenomenon, progressing as metaphor progresses from the concrete to the abstract. This then seemed to come full circle in the case of PTSD and nervous shock, as all the conceptual and practical problems involved with abstraction and invisibility made themselves felt and a neurological version of this wound restored its visibility. The first half of this process, with variations, seemed to be repeated in the case of the inward turn in our categorisation of child abuse, only to come full circle again in the story of attachment theory.

However, further study of the changing practices and the thought processes of those involved in these major shifts of discourse, revealed something else – perhaps, in the end, a more important story. This was not about body and soul, and their various combinations, but about the dramatic way these discourses of the wound have contributed to, or been shaped by, how we construe what was traditionally called 'the social' – 'the social' that was posited and theorised in studies of 'the socialisation process'. This 'social' might include a shared language, culture and moral imperatives and the organisation of production and reproduction with all its implications for group stratification and wealth distribution. A human way of being which, at birth, was seen as written onto the tabula rasa of the new child, who was just a bundle of animal instincts, essentially savage.

The story, as it emerges from this thesis, seems to run something like this. In Chapter 2, in which the implications of the invisible wound metaphor as a form of defensive individualism are laid out, a critique of the discourse of wounds is described at some length. In this, it is claimed, 'the social' is reduced to the interpsychic and national upheaval and change to the medical language of wounding and healing. In the straightforwardly medico-legal version of invisible wounds in the next two chapters on PTSD and nervous shock, 'the social' hardly makes an appearance, but then it re-emerges at a local level in the two chapters on emotional abuse. Here, the gradual shifting of the professional gaze from wounds on the body to wounds on the soul is facilitated by consideration of the psycho-social conditions of physical or sexual violence. But 'social' considerations like poverty and inequality were specifically eliminated from accounts of the causes and consequences of all forms of abuse, partly because of prevailing political conditions. This allowed the psychological its full range. Again, the interpersonal stands in for wider social considerations and this seems like a reductive process to which the critique in Chapter 1 could apply.

Then we come to attachment theory, where the interpersonal or the socio-psychological is *embodied* in the primal relationship between mother and child. This mutual relationship of complex interaction is said to be genetically programmed, and therefore natural, and exhibits a range of cross species features. It was Ainsworth who pointed out in her contribution to Martin Richard's *The Integration of a Child into a Social World* (Ainsworth, *et al.*, 1974) that attachment theory turns the old version of 'socialisation' on its head.[2] For the child is not *inducted* into the social world. This world is there in the child already! And attachment problems are this potential for sociality cut off or spoiled. Furthermore, this version of invisible wounds as an essential feature of attachment theory is not undermined by the recent neurological version, as the psychic harm version of PTSD seems to be. On the contrary, the affective turn to neuroscience seems to provide a new holism. The narrative is expansive rather than reductive. The inner space of attachment spreads to inhabit the brain as well, where it can be seen and read by new techniques. It strengthens attachment's natural version of the social as the basis on which the human 'social' world is built. The nursing dyad, ventrum to ventrum, or right brain to right brain, is the prototype of human spirituality, ethics, communication and co-operative organisation, as well as all the complex affective and cognitive capacities of the human mind. The basis of human society is a love relationship – the instinct for gift exchange rather than the rape and capture of women or the co-operative gaming of rational self interest. A truly Romantic theory and one in which, after centuries of cultivating his unique inner life, man can take his place in the animal kingdom once more.

This natural idyll has a terrible downside, however – children cut off from all the potential of their conception and the extremes of disorder in young and old alike. It stands as a constant warning to mothers and a continual, never-ending source of work for our mother substitutes – those psy professionals in the therapeutic domain. For whether they are experts on body or soul, brain or mind seems hardly to matter. We are continually learning new versions of our inner lives from new experts with new techniques, as we add to our explanatory repertoires. It is likely that, as individuals, we are still 'bricoleurs'[3] who will call, opportunistically, on different experts and different versions of the wound, whatever comes to mind, as it is useful to make a point or relieve distress. But these growing numbers of technicians of the psy and neuro-psy are what we need to service our way of being as (neuro) psychological individuals. For what is certain is that we will go on peering anxiously deep inside ourselves to appraise and improve our mind/brains, much as we work on our outer bodies, through practice, exercise, regimes for shaping and strengthening and pharmacological and surgical enhancement. We will call on a host of trainers who will coach us in confidence and self sufficiency and lessen our vulnerability to external pressure and hostility. And, if the worst happens, there will be others there to bathe our wounds, sew them up and set us on the pathway to healing.

This book is an account of some of the language, the narratives and the practices that feed into our thinking about ourselves and our psychic vulnerability. It has been written to assert the contingency of this language, its historical nature or ontological subjectivity. Our explorers of the interior could have come back with different stories. We could have seen ourselves differently. It is only in that thought that our freedom lies.

Notes

1 Introduction

1. The child protection system is now called 'Safeguarding Children'. Its title has varied over time and culture, but I use it here, for the sake of simplicity, to refer to all medico-administrative and legal systems devised to protect children.
2. This is considered in Chapter 4.
3. As I write, the UK is just recovering from extensive flooding. The spokesperson for the Institute for Environmental Management and Assessment (the largest professional membership body for the environment), while roundly rebutting accusations that flood defences were inadequate, identified the psychological distress of the victims as the area which had not been sufficiently studied or prepared for.
4. For an analysis and critique of this approach, see Douglas (1986).
5. Medical insurance both in the USA and the UK will cover treatment for clinically diagnosed psychiatric illness.
6. See an ethnographic study of such psychiatric services in France and by French psychiatrists in Palestine during the second Intifada (Fassin and Rechtman, 2009). This book is about the politics of victimhood and how it has become woven into the moral fabric of the contemporary world. Such therapeutic debriefing has not gone unquestioned (Rose *et al.*, 2003).
7. A recent book estimating the economic cost of the Iraq war (Stiglitz and Bilmes, 2008) includes the cost of care and loss of manpower to the economy from PTSD, as a diagnosed medical condition, attributed to returning troops.
8. The Diagnostic and Statistical Manual of Mental Disorders. (3rd edition) – the profession-wide diagnostic rubric of the American Psychiatric Association (1980).
9. See Chapter 3.
10. See Chapter 2.
11. For an example of such lists see Slovic (1987).
12. The Criminal Justice and Immigration Bill passed by the British parliament in 2008 contains provision for longer sentencing for crimes of violence or incitement, aggravated by 'hate', i.e. motivations of hostility on the grounds of race, gender, sexual orientation or abilities – a rationale for punishment, resting on intention rather than the nature of the harm. Harassment on these grounds appears in Employment Law, in tribunal cases in which aggravated damages are awarded for 'injury to feelings', as well as 'injury to health', cost of care, loss of earnings and the rest.
13. See the case of Sally Thornton, whose 1990 conviction for murdering her husband was converted to that of manslaughter in 1996 because of responsibility 'diminished by abnormality of mind' (Bennett, 1996).

14. See DHSS (1980).
15. But see Munro (2007).
16. For example, 'energy security' involves a nation making sure of its supplies of oil, gas etc.
17. The UN Advisory Committee on Human Security was established in the UN Secretariat in 2004.
18. Selective Serotonin Re-Uptake Inhibitors. Trade names: Prozac, Seroxat etc.
19. This is the thinking behind the Layard Depression Report (Layard, 2006).
20. See Chapter 8, The Emotional Right Brain.
21. See, for example, Rutter (1985).
22. See the American Psychological Association's 'Road to Resilience' program, devised in response to the events of 9/11 (Young, 2006).
23. See Chapters 7 and 8.
24. Gerrymandering is an electoral practice in which the boundaries of a constituency are moved to alter the demographic characteristics of its electorate, which may then favour the party in power.
25. 'Irrealism' or an indifference to metaphysics is Nelson Goodman's term, which, Hacking points out, is also a metaphysical position. See Hacking (1999): 60 and 61.
26. This context is stretched a little in Chapters 2 and 8 to include the text on internet sites of less official groups and organisations.

2 Invisible wounds

1. Like the sufferers from PTSD or Nervous Shock detailed in Chapter 3.
2. As in developmental versions such as attachment theory, discussed. in Chapters 7 and 8.
3. This is a contested question of the utmost complexity. See S. Rose (2001) and Searle (2005).
4. The DSM IV committee reflected on the title concept, 'mental' disorder (their inverted commas), and the unfortunate nature of the implicit distinction that it draws with 'physical' disorder, which they ascribed to 'a reductionistic anachronism of mind/body dualism'. American Psychiatric Association (1994): 21.
5. For example, see Butler (1993), Grosz (1994) and Nedelsky (1995).
6. See Chapter 3.
7. For an account of the status of 'nerves' in the late 19th and early 20th century see Shephard (2002).
8. See 'The Bargain', a poem by Philip Sidney in J. Wain ed. (1986a).
9. For a fuller discussion of this process of repression see Chapter 3 on Traumatic Memory.
10. For Freud, this emotion was 'unpleasure', in Freud (1966 [1895]).
11. 'I suffer, therefore we are.' This is a corruption of a corruption – a version of Descartes' original 'cogito' by the constructivist philosopher, Heinz von Foerster (von Foerster, 1991): 67, in which he discusses the linguistic and therefore essentially social nature of thought. *Cogito ergo sumus*: 'I think therefore we are.'

12. See Kenneth Arrow's 'Impossibility Theorem' for a discussion of the irrationalities that arise in any attempt to add the preferences of individuals (Arrow, 1974).
13. For an excellent discussion of the limits of the of 'the social' in traditional social psychology, as it comprises the interpersonal, rather than wider political and cultural considerations, see Riley (1983) and Burman (2008).
14. This point about the innate conservatism of the therapeutic model in politics, is also made by Wendy Brown in her book on identity politics, *States of Injury*, where she points out that the so-called. 'radical' new political movements, organised. around claims to injury, paradoxically reinforce the authority of the existing state (Brown, 1995).
15. See Kapur (2005). In Chapter 4 she makes this point at a more theoretical level.
16. See also Das (2003): 293 for a discussion of an alternative to anchoring narratives of violence to juridical discourses – finding 'forms of making the experience knowable, when saying gives way to showing'.

3   Suffering from nerves: The management of subjectivity in PTSD

1. *The Diagnostic and Statistical Manual of Mental Disorders of the American Psychiatric* Association (DSM I – IV) is an authoritative compendium of diagnoses used across American and then western psychiatry for the purposes of clinical consistency and epidemiological research. The only alternative system to be so widely used. is the World Health Organization's *International Classification of Diseases*, ICD 10. (WHO, 1992).
2. For example, Jones and Wessely (2005).
3. In the dualistic enlightenment philosophy of Locke and Hume (Hacking, 1995), memory, its content of words and images, the capacity for retrieval and the location in which these are stored, was that which formed identity and held together momentary flashes of self consciousness and sense data reception into some continuous subject with will and responsibility for the behaviour of the body.
4. After 1864, when the provisions of the Campbell Act, 1846 (under which compensation was paid to the families of those killed by accidents caused by the negligence of a second party, was extended to the victims of railway accidents), both Erichsen and his colleague, Page, recognised that desire for compensation might be a powerful psychological cause of the symptoms of nervous shock, even, according to Page, working at an unconscious level (Page, 1883).
5. In Barker (1991).
6. Commotional shock is defined as delivered by an explosive and concussive force (Young, 1995).
7. They also extended Page's understanding of fear reactions to include the vital notion of pain and the memory of pain, understanding that fear was not fear of injury per se but of the pain that goes with it.

8. Essentially, death from a prolonged state of fear, induced in someone by the belief that he/she was the object and victim of voodoo magic, as practised in South and Central America.

9. See his descriptions of his experiments with Leonie, a middle-aged woman who had been a somnambulist since the age of three years (Janet, 1889: 243–4).

10. Both Freud's and Horowitz's version of traumatic memory is also criticised as failing to generate the depressive symptoms which feature in the PTSD constellation.

11. Lately, other theories of memory function in PTSD have been put forward, including that of Chris Brewin (Brewin 2003) which suggests that 'repressed memory' and the theories that go with it 'are no longer credible features of PTSD' (Young, 2005: 155–157).

12. In one session, the neurologists speculated on what the psychiatrists could possibly find to talk about and were much amused when someone suggested. that they were exchanging information on a new sort of Chubb lock (Shephard, 2002).

13. In 1974, the American Psychiatric Association set up a task force to devise a revision of DSM-II, headed by Roger Spitzer, who is seen as a leading force in 'the DSM Revolution' (Young, 1995: 89–117).

14. The reformulation of diagnostic categories for DSM-III purely as symptom clusters is widely attributed to the writings and methodology of Kraepelin. In fact, he favoured the use of case studies, which included the consideration of aetiological histories and outcomes as well as symptoms, as a way of formulating a set of diagnostic categories.

15. The DSM methodology has remained a subject of contention, especially in the UK. See also Horwitz and Wakefield (2007).

16. For a history see Danziger (1997).

17. For example, Brown and Harris (1978). See, also, the 1970s work of Paykel (1978) on depression, Vaughn and Leff (1976) on social factors influencing schizophrenia and depression and Michael Rutter on a career of studying the social causes of child psychopathology (Rutter, 1989).

18. See Child Sexual Abuse, Battered Wife Syndrome etc in DSM-IV.

19. This refers to the controversial claim that memories of childhood abuse can be recovered by adults in therapy. This is contentious partly because of the fact vs fantasy dispute in psychoanalytic theories of the origins of neuroses, and partly because of its concrete result in the retrospective prosecution of parents. For accounts see Segal (1999: 131–3) and Hacking (1995b: Chapter 8).

20. This is a difficulty not confined to neurological research on PTSD.

21. For example, MacFarlane (1986).

22. For a definition of the reliability and validity of a diagnostic category see Young (1995): 102–107.

23. See, for example, Mayou (1996).

24. McNally, (2004: 3).

25. And even cognitive or cognitive-behavioural versions have to include some version of repression like 'cognitive dissonance'.

26. See Chapter 7.
27. See Segal (1999: 131–3) and Hacking (1995b: Chapter 8).

4   Negligently inflicted psychiatric illness or nervous shock

1. Nicola Lacey, for example, has looked at this historical movement in 'black letter law' as well as contemporary literature (Lacey, 1998).
2. This is the nearest the English Common Law approaches to the French '*crime passionelle*'.
3. The principle of 'consent' still dominates the prosecution of trials for rape in the UK, hence a raft of work by feminist legal scholars, insisting that the harm in sexual assault is inscribed also on a psychological space, or, in the more holistic, thinking of some feminist philosophers recently, on the whole person. See Butler (1993), Grosz (1994) and Lacey (1998).
4. For a gripping account of the politics of Hillsborough see Scraton (1999).
5. For instance, Handford (2006).
6. See *Alcock v Chief Constable of South Yorkshire* [1991] House of Lords 310. The Law commission report, *Liability for Psychiatric Illness* (1998: 39–51) suggests that, while PTSD is the diagnosis most favoured by claimants because, in its cause-and-effect form, it is most suitable for establishing liability, many of the psychiatric consultants to the Commission's inquiry pointed out its inadequacy in capturing all the symptomatic consequences of shock.
7. There are some exceptions to this generalisation. For example, Lord Hoffmann was brought up in South Africa.
8. This has interesting parallels with the crime of Psychic Assault. Discussion of Clause 4 of The Offences Against the Person Bill, which proposed a definition of assault in the following terms:
   'a person is guilty of assault if –

   a) he intentionally or recklessly applies force to or causes impact on the body of another … or …
   b) he intentionally or recklessly, without the consent of the other, causes the other to believe that any such force or impact is imminent.'

   In a discussion of this legislation, Jeremy Horder proposes that it is not the belief per se that constitutes the assault but the fear which goes with the belief. That is, that the crime of assault is the production of an affective rather than cognitive state. Horder (1998).
9. As opposed to a psychodynamic dualism in which the emotions move from the body to the inner life of an individual.

5   The emotional abuse of children: An inward turn

1. A study of the legal processing of cases in the English Family Courts, where emotional abuse has been registered, was beyond the scope of this book. It would involve extensive interviewing and ethnography. Meanwhile there is little UK research to call on and the DOH/DfES statistics on

care proceedings and numbers looked after do not relate to registration categories.

2. Both physical and sexual abuse are diagnostic categories in DSM IV.

3. Only the other 'hard to define' category of neglect has shown similar growth.

4. NSPCC is the National Society for the Prevention of Cruelty to Children, founded in London in 1884 to help to combat the cruel conditions suffered by too many children in Victorian England. It has undergone many transformations since this time, but is still the major child protection charity in the UK, complementing the activities of the state with some direct services, including national helplines, acting as a political pressure group and funding research and major publications in the area.

5. In the USA the states are responsible for reporting laws, which define child abuse and specify who is mandated to report it, whether to the courts or to the welfare services. They also make provision for the protective custody of children and the prosecution of abusers, if appropriate.

6. For a list of Court's articles see Parton (1985), Ch 3, Note 50: 213.

7. See Tunbridge Wells Study Group and Franklin (1973).

8. For an analysis of the issues of this crucial case see Nigel Parton's account of what he calls 'the catalyst for the rapid emergence of a "moral panic"' (Parton, 1985: 97).

9. See Chapter 5.

10. See Dingwall *et al.* (1983) for a discussion of what the authors call 'cultural relativism'.

11. See Chapter 1.

12. There was, however, an earlier, untranslated book, *Die Seelische Kindermisshandlung* by G. V. Levetzow, published in 1934.

13. See Chapters 7 and 8.

14. There is little literature on the subject – an isolated. article like Whiting (1976) – but Barbara Nelson (Nelson, 1984) notes that following the passing of the Child Abuse Prevention and Treatment Act (CAPTA) in 1974, increasing numbers of children were being taken into custodial protection under the category of 'emotional neglect'.

15. See also the work of Harry Hendrick on medical accommodation to the idea that psycho-social variables have measurable physical effects on babies and children. See Hendrick (2003).

16. For a description and history of the Family Unit at the Park Hospital, see Dingwall (1987): 51 Note 3.

17. For example, Baldwin and Oliver (1975), Smith (1975), and Starr (1982).

18. This was institutionalised as 'the Ounsted Round', named after Dr Kit Ounsted, the paediatrician and director of the Park Hospital, Oxford.

19. Dean (1979), Patterson and Thompson (1980), Besharov (1981) and Kavanagh (1982).

20. For example, the Family Rights Group and Justice for Children. See also the Children's Legal Centre. (1988) and Parents Against INjustice. (1986).

21. For a critique, see Fawcett *et al.* (2004).

22. By 2001, the general figure on the Child Abuse Registers were down by 11 per cent. The DOH statistician attributes this to a slight re-jigging of the categories (DOH (2001a), but the DOH report on the Children Act 2001, made to Parliament in June, 2002 attributes it to a shift in resources from

the Child Protection system to children in need. and child welfare generally (DOH, 2002).

23. The Green Paper also introduces a new system for the collection, management and multi-professional availability of data on all children about whom there is any professional concern. This has prompted questions about civil liberties. See Gallagher (2005) and Munro (2007).

24. Its recommendations are a wider, more contextualised assessment procedure; a less incident-driven response and one orientated to a plan of intervention rather than merely registration, all of which have largely been adopted.

25. For instance, in the organisational structure of most LASSDs, within the children's directorate, 'safeguarding' and 'family support' are the work of different social work teams and their leaders.

26. The use of the Child Protection Register was phased out (in England only) in 2007, to be substituted for by a list of children in need of a child protection plan. It would seem, however, that the categories of abuse have not been dropped.

27. See Chapter 7.

6   The heart of all harm: The emotional abuse literature, 1980–2006

1. The proportion of psychological maltreatment to other forms of abuse only entered the US figures in 2002 at 7 per cent. Neglect was 60 per cent, physical abuse 20 per cent and sexual abuse 10 per cent. These proportions seem to be roughly constant since then. If anything, psychological maltreatment has declined further as a percentage and has certainly not increased as it has in the UK figures.

2. As with emotional abuse, definitions varied from state to state. See Wolf and Pillemer (1988).

3. This is the title of a journal launched in 2000: *Trauma, Violence, and Abuse.* Sage Publications.

4. See the special edition of *Development and Psychopathology*: 3 (01).

5. *The Psychologically Battered Child* (Garbarino et al., 1986).

6. Perhaps emblematic of this merging of psychological abuse and violence is the take-over of the *Journal of Emotional Abuse* by the *Journal of Aggression, Maltreatment and Trauma* in 2008, both Taylor and Francis publications.

7. Research from Victoria, Australia (which has a similar legal system to the UK) shows that emotional abuse is the hardest category to process legally as a simple abuse type registration, yet, as an additional registration with another physical category, it makes care proceedings more likely to succeed. It is hard to make a case with just the sort of welfare evidence needed to support claims to emotional abuse. But hard evidence, incidents etc., can be subject to legal quibble and then the soft evidence of a child's general emotional state may swing the case (Sheehan, 2001 and 2006).

8. This view is part of what Gregory Bateson called. 'second-order cybernetics'. For a summary, see von Foerster (1974).

9. In welfare economics it is assumed that most economic agents have a 'time preference', so that, when thinking of future consumption, they discount future income streams at a cumulative rate.

7 Attachment: An 'internalised something' and the natural world

1. In the UK, from being the subject matter of the Family Doctor broadcasts of the 1950s, attachment has made it back into Family Doctor advice, this time in a self-help book series of this name, published in conjunction with the BMA, as the basis for psychotherapy for stress sufferers. Wilkinson's (2005) booklet on *Stress* boasts sales of 200,000.

2. The awesome responsibilities of motherhood posited by this theory can be seen as one of a long line of 'discourses of endangerment' that have served. to regulate the behaviour of women in the perinatal period (Brooks Gardner, 1994).

3. British attachment literature is much less profuse and has a more professional bias – in somewhat the same relationship to the US literature as for the emotional abuse literature.

4. This enhanced socialisation was not to be achieved by any seismic social shifts, however. The basic social and economic hierarchies of the UK remained, untouched by the redistribution of income, health and education at the margins, as did the biologically based assumptions about the naturalness of gender, racial, sexual and age differences.

5. Bowlby worked from the start of the war with other analysts on the Cambridge Evacuation Project, a report on evacuation for the Fabian Society. After the war, he was the compiler of the Report of the Expert Committee on Mental health of the WHO. He immediately applied this insight in an astute political operation in which he achieved some solution to the refugee problem and later improved the treatment of children in hospital.

6. Hugh Jolly in the 'Family Doctor' broadcasts, or Winnicot herself.

7. Note Denise Riley's (1983, Chapter 6) careful examination of the complex connection between theory, government propaganda and the position of women, where, she maintains, no directly causal relationships can be established.

8. This was a feature of the 1948 Children Act.

9. After the report of the Maria Colwell enquiry, 1974.

10. There was much initial hostility to Bowlby and attachment theory from the psychoanalytic movement, although post-Freudianism had taken a developmental turn with Margaret Mahler and ego psychologists like Erickson in the USA and Anna Freud, Joseph Sandler and the Bion–Klein School in Britain.

11. Here she brought a psychoanalytic framework to bear in her emphasis on coding her respondents' behaviour only as seen and interpreted within its interpersonal context; that is, it was given meaning as opposed to being mechanically observed and counted (Main, 1999b).

12. See section 7.3.

13. See Mahler's theories of infantile ambivalence as normative, described in Fonagy (2001).

14. The Grossmanns' results from the Bielefeld cohort in North Germany showed the A (insecure avoidant) group as the largest group in their Strange Situation test.

15. For a popular explanation of Hamilton's work, see Dawkins (1989).

16. For further explanation of this point see Allsopp (2009): 29 and note 268.

17. See Chapter 3.

18. For an account of criticisms of 'Bowlbyism' see Riley (1983): 106–108.
19. For example, Sir Keith Joseph , thought of as the guru of the new free market conservatism under Margaret Thatcher, frequently quoted the views of Charles Murray, summarised in Murray (1990).
20. For example, Penelope Leach's bestselling book, first published. in 1977, Leach (1994).
21. See Cassidy and Shaver (1999).
22. *Journal of Consulting and Clinical Psychology*, 1996 (and 2006), Monographs of the Society for Research in Child Development, (1985), *Child Abuse and Neglect* 22, (1998), *Psychoanalytic Inquiry*, (1999), *Child Abuse Review*, 1997, *Infant Mental Health* 22, 2001.
23. For a list of Ainsworth's students see Bretherton (1991).
24. It would also be conceded that temperament or innate characteristics might make a difference to how the attachment bond is experienced by mother and child, though the two dimensions are not highly correlated.
25. Main was and is perhaps the most important of Ainsworth's students, having been, initially, an unwilling worker in her professor's Baltimore study, because of the 'apprenticeship' system for PhD students at Johns Hopkins. She had wanted to study psycholinguistics.
26. The three AAI-organised categories were 'Secure /Autonomous', 'Insecure/Dismissive' and 'Insecure/ Preoccupied'.
27. See Waters, T. (2004).
28. Except for one airport-based study of parting couples by Fraley and Shaver, initially entitled: 'I'm Leaving on a Jet Plane' (Fraley and Shaver, 1998).
29. For a review of Adult Attachment Style measures, see Crowell and Fraley (1999).
30. For an elaboration of this IWM and supportive research, see Fonagy (2001).
31. Although there is a body of literature which suggests a concurrent correlation with disorganisation and psychological disturbance, it is less reliable because of the problems of cross-contamination of the data, and especially relating attachment problems to specific diagnoses, where the presence of co-morbidity is ever a problem (Greenberg, 1999).
32. This is found among Romanian orphans, who are emblematic of this group of children and the subject of much psychological and neurophysiological research (Rutter *et al.*, 2007).
33. With apologies to Robert O'Brien, author of the classic children's story, *Mrs Frisby and the Rats of NIMH.*

8   Risk and resilience: Attachment at the turn of the century

1. Note the resurgence of these theories plus their intergenerational and geographical enhancement in government 'social exclusion' thinking.
2. A search was run for all articles or book sections with 'attachment' in the abstract. The results were then further broken down by author and author's academic base. Besides this, information on the social organisation of the 'attachment world' comes from the internet, using Google as a search

engine, following links and mapping a network, and from some participant observation.

3. For an account of the UK attachment personnel, see Allsopp (2009) note 293.
4. It specialises in running courses for child therapists and child care professionals on the latest findings in the neurophysiology of the emotions.
5. It is hard to find instances of the diagnosis of RAD being used in the NHS. For instance a report on the mental health of children and young people, published by the Office of National Statistics in 2004, did not use this classification (DOH, 2005).
6. For example, Pat Crittenden, from the University of Miami – another Ainsworth graduate student; Allan Schore, a psychoanalyst on the clinical faculty of the Department of Psychiatry and Biobehavioral Sciences, UCLA David Geffen School of Medicine; Bruce Perry (The Child Trauma Academy, Houston, Texas) and Daniel Siegel, (part-based at UCLA).
7. It is also used, though less widely, to inform CBT with an affective dimension.
8. See the work of Phyllis Booth, founder of the Theraplay Institute, USA, promoting a method 'used successfully for over 35 years' to help children and families'.
9. The Cascade Centre is now closed, following litigation (*Deseret News*, 2008).
10. See Allsopp (2009): 333 for further discussion.
11. This was called 'Child and Family Training', although known in the trade as 'Arnon's Roadshow'.
12. Developed in Conjunction with the Lifespan Research Group, Royal Holloway College, University of London (CAFT, 2007).
13. Apart from the Suomi and Hofer articles referred to in Chapter 7, there is just one: Fox and Card, 1999.
14. The techniques of psychophysiological measurement of cognitive and affective processes in the individual are measuring heart rate (HR); blood and urine cortisol levels; an electroencephalogram (EEG), recording electrical activity in the brain; functional magnetic resonance imaging (fMRI) for mapping brain activity and positron emission tomography (PET) which provides a three-dimensional brain map. See Fox and Card (1999) for a careful description of the uses and the limits of these measures.
15. For these see Fox and Card (1999).

9 Conclusion

1. See Brown (1995). This presents a critique of Foucault's categorisation of power in the light of modern politics.
2. See also Riley (1983), Chapter 2, for an exposition.
3. See Levi-Strauss (1968) *The Savage Mind*. Chicago: University of Chicago Press. 'Bricoleur' is French for 'do-it-yourself man'. 'Bricolage' was a word used by Claude Levi Strauss in this book to describe the non-scientific building of imaginative worlds and world views with whatever bits and pieces come to mind.

References

Books and articles

Aaronson, C. J., Bender, D. S., Skodol, A. E. and Gunderson, J. G. (2006) Comparison of Attachment Styles in Borderline Personality Disorder and Obsessive–Compulsive Personality Disorder. *Psychiatric Quarterly*, **77**, 69–80.

Aber, J. L., Allen, J. P., Carlson, V. and Cicchetti, D. (1989) The Effects of Maltreatment on Development During Early Childhood: Recent Studies and Their Theoretical, Clinical, and Policy Implications. In *Child Maltreatment: Theory and Research on the Causes and Consequences of Child Abuse and Neglect* (eds V. Carlson and D. Cicchetti), 579–619. New York: Cambridge University Press.

Aber, J. L. and Zigler, E. (1981) Developmental Consideration in the Definition of Child Maltreatment. In *Developmental Perspectives on Child Maltreatment. New Directions for Child Development* (eds R. Rizley and D Cicchetti), **11**. San Francisco, CA: Jossey-Bass.

Ace, K. J., Tepper, M. S. and Owens, A. F. (2007) The Direct and Indirect Impact of Childhood Abuse and Neglect on Sexuality. In *Sexual Health Vol 1: Psychological Foundations*, 301–329. Westport, CT: Praeger Publishers/Greenwood Publishing Group.

Adenzato, M., Ardito, R. B. and Izard, E. (2006) Impact of Maternal Directiveness and Overprotectiveness on the Personality Development of a Sample of Individuals with Acquired Blindness. *Social Behavior and Personality*, **34**, 17–26.

Agamben, G. (1999) *Remnants of Auschwitz: The Witness and the Archive* (Translated by Daniel Heller Roazen). New York: Zone Books.

Agger, I. and Sorenson, J. (1990) Testimony as Ritual and Evidence in Psychotherapy. *Journal of Traumatic Stress*, **3**, 115–130.

Ahern, J., Galea, S., Resnick, H. and Vlahov, D. (2004) Television Images and Probable Posttraumatic Stress Disorder after September 11: The Role of Background Characteristics, Event Exposures, and Peri-Event Panic. *Journal of Nervous and Mental Disease*, **192**, 217–226.

Ainsworth, M. D. (1967) *Infancy in Uganda: Infant Care and the Growth of Love.* Oxford, England: Johns Hopkins University Press.

Ainsworth, M. D. (1969) Object Relations, Dependency, and Attachment: A Theoretical Review of the Infant–Mother Relationship. *Child Development*, **40**, 969.

Ainsworth, M. D. and Bell, S. M. (1970) Attachment, Exploration, and Separation: Illustrated by the Behavior of One-Year-Olds in a Strange Situation. *Child Development*, **41**, 49–67.

Ainsworth, M. D., Bell, S. M. and Stayton, D. F. (1974) Infant–Mother Attachment and Social Development: Socialization as a Product of Reciprocal Responsiveness to Signals. In *The Integration of a Child into a Social World* (ed. M. P. Richards), 99–135. New York: Cambridge University Press.

Ainsworth, M. S., Blehar, M. C., Waters, E. and Wall, S. (1978) *Patterns of Attachment: A Psychological Study of the Strange Situation.* Oxford, England: Lawrence Erlbaum.

Aldgate, J. and Hill, M. (1996) *Child Welfare Services: Developments in Law Practice, Policy and Research.* London: Jessica Kingsley.

Aldgate, J. and Tunstill, J. (1995) *Making Sense of Section 17: Implementing Services for Children in Need, within the 1989 Children Act: A Study for the Department of Health.* London: HMSO.

Alegre, J. N. and Juaneda, C. (2006) Destination Loyalty: Consumers' Economic Behavior. *Annals of Tourism Research,* **33**, 684–706.

Ali, A. N. (2000) Depression in Women: Effects of Life Events, Support, Emotional Abuse and Self-Silencing. In *Dissertation Abstracts International: Section B: The Sciences and Engineering,* 4873–4873. US: ProQuest Information and Learning.

Allsopp, M. (2009) Invisible Wounds: a Genealogy of Emotional Abuse and other Psychic Harms. PhD thesis. London School of Economics and Political Science.

Allsopp, M. and Stevenson, O. (1995) Social Workers' Perceptions of Risk in Child Protection. University of Nottingham.

American Journal of Orthopsychiatry. Washington, DC: Educational Publishing Foundation.

American Psychiatric Association (1980) *Diagnostic and Statistical Manual of Mental Disorders.* (3d edn). Washington, DC: American Psychiatric Association.

——(1987) *Diagnostic and Statistical Manual of Mental Disorders.* (3rd Revised edn). Washington, D. C.: American Psychiatric Association.

——(1994) *Diagnostic and Statistical Manual of Mental Disorders.* (4th edn). Washington, D. C.: American Psychiatric Association.

Amini, F., Lewis, T, Lannon, R., Louie, A., Baumbacher, G., McGuinness, T. and Schiff E. Z. (1996) Affect, attachment, memory: contributions toward psychobiologic integration. *Psychiatry,* 59:213–39.

Anyanwu, E. and Campbell, A. (2001) Childhood Emotional Experiences Leading to Biopsycho-socially Induced Dyslexia and Low Academic Performance in Adolescence. *International Journal of Adolescent Medicine and Health,* **13**, 191–203.

Archer, C. (1999) *First Steps in Parenting the Child Who Hurts: Tiddlers and Toddlers.* London: Jessica Kingsley.

Archer, J. (1999) Assessment of the Reliability of the Conflict Tactics Scales: A Meta-Analytic Review. *Journal of Interpersonal Violence,* **14**, 1263–1289.

Aristotle, *The Oxford Translation of Aristotle* (ed. W. D. Ross, 1925) 9 (*Poetics,* translated by Ingram Shaw), Chapter 21, 1457b1–30.

Arrow, K. (1974) *The Limits of Organisation.* New York: Norton.

Bacon, H. and Richardson, S. (2001) Attachment Theory and Child Abuse: An Overview of the Literature for Practitioners. *Child Abuse Review,* **10**, 377.

Bailey, T. F. and Bailey, W. H. (1986) *Operational Definitions of Child Emotional Maltreatment: Final Report.* Washington, DC: National Centre on Child Abuse and Neglect (DHSS90–CA–0958) US Government Printing Office.

Baldwin, J. A. and Oliver, J. E. (1975) Epidemiology and Family Characteristics of Severely Abused Children. *British Journal of Social and Preventive Medicine,* **29**, 205–221.

Bandura, A. (1963) *Social Learning and Personality Development.* New York: Holt, Rinehart and Winston.

——(1977) *Social Learning Theory*. Englewood Cliffs, NJ: Prentice Hall.

Banyard, V. L., Cross, C. and Modecki, K. L. (2006) Interpersonal Violence in Adolescence: Ecological Correlates of Self-Reported Perpetration. *Journal of Interpersonal Violence*, **21**, 1314–1332.

Barefoot Doctor (2003) Heart of the Matter. *Observer Magazine*, 25 May.

Barclay, P. M./NISW (1982) *Social Workers: Their Role and Tasks*. London: National Institute of Social Work.

Barker, P. (1991) *Regeneration*. Harmondsworth: Penguin.

Barnett, D., Manly, J. T. and Cicchetti, D. (1991) Continuing toward an Operational Definition of Psychological Maltreatment. *Development and Psychopathology*, **3**, 19–29.

Barossa, J. (2001) *Ideas in Psychoanalysis: Hysteria*. Cambridge: Icon Books.

Barry, A., Osbourne, T. and Rose, N. (eds) (1996) *Foucault and Political Reason: Liberalism, Neo-Liberalism and Rationalities of Government*. London: UCL Press.

Bateson, G. (1979) *Mind and Nature: A Necessary Unity*. Cresskill, NJ: Hampton Press.

Bauman, Z. (1994) Review: [Untitled]. *The British Journal of Sociology*, **45**, 143–144.

Beck, A. (1976) *Cognitive Therapy and the Emotional Disorders*. New York: International Universities Press.

Beck, U. (1992) *Risk Society: Towards a New Modernity*. London: Sage.

Beck, U., Giddens, A. and Lasch, S. (1994) *Reflexive Modernisation*. Palo Alto: Stanford University Press.

Behrens, K. Y., Hesse, E. and Main, M. (2007) Mothers' Attachment Status as Determined by the Adult Attachment Interview Predicts Their 6-Year-Olds' Reunion Responses: A Study Conducted in Japan. *Developmental Psychology*, **43**, 1553–1567.

Bell, D. (1978) *The Cultural Contradictions of Capitalism*. New York: Basic Books.

Belsky, J. (1991) Psychological Maltreatment: Definitional Limitations and Unstated Assumptions. *Development and Psychopathology*, **3**, 31–36.

——(1999a) Interactional and Contextual Determinants of Attachment Security. In *Handbook of Attachment: Theory, Research, and Clinical Applications*. (eds J. Cassidy and P. R. Shaver). New York: Guilford Press.

——(1999b) Modern Evolutionary Theory and Patterns of Attachment. In *Handbook of Attachment: Theory, Research, and Clinical Applications*. (eds J. Cassidy and P. R. Shaver), 141–161. New York: Guilford Press.

Belsky, J. and Cassidy, J. (1994) Attachment: Theory and Evidence. In *Development Through Life: A Handbook for Clinicians* (eds M. Rutter and D. Hays), 373. Oxford: Blackwell Scientific.

Belsky, J., Steinberg, L. and Draper, P. (1991) Childhood Experience, Interpersonal Development and Reproductive Strategy. An Evolutionary Theory of Socialization. *Child Development*, **62**, 647–670.

Bennett, W. (1996) *The Independent*, 31 May.

Bentovim, A. (1986) 'The Towers of Silence: Creative and Destructive Issues for Therapeutic Teams Dealing with Sexual Abuse': A Commentary. *Journal of Family Therapy*, **8**, 27–30.

Bentovim, A. and Tranter, M. (1984) A Family Therapy Approach to Decision-Making. *Adoption and Fostering*, **8**, 25–32.

Bernstein, D. P., Fink, L., Handelsman, L. and Foote, J. (1994) Initial Reliability and Validity of a New Retrospective Measure of Child Abuse and Neglect. *American Journal of Psychiatry*, **151**, 1132–1136.

Bernstein, D. P., Stein, J. A. and Handelsman, L. (1998) Predicting Personality Pathology among Adult Patients with Substance Use Disorders: Effects of Childhood Maltreatment. *Addictive Behaviors*, **23**, 855–868.

Berry, K., Wearden, A., Barrowclough, C. and Liversidge, T. (2006) Attachment Styles, Interpersonal Relationships and Psychotic Phenomena in a Non-Clinical Student Sample. *Personality and Individual Differences*, **41**, 707–718.

Besharov, D. (1981) Toward Better Research on Child Abuse and Neglect: Making Definitional Issues an Explicit Methodological Concern. *Child Abuse and Neglect*, **5**, 383–390.

Best, J. (ed) (1989) *Images of Issues: Typifying Contemporary Social Problems*. New York: de Gruyter.

——(2008) *Social Problems*. New York: Norton.

Bogels, S. M. and Brechman-Toussaint, M. L. (2006) Family Issues in Child Anxiety: Attachment, Family Functioning, Parental Rearing and Beliefs. *Clinical Psychology Review*, **26**, 834–856.

Boulton, S. and Hindle, D. (2000) Emotional Abuse: The Work of a Multidisciplinary Consultation Group in a Child Psychiatric Service *Clinical Psychology and Psychiatry*, **5 (3)**, 439–452.

Bowlby, J. (1940) The Influence of Early Environment in the Development of Neurosis and Neurotic Character. *International Journal of Psychoanalysis*, **21**, 154–178.

——(1946) *Forty-Four Juvenile Thieves; Their Characters and Home-Life*. Oxford, England: Bailliere, Tindall and Cox.

——(1953a) *Child Care and the Growth of Love*. Harmondsworth, UK: Penguin.

——(1953b) Some Pathological Processes Set in Train by Early Mother–Child Separation. *Journal of Mental Science*, **99**, 265–272.

——(1958) The Nature of the Child's Tie to His Mother. *International Journal of Psychoanalysis*, **39**, 350–373.

——(1969) *Attachment and Loss: Vol. 1: Attachment*. New York: Basic Books.

——(1973) *Attachment and Loss: Vol. 2. Separation*. New York: Basic Books.

——(1980) *Attachment and Loss: Vol. 3. Loss, Sadness, and Depression*. New York: Basic Books.

——(1988) *A Secure Base*. London: Routledge.

Bowman, M. and Yehuda, R. (2004) Risk Factors and the Adversity Stress Model. In *Post-Traumatic Stress Disorder: Issues and Controversies* (ed. G. M. Rosen). London: Wiley.

Braithwaite, J. (1996) Restorative Justice and a Better Future (Crime, Punishment and the Criminal Justice System). *Dalhousie Review*, **76**, 9–31.

Brandon, M., Lewis, A. and Thoburn, J. (1996) The Children Act Definition of Significant Harm: Interpretations in Practice. *Health and Social Care in the Community*, **4(1)**, 11–20.

Brassard, M. R., Germain, R. and Hart, S. N. (1987) *Psychological Maltreatment of Children and Youth*. New York; Oxford: Pergamon.

Brassard, M. R., Hardy, D. B., Helfer, M. E., Kempe, R. S. and Krugman, R. D. (1997) Psychological Maltreatment. In *The Battered Child (5th Edn., Rev.& Exp.)*, 392–412. Chicago, IL: University of Chicago Press.

Brassard, M. R., Hart, S. N. and Hardy, D. B. (1993) The Psychological Maltreatment Rating Scales. *Child Abuse and Neglect*, 17, 715–729.

Brennan, K. A., Clark, C. L., Shaver, P. R., Simpson, J. A. and Rholes, W. S. (1998) Self-Report Measurement of Adult Romantic Attachment: An Integrative Overview. In *Attachment Theory and Close Relationships*, 46.

Breslau, N. and Kessler, R. C. (2001) The Stressor Criterion in DSM-IV Post-Traumatic Stress Disorder: An Empirical Investigation. *Biological Psychiatry*, 50, 699–704.

Bretherton, I. (1991) The Roots and Growing Points of Attachment Theory. In *Attachment Across the Life Cycle*. (eds C. M. Parkes, J. Stevenson-Hinde and P. Marris), 9–32. New York: Tavistock/Routledge.

Bretherton, I., Gunnar, M. R. and Sroufe, L. A. (1991) Pouring New Wine into Old Bottles: The Social Self as Internal Working Model. In *Self Processes and Development*, 1–41. Hillsdale, NJ: Lawrence Erlbaum Associates.

Bretherton, I. and Munholland, K. A. (1999) Internal Working Models in Attachment Relationships: A Construct Revisited. In *Handbook of Attachment: Theory, Research, and Clinical Application* (eds J. Cassidy and P. R. Shaver), 89–111. New York: Guilford Press.

Bretherton, I. and Waters, E. (1985) Growing Points of Attachment Theory and Research. *Monographs of the Society for Research in Child Development*, **50 (1–2, serial no. 209)**.

Brett, E. A., Wilson, J. P. and Raphael, B. (1993) Psychoanalytic Contributions to a Theory of Traumatic Stress. In *International Handbook of Traumatic Stress Syndromes*, 61–68. New York: Plenum Press.

Breuer, J. and Freud, S. (1955 [1893–1895]) Studies on Hysteria. *Standard Edition of the Complete Works of Sigmund Freud 2*.

——1956 [1893]) On the Psychical Mechanism of Hysterical Phenomena. *International Journal of Psychoanalysis*, 37, 8–13.

Brewin, C. R. (2003) *Post-traumatic Stress Disorder: Malady or Myth*. New Haven, CT: Yale University Press.

Brook, D. W. (2006) Review of Addiction as an Attachment Disorder. *International Journal of Group Psychotherapy*, 56, 511–515.

Brooks Gardner, C. (1994) The Social Construction of Pregnancy and Fetal Development: Notes on a Nineteenth Century Rhetoric of Endangerment. In *Constructing the Social* (eds T. R. Sarbin and J. L. Kitsuse). London: Sage.

Brown, G. W. and Harris, T. (1978) *Social Origins of Depression: A Study of Psychiatric Disorder in Women*. London: Tavistock.

Brown, W. (1995) *States of Injury: Power and Freedom in Late Modernity*. Princeton, NJ: Princeton University Press.

Browne, C. J. and Shlosberg, E. (2006) Attachment Theory, Ageing and Dementia: A Review of the Literature. *Aging and Mental Health*, 10, 134–142.

Browne, K. and Lynch, M. (eds) (1997) *Child Abuse Review*. 6 (5): 313–390.

Bryant, S. and Range, L. (1996) Suicidality in College Women Who Report Multiple Versus Single Types of Maltreatment by Parents: A Brief Report. *Journal of Child Sexual Abuse*, 4, 87–94.

Burke, J. (2000) Harsh Words Can Deform Children's Brains for Life. *The Observer*. 31 December.

Burman, E. (2008) *Deconstructing Developmental Psychology (2nd Ed.)*. New York: Routledge/Taylor and Francis Group.

Butler-Sloss, E. (1988) *Report of the Inquiry into Child Abuse in Cleveland 1987.* London: HMSO.

Butler, J. (1993) *Bodies That Matter.* London: Routledge.

Calam, C. and Franchi, F. (1989) Setting Basic Standards. In *Child Abuse and Neglect: Facing the Challenge* (eds S. Rogers, D. Hevey and E. Ashe). Milton Keynes: Open University.

Campbell, B. (1988) *Child Abuse: The Cleveland Case and After.* London: Virago.

Canguilhem, G. (1991) *The Normal and the Pathological.* New York: Zone Books.

Cannon, W. B. (1914) The Interrelations of Emotions as Suggested by Recent Physiological Research. *American Journal of Psychiatry,* **25,** 256–281.

——(1929) *Bodily Changes in Pain, Hunger, Fear and Pain.* Boston: Charles T. Branford.

——(1942) "Voodoo" Death. *American Anthropologist,* **44,** 169–181.

Cantwell, H. (1980) Child Neglect. In *The Battered Child* (eds R. E. Helfer and C. H. Kempe). Chicago, IL: Chicago University Press.

Carlson, E. A. (1998) A Prospective, Longitudinal Study of Disorganized/Disoriented Attachment. *Child Development,* **69,** 1107–1128.

Cassidy, J. and Marvin, R. S. (1992) Attachment in Preschool Children: Coding Guidelines. Seattle: MacArthur Working Group on Attachment. Unpublished Coding Manual.

Cassidy, J. and Shaver, P. R. (1999) *Handbook of Attachment: Theory, Research, and Clinical Applications.* New York: Guilford Press.

Cawson, P., Wattam, C., Brooker, S. and Kelly, G. (2000) *Child Maltreatment in the United Kingdom: A Study of the Prevalence of Child Abuse and Neglect.* London: NSPCC.

Charcot, J. M. (1889) *Clinical Lectures on Diseases of the Nervous System Delivered at the Infirmary of La Salpetriere.* London: New Sydenham Society.

Chessick, R. D. (2006) Review of a Developmental Model of Borderline Personality Disorder: Understanding Variations in Course and Outcome. *The Journal of the American Academy of Psychoanalysis and Dynamic Psychiatry,* **34,** 385–388.

Children's Legal Centre. (1988) *Child Abuse Procedures – the Child's Viewpoint: Policy Proposals from the Children's Legal Centre (2nd rev. edn.).* London: Children's Legal Centre.

Chirichella-Besemer, D. and Motta, R. W. (2008) Psychological Maltreatment and Its Relationship with Negative Affect in Men and Women. *Journal of Emotional Abuse,* **8,** 423–445.

Chisholm, J. S. (1996) The Evolutionary Ecology of Attachment Organisation. *Human Nature,* **7,** 1–38.

Cicchetti, D. (2007) Intervention and Policy Implications of Research on Neurobiological Functioning in Maltreated Children. In *Child Development and Social Policy: Knowledge for Action* (eds J. L. Aber, S. J. Bishop-Josef, S. M. Jones, K. T. McLearn and D. A. Phillips), 167–184. Washington, DC: American Psychological Association.

Cicchetti, D. and Carlson, V. (1989) *Child Maltreatment: Theory and Research on the Causes and Consequences of Child Abuse and Neglect.* Cambridge; New York: Cambridge University Press.

Cicchetti, D. and Cohen, D. J. (eds) (2006) *Developmental Psychopathology, Vol 2: Developmental Neuroscience (2nd Ed.).* Hoboken, NJ: John Wiley and Sons.

Cicchetti, D. and Curtis, W. (2006) The Developing Brain and Neural Plasticity: Implications for Normality, Psychopathology, and Resilience. In *Developmental Psychopathology, Vol 2: Developmental Neuroscience* (eds D. Cicchetti and D. J. Cohen), 1–64. Hoboken, NJ: John Wiley and Sons.

Cicchetti, D. and Posner, M. I. (2005) Editorial: Cognitive and Affective Neuroscience and Developmental Psychopathology. *Development and Psychopathology*, **17**, 569–575.

Cicchetti, D., Rogosch, F. A. and Toth, S. L. (1998) Maternal Depressive Disorder and Contextual Risk: Contributions to the Development of Attachment Insecurity and Behavior Problems in Toddlerhood. *Development and Psychopathology*, 10, 283–300.

Cicchetti, D. and Sroufe, L. A. (2000) The Past as Prologue to the Future: The Times, They've Been a-Changin'. *Development and Psychopathology*, **12**, 255–264.

Cicchetti, D., Toth, S. L. and Lynch, M. (1995) Bowlby's Dream Comes Full Circle – the Application of Attachment Theory to Risk and Psychopathology. In *Advances in Clinical Child Psychology, Vol 17*, pp. 1–75. New York: Plenum Press Div Plenum Publishing Corp.

Ciechanowski, P. and Katon, W. J. (2006) The Interpersonal Experience of Health Care through the Eyes of Patients with Diabetes. *Social Science and Medicine*, **63**, 3067–3079.

Ciechanowski, P. S., Russo, J. E., Katon, W. J., Von Korff, M., Simon, G. E., Lin, E. H. B., Ludman, E. J. and Young, B. A. (2006) The Association of Patient Relationship Style and Outcomes in Collaborative Care Treatment for Depression in Patients with Diabetes. *Medical Care*, **44**, 283–291.

Clarke, J. (2004) *Changing Welfare, Changing States: New Directions in Social Policy*. London: Sage.

Claussen, A. H. and Crittenden, P. M. (1991) Physical and Psychological Maltreatment – Relations among Types of Maltreatment. *Child Abuse and Neglect*, **15**, 5–18.

Cleaver, H., Unell, I. and Aldgate, J. (1999) *Children's Needs – Parenting Capacity; The Impact of Parental Mental Illness, Problem Alcohol and Drug Use, and Domestic Violence on Children's Development*. London: HMSO.

Cohen, S. (1985) *Visions of Social Control*. Cambridge: Polity Press.

Connor, K. M. and Davidson, J. R. T. (2003) Development of a New Resilience Scale: The Connor–Davidson Resilience Scale (CD–RISC). *Depression and Anxiety*, **18**, 76–82.

Crittenden, P. M. and Ainsworth, M. D. (1989) Child Maltreatment and Attachment Theory. In *Child Maltreatment: Theory and Research on the Causes and Consequences of Child Abuse and Neglect* (eds D. Cicchetti and V. Carlson), 432–463. New York: Cambridge University Press.

Crittenden, P. M. (2000) A Dynamic–Maturational Approach to Continuity and Change in Pattern of Attachment. In *The Organization of Attachment Relationships* (eds P. M. Crittenden and A. H. Claussen), 343–358.

Crittenden, P. M., Partridge, M. F. and Claussen, A. H. (1991) Family Patterns of Relationship in Normative and Dysfunctional Families. *Development and Psychopathology*, **3**, 491–512.

Crowell, J. A., Fraley, R. C. (1999) Measurement of Individual Differences in Adolescent and Adult Attachment. In *Handbook of Attachment: Theory, Research, and Clinical Applications* (eds J. Cassidy and P. R. Shaver), 434–465. New York: Guilford Press.

Damasio, A. R. (1994) *Descartes' Error*. New York: Grosset Putnam.

Dance, C., Rushton, A. and Quinton, D. (2002) Emotional Abuse in Early Childhood: Relationships with Progress in Subsequent Family Placement. *Journal of Child Psychology and Psychiatry and Allied Disciplines*, **43**, 395–407.

Daniel, B., Wassell, S., Ennis, J., Gilligan, R. and Ennis, E., Critical Understanding of Child Development:the development of a module for a post qualifying certificate course in child protection studies. *Child and Family Social Work*, **2 (4)**, 209–219.

Danziger, K. (1997) *Naming the Mind: How Philosophy Found Its Language*. London: Sage.

Das, V. (2003) Trauma and Testimony: Implications for Political Community. *Anthropological Theory*, **3(3)**, 293–307.

Davidson, J. R. T., Payne, V. M., Connor, K. M., Foa, E. B., Rothbaum, B. O., Hertzberg, M. A. and Weisler, R. H. (2005) Trauma, Resilience and Saliostasis: Effects of Treatment in Post-traumatic Stress Disorder. *International Clinical Psychopharmacology*, **20**, 43–48.

Dawkins, R. (1989) *The Selfish Gene. (2nd Edition)*. Oxford: Oxford Paperbacks.

Dean, D. (1979) Emotional Abuse of Children. *Children Today*, **8 (4)**, 18–20.

Demare, D. (2001) Examining Long-Term Correlates of Psychological, Physical, and Sexual Childhood Maltreatment: Validation of the Childhood Maltreatment Questionnaire. In *Dissertation Abstracts International: Section B: The Sciences and Engineering*, 5557–5557. US: ProQuest Information and Learning.

DfES (2003) *Referrals, Assessments and Children and Young People on the Child Protection Registers. Year Ending 31st March 2003. England*. London: DfES.

DHSS (1970) *The Battered Baby*. CMO2 (70) London: HMSO.

——(1974a) *Non Accidental Injury to Children*. LASSL (74) 13, CMO (74) 8, London: DHSS.

——(1974b) *Report of the Committee of Inquiry into the Care and Supervision Provided in Relation to Maria Colwell*. London: HMSO.

——(1980) *Child Abuse: Central Register Systems*. LASSL (80) 4 London: HMSO.

——(1985) *Social Work Decisions in Childcare: Recent Research Findings and Their Implications*. London: HMSO.

Di Tella, R., MacCulloch, R. J. and Oswald, A. J. (2003) The Macroeconomics of Happiness. *Review of Economics and Statistics*, **85**, 809–827.

Dingwall, R. (1986) The Jasmine Beckford Affair. *Modern Law Review*, **49**, 489–507.

——(1987) Predicting Child Abuse and Neglect. In *Child Abuse: Professional Practice and Public Policy* (ed. O. Stevenson). London: Harvester Wheatsheaf.

Dingwall, R., Eekelaar, J. and Murray, T. (1983) *The Protection of Children : State Intervention and Family Life*. Oxford: Basil Blackwell.

DOH [Department of Health] (1988) *Protecting Children: A Guide for Social Workers Undertaking a Comprehensive Assessment in Cases of Child Protection*. London: HMSO.

——(1989a) *An Introduction to the Children Act (1989)*. London: HMSO.

——(1989b) *Working Together under the Children Act, 1989*. London: HMSO.

——(1995) *Child Protection Messages from Research*. London: HMSO.

——(1998) *The Quality Protects Programme: Transforming Children's Services*.

——(1999) *Children and Young People on the Child Protection Registers. Year Ending 31st March 1999. England.* London: Department of Health.

——(2000a) *Assessing Children in Need and Their Families: Practice Guidance.* London: HMSO.

——(2000b) *Framework for the Assessment of Children in Need and Their Families.*

——(2001a) *Children and Young People on the Child Protection Registers. Year Ending 31st March 2001. England.* London: Department of Health.

——(2001b) *Studies Informing the Framework for the Assessment of Children in Need and Their Families.* London: HMSO.

——(2002) *The Children Act Report 2001.* London: HMSO.

——(2004) *The Integrated Children's System (ICS): A Conceptual Framework to Lead Work with Children and Families in Need into the Twenty-First Century.* London: HMSO.

DOH; HO; DfES (2003) *Keeping Children Safe: The Government's Response to the Victoria Climbie Inquiry Report and Joint Inspectors' Report Safeguarding Children.* London: HMSO.

DOH; DfES (2006) *The Common Assessment Framework.* London: HMSO.

Donzelot, J. (1979) *The Policing of Families.* New York: Pantheon.

Double, D. (2002) The Limits of Psychiatry. *British Medical Journal,* **324**, 900–904.

Douglas, K. (1996) *Invisible Wounds: A Self-Help Guide for Women in Destructive Relationships.* London: The Women's Press.

Douglas, M. (1986) *Risk Acceptability According to the Social Sciences.* London: Routledge.

——(1992) *Risk and Blame: Essays in Cultural Theory.* London: Routledge.

Doyle, C. (1997a) Emotional Abuse of Children: Issues for Intervention. *Child Abuse Review,* **6**, 330–342.

——(1997b) *Emotional Abuse of Children: Issues for Intervention: Summary Report.* Northampton: Nene Centre for Research.

Dozier, M., Stovall, K. C., Albus, K. E. (1999) Attachment and Psychopathology in Adulthood. In *Handbook of Attachment: Theory, Research, and Clinical Applications* (eds J. Cassidy and P. R. Shaver), 497–519. New York: Guilford Press.

Dreyfus, H. L. and Rabinow, P. (1982) *Michel Foucault: Beyond Structuralism and Hermeneutics.* London: Harvester Wheatsheaf.

Duff, A. (2006) *The Trial on Trial: Judgement and Calling to Account.* Oxford: Hart Publishing.

Dupart, T. (2006) Attachment Styles in Caregivers of Loved Ones with Alzheimer's Disease. In *Dissertation Abstracts International: Section B: The Sciences and Engineering,* 3447–3447. US: ProQuest Information and Learning.

Durkheim, E. and Mauss, M. (1963) *Primitive Classification* (Translated by Rodney Needham). Chicago, IL: Chicago University Press.

Dwivedi, K. N. (2000) *Post-traumatic Stress Disorder in Children and Adolescents.* London: Whurr Publishers.

Eager, C. 2003 'The War is over but the Sarajevans cannot find the peace they seek'. *Daily Telegraph,* 6th September.

Eagleton, T. (1990) *The Ideology of the Aesthetic.* Oxford, UK: Blackwell.

——(2001) *The Gatekeeper: A Memoir.* Harmondsworth, UK: Allen Lane.

Eberhart, N. K. and Hammen, C. L. (2006) Interpersonal Predictors of Onset of Depression During the Transition to Adulthood. *Personal Relationships,* **13**, 195–206.

Edkins, J. (2003) *Trauma and the Memory of Politics*. Cambridge, UK: Cambridge University Press.

Elgin, J. and Pritchard, M. (2006) Adult Attachment and Disordered Eating in Undergraduate Men and Women. *Journal of College Student Psychotherapy*, **21**, 25–40.

Erichsen, J. E. (1866) *On Railway and Other Injuries of the Nervous System*. London: Walton and Maberly.

——(1883) *On Concussion of the Spine, Nervous Shock and Other Obscure Injuries in the Clinical and Medico-Legal Aspects*. New York: William Wood.

Excell, R. (2004) *Financial Times*, 1 March.

Fahlberg, V. (1981a) *Attachment and Separation*: British Agencies for Adoption and Fostering.

——(1981b) *Helping Children When They Must Move*. London: British Agencies for Adoption and Fostering.

Fairbairn, W. R. D. (1952) An Object–Relations Theory of the Personality. London: Tavistock.

Fanthorpe, U. A. (1989) *Selected Poems*. Harmondsworth: Penguin Books.

Farge, S. (2006) Clinical Recommendations for the Assessment and Treatment of Primary Caregivers and Pediatric Cancer Patients. In *Dissertation Abstracts International: Section B: The Sciences and Engineering*, 540–540. US: ProQuest Information and Learning.

Farmer, E. and Owen, M. (1995) *Child Protection Practice: Private Risks and Public Memories*. London: HMSO.

Fassin, D. and Rechtman, R. (2009) *The Empire of Trauma: An Inquiry into the Condition of Victimhood* (translated by Rachel Gomme). Princeton N. J: Princeton University Press.

Fawcett, B., Featherstone, B. and Goddard, J. (2004) *Contemporary Childcare Policy and Practice*. Basingstoke: Palgrave Macmillan.

Felthous, A. R. (1980) Aggression against Cats, Dogs and People. *Child Psychiatry and Human Development*, **10**, 169–177.

Ferguson, B. B. (2006) Bulimia and Binge-Eating-Disorder and Their Relationship to Family Characteristics, Attachment, Depression, and Self-Esteem. In *Dissertation Abstracts International: Section B: The Sciences and Engineering*, 5084–5085. US: ProQuest Information and Learning.

Field, L. H. (1999) Post-traumatic stress disorder: A Reappraisal. *Journal of the Royal Society of Medicine*, **92**.

Figlio, K. M. (1976) The Metaphor of Organisation. An Historical Perspective on the Bio-Medical Sciences of the Early Nineteenth Century. *History of Science*, **14**, 17–53.

Finzi-Dottan, R., Dekel, R., Lavi, T. and Su'ali, T. (2006) Post-traumatic stress disorder Reactions among Children with Learning Disabilities Exposed to Terror Attacks. *Comprehensive Psychiatry*, **47**, 144–151.

Fivush, R. and Sales, J. M. (2006) Coping, Attachment, and Mother–Child Narratives of Stressful Events. *Merrill-Palmer Quarterly*, **52**, 125–150.

Fleming, W. M., Jory, B. and Burton, D. L. (2002) Characteristics of Juvenile Offenders Admitting to Sexual Activity with Nonhuman Animals. *Society and Animals*, **10 (1)**, 31–45.

Foa, E. B. and Kozak, M. J. (1986) Emotional Processing of Fear: Exposure to Corrective Information. *Psychological Bulletin*, **99**, 20–35.

Fogarty, M. (1980) Emotional Abuse to Be Included in Registers. *Social Work Today*, **12**, (1) 4.

Fonagy, P. (2001) *Attachment Theory and Psychoanalysis*. New York: Other Press.

Fonagy, P. and Bateman, A. W. (2006) Mechanisms of Change in Mentalization-Based Treatment of BPO. *Journal of Clinical Psychology*, **62**, 411–430.

Fonagy, P., Target, M. and Gergely, G. (2000) Attachment and Borderline Personality Disorder: A Theory and Some Evidence. *Psychiatric Clinics of North America*, **23**, 103–122.

Foucault, M., (1973) *The Order of Things: An Archeology of the Human Sciences* (translated by A. M. Sheridan Smith). New York: Vintage/Random House.

——(1977) Nietzsche, Genealogy, History (1971). In *Michel Foucault: Language, Counter Memory, Practice: Selected Essays and Interviews*. Ithaca, NY: Cornell University Press.

——(1978) About The Concept of The Dangerous Individual in 19th-Century Legal Psychiatry. *International Journal of Law and Psychiatry*, **1**, 1–18.

——(1979) On Governmentality. *Ideology and Consciousness*, 5–21.

——(1980a) Canguilhem, Georges – Philosopher of Error. *Ideology and Consciousness*, 51–62.

——(1980b) *The History of Sexuality: Vol 1: An Introduction* (translated by Robert Hurley). New York: Vintage/Random House.

——(1982) The Subject and Power. *Critical Inquiry*, **8**, 777–795.

——(1985) Why Study Power – a Question of the Subject. *Aut Aut*, 2–10.

Fox, N. A. and Card, J. A. (1999) Psycho-physiological Measures in the Study of Attachment. In *Handbook of Attachment: Theory, Research, and Clinical Applications* (eds J. Cassidy and P. R. Shaver), 226–245. New York: Guilford Press.

Fraley, R. C., Fazzari, D. A., Bonanno, G. A. and Dekel, S. (2006) Attachment and Psychological Adaptation in High Exposure Survivors of the September 11th Attack on the World Trade Center. *Personality and Social Psychology Bulletin*, **32**, 538–551.

Fraley, R. C. and Shaver, P. R. (1998) Airport Separations: A Naturalistic Study of Adult Attachment Dynamics in Separating Couples. *Journal of Personality and Social Psychology*, **75**, 1198–1212.

Franklin, A. W. (1979) Summing Up. *Child Abuse and Neglect*, **3** (1), xvii–xx.

Fraser, S. (2002) Patterns of Substance Use in Adolescent Male Young Offenders: Relationships with Child Maltreatment Experiences and Their Inculcation of Antisocial Identities. In *Dissertation Abstracts International: Section B: The Sciences and Engineering*, 4205–4205. US: ProQuest Information and Learning.

Freud, S. (1923) The Ego and the Id. In *Standard Edition of the Complete Psychological Works of Sigmund Freud. Vol 19* (ed. J. Strachey). London: Hogarth Press.

——(1924) Neurosis and Psychosis. In *Standard Edition of the Complete Psychological Works of Sigmund Freud. Vol 19* (ed. J. Strachey). London: Hogarth Press.

——(1950 [1920]) Beyond the Pleasure Principle. In *The Standard Edition of the Complete Psychological Works of Sigmund Freud. Volume 18* (ed. J. Strachey), 3–64. London: Hogarth Press.

——(1953 [1900]) The Interpretation of Dreams. In *The Standard Edition of the Complete Psychological Works of Sigmund Freud. Volumes 4 and 5* (ed. J. Strachey). London: Hogarth Press.

——(1966 [1892–94]) Extracts from Freud's Footnotes to His Translation of Charcot's Tuesday Lectures. In *The Standard Edition of the Complete Psychological Works of Sigmund Freud. Volume 1* (ed. J. Strachey), 137–143. London: Hogarth Press.

——(1966 [1895]) Project for a Scientific Psychology. In *The Standard Edition of the Complete Psychological Works of Sigmund Freud. Volume 1* (ed. J. Strachey), 281–397. London: Hogarth Press.

Friedrich, W. N., Talley, N. J., Panser, L., Zinsmeister, A. and Fett, S. (1997) Concordance of Reports of Childhood Abuse by Adults. *Child Maltreatment*, 2, 164–171.

Furedi, F. (2004) *Therapy Culture: Cultivating Vulnerability in an Uncertain Age.* London: Routledge.

Gallagher, B. (2005) New Technology: Helping or Harming Children? *Child Abuse Review*, 14, 367–373.

Garbarino, J. (1978) The Elusive Crime of Emotional Abuse. *Child Abuse and Neglect*, 2, 89–99.

Garbarino, J. (1995) The American War Zone: What Children Can Tell Us About Living with Violence. *Journal of Developmental and Behavioral Pediatrics*, 16, 431–435.

Garbarino, J., Guttman, E. and Wilson Seely, J. (1986) *The Psychologically Battered Child.* San Francisco, CA: Jossey Bass.

Garland, C. (1998) *Understanding Trauma: A Psychoanalytical Approach.* London: Tavistock.

Garno, J. L., Gunawardane, N. and Goldberg, J. F. (2008) Predictors of Trait Aggression in Bipolar Disorder. *Bipolar Disorders*, 10, 285–292.

Gelles, R. J. (1979a) *Family Violence.* Beverly Hills: Sage Publications.

——(1979b) Psychopathology as Cause: A Critique and Reformulation. In *Violence against Children* (ed. D. G. Gil). Cambridge, Mass: Harvard University Press.

George, C., Kaplan, N. and Main, M. (1984) Adult Attachment Interview.

——(1985) The Adult Attachment Interview Protocol (2nd Ed.). Unpublished Manuscript. University of California, Berkeley. Department of Psychology.

——(1996) The Adult Attachment Interview Protocol (3rd Ed.). Unpublished Manuscript. University of California, Berkeley. Department of Psychology.

Gergen, K. and Shotter, J. (1989) *Texts of Identity.* London: Sage.

Gerhardt, S. (2004) *Why Love Matters: How Affection Shapes a Baby's Brain.* London: Brunner–Routledge.

Gervis, M. and Dunn, N. (2004) The Emotional Abuse of Elite Child Athletes by Their Coaches. *Child Abuse Review*, 13, 215–223.

Gibbons, J., Conroy, S. and Bell, C. (1995) *Operating the Child Protection System.* London: HMSO.

Giddens, A. (1998) *The Third Way: The Renewal of Social Democracy.* London: Polity Press/Blackwell.

Glaser, D. (2002) Emotional Abuse and Neglect (Psychological Maltreatment): A Conceptual Framework. *Child Abuse and Neglect*, 26, 697–714.

Glaser, D. (1993) Emotional Abuse. In *Clinical Paediatrics: Child Abuse* (eds C. Hobbs and J. Wynne), 251–267. London: Bailliere Tindall.

Glaser, D. and Prior, V. (1997) Is the Term Child Protection Applicable to Emotional Abuse? *Child Abuse Review*, 6, 315–329.

Glaser, D., Prior, V., Lynch, M. A. and British Association for the Study and Prevention of Child Abuse and Neglect (2001) *Emotional Abuse and Emotional Neglect: Antecedents, Operational Definitions and Consequences.* York: BASPCAN.

Godwin, G. (2002) *Heart: A Personal Journey through Its Myths and Meanings.* London: Bloomsbury.

Goodman, N. (1979) *Ways of Worldmaking.* Indianapolis, IN: Hackett.

Gopfert, M. (2006) Cognitive Analytic Therapy and Parents in Prison. In *Cognitive Analytic Therapy for Offenders: A New Approach to Forensic Psychotherapy* (eds P. H. Pollock, M. Stowell-Smith and M. Gopfert), 139–157. New York: Routledge/Taylor and Francis Group.

Greenberg, M. T. (1999) Attachment and Psychopathology in Childhood. In *Handbook of Attachment: Theory, Research, and Clinical Applications* (eds J. Cassidy and P. R. Shaver), 469–496. New York: Guilford Press.

Griffiths, P. E. (1997) *What Emotions Really Are.* Chicago, IL: University of Chicago Press.

Grossman, K. E. and Grossmann, K. (1999) Mary Ainsworth: Our Guide to Attachment Research. *Attachment and Human Development*, **1**, 224–228.

Grossmann, K. E., Grossmann, K., Huber, F. and Wartner, U. (1981) German Children's Behaviour Towards Their Mothers at Twelve Months and Their Fathers at Eighteen Months in Ainsworth's Strange Situation. *International Journal of Behavioural Development*, **4**, 157–181.

Grossmann, K. E., Grossmann, K. and Waters, E. (2005) *Attachment from Infancy to Adulthood: The Major Longitudinal Studies.* New York: Guilford Press.

Grosz, E. (1994) *Volatile Bodies: Toward a Corporeal Feminism.* Bloomington and Indianapolis, IN: Indiana University Press.

Gurr, R. and Quiroga, J. (2001) Approaches to Torture Rehabilitation. *Torture: Supplementum No. 1*, **1(a)**.

Hacking, I. (1995a) The Looping Effects of Human Kinds. In *Causal Cognition: A Multidisciplinary Approach* (eds D. Sperber, D. Premack and A. J. Premack). Oxford, UK: Clarendon Press.

——(1995b) *Rewriting the Soul: Multiple Personality and the Sciences of Memory.* Princeton, NJ: Princeton University Press.

——(1997) John Searle's Building Blocks. *The History of the Human Sciences*, **10 (4)**, 83–92.

——(1999) *The Social Construction of What?* Cambridge, Mass: Harvard University Press.

Hamama-Raz, Y. and Solomon, Z. (2006) Psychological Adjustment of Melanoma Survivors: The Contribution of Hardiness, Attachment, and Cognitive Appraisal. *Journal of Individual Differences*, **27**, 172–182.

Hamarman, S., Pope, K. H. and Czaja, S. J. (2002) Emotional Abuse in Children: Variations in Legal Definitions and Rates across the United States. *Child Maltreatment*, **7**, 303–311.

Hamilton, W. (1964) The Genetical Theory of Social Behaviour. *Journal of Theoretical Biology*, **7**, 1–52.

Hancock, P. (1998) Emotional Abuse Treatment and Prevention, a Specialist Health Visitor's Intervention. *Child Abuse Review*, **7**, 58–62.

Handford, P. R. (2006) *Mullany and Handford's Tort Liability for Psychiatric Damage* (2nd edn). Sidney: Thompson Lawbook Co.

Harlow, C. (2005) *Understanding Tort Law* (3rd edn). London: Sweet and Maxwell.

Harlow, H. F. (1961) The Development of Affectional Patterns in Infant Monkeys. In *Determinants of Infant Behaviour* (ed. B. M. Foss). London: Methuen.

Harlow, H. F. and Zimmermann, R. R. (1958) The Development of Affectional Responses in Infant Monkeys. *Proceedings of the American Philosophical Society*, **102**, 501–509.

Harper, F. W. K. and Arias, I. (2004) The Role of Shame in Predicting Adult Anger and Depressive Symptoms among Victims of Child Psychological Maltreatment. *Journal of Family Violence*, **19**, 367–375.

Harris, R. (1989) *Murders and Madness: Medicine, Law and Society in the Fin De Siecle*. Oxford, UK: Clarendon Press.

Hart, H. (1961) *The Concept of Law*. Oxford, UK: Clarendon Press.

Hart, S., Germain, R. and Brassard, M. (eds) (1983) *Proceedings Summary of the International Conference on the Psychological Abuse of Children and Youth*. Office for the Psychological Rights of the Child: Indiana University.

Hart, S. N. and Brassard, M. R. (1986) *Developing and Validating Operationally Defined Measures of Emotional Maltreatment: A Multimodal Study of the Relationship between Caretaker Behaviors and Children Characteristics across Three Developmental Levels (Grant No. DHHS90ca1216)*.

——(1991) Psychological Maltreatment: Progress Achieved. *Development and Psychopathology*, **3**, 61–70.

Hart, S. N., Binggeli, N. J. and Brassard, M. R. (1997) Evidence for the Effects of Psychological Maltreatment. *Journal of Emotional Abuse*, 1, 27–58.

Hart, S. N., Brassard, M. R., Binggeli, N. J., Davidson, H. A., Myers, J. E. B., Berliner, L., Briere, J., Hendrix, C. T. and Jenny, C. (2002) Psychological Maltreatment. In *The APSAC Handbook on Child Maltreatment (2nd Ed.)*, 79–103. Thousand Oaks, CA: Sage Publications.

Hart, S. N., Brassard, M. R., Karlson, H., J. Briere, L. B. J. B. C. J. and Reid, T. (1996) Psychological Maltreatment. In *The APSAC Handbook on Child Maltreatment*, 72. Thousand Oaks, CA: Sage Publications.

Hazan, C. and Shaver, P. (1987) Romantic Love Conceptualised as an Attachment Process. *Journal of Personality and Social Psychology*, **52**, 511–524.

Heidegger, M. (1977) The Question Concerning Technology. In *The Question Concerning Technology and Other Essays*. New York: Harper and Row.

Helfer, M. E., Kempe, R. S. and Krugman, R. D. (1997) *The Battered Child* (5th edn). Chicago, IL; London: University of Chicago Press.

Helfer, R. E. and Kempe, C. H. (1968) *The Battered Child*. Chicago, IL: University of Chicago Press.

——(1974) *The Battered Child* (2d edn). Chicago, IL: University of Chicago Press.

——(1980) *The Battered Child* (3d edn). Chicago, IL: University of Chicago Press.

——(1987) *The Battered Child* (4th edn). Chicago, IL: University of Chicago Press.

Hendrick, H. (2003) *Child Welfare: Historical Dimensions, Contemporary Debate*. Bristol: Policy Press.

Her Majesty's Government (2003) *Every Child Matters*. London: HMSO.

Herbert, M. (1996) *Bonding: Infantile and Parental Attachments*. Leicester: The British Psychological Society.

Herman, J. (1992) *Trauma and Recovery*. New York: Basic books.

Hesse, E. (1999) The Adult Attachment Interview: Historical and Current Perspectives. In *Handbook of Attachment: Theory, Research, and Clinical Applications* (eds J. Cassidy and P. R. Shaver), 395–433. New York: Guilford Press.

Higgins, D. J. and McCabe, M. P. (2000) Multi-Type Maltreatment and the Long-Term Adjustment of Adults. *Child Abuse Review*, 9, 6–18.

——(2001) Multiple Forms of Child Abuse and Neglect: Adult Retrospective Reports. *Aggression and Violent Behavior*, 6, 547–578.

Hinde, R. A. and Rutter, M. (1988) Continuities and Discontinuities: Conceptual Issues and Methodological Considerations. In *Studies of Psychosocial Risk: The Power of Longitudinal Data*, 367–383.

Hirigoyen, M.-F. (2000) *Stalking the Soul: Emotional Abuse and the Erosion of Identity*. New York, NY US: Helen Marx Books.

Hirschi, T. (1969) *The Causes of Delinquency*. Berkely, CA: University of California Press.

Hodson, C., Newcomb, M. D., Locke, T. F. and Goodyear, R. K. (2006) Childhood Adversity, Poly-Substance Use, and Disordered Eating in Adolescent Latinas: Mediated and Indirect Paths in a Community Sample. *Child Abuse and Neglect*, 30, 1017–1036.

Hofer, M. A. (1995) Hidden Regulators – Implications for a New Understanding of Attachment, Separation, and Loss. *Attachment Theory*, 203–230.

——(1996) On the Nature and Consequences of Early Loss. *Psychosomatic Medicine*, 58, 570–581.

Holmes, J. (2001) *The Search for the Secure Base: Attachment Theory and Psychotherapy*. Hove: Brunner–Routledge.

Horder, J. (1998) Reconsidering Psychic Assault. *Criminal Law Review*, 392–403.

Horowitz, M. (1976) *Stress Response Reactions* (2nd edn). New York: Basic Books.

Horwitz, A. V. and Wakefield, J. C. (2007) *The Loss of Sadness: How Psychiatry Transformed Normal Sorrow into Depressive Disorder*. New York: Oxford University Press.

House of Commons (1977) Select Committee on Violence in the Family: Violence to Children: Session 1976–77. London: House of Commons.

——(1978) Violence to Children: A Response to the First Report of the Select Committee on Violence in the Family. Session 1976–77. London: House of Commons.

House of Commons (HC 360). Social Services Committee. (1984) *Children in Care: Second Report from the Social Services Committee, House of Commons, Session 1983–84*. London: HMSO.

Howe, D. (1992) Child Abuse and the Bureaucratisation of Social Work. *Sociological Review*, 40, 491.

——(2006a) Developmental Attachment Psychotherapy with Fostered and Adopted Children. *Child and Adolescent Mental Health*, 11, 128–134.

——(2006b) Disabled Children, Parent–Child Interaction and Attachment. *Child and Family Social Work*, 11, 95–106.

Hyde, A. (1997) *Bodies of Law*. Princeton, NJ: Princeton University Press.

Ignatieff, M. (1996) Articles of Faith. *Index on Censorship*, 25, No 5, 110–122.

Iwaniec, D. (1983) Social and Psychological Features in the Etiology and Management of Children Who Fail to Thrive. PHD in the Department of Psychology, University of Leicester.

——(1995) *The Emotionally Abused and Neglected Child: Identification, Assessment, and Intervention*. Chichester; New York: J. Wiley and Sons.

——(1997) An Overview of Emotional Maltreatment and Failure to Thrive. *Child Abuse Review*, 6, 370–388.

Jackson, J. H. (1931a) *Selected Writings of John Hughlings Jackson. Volume 1.* London: Hodder and Stoughton.

——(1931b) *Selected Writings of John Hughlings Jackson. Volume 2.* London: Hodder and Stoughton.

Jackson, M. (2005) Storytelling Events, Violence, and the Appearance of the Past. *Anthropological Quarterly,* **78,** 355–375.

James, O. (2007) *Affluenza.* London: Vermilion/Ebury Publishing.

James, W (1894) *Psychological Review,* **1:** 199.

Janet, P. (1889) *L'automatisme Psychologique: Essai De Psychologie Experimentale Sur Les Formes Inferieures De L'activite Humaine.* Paris: Alcan.

——(1901) *The Mental State of Hystericals: A Study of Mental Stigmata and Mental Accidents.* New York: G. P. Putnam.

——(1925) *Psychological Healing.* New York: Macmillan.

Jaret, P. (1986) Our Immune System: The Wars Within. *National Geographic,* **169,** 702–735.

Jones, E. and Wessely, S. (2005) *Shell Shock to PTSD: Military Psychiatry From 1900 to the Gulf War.* Hove: Maudsley Monograph, Psychology Press.

Jones, S., Davidson, W. S., II, Bogat, G. A., Levendosky, A. and von Eye, A. (2005) Validation of the Subtle and Overt Psychological Abuse Scale: An Examination of Construct Validity. *Violence and Victims,* **20,** 407–416.

Jordan, E. F. (1880) *Surgical Inquiries, Including the Hastings Essay on Shock, the Treatment of Surgical Inflammations, and Clinical Lectures.* London: J. and A. Churchill.

Kang, S.-Y., Deren, S. and Goldstein, M. F. (2002) Relationships between Childhood Abuse and Neglect Experience and HIV Risk Behaviors among Methadone Treatment Drop-Outs. *Child Abuse and Neglect,* **26,** 1275–1289.

Kaplan, S. J., Pelcovitz, D. and Labruna, V. (1999) Child and Adolescent Abuse and Neglect Research: A Review of the Past 10 Years. Part I: Physical and Emotional Abuse and Neglect. *Journal of the American Academy of Child and Adolescent Psychiatry,* **38,** 1214–1222.

Kapur, R. (2005) *Erotic Justice: Law and the New Politics of Postcolonialism.* London: Glass House Press.

Kardiner, A. (1941) *The Traumatic Neuroses of War.* Washington, DC: National Research Council.

Kardiner, A. and Spiegel, H. (1947) *War Stress and Neurotic Illness.* New York: Paul B. Hoeber.

Karesh, D. M. (1996) The Relationship between Adult Neuroticism and Childhood Experiences of Psychological Maltreatment, Physical Punishment, and Intergenerational Sexual Contact. In *Dissertation Abstracts International: Section B: The Sciences and Engineering,* 6418–6418. US: ProQuest Information and Learning.

Kavanagh, C. (1982) Emotional Abuse and Mental Injury: A Critique of the Concepts and a Recommendation for Practice. *Journal of the American Academy of Child Psychiatry,* **21,** 171–177.

Keen, S. (1992) *Inward Bound: Exploring the Geography of Your Emotions.* New York: Bantam Doubleday.

Kempe, C. H. (1979) Recent Developments in the Field of Child Abuse. *Child Abuse and Neglect,* **3(1),** ix–xv.

Kempe, C. H., Silverman, F. N., Steele, B. F., Droegemueller, W. and Silver, H. K. (1962) The Battered Child Syndrome. *Journal of the American Medical Association*, **181**, 17–24.

Kennedy, H. (1993) *Eve Was Framed: Women and British Justice*. London: Chatto and Windus/Secker and Warburg.

Kinard, E. M. (1994) Methodological Issues and Practical Problems in Conducting Research on Maltreated Children. *Child Abuse and Neglect*, **18**, 654–656.

King, M. and Piper, C. (1990) *How the Law Thinks About Children*. Aldershot, Hants. Gower.

King, P. and Steiner, R. ed. (1944) *The Freud–Klein Controversies1941–45*, Routledge/Tavistock. London.

Klein, M. (1932) The Psychoanalysis of Children. Revised edition 1984. New York: The Free Press.

Kostelny, K. and Garbarino, J. (2001) The War Close to Home: Children and Violence in the United States. In *Peace, Conflict, and Violence: Peace Psychology for the 21st Century* (eds D. J. Christie, R. V. Wagner and D. D. N. Winter), 110–119. Upper Saddle River, NJ: Prentice Hall/Pearson Education.

Kotov, K. M. (2006) Insecure Attachment and College-Age Alcohol Use Disorders. A Case Report. *International Journal of Adolescent Medicine and Health*, **18**, 203–206.

Kraemer, G. (1992) A Psychological Theory of Attachment. *Behavioural and Brain Sciences*, **15**, 493–541.

Kraemer, S. and Roberts, J. (eds) (1996) *The Politics of Attachment: Towards a Secure Society*. London: Free Association Books.

Lacey (1998) *Unspeakable Subjects*. Oxford: Hart Publishing.

Laing, R. D. (1961) *The Self and Others*. London: Tavistock.

——(1964) *Sanity, Madness and the Family*. London: Penguin Books.

Lamb, M., Thompson, R., Gardner, W. and Charnov, E. (1984) Security of Infantile Attachment as Assessed in The "Strange Situation". Its Study and Biological Interpretation. *Behavioural and Brain Sciences*, **7**, 127–171.

Lanchester, J (2006) *Introduction to The Driver's Seat by Muriel Spark*. Harmondsworth: Penguin Classics.

Lang, A. J., Craske, M. G., Brown, M. and Ghaneian, A. (2001) Fear-Related State Dependent Memory. *Cognition and Emotion*, **15**, 695–703.

Latour, B. (1988 [1984]) *The Pasteurisation of France*. Cambridge, MA: Harvard University Press.

Layard, R. (2007) Setting Happiness as a National Goal. *Futurist*, **41**, 37–37.

——(2008) Special Issue: Happiness and Public Economics – Introduction. *Journal of Public Economics*, **92**, 1773–1776.

Leach, P. (1994) *Your Baby and Child: From Birth to Age Five*. New York: Knopf.

Levine, S. (1994) The Ontogeny of the Hypothalamic–Pituitary–adrenal Axis. The Influence of Maternal Factors. *Annals of the New York Academy of Science*, **746**, 275–288; discussion 289–293.

Liotti, G. (1992) Disorganized/Disoriented Attachment in the Etiology of the Dissociative Disorders. *Dissociation: Progress in the Dissociative Disorders*, **5**, 196–204.

Lopez-Corvo, R. E. (2003) *The Dictionary of the Work of W. R. Bion*. London: Karnac Books.

Lord Laming (2003) *The Victoria Climbie Inquiry. Report of an Inquiry by Lord Laming.* London: HMSO.

Lorenz, K. Z. (1958) The Evolution of Behavior. *Scientific American,* **199,** 67–70.

Lourie, I. S. and Stephano, I. (1978) On Defining Emotional Abuse: Results of a NIMH–CCAN Workshop. In *Child Abuse and Neglect: Issues on Innovation and Implementation. Proceedings of the Second Annual Conference on Child Abuse and Neglect, April 1977* (eds M. L. Launderdale, R. N. Anderson and S. E. Cramer). Washington, DC: US Department of Health Education and Welfare.

Luborsky, L., Singer, B. and Luborsky, L. (1975) Comparative Studies of Psychotherapies: Is It True That 'Everyone Has Won and All Must Have Prizes'? *Archives of General Psychiatry,* **32,** 995–1008.

Luhmann, N. (1988) Closure and Openness: On Reality in the World of Law. In *Autopoietic Law: A New Approach to Law and Society* (ed. G. Teubner). Berlin: de Gruyter.

——(1993) *Risk: A Sociological Theory.* Berlin: de Gruyter.

Lynch, M. A. (1976) Child Abuse: The Critical Path. *Journal of Maternal and Child Health,* **July,** 25–29.

Lynch, M. A. (1978) Prognosis of Child-Abuse. *Journal of Child Psychology and Psychiatry and Allied Disciplines,* **19,** 175–180.

Lynch, M. A. and Roberts, J. (1977a) Predicting Child Abuse. *Nursing Mirror,* **145,** 18–19.

——(1977b) Predicting Child-Abuse – Signs of Bonding Failure in Maternity Hospital. *British Medical Journal,* **1,** 624–626.

——(1982) *Consequences of Child Abuse.* London: Academic Press.

Lynch, M. A., Steinberg, D. and Ounsted, C. (1975) Family Unit in a Children's Psychiatric Hospital. *British Medical Journal,* **2,** 127–129.

Lyons-Ruth, K., Alpern, L. and Repacholi, B. (1993) Disorganized Infant Attachment Classification and Maternal Psycho–social Problems as Predictors of Hostile–Aggressive Behavior in the Preschool Classroom. *Child Development,* **64,** 572–585.

Lyons-Ruth, K. and Block, D. (1996a) The Disturbed Caregiving System: Relations among Childhood Trauma, Maternal Caregiving, and Infant Affect and Attachment. *Infant Mental Health Journal,* **17,** 257–275.

Lyons-Ruth, K., Bronfman, E. and Parsons, E. (1999a) Maternal Frightened, Frightening, or Atypical Behavior and Disorganized Infant Attachment Patterns. *Monographs of the Society for Research in Child Development,* **64,** 67.

Lyons-Ruth, K., Jacobvitz, D. (1999b) Attachment Disorganization: Unresolved Loss, Relational Violence, and Lapses in Behavioral and Attentional Strategies. In *Handbook of Attachment: Theory, Research, and Clinical Applications* (eds J. Cassidy, J. and P. R. Shaver), 520–554. New York: Guilford Press.

Lyons-Ruth, K., Repacholi, B., McLeod, S. and Silva, E. (1991) Disorganized Attachment Behavior in Infancy: Short-Term Stability, Maternal and Infant Correlates, and Risk-Related Subtypes. *Development and Psychopathology,* **3,** 377–396.

Lyons-Ruth, K., Zeanah, C. H., Benoit, D., Mash, E. J. and Barkley, R. A. (1996b) Disorder and Risk for Disorder During Infancy and Toddlerhood. In *Child Psychopathology,* 457–491. New York: Guilford Press.

Maccoby, E. E. and Feldman, S. S. (1972) Mother-Attachment and Stranger-Reactions in the Third Year of Life. *Monographs of the Society for Research in Child Development*, **37**.

Macfarlane, A. C. (1986) Post Traumatic Morbidity of a Disaster: A Study of Cases Presenting for Psychiatric Treatment. *Journal of Nervous and Mental Disease*, **174**, 4–14.

Maciejewski, P. K. and Mazure, C. M. (2006) Fear of Criticism and Rejection Mediates an Association between Childhood Emotional Abuse and Adult Onset of Major Depression. *Cognitive Therapy and Research*, **30**, 105–122.

Mahler, M. S. (1967) On Human Symbiosis and the Vicissitudes of Individuation. *Journal of the American Psychoanalytic Association*, **15**, 740–763.

Main, M. (1991) Metacognitive Knowledge, Metacognitive Monitoring, and Singular (Coherent) Vs. Multiple (Incoherent) Model of Attachment: Findings and Directions for Future Research. In *Attachment across the Life Cycle* (eds C. M. Parkes, J. Stevenson-Hinde and P. Marris), 127–159. New York: Tavistock/Routledge.

——(1995) Discourse, Prediction, and Recent Studies in Attachment: Implications for Psychoanalysis. In *Research in Psychoanalysis: Process, Development, Outcome* (eds T. Shapiro and R. N. Emde), 209–244. Madison, CT: International Universities Press, Inc.

——(1996) Introduction to the Special Section on Attachment and Psychopathology, 2. Overview of the Field of Attachment. *Journal of Consulting and Clinical Psychology*, **64**, 237–243.

——(1999a) Epilogue: Attachment Theory: Eighteen Points. In *Handbook of Attachment: Theory, Research and Clinical Applications* (eds J. Cassidy and P. R. Shaver). New York: Guilford Press.

——(1999b) Mary D. Salter Ainsworth: Tribute and Portrait. *Psychoanalytic Inquiry*, **19**, 682–736.

Main, M. and Cassidy, J. (1988) Categories of Response to Reunion with the Parent at Age 6: Predictable from Infant Attachment Classifications and Stable over a 1-Month Period. *Developmental Psychology*, **24**, 415–426.

Main, M. and Hesse, E. (1990) Parents' Unresolved Traumatic Experiences Are Related to Infant Disorganized Attachment Status: Is Frightened and/or Frightening Parental Behavior the Linking Mechanism? In *Attachment in the Preschool Years: Theory, Research, and Intervention* (eds M. T. Greenberg, D. Cicchetti and E. M. Cummings), 161–182. Chicago, IL: University of Chicago Press.

Main, M., Kaplan, N. and Cassidy, J. (1985) Security in Infancy, Childhood, and Adulthood: A Move to the Level of Representation. *Monographs of the Society for Research in Child Development*, **50**, 66–104.

Main, M. and Morgan, H. (1996) Disorganization and Disorientation in Infant Strange Situation Behavior: Phenotypic Resemblance to Dissociative States. In *Handbook of Dissociation: Theoretical, Empirical, and Clinical Perspectives* (eds L. K. Michelson and W. J. Ray), 107–138. New York: Plenum Press.

Main, M. and Solomon, J. (1990) Procedures for Identifying Infants as Disorganized/Disoriented During the Ainsworth Strange Situation. In *Attachment in the Preschool Years: Theory, Research, and Intervention* (eds M. T. Greenberg, D. Cicchetti and E. M. Cummings), 121–160. Chicago, IL: University of Chicago Press.

Main, M., Solomon, J. (1986) Discovery of an Insecure-Disorganized/Disoriented Attachment Pattern: Procedures, Findings, and Implications for the Classification of Behavior. In *Affective Development in Infancy* (eds T. B. Brazelton and M. Yogman), 95–124.

Manier, E. (1980) History, Philosophy and Sociology of Biology. A Family Romance. *Studies in the History and Philosophy of Science*, **11**(1), 1–24.

Marcil, R. R., Jr. (1996) The Development of a Childhood Stress Inventory: Establishing Reliability, Validity, and Normality. In *Dissertation Abstracts International: Section B: The Sciences and Engineering*, 4635–4635. US: ProQuest Information and Learning.

Marini, Z. A., Dane, A. V., Bosacki, S. L. and Ylc, C. (2006) Direct and Indirect Bully-Victims: Differential Psycho-social Risk Factors Associated with Adolescents Involved in Bullying and Victimization. *Aggressive Behavior*, **32**, 551–569.

Martin, E. (1990) Toward an Anthropology of Immunology – the Body as Nation State. *Medical Anthropology Quarterly*, **4**, 410–426.

Masters, J. C. and Wellman, H. M. (1974) The Study of Human Infant Attachment: A Procedural Critique. *Psychological Bulletin*, **81**, 218–237.

Maturana, H. and Varela, F. J. (1980) *Autopoiesis and Cognition: The Realisation of the Living*. New York: Springer.

Mayou, R. (1996) Accident Neurosis Revisited. *British Journal of Psychiatry*, **168**, 399–403.

Mazzeo, S. E. and Espelage, D. L. (2002) Association between Childhood Physical and Emotional Abuse and Disordered Eating Behaviors in Female Undergraduates: An Investigation of the Mediating Role of Alexithymia and Depression. *Journal of Counseling Psychology*, **49**, 86–100.

McCarthy, D. (1979) Recognition of Signs of Emotional Deprivation. *Child Abuse and Neglect*, **3**, 423–428.

Mcfarlane, A. C. (1986) Post-traumatic Morbidity of a Disaster: A Study of Cases Presenting for Psychiatric Treatment. *Journal of Nervous and Mental Disease*, **174**, 4–14.

McGee, R. A. and Wolfe, D. A. (1991a) Between a Rock and a Hard Place: Where Do We Go from Here in Defining Psychological Maltreatment? *Development and Psychopathology*, **3**, 119–124.

——(1991b) Psychological Maltreatment: Toward an Operational Definition. *Development and Psychopathology*, **3**, 3–18.

McGee, R. A., Wolfe, D. A. and Wilson, S. K. (1997) Multiple Maltreatment Experiences and Adolescent Behavior Problems: Adolescent Perspectives. *Development and Psychopathology*, **9**, 131–149.

McGee, R. A., Wolfe, D. A., Yuen, S. A. and Wilson, S. K. (1995) The Measurement of Maltreatment: A Comparison of Approaches. *Child Abuse and Neglect*, **19**, 233–249.

McMahon, C. A., Barnett, B., Kowalenko, N. M. and Tennant, C. C. (2006) Maternal Attachment State of Mind Moderates the Impact of Postnatal Depression on Infant Attachment. *Journal of Child Psychology and Psychiatry*, **47**, 660–669.

McNally, R. J. (2004) Conceptual Problems with the DSM–IV Criteria for Post-traumatic stress disorder. In *Post-traumatic Stress Disorder: Issues and Controversies* (ed. G. Rosen), 1–14. London: Wiley.

McWilliams, L. A. (2006) Evaluating Attachment Theory as a Framework for Understanding Pain-Related Appraisals and Interpersonal Concerns. In *Dissertation Abstracts International: Section B: The Sciences and Engineering*, pp. 5690–5690. US: ProQuest Information and Learning.

Meaney, M. J. (2001) Maternal Care, Gene Expression, and the Transmission of Individual Differences in Stress Reactivity across Generations. *Annual Review of Neuroscience*, **24**, 1161.

Meredith, P., Strong, J. and Feeney, J. A. (2006a) Adult Attachment, Anxiety, and Pain Self-Efficacy as Predictors of Pain Intensity and Disability. *Pain*, **123**, 146–154.

Meredith, P. J., Strong, J. and Feeney, J. A. (2006b) The Relationship of Adult Attachment to Emotion, Catastrophizing, Control, Threshold and Tolerance, in Experimentally Induced Pain. *Pain*, **120**, 44–52.

Minzenberg, M. J., Poole, J. H. and Vinogradov, S. (2006) Adult Social Attachment Disturbance Is Related to Childhood Maltreatment and Current Symptoms in Borderline Personality Disorder. *Journal of Nervous and Mental Disease*, **194**, 341–348.

Molcar, C. C. (2006) The Relationship of Place Attachment to Spiritual Well-Being across the Lifespan. In *Dissertation Abstracts International: Section B: The Sciences and Engineering*, 2840–2840. US: ProQuest Information and Learning.

Mollica, R. F. (2000) 'Invisible Wounds: Waging a New Kind of War', *Scientific American*. June 2000; 282 (6): 54–57.

——(2006) *Healing Invisible Wounds*. Orlando FL: Harcourt.

Moran, P. B., Vuchinich, S. and Hall, N. K. (2004) Associations between Types of Maltreatment and Substance Use During Adolescence. *Child Abuse and Neglect*. **28**, 565–574.

Morgan, S. R. (1987) *Abuse and Neglect of Handicapped Children*. Boston: College Hill.

Moss, E., Smolla, N., Guerra, I., Mazzarello, T., Chayer, D. and Berthiaume, C. (2006) Attachement et Problemes de Comportements Interiorises et Exteriorises Auto-Rapportes a La Periode Scolaire. *Canadian Journal of Behavioural Science/Revue Canadienne des Sciences du Comportement*, **38**, 142–157.

Mulford, J. (1958) The Emotional Neglect of Children. Denver, CO: The American Humane Society, Denver Branch.

Mullen, P. E., Martin, J. L., Anderson, J. C., Romans, S. E. and Herbison, G. P. (1996) The Long Term Impact of the Physical, Emotional, and Sexual Abuse of Children: A Community Study. *Child Abuse and Neglect*, **20**, 7–21.

Munro, E. (2007). Confidentiality in a Preventive Child Welfare System. Ethics and *Social Welfare*, 1(1): 41–55.

Murray, C. (1990) The British Underclass. *Public Interest*, 4–28.

Murray, L., Halligan, S. L., Adams, G., Patterson, P. and Goodyer, I. M. (2006) Socio-emotional Development in Adolescents at Risk for Depression: The Role of Maternal Depression and Attachment Style. *Development and Psychopathology*, **18**, 489–516.

Naffine, N. (1998) The Legal Structure of Self-Ownership: Or the Self-Possessed Man and the Woman Possessed. *Journal of Law and Society*, **25**, 193–212.

Navarre, E. (1987) Psychological Maltreatment: The Core Component of Child Abuse. In *Psychological Maltreatment of Children and Youth* (eds M. Brassard, R. Germain and S. Hart), 45–58. New York: Pergamon.

Nedelsky, J. (1990) Law, Boundaries, and the Bounded Self. *Representations*, 162–189.

——(1995) Meditations on Embodied Autonomy. *2 Graven Images*, **159**.

Nelson, B. (1984) *Making an Issue of Child Abuse: Political Agenda Setting for Social Problems*. Chicago: University of Chicago Press.

Nelson, C. A. and Carver, L. J. (1998) The Effects of Stress and Trauma on Brain and Memory: A View from Developmental Cognitive Neuroscience. *Development and Psychopathology*, **10**, 793–809.

Nillson, L. (1987) *The Body Victorious: The Illustrated Story of Our Immune System*. New York: Delacorte Press.

Nolan (1998) *The Therapeutic State: Justifying Government at Century's End*. New York: New York University Press.

Nuckolls, C. W. (2006) Ambivalence and Anxiety in the Psychiatric Systems of the United States and Japan. *Anthropology and Medicine*, **13**, 173–186.

Nussbaum, M. J. (2004) *Hiding from Humanity: Shame Disgust and the Law*. Princeton, NJ: Princeton University Press.

O'Hagan, K. (1993) *Emotional and Psychological Abuse of Children*. Buckingham: Open University Press.

——(1995) Emotional and Psychological Abuse: Problems of Definition. *Child Abuse and Neglect*, **19**, 449.

Ogata, S. and Sen, A. (2003) Human Security Now. New York: United Nations Commission on Human Security

Ogawa, J. R., Sroufe, L. A., Weinfield, N. S., Carlson, E. A. and Egeland, B. (1997) Development and the Fragmented Self: Longitudinal Study of Dissociative Symptomatology in a Nonclinical Sample. *Development and Psychopathology*, **9**, 855–879.

Onnis, L., Galluzzo, W., Barbara, E., Bernardini, M., Leonelli, A. and Vietri, A. (2006) Dissociated Voices. Auditive Hallucinations in a Systemic and Relational Approach. *Rivista Sperimentale di Freniatria: La Rivista della Salute Mentale*, **130**, 88–110.

Ounsted, C., Oppenheimer, R. and Lindsay, J. (1974) Aspects of Bonding Failure: The Psychopathology and Psychotherapeutic Treatment of Families of Battered Children. *Developmental Medicine and Child Neurology*, **16**, 447–456.

Page, H. W. (1883) *Injuries of the Spine and Spinal Cord without Apparent Mechanical Lesion, and Nervous Shock, in Their Surgical and Medico-Legal Aspects*. London: J. and A. Churchill.

Panksepp, J. (1998) *Affective Neuroscience: The Foundation of Human and Animal Emotions*. New York: Oxford University Press.

Papolos, J. (2002) *The Bipolar Child*. New York: Broadway Books.

Parents Against INjustice (1986) *A Response to Child Abuse: Working Together: A Draft Guide to Arrangements for Inter-Agency Co-Operation for the Protection of Children*. Bishop's Stortford, Herts: Parents Against INjustice.

Parton, N. (1985) *The Politics of Child Abuse*. London: Macmillan.

——(1991) *Governing the Family*. London: Macmillan.

Parton, N., Thorpe, D. and Wattam, C. (1997) *Child Protection: Risk and the Moral Order*. Basingstoke: Macmillan Press.

Patterson, P. and Thompson, M. (1980) Emotional Abuse and Neglect: An Exercise in Definition. In *The Maltreatment of the School-Aged Child* (eds R. Volpe, M. Breston and J. Milton). Lexington, MASS: Lexington Books.

Pavlov, I. (1927) *Conditioned Reflexes: An Account of the Physiological Activity of the Cerebral Cortex*. London: Oxford University Press.

Patterson, P. and Thompson, M. (1980) Emotional Abuse and Neglect: An Exercise in Definition. In *The Maltreatment of the School-Aged Child* (eds R. Volpe, M. Breston and J. Milton). Lexington, MA: Lexington Books.

Paykel, E. S. (1978) Contribution of Life Events to Causation of Psychiatric Illness. *Psychological Medicine*, **8**, 245–253.

Pederson, D. R., Gleason, K. E., Moran, G. and Bento, S. (1998) Maternal Attachment Representations, Maternal Sensitivity, and the Infant–Mother Attachment Relationship. *Developmental Psychology*, **34**, 925–933.

Perrow, C. (1984) *Normal Accidents: Living with High Risk Technology*. New York: Basic Books.

Perry, B. D. (1997) Incubated in Terror: Neurodevelopmental Factors in the 'Cycle of Violence'. In *Children in a Violent Society* (ed. J. D. Osofsky), 124–149. New York: Guilford Press.

Pfohl, S. J. (1977) The Discovery of Child-Abuse. *Social Problems*, **24**, 310–323.

Phillips, D. A. and Styfco, S. J. (2007) Child Development Research and Public Policy: Triumphs and Setbacks on the Way to Maturity. In *Child Development and Social Policy: Knowledge for Action* (eds J. L. Aber, S. J. Bishop-Josef, S. M. Jones and K. T. McLearn), 11–27. Washington, DC: American Psychological Association.

Pitman, R. K., van der Kolk, B. A., Orr, S. P. and Greenburg, M. S. (1990) Naxalone-Reversible Analgesic Response to Combat-Related Stimuli in Post-traumatic stress disorder. *Archives of General Psychiatry*, **47**, 541–544.

Polan, H. J., Hofer, M. A. (1999) Psycho-biological Origins of Infant Attachment and Separation Responses. In *Handbook of Attachment: Theory, Research, and Clinical Applications* (eds J Cassidy and P. R. Shaver), 162–180. New York: Guilford Press.

Pollak, S. D. (2005) Early Adversity and Mechanisms of Plasticity: Integrating Affective Neuroscience with Developmental Approaches to Psychopathology. *Development and Psychopathology*, **17**, 735–752.

Posada, G., Waters, E., Crowell, J. A. and Lay, K.-L. (1995) Is It Easier to Use a Secure Mother as a Secure Base? Attachment Q-Sort Correlates of the Adult Attachment Interview. *Monographs of the Society for Research in Child Development*, **60**, 133–145.

Pringle, M. L. K. and DHSS (1975) *The Needs of Children: A Personal Perspective Prepared for the Department of Health and Social Security*. London: Hutchinson.

Pupavac, V. (2004) War on the Couch: The Emotionology of the New International Security Paradigm. *European Journal of Social Theory*, **7**(2), 149–170.

QCA/DFE (1999) *The Review of the National Curriculum in England The Secretary of State's Proposals*. Suffolk: QCA Publications.

Raikes, H. A. and Thompson, R. A. (2005) Links between Risk and Attachment Security: Models of Influence. *Journal of Applied Developmental Psychology*, **26**, 440–455.

Reder, P. and Duncan, S. (2001) Abusive Relationships, Care and Control Conflicts and Insecure Attachments. *Child Abuse Review*, **10**, 411–427.

Reid, W. J. and Epstein, L. (1972) *Task-Centered Casework*. New York: Columbia University Press.

——(1977) *Task-Centered Practice*. New York: Columbia University Press.
Reid, W. J. and Shyne, A. W. (1969) *Brief and Extended Casework*. New York: Columbia University Press.
Reiff, P. (1967) *The Triumph of the Therapeutic: Uses of Faith after Freud*. Chicago, IL: University of Chicago Press.
Rheinberger, H.-J. (2000) Beyond Nature and Culture: Modes of Reasoning in the Age of Molecular Biology and Medicine. In *Living and Working with the New Medical Technologies* (eds M. Lock, A. Young and A. Cambrosio). Cambridge, UK: Cambridge University Press.
Ribbens, J. and Edwards, R. (1995) Introducing Qualitative Research on Women in Families and Households. *Women's Studies International Forum*, **18**, 247–258.
Ribot, T. A. (1883) *Diseases of Memory: An Essay in the Positive Psychology*. London: Kegan Paul, Trench.
Riley, D. (1983) *War in the Nursery: Theories of the Child and Mother*. London: Virago Press.
Rittner, B. and Wodarski, J. S. (1995) Clinical Assessment Instruments in the Treatment of Child Abuse and Neglect. *Early Child Development and Care*, **106**, 43–58.
Rivers, W. H. R. (1920) *Instinct and the Unconscious: A Contribution to a Biological Theory of the Psycho-Neuroses*. Cambridge, UK: Cambridge University Press.
Robertson, J. (1953a) Some Responses of Young Children to Loss of Maternal Care. *Nursing Care*, **49**, 382–386.
——(1953b) *A Two-Year-Old Goes to Hospital* [Film].
Robins, L. N. and Heltzer, J. E. (1986) Diagnostic and Clinical Assessment: The Current State of Psychiatric Diagnosis. *Annual Review of Psychology*, **37**, 409–432.
Ronnlund, M. and Karlsson, E. (2006) The Relation between Dimensions of Attachment and Internalizing or Externalizing Problems During Adolescence. *Journal of Genetic Psychology*, **167**, 47–63.
Rose, N. (1999) *Governing the Soul: The Shaping of the Private Self* (2 edn). London: Free Association Press.
——(2001) The Politics of Life Itself. *Theory, Culture and Society*, **18**, 1–30.
——(2007) *The Politics of Life Itself: Biomedicine, Power and Subjectivity in the Twenty First Century*. Princeton: Princeton University Press.
Rose, S. (2001) *The Future of the Brain: The Promise and the Perils of Tomorrow's Neuroscience*. New York: Oxford University Press.
Rose, S., Bisson, J. and Wessely, S. (2003) A Systematic Review of Single-Session Psychological Interventions ("Debriefing") Following Trauma. *Psychotherapy and Psychosomatics*, **72(4)**, 176–184.
Ross, F. (2003) On Having Voice and Being Heard. *Anthropological Theory*, **3 (3)**.
Rossman, B. B. and Rosenberg, M. S. (1998) *Multiple Victimization of Children: Conceptual, Developmental, Research, and Treatment Issues*. New York: Taylor and Francis.
Royal College of Psychiatry (2008) *Mental Health and Work*. London: Royal College of Psychiatry.
Rutter, M. (1972) *Maternal Deprivation Revisited*. Harmondsworth: Penguin.
——(1985) Resilience in the Face of Adversity: Protective Factors and Resistance to Psychiatric Disorder. *British Journal of Psychiatry*, **147**, 598–611.

——(1989) Isle of Wight Revisited: Twenty-Five Years of Child Psychiatric Epidemiology. *Journal of the American Academy of Child and Adolescent Psychiatry*, **28**, 633–653.

Rutter, M., Beckett, C., Castle, J., Colvert, E., Kreppner, J., Mehta, M., Stevens, S. and Sonuga-Barke, E. (2007) Effects of Profound Early Institutional Deprivation: An Overview of Findings from a UK Longitudinal Study of Romanian Adoptees. *European Journal of Developmental Psychology*, **4**, 332–350.

Rutter, M., O'Connor, T. G. (1999) Implications of Attachment Theory for Child Care Policies. In *Handbook of Attachment: Theory, Research, and Clinical Applications.*, (eds J. Cassidy and P. R. Shaver), 823–844. New York: Guilford Press.

Rutter, M. and Quinton, D. (1984) Parental Psychiatric Disorder: Effects on Children. *Psychological Medicine*, **14**, 853–880.

Rutter, M. and Sroufe, L. A. (2000) Developmental Psychopathology: Concepts and Challenges. *Development and Psychopathology*, **12**, 265–296.

Sameroff, A. J. and Fiese, B. (2000) Models of Development and Developmental Risk. In *Handbook of Infant Mental Health* (ed. C. H. Zeanah), 3–19.

Samuels, A. (2002) *Politics on the Couch: Citizenship and the Internal Life*. New York: Karnac Books.

Sar, V., Akyuz, G., Kugu, N., Ozturk, E. and Ertem-Vehid, H. (2006) Axis I Dissociative Disorder Comorbidity in Borderline Personality Disorder and Reports of Childhood Trauma. *Journal of Clinical Psychiatry*, **67**, 1583–1590.

Sarbin, T. R. and Kitsuse, J. L. (eds) (1994) *Constructing the Social*. London: Sage.

Scarry, E. (1985) *The Body in Pain: The Making and Unmaking of the World*. Oxford, UK: Oxford University Press.

Schäfer, I., Harfst, T., Aderhold, V., Briken, P., Lehmann, M., Moritz, S., Read, J. and Naber, D. (2006) Childhood Trauma and Dissociation in Female Patients with Schizophrenia Spectrum Disorders: An Exploratory Study. *Journal of Nervous and Mental Disease*, **194**, 135–138.

Scheff, T. J. (1966) *On Being Mentally Ill: A Sociological Theory*. London: Weidenfeld and Nicholson.

Schindler, L. W. (1988) *Understanding the Immune System*. Washington, DC: US Department of Health and Human Services.

Schore, A. N. (1994) *Affect Regulation and the Origin of the Self: The Neurobiology of Emotional Development*. Mahwah, NJ: Laurence Erlbaum Associates.

——(1999) Commentary on Emotions: Neuro–Psychoanalytic Views. *Neuro–Psychoanalysis*, **1(1)**, 49–55.

——(2000) Attachment and the Regulation of the Right Brain. *Attachment and Human Development*, **2**, 23–47.

——(2001a) Effects of a Secure Attachment Relationship on Right Brain Development, Affect Regulation, and Infant Mental Health. *Infant Mental Health Journal*, **22**, 7–66.

——(2001b) The Effects of Early Relational Trauma on Right Brain Development, Affect Regulation, and Infant Mental Health. *Infant Mental Health Journal*, **22**, 201–269.

——(2005) Developmental Affective Neuroscience Describes Mechanisms at the Core of Dynamic Systems Theory. *Behavioral and Brain Sciences*, **28**, 217–218.

Scraton, P. (1999) *Hillsborough: The Truth*. Edinburgh: Mainstream Publishing Projects.

Scull, A. (2005) *Most Solitary of Afflictions: Madness and Society in Britain 1700–1900*. New Haven, CT, CT: Yale University Press.

Searle, J. R. (1995) *The Construction of Social Reality*. New York: The Free Press.

——(2005) Consciousness: What We Still Don't Know. *The New York Review of Books*, 13 January: 36–9.

Seebohm Committee (1968) *Report of the Committee on Local Authority and Allied Personal Social Services, Cmnd 3703*.

Sheehan, R. (2001) *Magistrates' Decision Making in Child Abuse Cases*. Aldershot, UK: Ashgate Publishing.

——(2006) Emotional Harm and Neglect: The Legal Response. *Child Abuse Review*, **15**, 38–54.

Sheldon, B. (1978) Theory and Practice in Social Work: Re-Examination of a Tenuous Relationship. *British Journal of Social Work*, **8**, 1–22.

Shengold, L. L. (1979) Child Abuse and Deprivation: Soul Murder. *Journal of the American Psychoanalytic Association*, **27**, 533–559.

Shephard, B. (2002) *A War of Nerves: Soldiers and Psychiatrists in the Twentieth Century*. Cambridge, Mass: Harvard University Press.

Sheppard, M. (1982) *Perceptions of Child Abuse: A Critique of Individualism*. Norwich: University of East Anglia (in association with the weekly journal, *Social Work Today*).

Shine, J. (2006) Review of a Matter of Security: The Application of Attachment Theory to Forensic Psychiatry and Psychotherapy. *British Journal of Forensic Practice*, **8**, 48–50.

Shorey, H. S. and Snyder, C. R. (2006) The Role of Adult Attachment Styles in Psychopathology and Psychotherapy Outcomes. *Review of General Psychology*, **10**, 1–20.

Showalter, E. (1985) *The Female Malady*. New York: Pantheon.

Simpson, J. A. (1999) Attachment Theory in Modern Evolutionary Perspective. In *Handbook of Attachment: Theory, Research, and Clinical Applications*. (eds J. Cassidy and P. R. Shaver), 115–140. New York: Guilford Press.

Sinclair, R. and Carr-Hill, R. (1997) *Categorisation of Children in Need*. London: DOH.

Sivaramakrishnan, K. and Vaccaro, I. (2006) Introduction. Postindustrial Natures: Hyper-Mobility and Place-Attachments. *Social Anthropology/ Anthropologie Sociale*, **14**, 301–317.

Skuse, D. H. (1989) Emotional Abuse and Delay in Growth. *British Medical Journal*, **299**, 113–115.

Slovic, P. (1987) Perception of Risk. *Science*, New Series, **236**, 280–285.

Smith, A. (1976) *The Theory of Moral Sentiments* (eds D. D. Rafael and A. L. Mackie). Oxford: Clarendon Press.

Smith, R. (1984) *Trial by Medicine: Insanity and Responsibility in Victorian Trials*. Edinburgh: Edinburgh University Press.

Smith, S. (1975) *The Battered Child Syndrome*. London: Butterworth.

Solms, M. and Lechevalier, B. (2002) Neurosciences and Psychoanalysis. *International Journal of Psychoanalysis*, **83**, 233–237.

Solms, M. and Turnbull, O. (2002) *The Brain and the Inner World: An Introduction to the Neuroscience of Subjective Experience*. London: Karnac.

Sontag, S. (1991) *Illness as Metaphor and Aids and Its Metaphors*. Harmondsworth, UK: Penguin Books.

Spector, M. and Kitsuse, J. I. (1977) *Constructing Social Problems*. New York: Cummings.

Spilsbury, J. C., Drotar, D., Burant, C., Flannery, D., Creeden, R. and Friedman, S. (2005) Psychometric Properties of the Pediatric Emotional Distress Scale in a Diverse Sample of Children Exposed to Interpersonal Violence. *Journal of Clinical Child and Adolescent Psychology*, **34**, 758–764.

Spitz, R. A. (1945) Hospitalism: An Inquiry into the Genesis of Psychiatric Conditions in Early Childhood. *Psychoanalytic Study of the Child*, **1**, 53–74.

Spitzer, R. L., Gibbon, M., Williams, J. B. W., Kendler, K., Pincus, H. A. and Tucker, G. (1992) Dr Spitzer and Associates Reply. *American Journal of Psychiatry*, **149**, 1619–1620.

Springer, S. P. and Deutsch, G. (1997) *Left Brain, Right Brain: Perspectives from Cognitive Neuroscience*. New York: Freeman.

Sroufe, L. A. (1996) *Emotional Development; the Organisation of Emotional Life in the Early Years*. New York: Cambridge University Press.

Sroufe, L. A., Carlson, E. A., Levy, A. K. and Egeland, B. (1999) Implications of Attachment Theory for Developmental Psychopathology. *Development and Psychopathology*, **11**, 1–13.

Sroufe, L. and Waters, E. (1977a) Attachment as an Organizational Construct. *Child Development*, **48**, 1184–1199.

Sroufe, L. A. and Waters, E. (1977b) Heart Rate as a Convergent Measure in Clinical and Developmental Research. *Merrill-Palmer Quarterly*, **23**, 3–27.

Stapleton, J. (1994) 'In Restraint of Tort' in P. Birks (ed.), *The Frontiers of Liability* (1994) vol 2: 94–6,

Starr, R. H. (ed) (1982) *Child Abuse Predictions: Policy Implications*. Cambridge, Mass: Ballinger.

Steckley, P. L. (2006) An Examination of the Relationship between Clients' Attachment Experiences, Their Internal Working Models of Self and Others, and Therapists' Empathy in the Outcome of Process-Experiential and Cognitive-Behavioural Therapies. In *Dissertation Abstracts International Section A: Humanities and Social Sciences*, 2055–2055. US: ProQuest Information and Learning.

Steedman, C. (1995) *Strange Dislocations: Childhood and the Idea of Human Interiority, 1780–1930*. Cambridge, Mass: Harvard University Press.

Steele, M., Kenrick, J., Lindsey, C. and Tollemache, L. (2006) The 'Added Value' of Attachment Theory and Research for Clinical Work in Adoption and Foster Care. In *Creating New Families: Therapeutic Approaches to Fostering, Adoption, and Kinship Care.*, 33–42. London England: Karnac Books.

Stein, M. B., J.R. Walker, A.L. Hazen, and D.R.Forde (1997) Full and Partial Post-traumatic stress disorder: Findings from a Community Survey. *American Journal of Psychiatry*, 1114–1119.

Steinberg, D. R., Pianta, R. C. and Mayseless, O. (2006) Maternal Representations of Relationships: Assessing Multiple Parenting Dimensions. In *Parenting Representations: Theory, Research, and Clinical Implications*, 41–78. New York: Cambridge University Press.

Stevenson, O. (1996) Emotional Abuse and Neglect. *Child and Family Social Work*, **1**, 13–18.

——(1998) *Neglected Children: Issues and Dilemmas*. Oxford: Blackwell Science.

Stiglitz, J. and Bilmes, L. (2008) *The Three Trillion Dollar War: The True Cost of the Iraq Conflict*. Harmondsworth: Allen Lane.

Straus, M. A., Gelles, R. J. and Steinmetz, S. K. (1981) *Behind Closed Doors: Violence in the American Family*. Garden City, N.Y.: Anchor Books.

Strupp, H. H. and Hadley, S. W. (1979) Specific Vs Non-specific Factors in Psychotherapy: A Controlled Study of Outcome. *Archives of General Psychiatry*, **36**, 1125–1136.

Stuewig, J. and McCloskey, L. A. (2005) The Relation of Child Maltreatment to Shame and Guilt among Adolescents: Psychological Routes to Depression and Delinquency. *Child Maltreatment*, **10**, 324–336.

Summerfield, D. (1996) The Psychological Legacy of War and Atrocity: The Question of Long-Term and Transgenerational Effects and the Need for a Broad View. *Journal of Nervous and Mental Disease*, **184**, 375–377.

——(1999) A Critique of Seven Assumptions Behind Psychological Trauma Programmes in War-Affected Areas. *Social Science and Medicine*, **48**, 1449–1462.

——(2001) The Invention of Post-traumatic Stress Disorder and the Social Usefulness of a Psychiatric Category. *British Medical Journal*, **322**, 95–98.

——(2004) Cross-Cultural Perspectives on the Medicalization of Human Suffering. In *Post-traumatic Stress Disorder: Issues and Controversies* (ed. G. Rosen). Chichester: Wiley.

Sunderland, M. (2008) *The Science of Parenting*. London: DK Publishing.

Suomi, S. J. (1999) Attachment in Rhesus Monkeys. In *Handbook of Attachment: Theory, Research, and Clinical Applications* (eds J. Cassidy and P. R. Shaver), 181–197. New York: Guilford Press.

Sutherland, J. (1989) *Fairbairn's Journey into the Interior*. London: Free Association.

Szasz (1962) *The Myth of Mental Illness*. London: Secker and Warburg.

Target, M., Fonagy, P. and Shmueli-Goetz, Y. (2003) Attachment Representations in School-Age Children: The Development of the Child Attachment Interview (CAI). *Journal of Child Psychotherapy*, **29**, 171–186.

Taylor, C. (1989) *The Sources of the Self: The Making of Modern Identity*. Cambridge, UK: Cambridge University Press.

Teubner, G. (1989) How the Law Thinks: Towards a Constructivist Epistemology of Law. *Law and Society Review*, **23** 5, 727–756.

The Law Commission (1998) *Liability for Psychiatric Illness*. London: The Law Commission.

Thompson, R. A. and Raikes, H. A. (2003) Toward the Next Quarter-Century: Conceptual and Methodological Challenges for Attachment Theory. *Development and Psychopathology*, **15**, 691–718.

Thorpe, D. (1994) *Evaluating Child Protection*. Milton Keynes: Open University Press.

Tigges, L. M. (2006) Introduction: Community Cohesion and Place Attachment. *American Behavioral Scientist*, **50**, 139–141.

Trauma, Violence, and Abuse. London: Sage.

TRC (1998) *Truth and Reconciliation Commission of South Africa Report*. Cape Town: Juta.

Trimble, M. R. (1985) Post-traumatic stress disorder: History of a Concept. In *Trauma and Its Wake* (ed. C. R. Figley). New York: Brunner/Mazel.

Troisi, A., Di Lorenzo, G., Alcini, S., Nanni, R. C., Di Pasquale, C. and Siracusano, A. (2006) Body Dissatisfaction in Women with Eating Disorders: Relationship to Early Separation Anxiety and Insecure Attachment. *Psychosomatic Medicine*, **68**, 449–453.

Trowell, J. (1983) Emotional Abuse of Children. *Health Visitor*, **56**, 252–255.

Trowell, J., Hodges, S. and Leighton-Laing, J. (1997) Emotional Abuse: The Work of a Family Centre. *Child Abuse Review*, **6**, 357–369.

Tunbridge Wells Study Group. and Franklin, A. W. (1973) *The Tunbridge Wells Study Group on Non-Accidental Injury to Children*. London: TWSG.

Tutu, D. (1997) Foreword. In *To Remember and to Heal: Theological and Psychological Perspectives on Truth and Reconciliation* (eds H. Russell Botman and R. M. Peterson). Cape Town: Human and Rousseau.

Ursano, R. J. and Norwood, A. E. (2003) *Terrorism and Disaster: Individual and Community Mental Health Interventions*. Cambridge: Cambridge University Press.

van Brakel, A. M. L., Muris, P., Bagels, S. M. and Thomassen, C. (2006) A Multifactorial Model for the Etiology of Anxiety in Non-Clinical Adolescents: Main and Interactive Effects of Behavioral Inhibition, Attachment and Parental Rearing. *Journal of Child and Family Studies*, **15**, 569–579.

van der Kolk, B. A., Greenberg, A. M., Boyd, H. and Crystal, J. (1985) Inescapable Shock, Neurotransmitters and Addiction to Trauma: Towards a Psychobiology of Post-traumatic Stress. *Biological Psychiatry*, **20**, 314–325.

van der Kolk, B. A. and McFarlane, A. C. (1996) The Black Hole of Trauma. In *Traumatic Stress: The Effects of Overwhelming Stress on Mind, Body and Society* (eds B. A. van der Kolk, A. C. McFarlane and L. Weisaeth). New York: Guilford Press.

van der Kolk, B. A., McFarlane, A. C. and Weisaeth, L. (eds) (1996) *Traumatic Stress: The Effects of Overwhelming Stress on Mind, Body and Society*. New York: Guilford Press.

Van Ijzendoorn, M. H. (1995) Adult Attachment Representations, Parental Responsiveness, and Infant Attachment: A Meta-Analysis on the Predictive Validity of the Adult Attachment Interview. *Psychological Bulletin*, **117**, 387–403.

Vaughn, B. E. and Waters, E. (1990) Attachment Behavior at Home and in the Laboratory: Q-Sort Observations and Strange Situation Classifications of One-Year-Olds. *Child Development*, **61**, 1965–1973.

Vaughn, C. E. & Leff, J. P. (1976) The Influence of Family and Social Factors on the Course of Psychiatric Illness: A Comparison of Schizophrenic and Depressed Neurotic Patients. *British Journal of Psychiatry*, **129**, 125–137.

Veach, D. I. (1996) Posttraumatic Stress Disorder in Adults Who Experienced Parental Psychological Maltreatment, Physical Violence, and Physical Abuse as Adolescents and Children. In *Dissertation Abstracts International: Section B: The Sciences and Engineering*, 4595–4595. US: ProQuest Information and Learning.

Vissing, Y. M., Straus, M. A., Gelles, R. J. and Harrop, J. W. (1991) Verbal Aggression by Parents and Psycho-social Problems of Children. *Child Abuse and Neglect*, **15**, 223–238.

Volkan, V. (2000) *Traumatised Societies and Psychological Care: Expanding the Concept of Preventive Medicine*. Charlottesville, VA: Center for the Study of Mind and Human Interaction.

von Foerster, H. (1974) *Cybernetics of Cybernetics*. Urbana, IL: University of Illinois.

——(1991) Through the Eyes of the Other. In *Research and Reflexivity* (ed. F. Steier). London: Sage.

Wain, J. (ed) (1986a) *The Oxford Library of English Poetry: Volume 1*. Oxford, UK: Oxford University Press.

——(ed) (1986b) *The Oxford Library of English Poetry: Volume 2*. Oxford, UK: Oxford University Press.

Walker Bynum, C. (1992) *Fragmentation and Redemption: Essays on Gender and the Human Body in Medieval Religion*. New York: Zone Books.

Wang, H. and Tian, L.-F. (2006) Study on Relationship between Patients and Therapists in the Therapy of Borderline Personality Disorder. *Chinese Journal of Clinical Psychology*, **14**, 419.

Waters, E. and Deane, K. E. (1985) Defining and Assessing Individual Differences in Attachment Relationships: Q-Methodology and the Organization of Behavior in Infancy and Early Childhood. *Monographs of the Society for Research in Child Development*, **50**, 41.

Waters, T. (2004) Learning to Love: From Your Mother's Arms to Your Lover's Arms. *The Medium (Voice of the University of Toronto)*, **30 (19)**, 1–4.

Wattam, C. (1992) *Making a Case in Child Protection*. London: NSPCC/Longman.

Weir, T. (1992) *Casebook on Torts* 7th Edn. London: Sweet and Maxwell.

Wheeler, M. A., Stuss, D. T. and Tulving, E. (1997) Toward a Theory of Episodic Memory: The Frontal Lobes and Autonoetic Consciousness. *Psychological Bulletin*, **121**, 331–354.

Whiting, L. (1976) Defining Emotional Neglect: A Community Workshop Looks at Neglected Children. *Children Today*, **5**, 2–5.

WHO (1992) *The ICD–10 Classification of Mental and Behavioural Disorders: Clinical Descriptions and Diagnostic Guidelines*. Geneva: World Health Organisation.

——(2001) *The Invisible Wounds: The Mental Health Crisis in Afghanistan* www.who.int/disasters/repo/7399.pdf

——(2002) Breaking the Vicious Circle. *Health in Emergencies*, **12**.

Wilding, J. and Thoburn, J. (1997) Family Support Plans for Neglected and Emotionally Maltreated Children. *Child Abuse Review*, **6**, 343–356.

Wilkinson, G. and Smith, T (2005) *The British Medical Association Family Doctor Guide to Stress*. London: Dorling Kindersley.

Williams, P. (1987) Spirit Murdering the Messenger: The Discourse of Fingerpointing as the Law's Response to Racism. *University of Miami Law Reveiw*, **42**, 127.

Wilson, R. (2001) *The Politics of Truth and Reconciliation in South Africa: Legitimising the Post-Apartheid State*. Cambridge, UK: Cambridge University Press.

Witkiewitz, K. and Dodge-Reyome, N. (2001) Recollections of Childhood Psychological Maltreatment and Self-Reported Eating Disordered Behaviors in Undergraduate College Females. *Journal of Emotional Abuse*, **2**, 15–29.

Wolf, R. S. and Pillemer, K. A. (1988) Intervention, Outcome, and Elder Abuse. In *Coping with Family Violence: Research and Policy Perspectives* (eds G. T. Hotaling, D. Finkelhor, J. T. Kirkpatrick and M. A. Straus), 257–274. Thousand Oaks, CA: Sage Publications.

Wong, I. C. K., Murray, M. L., Novak, D. C. and Stephens, P. (2004) Increased Prescribing Trends of Paediatric Psychotropic Medications. *Archives of Disease in Childhood*, **89**, 1131–1132.

Woolgar, S. and Pawluch, D. (1985) Ontological Gerrymandering – the Anatomy of Social-Problems Explanations. *Social Problems*, **32**, 214–227.

Wootton, B. (1959) *Social Science and Social Pathology*. London: George Allen and Unwin.
Yehuda, R., Bryant, R., Marmar, C. and Zohar, J. (2005) Pathological Responses to Terrorism. *Neuro–psychopharmacology*, 30, 1793–1805.
Yehuda, R., Halligan, S. L. and Bierer, L. M. (2001) Relationship of Parental Trauma Exposure and PTSD to PTSD, Depressive and Anxiety Disorders in Offspring. *Journal of Psychiatric Research*, 35, 261–270.
Young, A. (1995) *The Harmony of Illusions: Inventing Post-traumatic Stress Disorder*. Princeton, NJ: Princeton University Press.
——(1999) W. H. R. Rivers and the War Neuroses. *Journal of the History of the Behavioral Sciences*, 35, 359–378.
——(2000) History, Hystery and Psychiatric Styles of Reasoning. In *Living and Working with the New Medical Technologies* (eds M. Lock, A. Young and A. Cambrosio). Cambridge, UK: Cambridge University Press.
——(2005) Review of Post-traumatic Stress Disorder: Malady or Myth? *Transcultural Psychiatry*, 42, 155–157.
——(2006) PTSD of the Virtual Kind – Trauma and Resilience in Post 9/11 America. Conference paper at *Embodiment and the State*, Institute of Public Health, University of Southern Denmark.
Zachrisson, H. D. and Kulbotten, G. R. (2006) Attachment in Anorexia Nervosa: An Exploration of Associations with Eating Disorder Psychopathology and Psychiatric Symptoms. *Eating and Weight Disorders*, 11, 163–170.
Zizek, S. (1997) *The Plague of Fantasies*. London: Verso.
——(1999) *The Absent Centre of Political Ontology*. London: Verso.

Electronic sources

American Values (2003) *Hardwired to Connect* http://www.americanvalues.org/html/hardwired.html and http://www.americanvalues.org/ExSumm-print.pdf [accessed 19 June 2012].
API (2007) http://www.attachmentparenting.org [accessed 19 June 2012].
APSAC (2006) *Report of the APSAC Task Force on Attachment Therapy, Reactive Attachment Disorder, and Attachment Problems*, http://depts.washington.edu/hcsats/PDF/AttachmentTaskForceAPSAC.pdf [accessed 19 June 2012].
Black, C. (2008) *Working for a healthier tomorrow* http://www.dwp.gov.uk/docs/hwwb-working-for-a-healthier-tomorrow.pdf [accessed 2 June 2012].
Teresa Brouwer (2006a) Shattered Words http://abusesanctuary.blogspot.co.uk/2006/12/shattered-words-by-teresa-brouwer-lot.www.suite101.com.html [accessed 5 June, 2012].
——(2006b) Emotional and Mental Rape, http://archive.suite101.com/article.cfm/women_abuse/110270 [accessed 16 January, 2006 – page no longer accessible].
CAFT (2007) http://www.childandfamilytraining.org.uk/attachmentstyleint.html [accessed 19 June 2012].
Catholic Advocate (2003) The Healer of Invisible Wounds, *News Letter*, 5th November http://www.rcan.org/index.cfm [accessed 19 June 2012].
CBC (2005) The Unseen Scars, http://www.cbc.ca/national/ [accessed 23 January, 2005].

CBS News (2007) http://www.cbsnews.com/stories/2007/11/13/terror/main3498789.shtml [accessed 2 June 2012].

Crittenden, P. (2009) Overview of Course: Attachment and Psychopathology, http://www.patcrittenden.com/Attach_and_Psycho-pathology.html [accessed 23 January, 2009, no longer accessible].

Cross, K. (2007) www.ksattach.us/attachmenttherapy.htm [accessed 19 June 2012].

Daily Press (2006) Invisible casualties, Daily Press.com [accessed 23 January, 2006].

Deseret News (2008) http://www.deseretnews.com/article/1,5143,635191573,00.html [accessed 19 June 2012].

DFE (2000) http://curriculum.qca.org.uk/ [accessed, 14th January, 2009].

Diana's Grove (2006) Invisible Knight, www.diana'sgrove.com [accessed 16 January 2006].

DOH (2005) *Mental Health of Children and Young People in Great Britain 2004*, http://www.ic.nhs.uk/webfiles/publications/mentalhealth04/MentalHealth ChildrenYoungPeople310805_PDF.pdf [accessed 20 June 2012].

Entertainment Weekly (1997) http://www.ew.com/ew/article/0,,289454_2,00.html [accessed 2 June 2012].

Fearnley, S. (2006) Now http://www.keyschildcare.co.uk/ [accessed 17 June 2012].

Fox News (1997) http://www.foxnews.com/story/0,2933,285456,00.html?sPage= fnc/world/diana# [accessed 2 June 2012].

Fraley, R. C. (2006) A Brief Overview of Adult Attachment Theory and Research http://internal.psychology.illinois.edu/~rcfraley/attachment.htm [accessed 17 June 2012].

Gospel, (2006) The Wounds of Spouse Abuse, www.gospel.com. [accessed 2 June 2006].

IACD (2006) http://www.instituteforattachment.org [accessed 6 June 2006].

Jones, L. (2006) 'Sierra Leone's invisible scars', http://news.bbc.co.uk/1/hi/world/africa/4058279.stm [accessed 2 June 2012].

Layard, R. (2006) http://cep.lse.ac.uk/research/mentalhealth/ [accessed 2 June 2012].

NPSA (2006) *Neuropsychoanalysis*, http://www.neuropsa.org.uk/journal [accessed 20 June 2012].

Piper Shafir, I. (2005) Trauma y reparación: Elementos para una retórica de la marca [Trauma and Reparation: Elements for a Rhetoric of Marks], http://www.psych.lse.ac.uk/socialpsychology/events/2004-05/fleshandblood/documents/trauma_r_isabelShafir_Esp.pdf [accessed 2 June 2012].

Pippin (2007) http://www.2-in-2-1.co.uk/services/pippin/ [accessed 20 June 2012].

Post Adoption Centre (2005) *Working with Severe Attachment Difficulties (AD)*. http://www.pac.org.uk/ [accessed 19 June 2012].

Quolkids (2007) http://www.quolkids.com/default.asp [accessed 19 June 2012].

Randolph, L. (2009) *Broken Hearts, Wounded Minds*, http://www.lizrandolph.com/rfrpublichtm.html [accessed 16 June 2012].

RTE Television (2004) The Afternoon Show, http://www.rte.ie/tv/theafternoonshow/2004/1117/stigmata.html (Accessed 2 June 2012).

Rutgers University (1983) http://www.sexetc.org/story/abuse/1983 [accessed 13 January 2006].

Ryan, J.E. (2009) *Broken Spirits, Lost Souls*, http://www.ebookmall.com/ebook/broken-spirits-lost-souls/jane-e-ryan/9780595297177 [accessed 16 June 2012].

Rygaard, N. P. (2007) www.attachmentdisorder.net [accessed 23 January 2007].

Santana Baptist Church (2001) Invisible Wounds. http://www.signonsandiego.com/news/metro/santana [accessed 16 January 2006].

Schrader, E. (2004) 'These unseen wounds cut deep', *Los Angeles Times* 14 November 2004 http://articles.latimes.com/2004/nov/14/nation/na-trauma14 [accessed 2 June 2012].

Shook, L. (2007) Changing History one Baby at a Time. Therapists Attempt to Resurrect Parents' Ancient Wisdom, http://www.waimh.org/Files/Signal/Signal_2001_9_4.pdf [accessed 20 June 2012].

Siegel, D (2007) http://www.mentalhelp.net [accessed 10th December 2007].

United Methodist Church (2006) *Clergy Depression*, http://www.umph.org/resources/publications/circuit_default.html [accessed 16 January 2006].

Vachss, A. (1994) You Carry the cure in Your Own Heart, *Parade Magazine*, 28 August, http://www.vachss.com/av_dispatches/disp_9408_a.html [accessed 20 June 2012].

Vega, M. (2006) 'Healing the Invisible Wounds of Violence', Inter Press Service, http://ipsnews.net/print.asp?idnews=26547 [accessed 2 June 2012].

Verrier, N. (1993) *The Primal Wound*, http://nancyverrier.com/the-primal-wound/ [accessed 16 June 2012].

Waters, E. (2002) The "Goodness" Of Attachment Assessment: There Is A "Gold Standard" But It Isn't as Simple as That. In *Attachment Theory and Research at Stonybrook*: http://www.psychology.sunysb.edu/attachment/measures/content/attachment_validity.html [accessed 20 June 2012].

WHO (2009) ICD10, http://www.who.int/classifications/apps/icd/icd10online/ [accessed 3 January,2009].

Will, G. (2003) Hardwired to Connect, http://townhall.com/columnists/georgewill/2003 [accessed 19 June 2012].

Index